Using Turbo Basic ®

Using Turbo Basic®

Frederick E. Mosher
and
David I. Schneider

BORLAND·OSBORNE/McGRAW·HILL
PROGRAMMING SERIES

Osborne **McGraw-Hill**
2600 Tenth Street
Berkeley, California 94710
U.S.A.

For information on translations and book distributors outside of the U.S.A., please write to Osborne **McGraw-Hill** at the above address.
   A complete list of trademarks appears on page 441.

Using Turbo Basic®

Copyright © 1988 by McGraw-Hill, Inc. All rights reserved. Printed in the United States of America. Except as permitted under the Copyright Act of 1976, no part of this publication may be reproduced or distributed in any form or by any means, or stored in a database or retrieval system, without the prior written permission of the publisher, with the exception that the program listings may be entered, stored, and executed in a computer system, but they may not be reproduced for publication.

234567890 DODO 8987

ISBN 0-07-881282-8

Information has been obtained by Osborne **McGraw-Hill** from sources believed to be reliable. However, because of the possibility of human or mechanical errors by our sources, Osborne **McGraw-Hill**, or others, Osborne **McGraw-Hill** does not guarantee the accuracy, adequacy, or completeness of any information and is not responsible for any errors or omissions or the results obtained from use of such information.

Contents

	Foreword	ix
	Preface	xi
1	**Introduction to Turbo Basic**	1
	Answers to Basic Questions	
2	**A First Look at Turbo Basic**	7
	Introduction	
	Getting Started	
	Creating and Running a Program: A Walkthrough	
	Compiling a Program	
	How to Perform Standard BASIC Tasks	
3	**The Turbo Basic Editor**	21
	Capabilities of the Turbo Basic Editor	
	The Editor Status Line	
	Editing Commands	
	An Editing Tutorial	
4	**Manipulating Data**	31
	Numbers	
	Strings	
	Further Discussion of Types	
	Arrays	

Inputting Data
Outputting Data to the Screen
Outputting Data to a Printer

5 Decisions and Repetition   69
Decision Making in Turbo Basic
Relational and Logical Operators
Decision Structures
Loops
Indentation and Nesting

6 Functions and Procedures   97
Stepwise Refinement
Single-line Functions
Multiline Functions
Subroutines
Procedures
Declaring Arrays
The Differences Between Functions and Procedures
Procedures and Functions That Invoke Each Other: Stepwise Refinement
Recursion

7 Data Files   133
The Three Types of Data Files
Sequential Files
Random Files
Binary Files

8 Graphics and Sound   163
Introduction
Graphics
Sound

9 A Closer Look at the Turbo Environment   229
The File Menu Commands
The Options Menu Commands
The Setup Menu Commands
The Window Menu Commands
The Debug Menu Commands
Adjusting Windows with SCROLL LOCK

10 Compiler Directives and System-Level Tools   **251**
     Directives
     Standalone Programs
     Special Instructions for the Compiler: Metastatements
     Event Trapping: $EVENT

11 Mathematics and Scientific Programming   **273**
     Predefined Mathematical Functions
     Techniques for Graphing Functions
     Random Numbers
     Creating Custom-designed Mathematical Characters
     Saving Graphs
     Matrices

12 Business Programming   **305**
     Financial Calculations
     Pie Charts
     Bar Charts
     Database Management

Appendixes   **351**

A	*ASCII Codes for the IBM PC*	**353**
B	*An Abridged Reference Manual of Turbo Basic*	**359**
C	*Converting BASICA Programs to Turbo Basic*	**397**
D	*Turbo Basic Reserved Words*	**407**
E	*Installing Turbo Basic*	**409**
F	*A Summary of Turbo Basic's Predefined Functions Grouped by Use*	**411**
G	*Editor Commands*	**421**
H	*The Differences Between WordStar and the Turbo Basic Editor*	**435**
	Index	**443**

Foreword

Readers of *Using Turbo Basic,* by Frederick E. Mosher and David I. Schneider, will progress from installation through advanced programming techniques in the fast, powerful, feature-rich programming-language environment of Turbo Basic.

Along the way they will learn the special uses of Turbo Basic, including math and scientific programming, business applications, and graphics development. Readers will be treated to an exceptionally clear discussion of looping, decision structure, and file handling. They will learn to use efficiently the many features of the fastest BASIC available.

Turbo Basic, developed by Borland International, Inc., is a complete development environment for IBM personal computers and true compatibles. Its integrated design permits quick program turnaround. Special features include floating-point support, multi-window environment, block-structured programming statements, full graphics support, and true recursion.

This book serves a broad range of users. It will be particularly helpful for beginning and intermediate programmers, and those who have used other BASIC compilers or other programming languages, but are new to Turbo Basic.

Mosher and Schneider, both authors of books on other BASIC compilers, present their material concisely and clearly. They demonstrate a knowledge of the language and a programming style worthy of imitation.

By the time readers reach the final page of *Using Turbo Basic*, they will be able to write solid, well-structured programs with maximum speed and efficiency.

Philippe Kahn
President
Borland International, Inc.

Preface

BASIC is the most popular computer language in the world. For example, a recent survey by the Boston Computer Society revealed that more than 80% of its programmer members use BASIC.* About 500,000 high school and college students enroll in BASIC courses each year. Hobbyists and recreational programmers like BASIC because it is easy to learn and allows the programmer to exercise all of the computer's capabilities. Professional programmers appreciate the speed and efficiency of developing programs in BASIC.

The last 20 years have witnessed the arrival of many fine programming languages. Languages like Pascal and C have control structures that permit beautifully designed and easily maintained programs. Unfortunately, these control structures are missing from most of the BASIC versions that have appeared since the language was invented at Dartmouth College in 1964.

Turbo Basic provides the best of both worlds. It is as easy to learn and use as the standard versions of BASIC and yet has the

---

*In "Developers Pick BASIC for High Productivity," *InfoWorld*, June 15, 1987.

essential control structures and power of the "serious" languages like Pascal and C. Among the features that make Turbo Basic so appealing are these:

- Full-featured editor
- Fast and efficient compilation
- Procedures
- Multiline functions
- Parameter passing
- Local, static, and global variables
- True recursion
- 8087 support
- **IF...THEN...ELSEIF...ELSE** blocks
- **SELECT CASE** blocks
- **DO** loops
- Optional line numbers

Prerequisites

This book assumes that the reader has a minimal knowledge of BASIC. If you already know what a program is and are familiar with the **LET**, **PRINT**, and **INPUT** commands, you have adequate preparation.

Turbo Basic builds on IBM PC BASIC. Therefore, if you already know IBM PC BASIC (or one of its equivalent formulations, such as GW BASIC), you have a head start. Actually, most programs that are written in IBM PC BASIC can be loaded as is into Turbo Basic and run.

Preface xiii

Overview of the Book

The first three chapters are preparatory. Chapter 1 answers some questions that you might have about Turbo Basic, Chapter 2 shows how to create and execute a program, and Chapter 3 gives an in-depth demonstration of the editor. You can skip Chapter 3 if you have used WordStar or Turbo Pascal.

The fundamental programming structures and statements of Turbo Basic are presented in Chapters 4, 5, and 6. Although the greatest emphasis is given to topics that are unique to Turbo Basic, all of the necessary concepts from Standard BASIC are reviewed.

Chapters 7 and 8 provide in-depth discussions of files, graphics, and sound. A knowledge of files is essential since most data used or generated by computer programs is stored in files. Graphics has steadily increased in importance as a programming tool because of the excellent graphics capabilities of microcomputers and the current interest in desktop publishing. Although the use of sound does not have the importance of files or graphics, it is included because it is fun. Some in-depth applications of graphics and files appear in Chapters 11 and 12.

Chapters 9 and 10 present advanced programming topics that many readers will just skim during their first reading of the book and refer to at a later time as they expand their horizons. Experienced programmers, who will be anxious to delve into the fine points of the Turbo Basic compiler, will probably read these chapters first.

Chapters 11 and 12 explore selected subjects in mathematics, scientific, and business programming. Some of the longer programs show how piecewise refinement is used to break a programming task into manageable chunks.

The appendixes contain a variety of reference materials. A table of ASCII codes is included in Appendix A. Appendix B is a quick reference manual of Turbo Basic's metastatements, statements, and functions. Appendix E shows you how to install Turbo Basic. The other appendixes are equally useful and are presented to save you valuable time while programming in Turbo Basic.

Programs

It is our conviction that programming concepts are best explained by illustrating them with carefully thought-out examples. Therefore, whenever possible, each new statement or structure is accompanied by a program or program segment that clarifies its use.

In addition, we present a number of comprehensive programs that not only demonstrate how large problems can be broken into manageable chunks, but also accomplish useful tasks.

Examine and edit any file—Program 7-14 This program allows you to see exactly what is in the files created by major spreadsheet and database software, and to alter their contents. Even non-ASCII files such as .EXE files may be examined and revised.

Graph a function—Program 11-8 This user-friendly graphing program will draw the graphs of functions with very large or undefined values. No matter what domain you specify for the function, the program guarantees that a pair of coordinate axes will be displayed. The scale range of values appearing as y-coordinates can be either given by the user or determined by the program.

Custom-design characters—Program 11-12 This program allows you to create up to 128 new characters that can be displayed in graphics mode.

Manipulate matrices—Programs 11-14 to 11-16 These generic procedures, which add, multiply, and invert matrices, can be included in mathematics programs to perform matrix operations.

Analyze a loan—Program 12-3 This program allows you to determine the amount that you can afford to borrow, the number of months it will take to pay off a loan, or the monthly payment on a loan. After the details of the loan are determined, the program displays a complete amortization schedule.

Preface

Draw a pie chart—Program 12-4 This generic program will produce a pie chart displaying up to ten values. The programmer merely has to place the values and their descriptions into **DATA** statements. The program will draw the pie chart along with identifying legends.

Draw a bar chart—Program 12-8 This generic program displays up to 37 user-supplied pieces of data in a vertical bar chart with descriptions below each bar. The program uses the largest data value to determine the vertical scale automatically. Also, procedures provide for a fast (non-screen-dump) printing of the chart.

Construct and manage a database—Program 12-22 This generic, menu-driven program provides the standard tools found in major database management programs. It allows you to create new databases by specifying field names and character counts, list the contents of the database, sort on a field in the database, and append, insert, or edit records. One program does it all; there is no need to write a new program for each database that you wish to create and maintain. You can add new features to this general program and have them available for every database you use or create.

Diskette

A diskette containing all the programs in this book can be obtained by sending a check or money order for $20.00 (Maryland residents add 5% sales tax) to

Turbosoft
P.O. Box 2656
College Park, Maryland 20740

An order form is provided following this preface.

Videotapes

A series of videotapes suitable for a short course based on this book is available for rental or purchase. For further information write to

Director of Instructional Television
Engineering Building
University of Maryland
College Park, Maryland 20742

—Frederick E. Mosher and
David I. Schneider

Disk Order Form

The companion disk includes more than 150 programs, all of those in *Using Turbo Basic*. The source code for each program is immediately available to be run or modified. Particularly valuable are the programs that permit you to determine the day of the week corresponding to any date, examine and edit any file, graph a function, custom-design characters, manipulate matrices, analyze a loan, draw pie and bar charts, and construct and manage a database.

The disk also contains the time-saving utility BASTOTB, which converts a BASICA program to a correct and efficient Turbo Basic format. This utility replaces essential line numbers with labels and removes unneeded line numbers. It finds all BASICA statements not supported by Turbo Basic and, if possible, replaces them with equivalent Turbo Basic statements. If there is no equivalent, the user is so alerted. In addition, BASTOTB finds all variable names that are reserved words in Turbo Basic and adds prefixes to the names.

To order your diskette, fill in the order form below and send it, along with a check or money order for $20.00 (Maryland residents add 5% sales tax), to

Turbosoft
P.O. Box 2656
College Park, Maryland 20740

-------------------------------------- (cut here) --------------------------------------

Please rush one companion disk for *Using Turbo Basic* to

Name _____

Address _____

City _____ State _____ ZIP _____

Enclosed find payment of $20.00 (plus sales tax if applicable).

This is solely the offering of the authors. Osborne/McGraw-Hill takes no responsibility for the fulfillment of this offer.

Acknowledgments

We are grateful to the staffs of Borland International, Inc., and Osborne/McGraw-Hill for their commitment to the production of a quality book. At Borland, Nan Borreson arranged access to information about Turbo Basic for us. Richard Guion's expert technical reviews of every chapter fine-tuned the accuracy of the book. At Osborne/McGraw-Hill, Liz Fisher, Fran Haselsteiner, and Pamela Webster worked diligently on the editorial and design tasks. Special thanks are offered to Jeff Pepper, senior editor at Osborne/McGraw-Hill. He not only initiated this project and participated in every stage of its development, but also his enthusiasm, advice, and friendship added immeasurably to the enjoyment of writing this book.

—F.E.M.
D.I.S.

1 Introduction to Turbo Basic

Answers to Basic Questions

No doubt you have seen the reviews that proclaim Turbo Basic as the most powerful version of BASIC ever. This chapter addresses some of the questions that you might have about Turbo Basic.

What is BASIC?

The original version of *BASIC* (Beginner's *A*ll-purpose Symbolic *I*nstruction *C*ode) was developed at Dartmouth College in 1964 as a teaching language. In subsequent years, BASIC underwent many revisions and enhancements. In 1978, a national standard was adopted that gave the minimal requirements of BASIC. This minimal language is called *Standard BASIC*.

What is BASICA?

BASICA is the enhanced version of BASIC that the Microsoft Corporation wrote for the IBM Personal Computer. An equivalent form, known as *GW BASIC,* is available for use with IBM PC compatibles. BASICA has about 190 commands and goes beyond most of the other versions of Standard BASIC.

Standard BASIC and BASICA are referred to as *interpreted languages.* **What is an interpreted language?**

In order for the computer to execute a program directly, the program instructions must be in *machine language,* which is a language that is difficult to write. An *interpreter* is a program with machine-language instructions that has been written to understand and act upon the instructions in another language, such as BASIC. When the computer RUNs a Standard BASIC program, it actually executes a program that must read, understand, and act upon each BASIC instruction. A language that is executed in this manner is called an *interpreted language.* One drawback to an interpreted language is that the computer must read and understand an instruction each time that it is encountered—even if the computer encounters the identical statement 1000 times in a loop! This repetition results in wasted time.

Turbo Basic is referred to as a *compiled language.* **What is a** *compiler*?

The Turbo Basic compiler is a program—actually a subprogram—within Turbo Basic. It reads and understands the instructions of a BASIC program, checks them for certain types of errors, and translates them into machine language. The compiler only needs to read and translate each instruction once—thereby making a compiler much more efficient than an interpreter. The compiler does not carry out the instructions that it translates, but does produce a set of machine-language instructions that the computer can execute directly and quickly to accomplish the task of the BASIC program. Two of the outstanding features of Turbo Basic are the speed and the efficiency with which it compiles programs.

Introduction to Turbo Basic 3

What are the strong points of Standard BASIC and BASICA?

Both versions of BASIC are easy to learn for three reasons: the statements use familiar words, you can introduce new variables at any time, and there are few complicated structures. BASICA has many advanced graphics, sound, and event-trapping capabilities that you cannot find in many other languages. Since Standard BASIC and BASICA interpret programs, you can debug them by stopping them at any point to analyze the values of the variables.

What are some limitations of Standard BASIC and BASICA?

First, in both versions, the need for line numbers sometimes makes programs hard to write and subroutines difficult to keep track of. Second, since all variables are *global,* which means that they maintain their values in all parts of the program, you cannot move subroutines easily from one program to another, and you must take care to avoid using the same variable in two different contexts. Third, the control statement **IF...THEN** does not provide enough flexibility and clarity. Fourth, Standard BASIC and BASICA are confined to 64K of memory, which must serve as both the workspace and the storage space for the values of the variables. Finally, since both versions of the language are interpreted, programs run slowly.

How does Turbo Basic improve on Standard BASIC and BASICA?

Computer scientists are in unanimous agreement that a modern programming language should not have line numbers, but should have extensive control structures, *local variables* (that is, variables that apply only to a portion of the program), and the ability to pass and receive values from a *procedure.* (A procedure is a portion of the program that is similar to a subroutine.) These features are available in Turbo Basic. For most programs, Turbo Basic can access the computer's entire memory. In addition, since Turbo Basic is a compiled language, programs run faster and can be executed directly from DOS.

Aren't line numbers necessary for certain programming tasks?

In Turbo Basic, line numbers are optional, and are only important in **GOTO** and **GOSUB** statements. The availability of procedures and extensive control structures removes the need for these statements. In addition, you can use another device, called a *label*, as a substitute for a line number in any line that is the target of a **GOTO** or **GOSUB** statement.

Will programs written in other versions of BASIC run in Turbo Basic?

You can load and execute most programs written in BASICA, Microsoft BASIC, or GW BASIC in Turbo Basic. You must make slight modifications in the use of a few statements such as **DRAW**, **PLAY**, **POKE**, and **USR**. However, you cannot use statements that apply to the program itself—such as **LIST**, **EDIT**, **RENUM**, and **AUTO**—in Turbo Basic.

How long will it take to learn Turbo Basic?

If you already know Standard BASIC, you can start programming almost immediately. You will need about one hour to learn the essentials of entering, executing, and modifying programs. Then you can write short programs exactly as you would in Standard BASIC. After that, you can read this book or the *Turbo Basic Owner's Handbook* to explore the new possibilities that Turbo Basic provides.

What is an *editor*?

An editor is a special-purpose word processor that you use to compose a program. The Turbo Basic editor has the power of the major word processors and uses the same type of instructions as WordStar.

Figure 1-1 shows the screen when Turbo Basic is first invoked. What is the significance of the eight words at the top of the screen and the four different windows?

Introduction to Turbo Basic

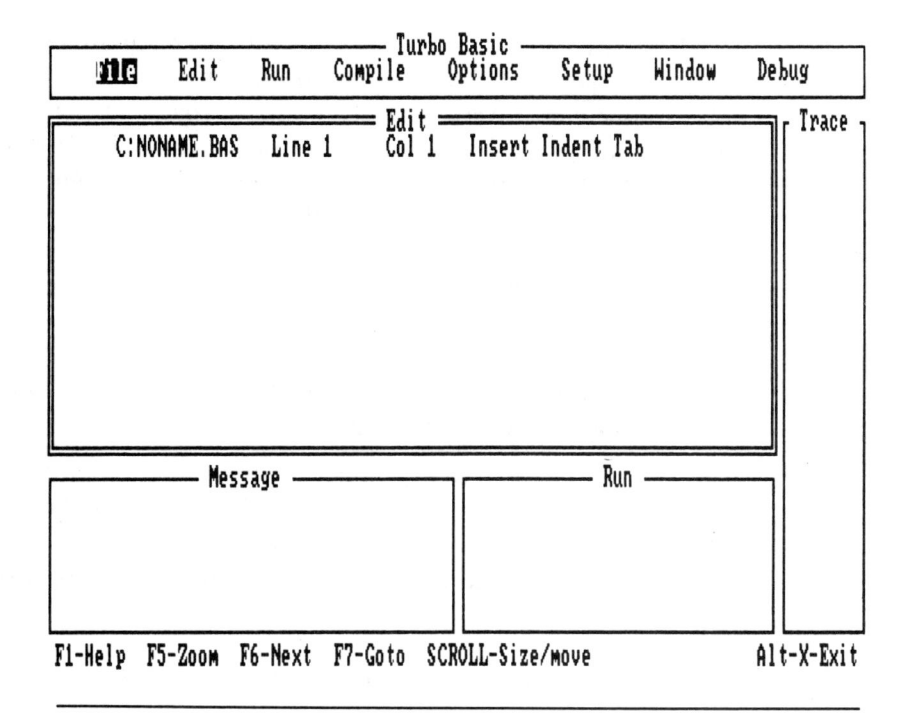

```
┌─────────────────── Turbo Basic ───────────────────┐
│  File   Edit   Run   Compile   Options   Setup   Window   Debug  │
├──────────────── Edit ────────────────┬─ Trace ─┐
│ C:NONAME.BAS   Line 1   Col 1   Insert Indent Tab │         │
│                                                   │         │
│                                                   │         │
│                                                   │         │
│                                                   │         │
│                                                   │         │
├─── Message ───────────┬─── Run ──────────────────┤
│                       │                          │
│                       │                          │
│                       │                          │
└───────────────────────┴──────────────────────────┘
 F1-Help  F5-Zoom  F6-Next  F7-Goto  SCROLL-Size/move      Alt-X-Exit
```

Figure 1-1. *Initial Turbo Basic screen*

The eight words at the top of the screen are the choices in the main menu. Of these, **Edit** invokes the editor, **Run** executes the current program, and **File** opens a pull-down list of options having to do with saving and loading programs. You use the last five choices less frequently and can ignore them for the time being.

Of the four windows, you will primarily use the Edit and Run windows. You compose programs in the Edit window. When the computer executes a program, its output appears in the Run window. The Message window offers information about the compiler; you use the Trace window for certain debugging procedures.

What are some of the consequences of writing programs for a compiler as opposed to an interpreter?

With an interpreted language, long variable names take up more memory space than short names; however, for compiled languages, all variable names use the same amount of space. Therefore, you as a programmer are free to use descriptive names in Turbo Basic. Standard BASIC uncovers errors only when the computer executes the program, so the language will uncover errors only in certain parts of your program after several well-planned runs. With Turbo Basic, the compiler scans the entire program and uncovers some types of errors prior to execution.

College computer-science departments stress structured programming. What is structured programming?

Structured programming is a strategy for creating programs that are easy to write, read, maintain, and debug. The strategy breaks problems down into smaller pieces that are dealt with one at a time. Structured programming requires the modern control structures and procedures that Turbo Basic provides.

Turbo Basic is advertised as having 8087 support. What does that mean?

The 8087 coprocessor, which you can add to any IBM PC-compatible computer, speeds up numeric calculations. Standard BASIC, BASICA, and many compiled versions of BASIC are not capable of using the coprocessor. However, Turbo Basic is.

What are the essential steps to create a program in Turbo Basic?

The steps are as follows:

1. Invoke Turbo Basic by entering **TB** and then pressing the spacebar to activate the main menu.

2. Press E to activate the editor.

3. Type in the program as you would on a word processor.

4. After writing the program, press ALT-R to run the program.

These insights into the capabilities and power of Turbo Basic can inspire you to explore the language further. We are pleased to have the opportunity to serve as your guides.

2 A First Look at Turbo Basic

Introduction

You write a Turbo Basic program by using a word processor called the *editor*. The word *edit* is used to describe both the process of writing and the process of revising a program. This chapter presents the essential information that you need to edit and run a program using Turbo Basic. Chapter 3 presents further capabilities of the editor.

Getting Started

As with any software package, you should first make a copy of the Turbo Basic Program Disk for day-to-day use and put the master disk away for safekeeping. Appendix E gives details for making backup copies or copying files into a subdirectory of a hard disk.

8 *Using Turbo Basic*

If the copy resides in a subdirectory of a hard disk designated as drive C, then you invoke Turbo Basic from the DOS prompt **C>** by entering

C> CD \ name of subdirectory

C> TB

If the copy resides on a floppy disk in a disk drive, then make that drive the current drive by entering (from DOS) its letter followed by a colon. You then enter **TB**. After the Borland copyright notice appears, press the space bar to get the main screen, which is shown in Figure 2-1.

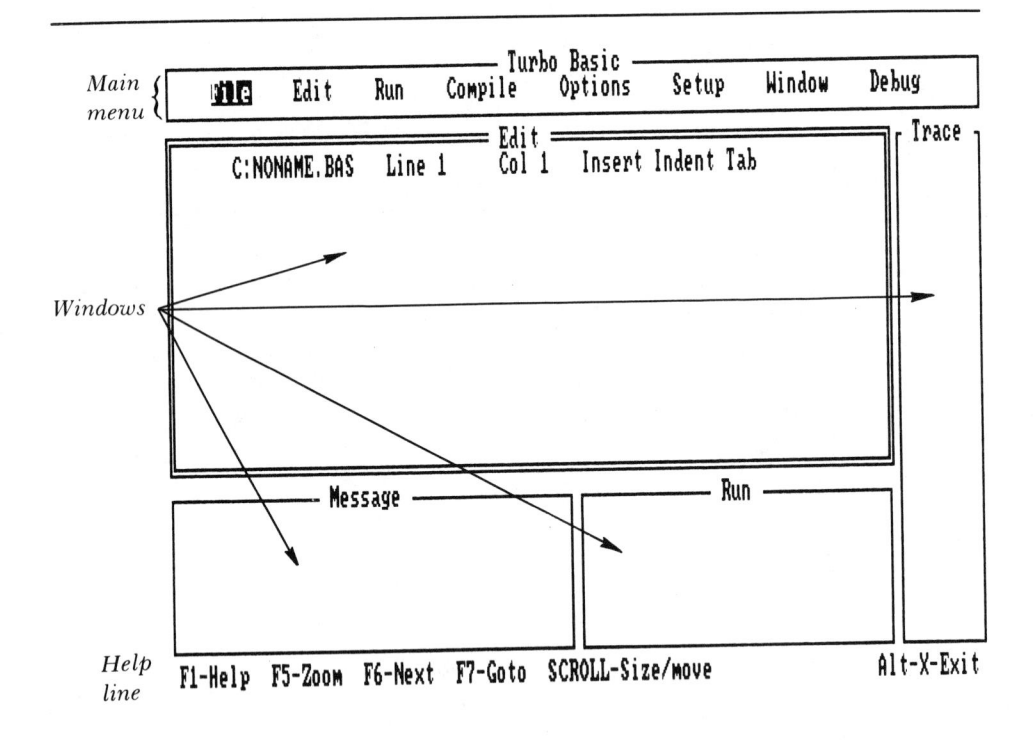

```
                    ┌──────── Turbo Basic ────────┐
 Main  {   File    Edit   Run   Compile   Options   Setup   Window   Debug
 menu
                    ┌═══════════ Edit ═══════════┐ ┌ Trace ┐
                      C:NONAME.BAS  Line 1  Col 1  Insert Indent Tab



Windows


                    ┌──── Message ────┐  ┌──── Run ────┐



  Help
  line     F1-Help  F5-Zoom  F6-Next  F7-Goto  SCROLL-Size/move        Alt-X-Exit
```

Figure 2-1. *The Main screen*

A First Look at Turbo Basic 9

The Main Screen

The eight items available from the *main menu* are as follows.

File Produces a pull-down menu of file-related tasks, such as loading or saving a program.

Edit Allows writing or revising of a program.

Run Runs the program currently in memory.

Compile Compiles the program currently in memory.

Options Produces a pull-down menu of special rules for the compiler to follow, such as the rule that permits a user to terminate programs by pressing CTRL-BREAK.

Setup Produces a pull-down menu of assorted tasks, such as changing the colors of the windows or telling Turbo Basic to save each program automatically.

Window Produces a pull-down menu of window-related tasks, such as changing the configuration of the windows so that Turbo Basic stacks them one on top of the other.

Debug Produces a pull-down menu of debugging tasks, such as tracing.

When one item is highlighted, as **File** is in Figure 2-1, Turbo Basic is waiting for you to choose one of the eight items.
   Let's now consider the four rectangular *windows* that appear in the Main screen.

Edit Window Holds text of current program.

Message Window Provides information about the compiling process during compilation.

Run Window Displays the output of executed programs.

Trace Window Holds useful information that Turbo Basic produces when tracing a program.

Finally, the *help line* at the bottom of the main screen displays the actions or commands that are associated with certain special keys. This information sometimes changes as you move from task to task. In addition, pressing one of the keys SHIFT, ALT, or CTRL for a moment displays actions associated with that key. A particularly useful key shown in the help line is the function key F1, which calls up Turbo Basic's context-sensitive help screens.

Using Turbo Basic's Menus

When you first invoke Turbo Basic, the main menu is *active,* which means that one of the selections is highlighted by a rectangular box and Turbo Basic is waiting for you to make a choice from the main menu. Regardless of where you are in Turbo Basic—except in the middle of running a program—you can always activate the main menu by pressing ESC one or more times. There are two methods for selecting an item from the main menu:

- Press the first letter of the item. (You can use either lowercase or uppercase.)

- Use the cursor-movement keys to move the highlighted rectangle to the desired item, and then press the Enter key.

For example, with the main menu active, pressing F selects **File** and pulls down another menu from under the word **File**, as shown in Figure 2-2. This menu is called a *pull-down menu.* At this point, pressing D selects the command **Directory** and causes the instruction **Enter Mask** to pop up on top of the full-down menu, as shown in Figure 2-3. Pressing ENTER produces a display of all files on the current disk drive or directory. From here, you can reactivate the main menu by pressing ESC twice.

A First Look at Turbo Basic 11

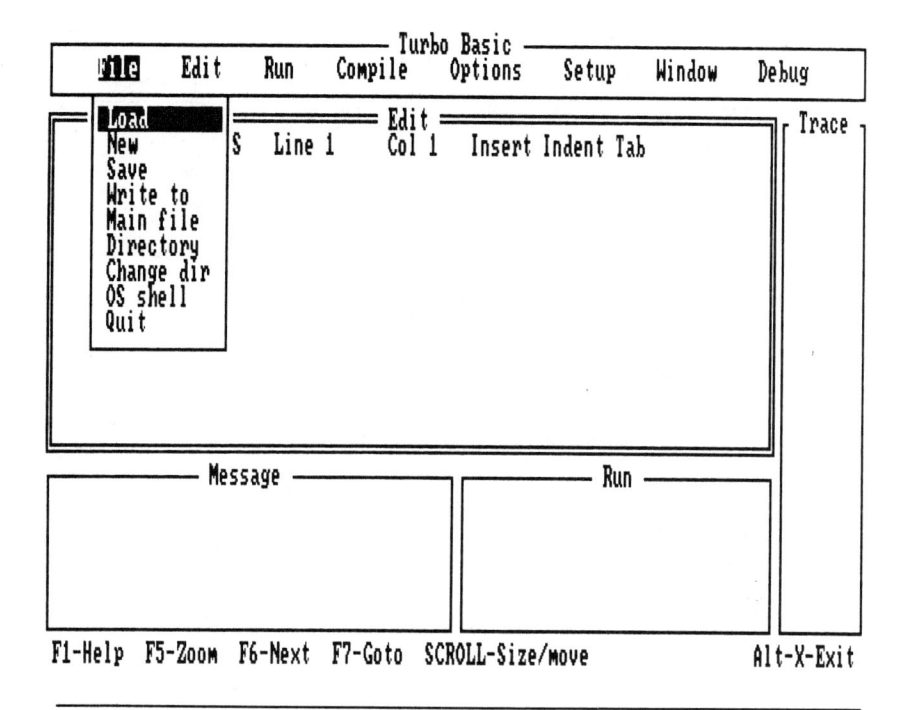

```
                        ┌─ Turbo Basic ─┐
  ▓File▓   Edit   Run   Compile   Options   Setup   Window   Debug
  ┌─Load──────┬────── Edit ──────────────────────────┬─ Trace ─┐
  │ New      │S  Line 1   Col 1   Insert Indent Tab │         │
  │ Save     │                                       │         │
  │ Write to │                                       │         │
  │ Main file│                                       │         │
  │ Directory│                                       │         │
  │ Change dir                                       │         │
  │ OS shell │                                       │         │
  │ Quit     │                                       │         │
  └──────────┴───────────────────────────────────────┴─────────┘
      ┌───── Message ─────┐      ┌───── Run ─────┐
      │                   │      │               │
      │                   │      │               │
      └───────────────────┘      └───────────────┘
  F1-Help  F5-Zoom  F6-Next  F7-Goto  SCROLL-Size/move    Alt-X-Exit
```

Figure 2-2. *The File menu*

Here is another example of using the menus. Activate the main menu and then press the right-arrow key a few times until **Options** is highlighted. Now, press ENTER to produce the pull-down menu shown in Figure 2-4. At this point, pressing the down-arrow key three times highlights the option **Keyboard break**, which you can toggle between ON and OFF states by pressing ENTER. You should select the ON state, which allows you to terminate the execution of a program by pressing the key combination CTRL-BREAK. As before, you can return to the main menu by pressing ESC twice.

You may now wish to select some other items from the main menu and explore their pull-down and pop-up menus. Later, Chapter 9 discusses the usefulness of most of the items. Note that the commands **Edit**, **Run**, and **Compile** in the main menu do not have any pull-down menus.

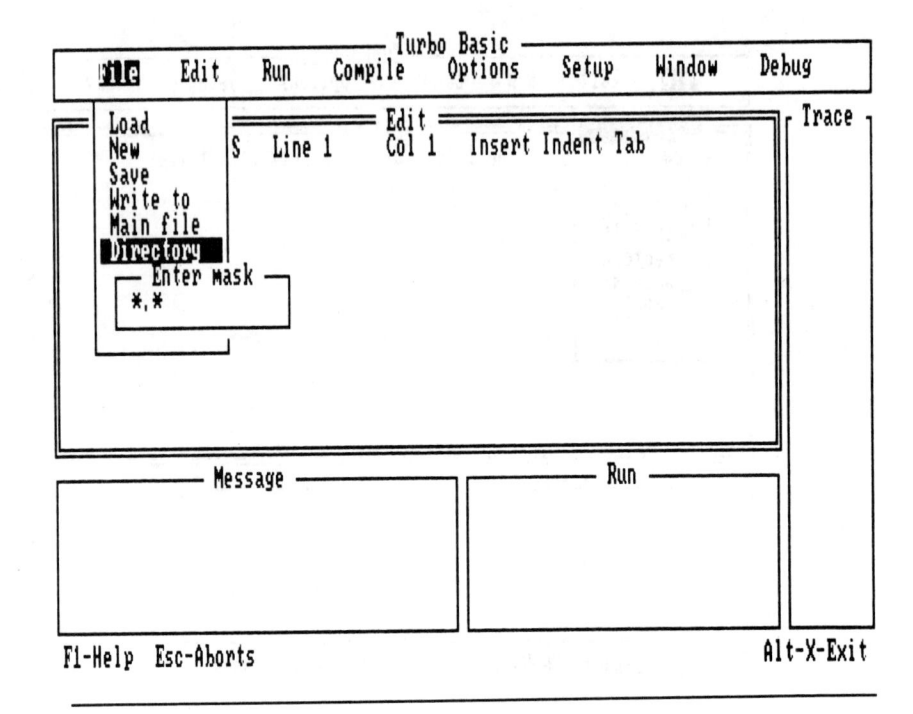

Figure 2-3. A pop-up menu

Using Turbo Basic's Help Screens

Turbo Basic provides easy access to an extensive system of context-sensitive help screens, which explain the use of the items in the various menus. To obtain a help screen, position the highlighting rectangle on an item in any menu and then press F1. Figure 2-5 shows the help screen that describes **Keyboard break**. To leave the help screen and return to the main menu, simply press ESC.

Turbo Basic's help system provides information on over 60 subjects. To see an index of these subjects, press F1 twice. Turbo Basic displays only part of the index at any time. To see additional topics, press END (which moves the highlighting rectangle to the words **Go**

A First Look at Turbo Basic 13

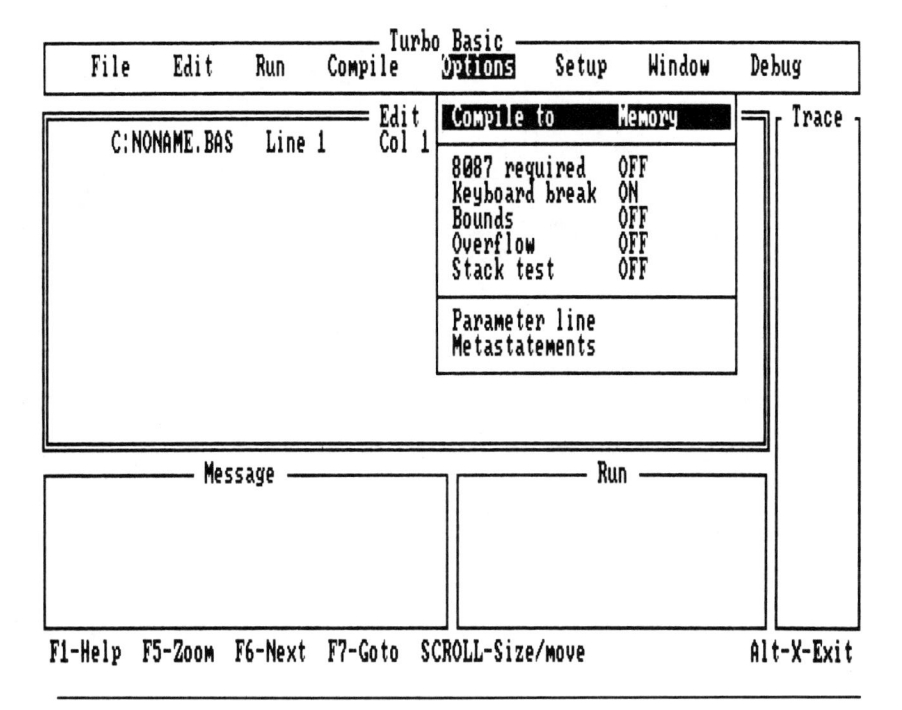

Figure 2-4. *The Options menu*

on...) and then press ENTER. You can obtain the help screen for any topic in the index by positioning the highlighting rectangle on the topic and then pressing ENTER.

Often, when displaying a help screen, Turbo Basic emphasizes one or more words of the text by displaying them in high-intensity white or in a special color. Highlighting one of the emphasized words and pressing ENTER calls up the help screen associated with that word. When you highlight **Go on...**, you can get additional information on the current subject by pressing ENTER.

As you move from topic to topic in the help system, you may decide to return to the previous help screen. You can do this by pressing ALT-F1. No matter how many help screens you have examined, pressing ESC once allows you to exit the help system.

14   Using Turbo Basic

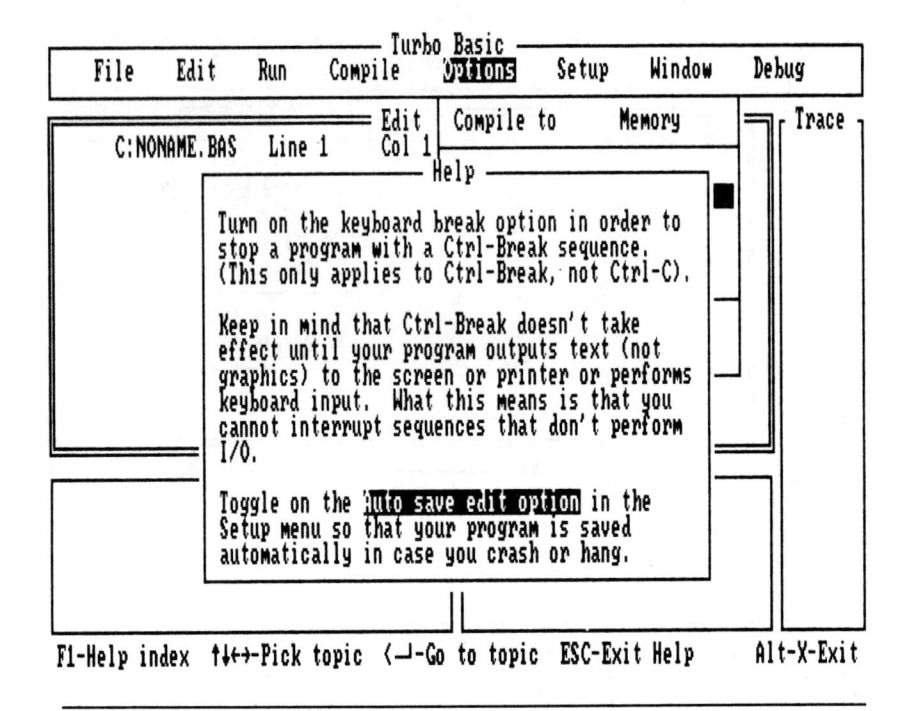

Figure 2-5.   *Help screen for the* **Keyboard break** *option*

Creating and Running a Program: A Walkthrough

You are now ready to write your first Turbo Basic program. To begin, select **Edit** from the main menu. A blinking cursor appears in the Edit window, which now has a double border around it. (The double border signifies that the Edit window is currently the active window.)

A First Look at Turbo Basic

Turbo Basic's word processor has many convenient features to help you type in a program. However, for now, the following elementary editing techniques will be sufficient.

- Type each line of the program as you would on a typewriter. After finishing a line, move to a new line by pressing ENTER.

- You can use the cursor-movement keys to move anywhere in the program.

- To erase a character, press either the backspace key to erase the character to the left of the cursor, or DEL to erase the character at the cursor.

- To insert a character, position the cursor at the desired location and type the character. Characters at and to the right of the cursor will automatically move to the right to accommodate the inserted character.

Type in the following program. Be careful to copy exactly what is shown here. (In Turbo Basic, line numbers are optional. This book does not use them.)

```
CLS
INPUT "What is your first name"; firstName$
LET message$ = "Welcome to Turbo Basic " + firstName$
FOR count = 1 TO 5
   PRINT message$
NEXT count
```

Now that the program is typed in, you can run it. The simplest method of leaving the Edit window and running the program is to press ALT-R. After you press the key combination, you should respond with the information that the **INPUT** statement requests.

If the program was not typed correctly and contains an error, Turbo Basic will display an error message at the top of the Edit window, and will position the cursor on the line that contains the error. If this happens, compare your program to the one shown above, correct the mistake, and press ALT-R again.

16   Using Turbo Basic

```
┌──────────────────────── Turbo Basic ────────────────────────┐
│     File    Edit    Run    Compile    Options    Setup    Window    Debug     │
├──────────────────────────── Edit ────────────────────────┬─ Trace ─┐
│     C:NONAME.BAS    Line 6    Col 11    Insert Indent Tab │         │
│ CLS                                                       │         │
│ INPUT "What is your first name"; firstName$              │         │
│ LET message$ = "Welcome to Turbo Basic " + firstName$    │         │
│ FOR count = 1 to 5                                        │         │
│   PRINT message$                                          │         │
│ NEXT count                                                │         │
│                                                           │         │
│                                                           │         │
│                                                           │         │
├──────── Message ────────┬──────────── Run ────────────────┤
│ Compiling: NONAME       │ Welcome to Turbo Basic Gabrie   │
│ Line:   6   Stmt:   8   │ Welcome to Turbo Basic Gabrie   │
│                         │ Welcome to Turbo Basic Gabrie   │
│                         │ Welcome to Turbo Basic Gabrie   │
└─────────────────────────┴─────────────────────────────────┘
Alt-F5-Zoom  Alt-F6-Next
```

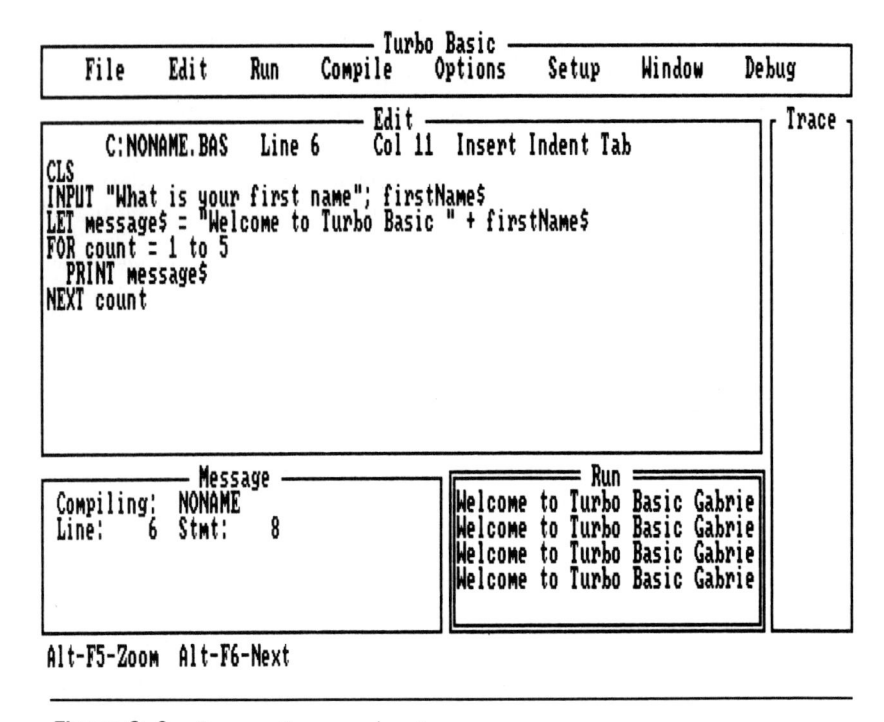

Figure 2-6. *Screen after running program*

After you run the correct program, the screen should appear as shown in Figure 2-6. If it does not, press ESC to leave the Run window and return to the main menu. Next, press E to go back to the Edit window and correct your mistakes. Finally, press ALT-R to rerun your program.

The Message window displays some information about the compilation of the program. Yes, Turbo Basic did compile the program—though, if you blinked, you missed it. Turbo Basic automatically compiles each program before running it. For now, the Message window is of little or no interest.

However, you should study the Run window. Note that the Run window now has a double border, which signals that the Run window is active. Since this window is rather small, some of the output from the program is not visible. To remedy this situation, press

A First Look at Turbo Basic

ALT-F5 (F5 is one function key, and not the separate keys F and 5). Voila! The Run window now fills the entire screen. Press ALT-F5 again: the Run window returns its original size. Pressing ALT-F5 is said to "zoom" the Run window—both *out* (to fill the screen) and *in* (to its original size). You can only use ALT-F5 to zoom the Run window, and then only from the time a program begins to run until the main menu is activated. Before continuing, zoom the Run window out and leave it that way.

Now that you have run the program, you are ready to make a few changes to it. To return to the editor, first press ESC to go back to the main menu, and then select **Edit**. The active Edit window reappears, covering part of the zoomed Run window.

Change the program to read as follows:

```
INPUT "What is your first name"; firstName$
LET message$ = "Welcome " + firstName$
CLS
FOR count = 1 to LEN(message$)
   PRINT TAB(2*count); MID$(message$,count,1)
NEXT count
```

After you have made all of the changes, run (and compile) the new program by pressing ALT-R.

When you have perfected the program, it is time to save it in a file on a disk. Note that the help line at the bottom of the screen indicates that pressing F2 saves your program. Press F2 now. Since you have not given a name to the program yet, Turbo Basic has been calling it by the temporary name NONAME.BAS. Now that you have requested to save your program, Turbo Basic gives you an opportunity to give it a permanent name. Let's call the program GREETING.BAS. Type in **GREETING**. (Notice that NONAME.BAS disappears as soon as you start to type the permanent name.) You do not need to include the .BAS ending; Turbo Basic will add it automatically. Pressing ENTER causes Turbo Basic to save the program in a file named GREETING.BAS. Note that the program is still in memory, ready for you to make additional changes.

To exit from Turbo Basic, simply press ALT-X. If you have made changes in the current program since the last save operation, Turbo Basic will give you the option of saving the current form of the program before exiting. In the future, if you wish to rerun or make changes to GREETING.BAS, start up Turbo Basic, select **Edit**, and follow the directions at the end of this chapter for loading a program.

Compiling a Program

Turbo Basic's compiler translates the program currently in the editor into machine language, which is the only language that the computer understands directly. Turbo Basic performs this task when you select **Compile** from the main menu or when you press ALT-C from inside the editor. The compilation process is very fast in Turbo Basic. Most of the programs in this book will compile in less than one second.

When you type the **Run** command, Turbo Basic first checks to see whether it has compiled the current program. If it has, it executes the program at once. If not, Turbo Basic first compiles the program and then executes it.

Compile-time Errors Versus Run-time Errors

While Turbo Basic's compiler translates a program into machine language, it can detect about 100 violations of the rules for Turbo Basic programs. An error in a program that the compiler catches is referred to as a *compile-time error*. When the compiler detects an error, it stops processing, invokes the editor, displays an error message at the top of the Edit window, and places the cursor at the point in the program where it detected the error. Some examples of errors caught at compile-time are trying to assign a number to a string variable or vice versa (*type mismatch*), forgetting the keyword **THEN** in an **IF** statement, and having more left parentheses than right parentheses in a numeric expression. Appendix E of the owners' handbook offers a complete list of errors and their explanations.

A First Look at Turbo Basic

Not all errors can be detected while the compiler is translating a program into machine language. Errors that do not show up until the program is actually run are referred to as *run-time errors*. When Turbo Basic detects a run-time error, it stops execution, activates the editor, displays an error message at the top of the Edit window, and places the cursor at the location in the program where it detected the error. Some examples of run-time errors are trying to **READ** a value for a numeric variable and having a string value in the **DATA** statement; trying to do a division of two variables when the divisor has the value zero; and trying to print information on a printer that you have not turned on.

How to Perform Standard BASIC Tasks

Here is a list of some common "direct" commands found in Standard BASIC. Following each command is a method to accomplish the same task when you use the Turbo Basic editor. (You may also perform some of these tasks outside of the editor, as Chapter 9 will describe.)

LIST A portion of the current program is always visible in the Edit window. To see other parts of the program, use the up-arrow, down-arrow, PGUP, PGDN, CTRL-PGUP, or CTRL-PGDN key.

SAVE Press F2. If you have not given a name to the program yet, Turbo Basic will prompt you to type a name in an input box.

RUN Press ALT-R. Turbo Basic will then compile (if it has not done so already) and execute the program. After the program has finished running, you can return to the editor by pressing ESC and then E.

LLIST To print the entire current program, press CTRL-KP. To print just a portion of the program, first mark the portion as a block. You do this by moving the cursor to the beginning of the portion and pressing F7, and then moving the cursor to the end of the portion and pressing F8. (The marked block of code will appear in reverse video.) After that, pressing CTRL-KP prints the marked block. After the code is printed, you can unmark the block by pressing CTRL-KH.

LOAD   Press F3 to execute the "load a **New** program" command. Pressing this key activates an input box entitled **Load File Name** that displays *.**BAS**. At this point, there are two options. You can load a program into memory by typing the name of the program over *.**BAS** and pressing ENTER. Or, you can request a selective listing of file names on a disk, as you would in DOS, by typing the desired specification over *.**BAS** and pressing ENTER. (Simply press ENTER to use the default specification *.**BAS**.) You can then select the program that you want to load from the list by using the cursor-movement and ENTER keys. If Turbo Basic queries you about saving the current program, respond as desired.

NEW   To erase the current program from memory and start work on a new program, press F3 and enter the name for the new program that you wish to create. If Turbo Basic queries you about saving the current program, respond as desired.

MERGE   To merge or incorporate a program residing on a disk into the program that you are currently editing, move the cursor to the place where you want to insert the merged material and then press CTRL-KR. Doing so activates an input box entitled **Read Block From File** that displays *.**BAS**. You can now proceed to request a program as described earlier with the Load command. The inserted material will appear marked as a block. Press CTRL-KH to unmark the block.

SYSTEM   To return to DOS, press ALT-X. If Turbo Basic queries you about saving the current program, respond as desired.

3 The Turbo Basic Editor

Capabilities of the Turbo Basic Editor

The main tasks that the editor can perform are common to most word processors, as shown here.

Cursor Movement You can move the cursor to any location in the program. The cursor-movement keys on the numeric keypad move the cursor one position in any direction. When used with CTRL, the left-arrow and right-arrow keys move the cursor to the beginning of the word to the left and right of the current cursor position. In addition, the editor has commands that move the cursor to the beginning or the end of the current line, or to the top or bottom of the Edit window.

Scrolling There are commands that scroll the program up or down one line, up or down an entire screen, and to the beginning or the end of the program.

Search or Replace The editor can search the program for the first occurrence of any character or word that you specify. You can repeat this search to find subsequent occurrences. As an enhancement of this process, Turbo Basic allows you to replace the found character or word (either automatically or with your consent) with specified text.

Block Manipulation You can mark as a block all of the material between two specified points in the program. (The text within the block will appear highlighted.) You can move a marked block to another place in the program and duplicate it elsewhere, as well as delete it, print it, or save it on a disk.

Deletion The backspace and DEL keys delete one character at a time. The editor has commands that delete the line that contains the cursor, all the text from the cursor to the end of the line, or the word to the right of the cursor.

Restoration You can restore the text or error message that has most recently been erased. Also, you can rescind most commands.

Save and retrieve Programs You can save on disk any program written with the editor and retrieve it at a later time.

One feature of word processors does not hold for the Turbo Basic editor: word-wrapping. With a word processor, when you type a word beyond the end of a line, the word processor automatically brings the word down to the beginning of the next line. However, the Turbo Basic editor scrolls the screen to the *right* to accommodate the text. Thus, one line can contain up to 247 characters. You can start a new program line only by pressing ENTER.

Turbo Basic provides a device that permits program lines both to contain many characters and to be easily read. If you place an underline character (_) at the end of a line on screen, then Turbo Basic will treat the next physical line on screen as a continuation of the preceding program line. If you use this capability, program lines can be of any length.

The Editor Status Line

The top line of the Edit window provides the status of various editing features, and is, therefore, referred to as the *status line*. When you first call up Turbo Basic, the status line appears as follows:

```
C:NONAME.BAS    Line 1      Col 1    Insert Indent Tab
```

Here is the significance of these six entries.

filespec   (as in **C:NONAME.BAS**) When Turbo Basic programs are saved, loaded, or begun with the command **New**, Turbo Basic asks you to provide a name for the program. The filespec, which is an abbreviation for *file specification,* consists of first the disk drive that contains (or will contain) the program and then the program name. Until you name the program, Turbo Basic knows it by the default name NONAME.BAS.

Line Number   The number given identifies the program line that contains the cursor. Turbo Basic counts lines by beginning with the first line of the program currently in memory—not with the line at the top of the screen—and includes all lines, including blank lines. Line numbers that may appear in the program have nothing to do with this count.

Col Number   The number given identifies the cursor's position in its line. Column 1 is the leftmost position in a line, and is usually the leftmost position in the Edit window.

Insert   This word appears when the editor is operating in *insert mode*. When insert mode is on, Turbo Basic moves any text located at the cursor position to the right as you enter new text. When the editor is not in insert mode, new text overwrites any old text that is located at the cursor position. Pressing the INS key will toggle the editor back and forth between the insert mode and the *overwrite mode*.

Indent This word appears when the editor is operating in *auto-indent mode*. When insert mode and auto-indent mode are on, pressing ENTER indents the next line so that it is aligned with the preceding line. When the editor is not in auto-indent mode, new lines begin at column 1. Pressing CTRL-OI toggles the editor back and forth between the auto-indent mode and the no-indent mode.

Tab This word appears when the editor is operating in *tab mode*. When tab mode is on, you may press TAB to move the cursor to the next tab stop on the right. Turbo Basic places an actual tab character in the program text, so that using a single backspace or delete will remove the space created by a tab. Turbo Basic sets tab stops in columns 9, 17, 25, 33, and so on. When the editor is not in tab mode, pressing TAB has no effect. Pressing the CTRL-OT key combination repeatedly will toggle the editor back and forth between the tab mode and the no-tab mode.

Editing Commands

The Turbo Basic command format was influenced by the widely used word processor WordStar. You can issue nearly every command by holding down CTRL and then pressing one or two other keys. For instance, holding down the CTRL key and pressing CTRL-F moves the cursor to the first character of the next word on the right. This command is written CTRL-F. Holding down the CTRL key and pressing Q and then D moves the cursor to the end of the line containing the cursor. This combination is written CTRL-QD. (You only need to hold down the CTRL key until Q is pressed. You can release it, if desired, before you press D.)

Appendix G contains all of the editor's commands. If you are a WordStar user, you will quickly identify the minor operational differences between WordStar and the Turbo Basic editor. Appendix H enumerates these differences.

An Editing Tutorial

This section presents a tutorial that introduces the most frequently used commands. To begin, start up Turbo Basic and press E to enter the editor. Carefully type the following line, including its obvious errors:

```
PRIMT "The ate is"; DATE$
```

The cursor should now be to the right of the dollar sign. Press either HOME or CTRL-QS: Turbo Basic moves the cursor to the beginning of the line and positions it under the **P** in **PRIMT**.

Let's change the **M** to an **N** so that the word is **PRINT**. To do this, press either the right-arrow key or CTRL-D three times to move the cursor under **M**. Delete the **M** by pressing DEL or CTRL-G once. Now type **N** to make the correction.

Next, you should add a space immediately after the word **is**. Press CTRL-right arrow or CTRL-F four times. Note that the cursor moves to the right to the beginning of a word each time you press one of these key combinations. The cursor should now be at the **D** in **DATE$**. Press the left-arrow key or CTRL-S three times to place the cursor under the quotation mark. Finally, press the space bar to insert a space after **is**.

Now, you are ready to change **ate** to **date**. Press CTRL-left arrow or CTRL-A twice. Note that the cursor moves to the left to the beginning of a word each time that you press one of these key combinations. The cursor should now be at the **a** in **ate**. Type **d** to correct the word to **date**.

Next, press ENTER. What was a single line now consists of two lines, with the cursor moving to the beginning of the second line. The cursor brings the **a** in **date** and all subsequent characters with it. Press the backspace key to delete the *new-line character* that pressing ENTER inserted. The two lines become one line again. Press CTRL-N: note that the effect is similar to pressing ENTER, except that the cursor does not move to the beginning of the new line, but rather stays at the end of the old line. Rejoin the two lines by pressing DEL.

Now press END or CTRL-QD to move to the end of the line, and then press ENTER to create a new line properly. Carefully type the following on the new line:

```
PRINT "Time waits for no one."
```

Move the cursor back to the first line by pressing either CTRL-E or the up-arrow key. Note that the cursor remains in the same column. Move the cursor back to the second line by pressing either CTRL-X or the down-arrow key. Now press CTRL-A or CTRL five times, and then press CTRL-D or the right-arrow key to move the cursor left to the beginning of **Time**. Press CTRL-T: note that the editor deletes the word **Time**. Press CTRL-T again to delete the space that was present between **Time** and **waits**. Press CTRL-T a third time to delete the word **waits**. CTRL-T deletes text from the cursor position to the right, to the end of the current word, or to the end of the current group of spaces, as is appropriate.

You should not have deleted the word **Time**. While you could retype it, use Turbo Basic's unique *restore-line command*. Press CTRL-QL: Turbo Basic restores the line to exactly the form it had when you moved the cursor back to the line by pressing CTRL-X or the down-arrow key.

Now press CTRL-right arrow or CTRL-A to move the cursor to the beginning of the word **waits**. Next, delete the remainder of the line by pressing CTRL-QY. Type **is money."** to complete the modifications to this line. The cursor should now be at the end of the line and the line should read

```
PRINT "Time is money."
```

Now you are ready to do some work with blocks of text. Press ENTER to create a third line. Press the up-arrow key or CTRL-E to move the cursor up one line so that it is at the **P** in **PRINT**. Press F7 or CTRL-KB to mark this point as the beginning of a block. Move the cursor to the beginning of the word **is**. Press F8 or CTRL-KK to mark the end of the block. Notice that the highlighted block does not include the **i** in **is**. Press the down-arrow key or CTRL-X to move the cursor down one line: the cursor stays in column 13 even though the third line is empty. Press CTRL-KC; Turbo Basic copies the highlighted block beginning at the cursor location.

Press HOME to move the cursor to the beginning of the line and then press CTRL-T. Notice that Turbo Basic deletes the leading blank spaces in the line. Move up to the beginning of the second line (by pressing the up-arrow key), and then press F7 to mark this point as the beginning of the block. The highlighted block now extends from the beginning of the second line to the end of the third line. Now save—that is, **Write**—just this highlighted block of text in a disk file. Press CTRL-KW, and at the prompt for a file name, type **TEMP** and press ENTER. Turbo Basic now saves the highlighted text in a disk file called TEMP.BAS. The current program has not been changed. Finally, delete the highlighted block of text by simply pressing CTRL-KY.

You are now ready to read the file TEMP.BAS into the program at a new location. Press ENTER three times to create three empty lines at the bottom of the program. Type **PRINT::PRINT** and move the cursor back to the second colon. Now press CTRL-KR and, at the prompt for a file name, type **TEMP** and press ENTER. The Edit window should now appear as shown in Figure 3-1. Turbo Basic inserts the text that you saved earlier into the program beginning at the cursor. Note that the inserted text is highlighted as a block. Press the up-arrow key and HOME to move the cursor to the beginning of the line above the highlighted block. Now press CTRL-KV to move the highlighted block from its current location to the point where the cursor is located.

So far, you have seen the way to mark, copy, delete, move, save, and recall a highlighted block of text. The final operation available for use on a block of text is printing. Before you print a block of text, it is best to make sure that Turbo Basic includes in the block

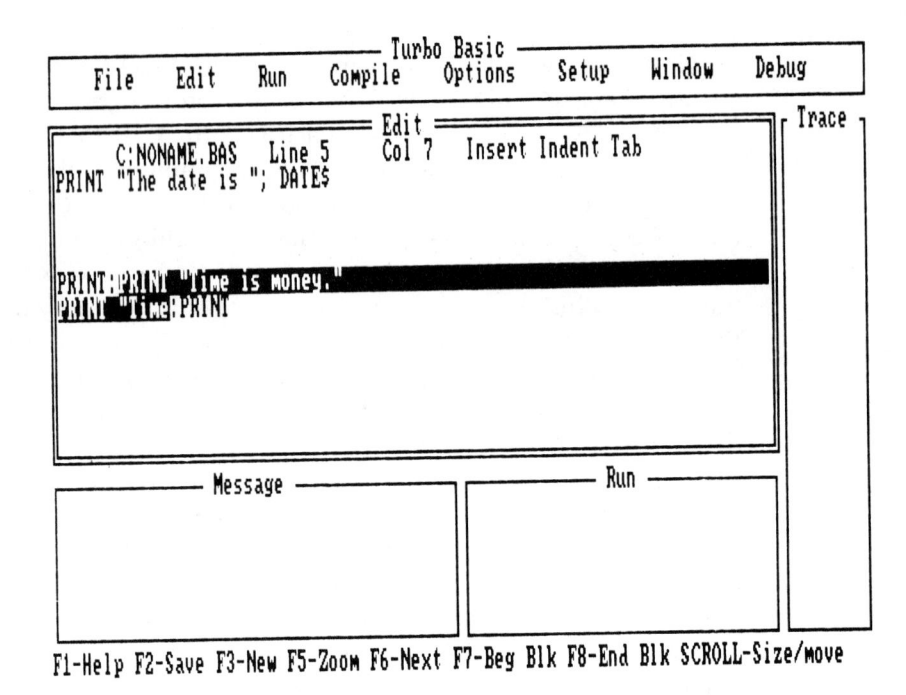

```
┌─────────────────────── Turbo Basic ───────────────────────┐
│   File    Edit    Run    Compile   Options   Setup   Window   Debug │
```

```
┌──────────────────────────── Edit ────────────────────────┐┌─ Trace ─┐
│       C:NONAME.BAS    Line 5    Col 7   Insert Indent Tab │
│PRINT "The date is "; DATE$                                │
│                                                           │
│                                                           │
│PRINT::PRINT "Time is money."                              │
│PRINT "Time::PRINT                                         │
│                                                           │
│                                                           │
│                                                           │
└───────────────────────────────────────────────────────────┘
```

```
┌────── Message ──────┐┌──────── Run ────────┐
│                     ││                     │
│                     ││                     │
│                     ││                     │
└─────────────────────┘└─────────────────────┘
```

F1-Help F2-Save F3-New F5-Zoom F6-Next F7-Beg Blk F8-End Blk SCROLL-Size/move

Figure 3-1. *The tutorial program after reading in TEMP.BAS*

the new-line character at the end of the last line. In order to do this, you must mark the end of the block at the beginning of the line that follows the last line you want to have as part of your block. Use the down-arrow key to move the cursor down two lines so that it is positioned under the first **P** in **PRINT::PRINT**. Now press F8 to mark this point as the end of the block. Notice how the highlighting changes. If your computer is attached to a printer, turn it on now and then press CTRL-KP. The printer will print the two lines of text in the highlighted block.

Move the cursor up one line (to the second of the highlighted lines). Press CTRL-Y twice to delete this line and the line that contains **PRINT::PRINT**. Now make 15 or so copies of the highlighted line by pressing CTRL-KC repeatedly. Now give the "move to end of program" command by pressing either CTRL-PGDN or CTRL-QC, and type in the line

```
PRINT "The time is "; time$
```

Move back to the beginning of the program by pressing CTRL-PGUP or CTRL-QR. Press ENTER to create a blank line at the top of the program. Then move the cursor to the beginning of this empty line and type

```
REM A timely program.
```

Now that the program is complete, save it in a disk file by pressing either F2 or CTRL-KS. Respond to the prompt for a name by typing **TIME** and pressing ENTER. Turbo Basic saves the program in the disk file TIME.BAS.

The program is also still in memory. Imagine that you want to create a version that prints the original message **Time waits for no one**. Let's use Turbo Basic's search and replace command to create this version. Press CTRL-QA. In response to the prompt for a string to search for, type **is money** and press ENTER. In response to the prompt for a replacement string, type **waits for no one** and press ENTER. Finally, in response to the prompt for options, type **GN** and press ENTER to request global replacement and no verification of each replacement. (Note: if you only want to *find* a specific string in the program, you can use the search command by pressing CTRL-QF.)

Press PGUP or CTRL-R and PGDN or CTRL-C to move up and down through the program to examine your new creation. Finally, return to the main menu by pressing ESC. The new version of the program resides in memory, but has not yet been saved on disk. To save this program in a new disk file (rather than overwriting the contents of TIME.BAS), use the **Write to** command in the Files menu.

4 Manipulating Data

Numbers

Turbo Basic can perform calculations with numbers as small as 10^{-307} and as large as 10^{308}. The results of these calculations can range in magnitude from 10^{-999} to 10^{999}. (These magnitudes are more than adequate for any physical measurements. For instance, there are less than 10^{100} atoms in the solar system.)

You can use a number in Turbo Basic either directly as a literal numeric value, as in the statement **PRINT 3.14159**; or indirectly by storing the number in a named place in memory, commonly referred to as a *variable,* and then using the name of the variable in statements, such as **LET pi = 3.14259** and **PRINT pi**. Variable names must begin with a letter and can consist of any number of letters and digits. The cases of the letters are irrelevant; for example, **pi** and **PI** refer to the same variable. Appendix D contains a list of words that Turbo Basic reserves for its own use and that you cannot use as variable names.

A good variable name makes the program easy to understand by indicating the role of the variable. Some suggestive names of variables are **averagePrice**, **costOfMaterials**, **answer**, and **milesDriven**.

In this book, we write variable names with lowercase letters, except for the first letters of new words.

To optimize execution time and make efficient use of memory, Turbo Basic has four types of numeric variables to which you can assign numbers. These types are known as *integer, long integer, single-precision floating-point,* and *double-precision floating-point.* You can specify the type of a numeric variable by appending one of the four *type-declaration tags*—%, &, !, and #—to the end of the variable name. If no type-declaration tag is present, Turbo Basic considers the variable to be single-precision. Figure 4-1 presents some examples.

Turbo Basic provides the eight arithmetic operations, which are shown in Table 4-1. Since the integer division and modulo operators are not as well known as the others, some further explanation is in order.

When you divide two whole numbers by using long division, you obtain an integer quotient and a remainder. For instance, as shown here, 122 divided by 5 produces an integer quotient of 24 and a remainder of 2.

$$
\begin{array}{r}
24 \\
5 \overline{\smash{)}122} \\
\underline{10} \\
22 \\
\underline{20} \\
2
\end{array}
$$

In general, if M and N are whole numbers and you divide M into N by long division, then $N \backslash M$ denotes the integer quotient and N **MOD** M denotes the remainder. Hence, **122 \ 5** is 24, and **122 MOD 5** is 2.

Turbo Basic defines integer division and **MOD** for any pair of numbers whose (possibly rounded) values are between -32768 and 32767. If M or N are not whole numbers, they are rounded to the nearest whole numbers. The value of $N \backslash M$ is the whole-number portion of the ordinary quotient, N/M. The value of N **MOD** M is $N - M*(N \backslash M)$. You can replace M and N by numeric variables of any type. However, unless the values assigned to the variables are in the proper range, Turbo Basic presents the error message **Error 6: Overflow.**

Manipulating Data

Variable Name	Variable Type
Count%	Integer
population&	Long integer
price!	Single-precision floating point
cost	Single-precision floating point
grossNationalProduct#	Double-precision floating point

Figure 4-1. *Examples of type-declaration tags*

Operator	Name	Example
+	Addition	2 + 3 is 5
−	Subtraction	3 − 2 is 1
*	Multiplication	2*3 is 6
/	Division	2/3 is .6666666666666667
^	Exponentiation	3^2 is 9
−	Negation	−(1.5) is −1.5
\	Integer division	17\5 is 3
MOD	Modulo	17 MOD 5 is 2

Table 4-1. *Arithmetic Operators*

Program 4-1 uses \ and **MOD** in an elementary change-making program that accepts an amount of money as input, and calculates the number of nickels and pennies required to make that amount of change.

Integer Variables and Long Integer Variables

Integer variables and long integer variables can only store whole numbers (both positive and negative) with restricted ranges. An integer variable can store whole numbers from −32768 through 32767, while long integer variables can store whole numbers from

```
REM Demonstrate integer division and MOD [4-1]
INPUT "Amount of money in cents"; money
nickels = money\5
pennies = money MOD 5
PRINT nickels; "nickels and"; pennies; "pennies"
END

Run
Amount of money in cents? 23
 4 nickels and 3 pennies

Run
Amount of money in cents? 35000
Error 6: Overflow
```

Program 4-1. *Integer division and* **MOD**

−2147483648 through 2147483647. You classify variables as integer or long integer by using the type-declaration tag % or &, respectively. Although long integers require more memory space and take longer to process than integers, long integers are often necessary. For instance, integer variables cannot hold the populations of the states in the United States.

When you assign a number that is not whole to an integer variable or a long integer variable, Turbo Basic rounds the number to the nearest whole number. If the number contains the decimal 0.5, Turbo Basic rounds it to the nearest even whole number. For instance, Turbo Basic rounds 2.5 to 2 and 3.5 to 4. If you assign a number outside of the allowable range to an integer or a long integer, an overflow error message results.

Program 4-2 assigns values to numeric variables and displays the value of one of the variables. The last statement causes the error message **Error 6: Overflow** to appear at the top of the Edit window. In the output shown here, we have displayed the error message in boldface since it appears in the Edit window rather than the Run window.

```
REM Working with integer and long integer variables [4-2]
castOfBenHur% = 25452
wordsInBible& = 773692
US1986medianAge% = 31.4
PRINT US1986medianAge%
US1985nationalDebt& = 2,000,000,000,000

Run
 31
Error 6: Overflow
```

Program 4-2. *Integer variables and long integer variables*

Floating-point Variables

You designate a single-precision numeric variable by using its name with either the type-declaration tag ! or no type-declaration tag. A single-precision numeric variable can store numbers—positive or negative—that have magnitude from 0 to 10^{38}. Turbo Basic treats values having magnitudes less than about 9×10^{-37} as zero. You designate a double-precision numeric variable by using its name followed by the type-declaration tag #. A double-precision numeric variable can store the value zero or any value of magnitude from about 10^{-306} to 1.67×10^{308}. The values of single-precision variables are accurate to 6 (and sometimes 7) significant figures, while the values of double-precision variables are accurate to 16 significant figures.

Turbo Basic converts the values of floating-point variables for storage to a special base 2 floating-point format, and then converts them back to base 10 format for display or printing. The conversions to and from the base 2 format alter some numbers slightly. Turbo Basic displays the values of floating-point variables either in

```
REM Demonstrate the use of numeric variables [4-3]
num = .2
weightOfEarthInTons = 6588*10^21
balance = 1234567.89
balance# = 1234567.89
googol# = 1E100             '1*10^100
PRINT num
PRINT weightOfEarthInTons
PRINT balance
PRINT balance#
PRINT googol#^5
googolplex# = 10^googol#    'Causes overflow
END

Run
 .2000000029802322
 6.588E+024
 1234567.875
 1234567.89
 1E+500
Error 6: Overflow:
```

Program 4-3. *The use of numeric variables*

scientific or standard notation. In scientific notation, Turbo Basic expresses each number as a number from 1 to 10 multiplied by 10 to a power, where 10 to a power is written as **E** followed by the power. Program 4-3 illustrates these concepts.

Note that you always begin a program with a descriptive **REM** statement. In addition, you can add a remark to the end of a line by preceding the remark with an apostrophe.

Numeric Functions

Turbo Basic provides a wide variety of predefined *numeric functions*, which act upon numeric values to produce new values. Some of these functions are shown in Table 4-2. Appendix F contains a complete list of Turbo Basic's predefined functions.

The function **CEIL** can be used to tabulate rates based on units plus fractions thereof. Program 4-4 demonstrates a use of **CEIL** in computing postage for first-class letters.

Manipulating Data

Function	Meaning	Example
ABS(x)	Absolute value of x, | x |	ABS(−3.2) is 3.2
CEIL(x)	Nearest whole number ≤ x	CEIL(3.2) is 4
FIX(x)	Whole number part of x	FIX(3.2) is 3
INT(x)	Nearest whole number ≥ x	INT(3.2) is 3
SGN(x)	Sign of x (−1, 0, or 1)	SGN(3.2) is 1

Table 4-2. *Some Predefined Numeric Functions*

You can use the function **INT** to round numbers. If x is a positive number, then

INT(x + .5)

is the value of x rounded to the nearest whole number.

The functions **ABS** and **SGN** can be used to round negative numbers. The value of **SGN**(x) is −1, 0, or 1, depending upon whether x is negative, zero, or positive, respectively. If x is any number, then

SGN(x)*INT(ABS(x)+.5)

is the rounded value of x.

For any x,

SGN(x)*INT(100*ABS(x)+.5)/100

```
REM Determine the proper postage for a first-class letter [4-4]
INPUT "Weight of letter in ounces"; weight
postage = .22 + .17*CEIL(weight - 1)
PRINT "The postage is"; postage
END

Run
Weight of letter in ounces? 2.3
The postage is .56
```

Program 4-4. *Using CEIL*

```
REM Round a number [4-5]
INPUT "Number to be rounded"; x#
INPUT "Number of decimal places"; n%
roundedValue# = SGN(x#)*INT(10^n%*ABS(x#)+.5)/10^n%
PRINT "The rounded value is"; roundedValue#
END

Run
Number to be rounded? -1.235
Number of decimal places? 2
The rounded value is -1.24
```

Program 4-5. *Rounding a number*

is the value of x rounded to two decimal places. To round x to N decimal places, replace 100 in the expression just given with 1 followed by N zeros. Program 4-5 illustrates this technique.

Numeric Expressions

A numeric expression consists of numeric constants, variables, and/or functions combined by numeric operators. Parentheses are helpful in clarifying the order that Turbo Basic uses to perform the operations. Turbo Basic evaluates expressions within parentheses first. In the event that parentheses are nested one pair inside another pair, the innermost expression takes precedence. Unless altered by parentheses, the arithmetic operations are evaluated in the order given in Table 4-3. First, Turbo Basic evaluates all exponentiations from left to right, and then all negations from left to right. After that, Turbo Basic evaluates the multiplications and divisions one after another from left to right. After evaluating the integer divisions and **MOD**s, Turbo Basic carries out additions and subtractions from left to right. Table 4-4 gives some expressions and their interpretations.

Manipulating Data

exponentiation
negation
multiplication and division
integer division
MOD
addition and subtraction

Table 4-3. Hierarchy of Arithmetic Operations

Expression	Interpretation	Value
2 + 3*4	2 + (3*4)	14
100 MOD 21/3	100 MOD (21/3)	2
−2^4	−(2^4)	−16
6*8/4+3	((6*8)/4)+3	15

Table 4-4. Operator Hierarchy Examples

Strings

A string constant is a sequence of characters. String constants often appear surrounded by quotation marks in programs. The string constant "", which has length zero, is referred to as the *null string*. Variables that hold string constants follow the same naming rules as numeric variables, but use the type-declaration tag $. Although a string constant in Turbo Basic can be as long as 32767 characters, the combined length of all strings stored in memory at one time cannot exceed 65536 characters.

The only operator available for strings is the *concatenation operator*, which is denoted by +. If a$ and b$ are strings, then the string a$ + b$ is the string that you obtain by joining the two strings. For instance, **"hand"** + **"book"** is **"handbook"**.

String Functions

Turbo Basic provides numerous functions that take strings as arguments. Table 4-5 presents some of the string functions available in Turbo Basic, and Appendix B offers a complete description of these functions and other predefined string functions.

Program 4-6 uses string functions to extract a person's first name from that person's full name, while Program 4-7 determines a person's age.

Function	Meaning	Example
INSTR(a$,b$)	First location of b in a$	INSTR("cat","a") is 2
LCASE$(a$)	a$ in lowercase letters	LCASE$("Cat") is "cat"
LEFT$(a$,n)	Leftmost n characters of a$	LEFT$("cat",2) is "ca"
LEN(a$)	Number of characters in a$	LEN("cat") is 3
MID$(a$,m,n)	n characters of a$ beginning with mth	MID$("cat",2,1) is "a"
RIGHT$(a$,n)	Rightmost n characters of a$	RIGHT$("cat",2) is "at"
UCASE$(a$)	a$ in uppercase letters	UCASE$("Cat") is "CAT"
DATE$	Current date	DATE$ might be "09-26-1987"
VAL(a$)	Converts a$ to number	VAL(MID$("04/06/37",4,2)) is 6

Table 4-5. *Some Predefined String Functions*

Manipulating Data

```
REM Extract first name [4-6]
INPUT "Enter your full name: ", fullName$
n = INSTR(fullName$," ")         'Location of first space
firstName$ = LEFT$(fullName$,n)
PRINT "Your first name is "; firstName$
END

Run
INPUT Enter your full name: George H. "Babe" Ruth
Your first name is George
```

Program 4-6. *Extracting a first name*

```
REM Determine a person's age on this year's birthday [4-7]
INPUT "Enter your date of birth (mm/dd/yyyy): ", birthday$
age = VAL(RIGHT$(DATE$,4)) - VAL(RIGHT$(birthday$,4))
PRINT "Your age is"; age; "this year."
END

Run   (Assume that this year is 1988.)
Enter your date of birth (mm/dd/yyyy): 04/06/1937
Your age is 51 this year.
```

Program 4-7. *Determining a person's age on this year's birthday*

Further Discussion of Types

As discussed earlier, placing a type-declaration tag—%, &, !, #, or $—at the end of a variable name explicitly specifies the type of the variable. You should also note that variables with the same name but different tags are distinct variables, as shown in Program 4-8.

```
REM Demonstrate that different tags produce distinct variables [4-8]
a% = 5: a& = 987654321
a! = 2.5: a# = 3.14159265358979
a$ = "Turbo Basic"
PRINT a%; a&
PRINT a!; a#
PRINT a$
END

Run
 5   987654321
 2.5  3.14159265358979
Turbo Basic
```

Program 4-8. *Different tags produce distinct variables*

Note that you can write several statements on the same line of a program as long as you separate them by using colons.

Turbo Basic specifies a variable whose name has no type-declaration tag as a single-precision variable; that is, Turbo Basic treats it as if the variable name had the tag !. Program 4-9 shows that Turbo Basic considers a tagless variable to be the same as the single-precision tagged variable of the same name.

If you find using type-declaration tags to be cumbersome, especially for numeric variables, you might be tempted to omit them and, thereby, use only single-precision numeric variables. In some circumstances, this practice is fine; but in others, it can slow down

```
REM Tagged and untagged variables of same name [4-9]
a = 2: b! = 3
PRINT a; a!; b; b!
END

Run
 2  2  3  3
```

Program 4-9. *Tagged and untagged variables of the same name*

Manipulating Data

a program or not provide adequate accuracy in calculations. Turbo Basic provides a better solution through its **DEF**type statements.

If *L1* is a letter, then the statement

DEFINT *L1*

specifies that all tagless variables whose names begin with the letter *L1* will be integer variables. If *L2* and *L3* are letters with *L2* preceding *L3*, then the statement

DEFINT *L2* − *L3*

specifies that all tagless variables whose names begin with any letter from *L2* through *L3* will be integer variables. In general, **DEFINT** statements can contain several letters, ranges, or both, separated by commas.

Program 4-10 demonstrates the use of **DEFINT**. Notice that the cases (uppercase versus lowercase) used in the **DEFINT** statement are immaterial.

In an analogous manner, you can designate tagless variables as long integer, single-precision, double-precision, and string by using the statements **DEFLNG**, **DEFSNG**, **DEFDBL**, and **DEFSTR**, respectively.

```
REM   Populations of states in millions [4-10]
DEFINT C, i, m - R
california = 23.7
illinois = 11.4
maryland# = 4.2
newYork = 17.6
texas = 14.2
PRINT california; illinois; maryland; newYork; texas
END

Run
 24   11   4.2   17   14.2
```

Program 4-10. *The use of DEFINIT*

```
REM Demonstrate the peril of delaying type declaration [4-11]
cost1 = 123.45          'Processed as cost1!
DEFDBL c
cost2 = 67.89           'Processed as cost2#
PRINT cost1; cost2      'Processed as cost1# and cost2#
PRINT cost1!
END

Run
 0  67.89
 123.45
```

Program 4-11. *The peril of delaying type declaration*

Although **DEF***type* statements may appear anywhere in a program, good programming practice mandates that you place them near the top of the program. Doing so avoids mistakes such as the confusion with the variable **cost1** that occurs in Program 4-11.

Arrays

An *array* is a collection of variables of the same type that share a common name, with each variable indexed by one or more whole numbers. The individual variables are the *elements* of the array.

One-Dimensional Arrays

You use one-dimensional arrays to hold a list of values, and index the elements in a one-dimensional array by using a sequence of successive nonnegative whole numbers. If *arrayName* is the name of a one-dimensional array, and the indices (or *subscripts*) range from M to N, then you write the elements of the array as *arrayName(M)*, *arrayName(M+1)*, and so on to *arrayName(N)*. You

```
REM Man of the Year award from Time magazine [4-12]
DIM manOfYear$(1979:1982)
manOfYear$(1979) = "Ayatollah Khomeini"
manOfYear$(1980) = "Ronald Reagan"
manOfYear$(1981) = "Lech Walesa"
manOfYear$(1982) = "The Computer"
INPUT "Enter year from 1979 to 1982: ", year
PRINT manOfYear$(year); " was named Man of the Year."
END

Run
Enter year from 1979 to 1982: 1982
The Computer was named Man of the Year.
```

Program 4-12. *Using a string array*

declare this array and its range by using the statement

DIM *arrayName(M:N)*

If you use an array in a program without first declaring it in a **DIM** statement, then Turbo Basic automatically assigns it a range of 0 through 10. Also, you can declare an array that has a range of 0 through *N* with the statement

DIM *arrayName(N)*

Each element of an array must be of the same variable type. You usually specify this type through a type-declaration tag at the end of the array name. Program 4-12 uses a string array to record *Time* magazine's Man of the Year awards.

Two-Dimensional Arrays

If you can think of a one-dimensional array as holding the values from a list, then you can think of a two-dimensional array as holding the values from a table. Think of the rows of the table as being

```
REM United States economic statistics [4-13]
DIM USstat#(1:3, 1981:1984)
USstat#(1,1981) = 10.4
USstat#(1,1982) = 6.1
USstat#(1,1983) = 3.2
USstat#(1,1984) = 4.3
USstat#(2,1981) = 7.5
USstat#(2,1982) = 9.5
USstat#(2,1983) = 9.5
USstat#(2,1984) = 7.4
USstat#(3,1981) = 25569
USstat#(3,1982) = 25216
USstat#(3,1983) = 25594
USstat#(3,1984) = 26433
INPUT "CPI or unemployment or income (1 or 2 or 3)"; category
INPUT "Year from 1981 through 1984"; year
PRINT USstat#(category,year)
END

Run
CPI or unemployment or income (1 or 2 or 3)? 2
Year from 1981 through 1984? 1983
 9.5
```

Program 4-13. *Using a two-dimensional array*

labeled *M* through *N*, and the columns of the table being labeled *S* through *T*. Then the value in the *r*th row and *c*th column of the table would be placed in *arrayName(r,c)*. The statement

DIM arrayName(*M:N,S:T*)

declares such an array. Program 4-13 illustrates the use of a two-dimensional array that provides access to the information given in Table 4-6.

	1981	1982	1983	1984
Percentage change in consumer price index	10.4	6.1	3.2	4.3
Unemployment rate	7.5	9.5	9.5	7.4
Median family income	25569	25216	25594	26433

Table 4-6. *United States Economic Statistics*

Higher-Dimensional Arrays

You can declare arrays with up to six indices by using a statement of the form

DIM *arrayName(M:N, S:T, ..., U:V)*

Such an array consists of $(N - M + 1)*(T - S + 1)* \ldots *(V - U + 1)$ elements. The name of each element has the form

arrayName(a,b,...,c)

where $M \leq a \leq N$, $S \leq b \leq T$, and $U \leq c \leq V$. If you use a two-dimensional or higher-dimensional array in a program without first declaring the array in a **DIM** statement, then Turbo Basic automatically assigns the range of 0 through 10 to each index. Also, the statement

DIM *arrayName(N,T,...,V)*

can declare an array with the first index ranging from 0 to N, the second index from 0 to T, and the last index from 0 to V.

Memory Considerations

When a **DIM** statement declares an array, Turbo Basic sets aside a portion of memory for the elements of the array. The memory reserved for a numeric array has enough space to hold all of the values that can potentially be assigned to the array elements. However, the memory reserved for a string array has no room for the values of the elements. Instead, the memory locations allotted to each element are intended to store the length and location (in string space) of the string that will be assigned. Table 4-7 lists the maximum number of elements in each type of array. Turbo Basic imposes no restriction on the number of arrays that you can declare; the only limitation depends on the amount of memory present in the computer.

Array Type	Maximum Number of Elements
String	32767
Integer	32767
Long integer	8191
Single-precision	8191
Double-precision	4091

Table 4-7. *Maximum Number of Array Elements*

Static Arrays Versus Dynamic Arrays

DIM statements can specify the ranges of their indices with constants or expressions. For instance, the statements **DIM arrayName(20)** and **DIM arrayName(3:100, 2:17)** use only constants, whereas the statements **DIM arrayName**(*a:b*, **15)** and **DIM arrayName(2∗***n***)** use one or more expressions.

Turbo Basic offers two different ways to assign arrays a portion of memory. The compiler allocates *static* arrays a portion of memory. Each time that you run the program, this memory space will be the same size and cannot be used for any other purpose. Turbo Basic allocates *dynamic* arrays a portion of memory at runtime. The size of this space might vary for each run of the program, and it can be liberated at any time. In Standard BASIC, all arrays are dynamic.

In Turbo Basic, all arrays will be static unless one or more of the following conditions occur:

1. A **DIM** statement specifies the array by using one or more expressions to specify ranges of indices.

2. You insert the word **DYNAMIC** into the **DIM** statement following the word **DIM**. A typical statement of this type is **DIM DYNAMIC arrayName(20)**.

Manipulating Data

3. The statement **$DYNAMIC** appears in the program prior to the dimensioning of the array. (Statements that begin with a dollar sign are referred to as *metastatements*. They give instructions to the compiler.)

4. You use the array in two or more **DIM** statements in the program.

You can completely remove a dynamic array from memory with the **ERASE** statement. Specifically, the statement

ERASE *arrayName*

frees up the portion of memory that has been allocated to the named array. When you apply the **ERASE** statement to a static array, Turbo Basic retains the portion of memory; however, it removes all values that have been assigned to the elements. (Thus, these values become 0 for numeric arrays and "" for string arrays.)

Dynamic arrays have greater flexibility than static arrays. In addition, they are memory-efficient since you can release their memory space for other purposes after the program no longer needs

---

```
REM Demonstrate the creation of static and dynamic arrays [4-14]
DIM a(1:25)             'Static array
INPUT n
DIM c(n)                'Dynamic array
DIM DYNAMIC d(17)       'Dynamic array
DIM b(50)               'Dynamic array (look at 8th line)
ERASE b
DIM b(20:50)            'Dynamic array
$DYNAMIC
DIM e(3,4,5)            'Dynamic array
a(22) = "ABC"
ERASE a
PRINT a(22) + "DEF"
END

Run
DEF
```

Program 4-14. *The creation of static arrays and dynamic arrays*

the array. However, static arrays have one important feature that justifies their inclusion in Turbo Basic: they can be accessed faster. This quality produces a significant time saving when you search and sort arrays.

Program 4-14 produces both static arrays and dynamic arrays.

Inputting Data

Programs, to be meaningful, must have data to process. Turbo Basic provides a wealth of statements for inputting data, including the **LET**, **INPUT**, **READ/DATA**, and **INPUT$** statements, which are discussed below.

LET and INPUT

You can assign data to variables in many ways. The **LET** and **INPUT** statements, which have already been used in this book, are the best known. The statement

LET *variable = expression*

or its abbreviated form

variable = expression

assigns the value of the expression to the variable. Remember that the value and the variable must be either both string or both numeric. If they are numeric of different precisions, then Turbo Basic converts the value to the precision of the variable. The statement

INPUT *variable*

Manipulating Data 51

causes a question mark to be displayed, pauses until you enter a response, and then assigns the response to the variable. The variation

INPUT "*prompt*"; *variable*

displays the message *prompt* prior to the question mark. If you replace the semicolon in this variation with a comma, Turbo Basic displays the message without the question mark. Variations of the form

INPUT "*prompt*"; *variable1*, *variable2*, ...

allow you to assign values to several variables. You type the values, separated by commas, and then press ENTER.

READ and DATA

DATA statements list values that **READ** statements assign to variables. Specifically, a statement of the form

READ *variable*

causes the computer to look for the first unassigned item of data in a **DATA** statement, and assign it to the variable. You can replace a sequence of statements such as

READ *variable1*
READ *variable2*
READ *variable3*

with the single statement

READ *variable1*, *variable2*, *variable3*

Each **DATA** statement holds one or more constants, with multiple constants separated by commas. Typically, each **DATA** statement

```
REM Demonstration of READ and DATA statements [4-15]
READ person$, yearOfBirth
PRINT "When the United States constitution was signed,"
PRINT person$;" was"; 1776 - yearOfBirth; "years old."
READ person$
READ yearOfBirth
PRINT "When the Civil War began, "; person$; " was";_
1861 - yearOfBirth; "years old."
REM ------------------------------------- Data: Person, Year of Birth
DATA Thomas Jefferson, 1743
DATA Abraham Lincoln, 1809
END

Run
When the United States constitution was signed,
Thomas Jefferson was 33 years old.
When the Civil War began, Abraham Lincoln was 52 years old.
```

Program 4-15. *READ and DATA statements*

holds several related items. It is good style to place the **DATA** statements together at the end of the program, and precede them with a **REM** statement that gives the categories of the information held in each **DATA** statement, as shown in Program 4-15.

INPUT$

If *a$* is a string variable and *n* is a whole number from 1 through 32767, then the statement

a$ = INPUT$(*n*)

causes the program to pause until you type *n* characters on the keyboard. Then the program assigns the string consisting of these *n* characters to the variable *a$* before continuing with the next line.

The **INPUT$** function is often used to make a selection from a menu. Unlike making a selection with **INPUT**, the typed letter does not appear on screen and you do not need to press ENTER. In

Manipulating Data

```
REM Demonstrate the INPUT$ function [4-16]
PRINT "Type a letter."
letter$ = INPUT$(1)
PRINT "The letter you typed is "; letter$
END

Run
Type a letter.
The letter you typed is T
```

Program 4-16. *The INPUT$ function*

Program 4-16, which illustrates the technique, the user types the letter **T** after the instruction appears.

Type Mismatches

Each of the input statements just given assigns a constant to a variable of a specified type. In the event that the constant is not of the same type as the variable, Turbo Basic accommodates as best as possible.

If the variable is numeric with a lower precision than the constant, then Turbo Basic rounds the constant, if possible, before assigning it to the variable. (An assignment for which rounding is not possible is **n%** = 41234.56. Such a statement causes the display of the message **Error 6: Overflow**.) Assigning a string constant to a numeric variable causes the message **Error 418: Numeric expression requires relational operator** to be displayed.

In a **LET** statement, the item on the right side of the equal sign can be either a constant or an expression. If this item is a numeric expression and the variable on the left of the equal sign is a string variable, then an error message results. In all other cases, assigning a number constant to a string variable with *any* input statement results in Turbo Basic recognizing the number as a string.

Outputting Data to the Screen

The **PRINT** statement, with help from the functions **TAB** and **LOCATE**, can position data at specific places on the screen. A variation of the **PRINT** statement, **PRINT USING**, is custom-designed to display data in an orderly and familiar form.

PRINT Zones

The screen can hold 25 rows of text, with each row consisting of at most 80 characters. Think of each row as being subdivided into five zones, as shown in Figure 4-2.

When several items separated by semicolons follow the **PRINT** statement, Turbo Basic displays the items one after the other. When you use commas instead of semicolons, Turbo Basic displays the items in consecutive zones. As usual, positive numbers are displayed with leading spaces, and all numbers are displayed with trailing spaces. Program 4-17 utilizes **PRINT** zones to produce a table that shows the various average annual expenditures for certain income groups.

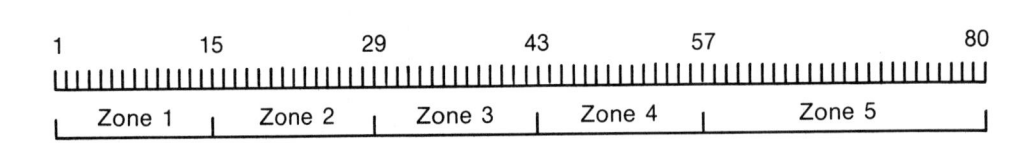

```
1        15        29        43        57              80
|||||||||||||||||||||||||||||||||||||||||||||||||||||||||||||||||||||||||||||||||
| Zone 1  | Zone 2  | Zone 3  | Zone 4  |     Zone 5     |
```

Figure 4-2. *PRINT* zones

Manipulating Data

```
REM Annual expenditures of urban consumer units [4-17]
PRINT , "Food", "Housing", "Transportation"
PRINT "Highest 20%", 4838, 10188, 6949
PRINT "Middle 20%", 2877, 5032, 3451
PRINT "Lowest 20%", 1753, 1730, 1231
END

Run
              Food           Housing         Transportation
Highest 20%   4838           10188           6949
Middle 20%    2877           5032            3451
Lowest 20%    1753           1730            1231
```

Program 4-17. *Using PRINT zones*

Note: You can put monitors attached to a graphics card, such as the Color/Graphics Adapter or the Enhanced Graphics Adapter, into a 40-column mode by using the statement **WIDTH 40**. (The statement **WIDTH 80** reinstates 80-column mode.) In 40-column mode, there are just two **PRINT** zones—one zone of length 14 and the other zone of length 26.

The TAB Function

While the use of **PRINT** zones permits data to be organized into columns beginning at every fourteenth position of the line, the **TAB** function gives access to every position of the line. If an item in a **PRINT** statement is preceded by

TAB(*n*)

where *n* is a whole number from 1 to 80, then Turbo Basic will display that item, if possible, beginning in the *n*th position of the line. Program 4-18 uses **TAB** to improve Program 4-17's output.

```
REM Annual expenditures of urban consumer units [4-18]
PRINT TAB(17) "Food"; TAB(26) "Housing"; TAB(37) "Transportation"
PRINT "Highest 20%"; TAB(16) 4838, TAB(25) 10188; TAB(36) 6949
PRINT "Middle 20%"; TAB(16) 2877; TAB(25) 5032; TAB(36) 3451
PRINT "Lowest 20%"; TAB(16) 1753; TAB(25) 1730; TAB(36) 1231
END

Run
                Food        Housing     Transportation
Highest 20%     4838        10188       6949
Middle 20%      2877        5032        3451
Lowest 20%      1753        1730        1231
```

Program 4-18. *Using* **TAB** *to improve output*

LOCATE

For text purposes, the screen is subdivided into 25 horizontal rows (numbered 1 to 25) and 80 (or 40) vertical columns (numbered 1, 2, 3, and so on). The statement

LOCATE r,c

moves the cursor to the rth row, cth column of the screen. The next **PRINT** statement will display its data beginning at that location. Program 4-19 displays the string **"Happy Birthday"** in the center of an 80-column screen.

```
REM Display a message in the center of the screen [4-19]
a$ = "Happy Birthday"
LOCATE 12, (80 - LEN(a$))\2
PRINT a$
END
```

Program 4-19. *Displaying a message in the center of the screen*

PRINT USING

You use the **PRINT USING** statement to display numeric data in a familiar form (with commas, an appropriate number of decimal places, and possibly a preceding dollar sign), and to coordinate the combined display of string and numeric data. **PRINT USING** statements use a string, called a *format string*, to specify the form of the display.

A typical numeric format string is "#####,###.##", which is a string of twelve characters. The statement

PRINT USING "#####,###.##"; n

reserves 12 positions, called a *field*, to display the number n. Turbo Basic will display the number right-justified in that space, rounded to two decimal places, and containing appropriate commas preceding groups of three digits to the left of the decimal point. Figure 4-3 shows three possible values of n and their display with the statement just given.

If the first character in a numeric format string is a dollar sign, then Turbo Basic will display the number with a dollar sign in the leftmost position of the field. If the first two characters are dollar signs, then Turbo Basic will display the number with a dollar sign directly preceding the first digit, as shown in Figure 4-4.

PRINT USING statements can combine text with numbers in several ways. One method is for the format string to contain the text with the special formatting characters. Turbo Basic will display the

n	Formatted Display
1234	1,234.00
12.345	12.35
1234567.89	1,234,567.89

Figure 4-3. *Effect of* **PRINT USING** *statement*

Statement	Display
PRINT USING "$####.##"; 45.78	$ 45.78
PRINT USING "$$###.##"; 45.78	$45.78

Figure 4-4. *Displaying dollar signs with* **PRINT USING**

text as it appears, and the numbers will conform to the rules of its formatting characters. Program 4-20 presents an example of this method.

You can use the backslash character, \, to format text with a format string. If *c$* is a string, then the statement

PRINT USING "\   \"; *c$*

displays the first *n* characters of *c$*, where *n* is the length of the string "\   \". In this string, there are *n* − 2 blank spaces between the backslashes. You use the exclamation mark, !, to extract the first character from a string. Figure 4-5 shows examples that use the backslash character and the exclamation mark.

Program 4-21 shows that a format string can contain several groups of string formatting characters, numeric formatting characters, or both. In the program, the values to be formatted appear in a sequence in which the items are separated by commas.

```
REM   Growth of a bank deposit earning 6% interest [4-20]
INPUT "Enter amount of deposit: "; principal
a$ = "The balance after one year is $$###,###.##"
PRINT USING a$; 1.06*principal
END

Run
Enter amount of deposit: 1234.56
The balance after one year is    $1,308.63
```

Program 4-20. *Combining text and format in* **PRINT USING**

Statement	Display
PRINT USING "\\nnell"; "Turbo Basic" PRINT USING "\ \"; "Turbo Basic" PRINT USING "!"; "Turbo Basic"	Tunnel Turbo T

Figure 4-5. *Displaying leading characters with* **PRINT USING**

```
REM Demonstrate several features of the PRINT USING statement [4-21]
a$ = "!!! sold ###,### PC's in \ \ ####"
PRINT USING a$; "International", "Business", "Machines", 158000,_
    "December", 1984
END

Run
IBM sold 158,000 PC's in Dec 1984
```

Program 4-21. *Several features of the* **PRINT USING** *statement*

Often, you use the **PRINT USING** statement to align numbers properly in columns. For instance, consider the Housing column in the output of Program 4-18. Ideally, the numbers should be aligned so that their rightmost digits appear in the same column. Program 4-22 utilizes **PRINT USING** to achieve this goal and to improve readability by placing commas where appropriate.

Table 4-8, which shows the result of **PRINT USING** *a$; n*, contains some additional symbols that you can use in formatting strings.

You can use the ampersand character, &, in a format string to display an entire string. If one of the formatting characters, such as # or \, appears in a format string preceded by an underline character, then the formatting character loses its special significance and is displayed literally. Program 4-23 illustrates the use of & and _.

```
REM Annual expenditures of urban consumer units [4-22]
PRINT "          Food       Housing    Transportation"
a$ = "\          \        #,###      ##,###         #,###"
PRINT USING a$; "Highest 20%", 4838, 10188, 6949
PRINT USING a$; "Middle 20%", 2877, 5032, 3451
PRINT USING a$; "Lowest 20%", 1753, 1730, 1231
END

Run
             Food      Housing    Transportation
Highest 20%  4,838     10,188     6,949
Middle 20%   2,877      5,032     3,451
Lowest 20%   1,753      1,730     1,231
```

Program 4-22. *Using **PRINT USING** to improve readability*

Symbol(s)	Meaning	n	a$	Result
**	Inserts asterisks in place of leading blanks	23	"**###"	***23
*	Displays an asterisk as the first character of the field	23	"*####"	* 23
^^^^	Displays the number in exponential form	23	"#.##^^^^"	2.30E+001
+	Reserves a space for the sign of the number	23 −23	"+###" "###−"	+23 23−

Table 4-8. *Additional Formatting Strings for **PRINT USING***

```
REM Illustrate the use of & and _ with PRINT USING [4-23]
b$ = "New York Giants"
PRINT USING "The _#1 team in 1987 was the &"; b$
END

Run
The #1 team in 1987 was the New York Giants
```

Program 4-23. *Using & and _ with **PRINT USING***

Special Effects with a Monochrome Display

Depending on the type of monitor used, you can display text on screen with special effects (such as underlined or blinking) or in color. A monochrome display is a special type of monitor that you can use with an IBM PC or an IBM PC compatible. Monochrome displays produce sharper text than other monitors, but are restricted to two colors, referred to as *white* and *black*. (Most likely, the actual colors will be green and black, or amber and black.) For each character that is displayed on screen, the color of the character itself is called the *foreground* color and the color of the portion of the screen surrounding the character is called the *background* color. You can use the **COLOR** statement to produce underlined, blinking, intense white, or reverse video text, or certain combinations thereof on a monochrome display. Table 4-9 shows every possible combination and a **COLOR** statement that produces each one. After you execute one of the **COLOR** statements in the table, Turbo Basic displays subsequent text with the corresponding foreground and background until you execute another **COLOR** statement. Several

Foreground	Background	Statement
White	Black	COLOR 7, 0
White, underlined	Black	COLOR 1, 0
White, blinking	Black	COLOR 23, 0
White, underlined, blinking	Black	COLOR 17, 0
High-intensity white	Black	COLOR 15, 0
High-intensity white, underlined	Black	COLOR 9, 0
High-intensity white, blinking	Black	COLOR 31, 0
High-intensity white, underlined, blinking	Black	COLOR 25, 0
Black	White	COLOR 0, 7
Black, blinking	White	COLOR 16, 7
White	White	COLOR 7, 7
Black	Black	COLOR 0, 0

Table 4-9. *Special Effects for Displaying Text on Monochrome Display*

```
REM Demonstrate different effects on the monochrome display [4-24]
COLOR 17, 0
PRINT "The letters in this line are underlined and blinking."
COLOR 0, 7
PRINT "The letters in this line are in reverse video."
COLOR 7, 7
PRINT "This line will be unreadable."
COLOR 7, 0
PRINT "This is a standard line having white on black letters."
END
```

Program 4-24. *The different effects on the monochrome display*

different effects can appear on the same screen. Program 4-24 demonstrates the different effects that you can produce with the monochrome display.

Displaying Color on a Color Monitor

Most color monitors are attached to either a Color/Graphics Adapter board (CGA) or an Enhanced Graphics Adapter board (EGA). With either of these boards, you can display text with foreground and background colors chosen from the 16 colors in Figure 4-6. In addition, you can also make the foreground blink. With an EGA board, up to 48 additional colors are available.

0	Black	4	Red	8	Gray	12	Light red
1	Blue	5	Magenta	9	Light blue	13	Light magenta
2	Green	6	Brown	10	Light green	14	Yellow
3	Cyan	7	White	11	Light cyan	15	High-intensity white

Figure 4-6. *Available colors on a color monitor*

Manipulating Data

```
REM Demonstrate the use of colors [4-25]
COLOR 14, 4
PRINT "The letters in this line are yellow on red."
COLOR 30, 4
PRINT "This line is the same as the first, but with blinking letters."
COLOR 7, 0
PRINT "The is a standard line having white on black letters."
END
```

Program 4-25. *The use of colors*

If f is a number from 0 through 15, and b is a number from 0 through 7, then the statement

COLOR *f,b*

causes all further characters displayed on screen to have a foreground of color f, and a background of color b (that is, the character itself will have color f and the small rectangle that contains the character will have color b). Characters placed on screen prior to this statement retain their original colors. Adding 16 to the number f causes the foreground to blink. Program 4-25 demonstrates some uses of the **COLOR** statement.

Displaying Color on an Enhanced Graphics Display

An Enhanced Graphics Display is a special type of color monitor, which is capable of displaying 64 different colors. The colors are numbered 0 through 63. Each of the colors blue, green, cyan, red, magenta, and yellow are available in six shades. There are four shades of gray that range from black to high-intensity white. Figure 4-7 gives the numbers of the colors in these groups. As a rule, in each group, the higher numbers correspond to lighter or brighter

Blues 1, 8, 9, 14, 15, 57
Greens 2, 16, 18, 21, 23, 58
Cyans 3, 24, 27, 31, 28, 59
Reds 4, 32, 35, 36, 39, 60
Magentas 5, 40, 42, 45, 47, 61
Yellows 6, 48, 49, 54, 55, 62
Grays 0 (black), 7, 56, 63 (high-intensity white)

Figure 4-7. *Shades of familiar colors*

hues than the lower numbers. Brown has the number 20. The colors associated with the remaining 23 numbers are difficult to name. Program 4-26 causes the display of all 64 colors. (This program uses statements that have not been discussed yet. You will learn about them later. For now, just run the program to see the variety of colors at your disposal.)

Turbo Basic utilizes two collections of numbers to control the choice of colors. The first collection is the set of numbers from 0 through 63 that identify the 64 different colors. Figure 4-8 shows 16 paint jars labeled 0 through 15. For each jar, Turbo Basic reserves a

```
REM The 64 colors available on an Enhanced Graphics Monitor [4-26]
DEFINT i, j
FOR i = 0 TO 63 STEP 8
  CLS
  FOR j = 0 TO 7
    PALETTE j + 1, i + j
    COLOR j + 1, 0
    PRINT USING "Color ##"; i + j
    PRINT
  NEXT j
  DELAY 4              'Pause 4 seconds
NEXT i
END
```

Program 4-26. *The 64 colors available on an enhanced graphics monitor*

Manipulating Data   65

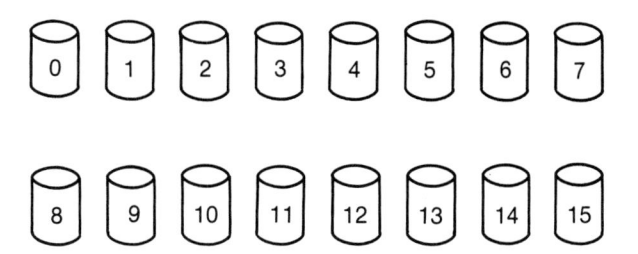

```
 ___   ___   ___   ___   ___   ___   ___   ___
| 0 | | 1 | | 2 | | 3 | | 4 | | 5 | | 6 | | 7 |

 ___   ___   ___   ___   ___   ___   ___   ___
| 8 | | 9 | |10 | |11 | |12 | |13 | |14 | |15 |
```

Figure 4-8. *A palette*

memory location that keeps track of the color in the jar. The list of jars and colors is referred to as a *palette*. You can change the color in a jar at any time. If m is a number from 0 through 15, and c is a number from 0 to 63, then the statement

PALETTE *m,c*

replaces the color currently in jar m with the color c. The default colors—that is, the colors in the jars before any **PALETTE** statements are executed—are shown in Table 4-10. Note: the numbers 0 through 15 that label the jars are often called *attributes*.

If f and b are any numbers from 0 through 15, then the statement

COLOR *f,b*

Jar	0	1	2	3	4	5	6	7	8	9	10	11	12	13	14	15
Color	0	1	2	3	4	5	20	7	56	57	58	59	60	61	62	63

Table 4-10. *The Default Palette*

```
REM Demonstrate the use of colors on an EGA monitor [4-27]
COLOR 6,15
PRINT "brown foreground, high intensity white background"
PALETTE 12,1
COLOR 12,15
PRINT "blue foreground, high intensity white background"
DELAY 5                                    'Pause for 5 seconds
PALETTE 15,4
PRINT "All characters now have a red background."
END
```

Program 4-27. *The use of colors on an EGA monitor*

causes all subsequent characters displayed on screen to have the color in jar f of the palette as foreground, and the color in jar b as background. Actually, the EGA board does not record two colors for each text position of the screen, but rather records the numbers of the two jars. The monitor continually looks at the palette list to determine the colors to use. Characters placed on screen prior to the execution of a **COLOR** statement retain their original colors. However, whenever you execute a **PALETTE** statement, Turbo Basic will change every character whose foreground or background is specified by the jar whose color is changed. At any time, at most 16 different colors can appear on screen. Program 4-27 shows the use of **COLOR** and **PALETTE** with the EGA Monitor.

Special Graphics Modes on the IBM PS/2

Turbo Basic supports two special graphics modes on IBM PS/2 computers. The statement SCREEN 11 selects the 640 by 480 black and white graphics screen mode. The statement SCREEN 12 selects the 640 by 480 color graphics screen mode. In SCREEN 12, the PALETTE statement may be used to assign any of the 256,000 available colors to the 16 palette jars for use by Turbo Basic's graphics statements.

Outputting Data to a Printer

The statement **LPRINT** sends data to the printer in much the same way that **PRINT** displays it on the screen. Semicolons suppress the carriage-return/line-feed combination, commas lay out the data into zones, the **TAB** function places data in specific positions on the line, and **LPRINT USING** formats the data with the same capabilities as **PRINT USING**. In addition, for appropriate print-

Statement	Effect
LPRINT CHR$(7);	Buzz the buzzer
LPRINT CHR$(9);	Move to next horizontal tab stop
LPRINT CHR$(11);	Move to next vertical tab stop
LPRINT CHR$(14);	Turn on double-width mode (5 characters/inch)
LPRINT CHR$(15);	Turn on compressed mode (16.5 characters/inch)
LPRINT CHR$(18);	Turn off compressed mode
LPRINT CHR$(20);	Turn off double-width mode
LPRINT CHR$(27) "A" CHR$(n);	Printer will advance $n/72$ of an inch after a line feed*
LPRINT CHR$(27) "C" CHR$(n);	Specify n lines per page
LPRINT CHR$(27) "E";	Turn on emphasized mode
LPRINT CHR$(27) "F";	Turn off emphasized mode
LPRINT CHR$(27) "G";	Turn on double-strike mode
LPRINT CHR$(27) "H";	Turn off double-strike mode
LPRINT CHR$(141);	Carriage return without a line feed
LPRINT CHR$(27) "B" CHR$($n1$) CHR$($n2$) ... CHR$(nr) CHR$(0)	Sets vertical tabs at lines $n1, n2, ..., nr$
LPRINT CHR$(27) "D" CHR$($n1$) CHR$($n2$) ... CHR$(nr) CHR$(0)	Sets horizontal tabs at lines $n1, n2, ..., nr$

* With certain printers, such as the IBM Graphics Printer, the desired change in line spacing will not take effect until the statement **LPRINT CHR$(27) "2";** is executed.

Table 4-11. Printer-control Statements

ers, **LPRINT** can control character size, font, line spacing, and page length. Table 4-11 contains printer-controlling statements that hold for IBM printers, Epson printers, and a number of other compatible dot matrix printers.

The **WIDTH** statement specifies the maximum number of characters to be printed on each line before Turbo Basic automatically performs a carriage return and line feed. If n is a positive integer, then the statement

WIDTH "LPT1:", n

specifies that each line contain n characters at most. The default value is 80 characters per line.

5 Decisions and Repetition

Decision Making in Turbo Basic

Standard BASIC relies on the **IF...THEN** statement to make decisions. Enhanced versions of BASIC also employ the statements **IF...THEN...ELSE**, **ON...GOTO**, and **ON...GOSUB**. By adding the **IF** block (including **ELSEIF**) and the **SELECT CASE** structure, Turbo Basic improves the clarity of code that chooses one of several possibilities.

Standard BASIC creates loops by using the **FOR...NEXT** and **GOTO** statements. Enhanced versions also contain the **WHILE ...WEND** loop that repeatedly executes a block of code as long as (or "while") a certain condition remains true. Turbo Basic upgrades the **WHILE...WEND** loop with the **DO** loop, which can test for a condition either at the beginning or the end of the loop.

Relational and Logical Operators

Computer programs are useful because of their ability to make decisions. In particular, a program can determine whether two numbers are the same and, if not, which number is the larger. In a program, symbols such as <, =, and > are called *relational operators* and are used to construct conditions that are evaluated as either "true" or "false." Table 5-1 presents a complete list of the relational operators.

You can determine the order of two numbers by comparing their positions on a number line. The number *a* is said to be *less than* the number *b* if *a* appears to the left of *b* on the number line. Here are three examples:

2   < 7
−3 < 1.5
−5 < −2

The process of ordering strings is similar to the process of alphabetizing words. A computer determines the order of two characters by their positions in the ASCII table (see Appendix A). The character with the lower ASCII value precedes (or is "less than") the other. For instance, according to the ASCII table, these relationships are true:

"a" < "g"
"9" < "A"
"Z" < "A"

To determine the orders of two strings, the computer compares their characters one at a time until two characters in the same position differ. For instance, here are three true string relationships:

"ball" < "bat"
"Hard" < "disk"
"9W"   < "nine"

Decisions and Repetition

Symbol	Meaning
<	Less than
>	Greater than
=	Equal to
<= (or =<)	Less than or equal to
>= (or =>)	Greater than or equal to
<> or ><	Not equal to

Table 5-1. *Relational Operators*

If the strings have different lengths, but agree for every position of the shorter string, then the computer takes the shorter string to be less than the longer string, as shown in this example:

"key" < "keyboard"

If the strings have the same length and identical characters in each position, then the strings are said to be *equal*.

A relational expression, or *condition*, consists of two expressions (either both numeric or both string), that are separated by a relational operator. A condition is *true* if the values of the expressions satisfy the relationship, or are *false* if the values do not. Some conditions and their truth values are shown in Table 5-2. In the table, assume that the variables **a**, **b**, **a$**, and **b$** have been assigned the values **4**, **6**, **"hello"**, and **"Goodbye"**.

The computer uses *logical operators*—such as **AND**, **OR**, and **NOT**—to build complex conditions out of simple conditions. The truth value of a complex condition depends both on the truth values of the simple conditions, and on the logical operators that join the simple conditions.

Table 5-3 gives the truth values of the simplest complex conditions using **AND**, **OR**, and **NOT**. The complex condition (*cond1* **AND** *cond2*) is true only when *both* of the simple conditions are true. **NOT** is called the *negation operator* and **OR** is called the

Condition	Truth value
2 < 3	True
INT(2.7) > 2	False
3 <= 3	True
a + 5 = b	False
−7 > a	False
"bit" < "byte"	True
"two" = "TWO"	False
b$ > a$	True
LEN(a$) <> 5	False

Table 5-2. Truth Values of Relational Expressions

cond1	cond2	NOT cond1	cond1 AND cond2	cond1 OR cond2
True	True	False	True	True
True	False	False	False	True
False	True	True	False	True
False	False	True	False	False

Table 5-3. Truth Tables for **AND**, **OR**, and **NOT**

inclusive OR operator. **NOT** *cond1* has the opposite truth value of *cond1*. The complex condition (*cond1* **OR** *cond2*) is true if either one or both of the two simple conditions are true.

Table 5-4 presents some conditions and their truth values. As before, assume that the variables **a**, **b**, **a$**, and **b$** have been assigned the values 4, 6, "hello", and "Goodbye".

Table 5-5 gives the truth values of the other logical operators available in Turbo Basic. The operator **XOR** is known as *exclusive OR*. The complex condition (*cond1* **XOR** *cond2*) is true if one or

Condition	Truth value
(2 < 3) OR (0 > 1)	True
(2 < 3) AND (0 > 1)	False
NOT (0 > 1)	True
(MID$(a$,2) < "Z") OR (a < > 4)	False
(LEN(b$) = 7) AND (a$ > b$)	True
NOT (a$ >= "hello")	False

Table 5-4. *Truth Values of Complex Conditions*

cond1	cond2	cond1 XOR cond2	cond1 EQV cond2	cond1 IMP cond2
True	True	False	True	True
True	False	True	False	False
False	True	True	False	True
False	False	False	True	True

Table 5-5. *Truth Tables for XOR, EQV, and IMP*

the other of the two simple conditions is true, but not both. You read the operators **EQV** and **IMP** as "is equivalent to" and "implies," respectively. Two conditions are equivalent if they have the same truth values. One condition is said to imply another as long as the second is true whenever the first is true. Some examples follow in Table 5-6.

Complex conditions might involve a combination of several arithmetic, relational, and logical operators. This text generously uses parentheses in order to avoid any ambiguity and to make the code easy to read. However, in the absence of parentheses, all versions of BASIC use the same operator hierarchy. First, the computer

Condition	Truth value
(1 < 2) XOR (3 < 4)	False
(1 = 2) EQV ("A" > "B")	True
(1 < 2) IMP (1 = 2)	False

Table 5-6. *Expressions using* **XOR, EQV,** *and* **IMP**

evaluates the arithmetic expressions with the precedence discussed in Chapter 4. Then the computer evaluates each relational operator as either true or false. Finally, the computer evaluates the logical operators in the order **NOT, AND, OR, XOR, EQV,** and **IMP**. For instance, the computer evaluates

NOT 2 + 3 < 6 AND "A" < "B" OR 4*5 + 2 < 23

as

((NOT ((2 + 3) < 6)) AND ("A" < "B")) OR (((4*5) + 2) < 23)

The ability to make decisions that affect the flow of a program is crucial to problem solving. The 12 relational and logical operators presented in this section are sufficient to express any condition needed to make a decision

Decision Structures

Most versions of BASIC, including Turbo Basic, support the single-line **IF...THEN...ELSE** statement. For example, suppose that *cond* is a condition (simple or complex), and that *action1* and

Decisions and Repetition

```
REM Determine eligibility to vote    [5-1]
a$ = "You are eligible to vote"
INPUT "Enter your age: ", age
IF age>=18 THEN PRINT a$ ELSE PRINT a$+"in";18-age;"years"
END

Run
Enter your age: 32
You are eligible to vote

Run
Enter your age: 15
You are eligible to vote in 3 years
```

Program 5-1. *Single-line* **IF...THEN...ELSE**

action2 are statements (or sequences of statements). Then the statement

IF *cond* THEN *action1* ELSE *action2*

executes *action1* or *action2*, depending upon whether the condition is true or false, respectively. Program 5-1 gives an example of a single line **IF...THEN...ELSE** statement.

IF Block

In the event that the actions in an **IF...THEN...ELSE** statement consist of several BASIC statements that are separated by colons, the single line can be too long to fit into a logical line or too difficult to understand. One way to handle this situation is first to replace each action by a **GOSUB** statement and then to place each sequence of statements in a subroutine. A more readable way is to use the **IF** block that Turbo Basic supplies. The format is

IF condition THEN

    .
    .
  statement(s)
    .
    .

ELSE

    .
    .
  statement(s)
    .
    .

END IF

Each of the two "action" blocks can consist of as many statements as desired. The blocks can even include other **IF** blocks. Note that, in an **IF** block, no statement can follow **THEN** or **ELSE** on the same line, but must be on a following line.

Program 5-2 accepts a year as input and decides if it is a leap year. Each year divisible by 4 is a leap year, with the exception of

```
REM Determine if a given year is a leap year   [5-2]
INPUT "Year (xxxx)"; year
IF year MOD 4 <> 0 THEN
    PRINT year; "is not a leap year."
  ELSE
    IF (year MOD 100 = 0) AND (year MOD 400 <> 0) THEN
        PRINT year; "is not a leap year."
      ELSE
        PRINT year; "is a leap year."
    END IF
END IF
END

Run
Year (xxxx)? 1800
  1800 is a leap year.
```

Program 5-2. Using **IF...THEN...ELSE** blocks

Decisions and Repetition 77

years that end in 00—that is, those years that are divisible by 100—and not divisible by 400. Recall that the **MOD** operator gives the remainder when the first number is divided by the second.

ELSEIF Statement

As Program 5-2 shows, you can use the **IF** block to select one of several possible options. This capability is made simpler with a further enhancement to the **IF** block—namely, the **ELSEIF** statement. A block of the general form

```
IF cond1 THEN
    statement(s)
  ELSEIF cond2
    statement(s)
  ELSEIF cond3
    statement(s)
  ELSE
    statement(s)
END IF
```

examines each condition, in order, and executes the statement or statements that follow the first true condition. If none of the conditions are true, the block executes the statement or statements following **ELSE**. The **IF** block can contain as many **ELSEIF** statements as desired. Note that the **ELSE** statement at the end of the **IF** block is optional. If all of the conditions are false and no **ELSE** statement is present, then the **IF** block takes no action.

Program 5-3 uses **ELSEIF** to improve the readability of Program 5-2, which determines leap years. In the first run, the condition after **IF** was false, but the condition following **ELSEIF** was true. In the second run, the conditions after **IF** and **ELSEIF** were false and so the program executed the statement after **ELSE**.

Program 5-4, which computes the social security tax that a company deducts from an employee's paycheck, uses two **ELSEIF** statements and no **ELSE** statement.

```
REM Determine if a given year is a leap year   [5-3]
INPUT "Year (xxxx)"; year
IF year MOD 4 <> 0 THEN
    PRINT year; "is not a leap year."
  ELSEIF (year MOD 100 = 0) AND (year MOD 400 <> 0)
    PRINT year; "is not a leap year."
  ELSE
    PRINT year; "is a leap year."
END IF
END

Run
Year (xxxx)? 1600
 1600 is not a leap year.

Run
Year (xxxx)? 1800
 1800 is a leap year.
```

Program 5-3. *Using ELSEIF*

```
REM Calculate social security tax   [5-4]
INPUT "Enter current earnings: ", pay
INPUT "Enter prior year-to-date earnings: ", priorYearToDate
IF yearToDate >= 33800 THEN
    PRINT "No tax due."
  ELSEIF pay + priorYearToDate <= 33800
    PRINT USING "Tax = $$#,###.##"; .0715*pay
  ELSEIF pay + priorYearToDate > 33800
    PRINT USING "Tax =$$#,###.##"; .0715*(33800 - priorYearToDate)
END IF
END

Run
Enter current earnings: 1600
Enter prior year-to-date earnings: 6000
Tax =    $114.40

Run
Enter current earnings: 2000
Enter prior year-to-date earnings: 36000
No tax due.
```

Program 5-4. *Using two ELSEIF statements*

Decisions and Repetition

Avoiding Ambiguity

In Standard BASIC, statements that contain multiple **IF**s, **THEN**s, and **ELSE**s are not immediately understandable. Consider

IF *condition1* THEN IF *condition2* THEN *action1* ELSE *action2*

Does **ELSE** go with the first **IF** or the second **IF**? The general rule in BASIC is that a program associates the first **ELSE** with the closest preceding **IF** and each subsequent **ELSE** with the closest unassigned preceding **IF**. The **IF** block not only allows you to determine the correct associations without a possibly tedious application of this rule, but also allows you to associate an **ELSE** with whichever preceding **IF** you desire. Figure 5-1 gives the statement just presented two different interpretations in the **IF** blocks. In the figure, the block on the left associates the **ELSE** with the first **IF**, whereas the block on the right associates the **ELSE** with the second **IF**.

SELECT CASE Structure

Often, the action that the program will take depends solely on the value of an expression. The **SELECT CASE** structure is custom-made for this task. Consider Program 5-5, which is written in

```
IF condition1 THEN              IF condition1 THEN
    IF condition2 THEN action2      IF condition2 THEN
ELSE                                    action1
    action2                         ELSE
END IF                                  action2
                                    END IF
                                END IF
```

Figure 5-1. *Nested* **IF...THEN** *blocks*

Using Turbo Basic

```
10 REM One, Two, Buckle My Shoe    [5-5]
20 LET a = 7: LET b = 8
30 INPUT "Enter a number from 1 to 10: ", n
40 IF (n = 1) OR (n = 2) THEN PRINT "Buckle my shoe.": GOTO 90
50 IF (3 <= n) AND (n <= 4)   THEN PRINT "Shut the door.": GOTO 90
60 IF n <= 6 THEN PRINT "Pick up sticks.": GOTO 90
70 IF n = a OR n = b THEN PRINT "Lay them straight.": GOTO 90
80 PRINT "Start all over again."
90 END
RUN
Enter a number from 1 to 10: 5
Pick up sticks.
Ok
```

Program 5-5. *A program with many decisions*

Standard BASIC. If you rewrite this program with the **SELECT CASE** structure, as was done in Program 5-6, the new version is not only easier to write and read, but also has greater flexibility.

The general **SELECT CASE** block begins with a statement of the form

SELECT CASE *expression*

```
REM One, Two, Buckle my shoe    [5-6]
a = 7: b = 8
INPUT "Enter a number from 1 to 10: ", n
SELECT CASE n
   CASE 1, 2
     PRINT "Buckle my shoe."
   CASE 3 TO 4
     PRINT "Shut the door."
   CASE <= 6
     PRINT "Pick up sticks."
   CASE a, b
     PRINT "Lay them straight."
   CASE ELSE
     PRINT "Start all over again."
END SELECT
END
```

Program 5-6. *Using SELECT CASE*

Decisions and Repetition

where the expression evaluates to either a number or a string. The block ends with the statement

END SELECT

which is possibly preceded by the statement

CASE ELSE

The standard **CASE** statements inside the block consist of one or more possibilities for the value of the expression. The different possibilities are separated by commas. Each possibility is one of these types:

- A constant

- A variable

- An inequality sign followed by a constant or a variable

- A range expressed in the form **"X TO Y"**, where **X** and **Y** are either constants or variables.

When encountering a **SELECT CASE** block, Turbo Basic evaluates the expression, and then looks for the first standard **CASE** statement that includes the value of the expression or otherwise for a **CASE ELSE** statement. If Turbo Basic finds either one, it executes the statements associated with it. After that, or in the event neither is present, Turbo Basic proceeds to the statement that follows the **SELECT CASE** block.

Program 5-7 contains multistatement actions and nested blocks. After you enter the month as a number from 1 to 12, the program determines the number of days in the month. The program also requests the year in the event that the month entered is February.

Program 5-8, which translates words into pig latin, uses a string expression in a **SELECT CASE** block. If the word to be translated into pig latin begins with an uppercase letter, the pig latin translation will also begin with an uppercase letter; the uppercase letter that is moved to the end of the word will now appear in lowercase.

```
REM Determine the number of days in a given month   [5-7]
INPUT "Number of month (Jan = 1, Feb = 2, etc.)"; month
SELECT CASE month
  CASE 9, 4, 6, 11
    numberOfDays = 30
  CASE 2
    REM Determine if a given year is a leap year
    INPUT "Year (xxxx)"; year
    IF year MOD 4 <> 0 THEN
       numberOfDays = 28
       ELSEIF (year MOD 100 = 0) AND (year MOD 400 <> 0)
       numberOfDays = 28
    ELSE
       numberOfDays = 29
    END IF
  CASE ELSE
    numberOfDays = 31
END SELECT
PRINT "The number of days in the month is"; numberOfDays
END

Run
Number of month (Jan = 1, Feb = 2, etc.)? 2
Year (xxxx)? 2000
The number of days in the month is 28
```

Program 5-7. *Using multistatement actions and nested blocks*

```
REM Translate a given word into pig latin   [5-8]
INPUT "Enter a word: ", word$
SELECT CASE LEFT$(word$,1)
  CASE "a", "e", "i", "o", "u", "A", "E", "I", "O", "U"
    pigword$ = word$ + "way"
  CASE "a" TO "z"
    pigword$ = MID$(word$,2,LEN(word$)) + LEFT$(word$,1) + "ay"
  CASE "A" TO "Z"
    pigword$ = UCASE$(MID$(word$,2,1) + MID$(word$,3,LEN(word$))) _
             + LCASE$(LEFT$(word$,1) + "ay"
END SELECT
PRINT "The pig latin translation is "; pigword$
END

Run
Enter a word: Computer
The pig latin translation is Omputercay
```

Program 5-8. *A SELECT CASE block with a string expression*

Loops

A loop repeats a sequence of statements either as long as or until a certain condition is true. The loop can check the condition before or after executing the sequence of statements. The standard loop in Turbo Basic is the **DO** loop, which has several variations.

When Turbo Basic encounters the block

DO UNTIL *condition*

   .
   .
   statement(s)
   .
   .

LOOP

it first checks whether the condition is true or false. If the condition is true, then the program will skip the statements in the block and will continue with the statement after the block. If the condition is false, the program will execute the sequence of statements and then will repeat the entire process. The flowchart in Figure 5-2 describes the procedure. Program 5-9 computes the average of a list of numbers that the user supplies. The block

DO

   .
   .
   statement(s)
   .
   .

LOOP UNTIL *condition*

also executes the sequence of statements repeatedly until the specified condition is true. However, in this case, the program checks the condition *after* executing the statements. Therefore, this **DO** loop structure guarantees that the sequence of statements will be executed at least once. The flowchart in Figure 5-3 describes the procedure.

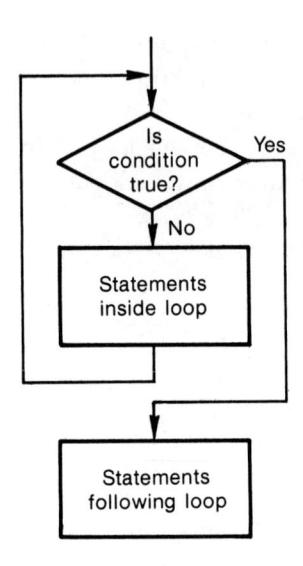

Figure 5-2. *A flowchart for **DO UNTIL** loop with the condition checked at the top*

Here is an example of the use of loops. Suppose that the 100 entries in the string array **cities$()** are in ascending order. Also, suppose that the array **pop()** contains the corresponding populations. Program 5-10 uses a *binary search* to find the population of a given city. At each pass through the loop, the program divides in half the range of subscripts that could possibly contain the city.

Decisions and Repetition

```
REM Find the average of a list of numbers   [5-9]
numberOfItems = 0: sum = 0
PRINT "Enter -1 after the entire list has been entered."
INPUT "Enter a number: ", number
DO UNTIL number = -1
  numberOfItems = numberOfItems + 1
  sum = sum + number
  INPUT "Enter a number: ", number
LOOP
IF numberOfItems > 0 THEN PRINT "The average is"; sum/numberOfItems
END

Run
Enter -1 after the entire list has been entered.
Enter a number: 89
Enter a number: 94
Enter a number: 87
Enter a number: -1
The average is 90
```

Program 5-9. *Using* **DO UNTIL**

Instead of looping *until* a certain condition is true, **DO** loops can loop *while* (or as long as) a condition is true. The syntax of the **DO** loop is one of the following:

```
DO WHILE condition         DO
    statement(s)               statement(s)
LOOP                       LOOP WHILE condition
```

You can write any **DO** loop that uses **UNTIL** so that it uses **WHILE** by replacing the condition with its negation. For instance, you can rewrite the **DO** in loops in Program 5-9 and Program 5-10 as shown in Figure 5-4.

DO loops can also involve two conditions—one condition checked at the top and the other checked at the bottom. However, such code can be difficult to understand and, if possible, should be rewritten. For instance, you could replace the code on the left in Figure 5-5 with the code on the right.

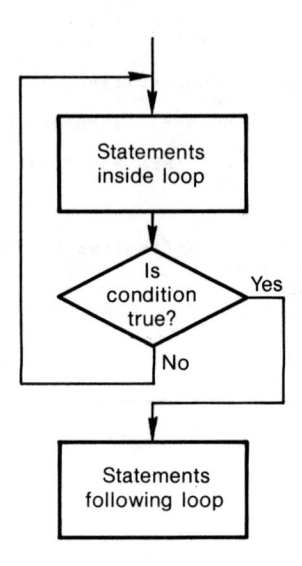

Figure 5-3. *A flowchart for a **DO UNTIL** loop with the condition checked at the bottom*

The **WHILE...WEND** loop that is available in many enhanced versions of Standard BASIC performs in the same way as a **DO** loop that begins with **DO WHILE** *condition*. For instance, you could

Decisions and Repetition

```
REM Binary Search   [5-10]
INPUT "Enter name of city", city$
low = 1: high = 100
DO
  middle = INT((low + high)/2)
  SELECT CASE cities$(middle)
    CASE1 < city$
      low = middle + 1
    CASE2 > city$
      high = middle - 1
    CASE3 city$
      PRINT city$; " has population"; pop(middle)
  END SELECT
LOOP UNTIL (cities$(middle) = city$) OR (low > high)
IF cities$(middle) <> city$ THEN PRINT "City not found."
```

Program 5-10. *A binary search*

```
DO WHILE number <> -1
   :
LOOP

DO
   :
LOOP WHILE (cities$(middle) <> city$) AND (low <= high)
```

Figure 5-4. *DO WHILE loops*

replace the **DO** loop in Program 5-9 with the **WHILE...WEND** loop shown in Figure 5-6.

```
DO UNTIL cond1
    statement(s)
LOOP UNTIL cond2

IF NOT cond1 THEN
    DO
        statement(s)
    LOOP UNTIL cond1 OR cond2
END IF
```

Figure 5-5. *Improving the readabililty of a* **DO** *loop*

The loops considered so far are called *condition-controlled loops*. The **FOR...NEXT** loop is referred to as a *counter-controlled loop*. You give a counter—that is, a numeric variable—an initial value that a program increases (or decreases) after each pass through the loop. The program executes statements within the

```
WHILE number <> -1
    numberOFItems = numberOFItems + 1
    sum = sum + number
    Input "Enter a number: ", number
WEND
```

Figure 5-6. *A* **WHILE...WEND** *loop*

Decisions and Repetition

loop repeatedly until the counter becomes less than (or greater than) a specified terminal value. Specifically, the loop

FOR j # a TO b STEP s
    statement(s)
NEXT j

initially assigns the value **a** to the variable **j**. Next, the loop does a test to see if **j** is less than or equal to **b**, when **s** is positive, or if **j** is greater than or equal to **b**, when **s** is negative. If so, the program executes the statements, replaces the value of **j** with the value **j** + **s**, and repeats the test. This process continues until the test fails, at which time the program exits the loop and executes the statement after the loop. In a general **FOR...NEXT** loop, **a**, **b**, and **s** can be numeric expressions. However, the program executes faster if they are variables, and fastest if they are constants. If **STEP s** is omitted from the **FOR** statment, the program increases the counter variable by 1 after each pass.

Program 5-11 uses a **FOR...NEXT** loop to add up the odd numbers from 1 to 99.

In many versions of Standard BASIC, the counter variable of a **FOR...NEXT** loop must be of either integer precision or single-precision. Turbo Basic permits the counter variable to be *any*

```
REM Sum the odd numbers from 1 TO 99   [5-11]
sum = 0
FOR number% = 1 TO 99 STEP 2
   sum = sum + number%
NEXT number%
PRINT sum
END

Run
 2500
```

Program 5-11. *A FOR...NEXT example*

numeric type. However, you must take care to avoid rounding errors when using single-precision and double-precision counters. For instance, you should replace the statement

```
FOR n# = 1 TO 2 STEP .01
```

with

```
FOR n# = 1 TO 2.005 STEP .01
```

since adding .01 one hundred times produces a number that is slightly larger than 1.

The execution time of a **FOR...NEXT** loop depends on the numeric type of the counter variable. Execution is fastest with integer variables, and then decreases in speed with long integer variables, single-precision variables, and double-precision variables, in that order. The difference in speed between those loops that have integer counter variables and those that have double-precision counter variables is considerable, especially for computers that lack 8087 coprocessors. You should always use the most elementary type possible.

Infinite Loops

The condition that causes a loop to terminate is called the *terminal condition*. It usually involves a variable whose value can be altered by the statements in the body of the loop. However, if there is no terminal condition or if the body of the loop cannot change the truth value of the terminal condition, the loop might repeat indefinitely. Examples of infinite loops are shown in Figure 5-7.

In Standard BASIC, you can always terminate an infinite loop, along with the program, by pressing CTRL-BREAK. With Turbo Basic, you can only do this some of the time. Turbo Basic requires the following two steps in order for a program to be "breakable."

1. Prior to compiling the program, you must select **Keyboard break ON** from the Options command pull-down menu. The default

```
DO
  PRINT "Hello";
LOOP

sum = 0
FOR j = 1 TO 5 STEP 0
  sum = sum + j
NEXT j

INPUT "Enter a number: ", n
DO UNTIL n*n < 0
  IF n < 10 THEN n = n - 1 ELSE n = n + 1
LOOP
```

Figure 5-7. *Infinite loops*

Keyboard break status is **OFF**. Check the status by returning to the main menu and typing **O** for the Options menu. Then, if necessary, change the **Keyboard break** status from **OFF** to **ON** by typing **K**.

2. The program must contain input or output statements in appropriate places. After you press CTRL-BREAK, execution terminates when the program reaches the next input or output statement. Program 5-12 displays **Hello**, makes five beeping sounds, and then displays **Goodbye**. If you press CTRL-BREAK after the first beep, the program will continue to execute until it reaches the output statement **PRINT "Goodbye"**. It will then terminate, without either displaying a break message or the string **"Goodbye"**.

If you change the third line of Program 5-12 to

```
FOR j = 1 TO 1000 STEP 0
```

you will create an unbreakable infinite loop. You could only stop this program either by turning off the computer or by pressing CTRL-ALT-DEL. (Pressing CTRL-ALT-DEL causes a system reset, in which everything is erased from memory, including Turbo Basic, and the computer reloads DOS.)

```
REM Beep five times   [5-12]
PRINT "Hello"
FOR j = 1 TO 1000
   IF (j MOD 200) = 0 THEN BEEP
NEXT j
PRINT "Goodbye"
END
```

Program 5-12. *Beep five times*

You can take the following steps to avoid losing a program due to an infinite loop:

1. Carefully read each loop to check that it will terminate.

2. If doubt whether the loop will terminate, temporarily insert an innocuous input or output statement (such as **Print** " ";) that will allow you to terminate the program by pressing CTRL-BREAK. You can remove this statement after you debug the program.

3. Save the program prior to execution so that it will not be lost in case you have to turn off the computer or do a system reset. Turbo Basic provides an option whereby the system saves the program in memory to disk whenever you give the **Run** command. To select this option, return to the Main Menu, type **S** for the Setup pull-down menu, then type **M** for the Miscellaneous pop-up menu, and finally type **A** to select the **Auto save edit ON** option.

Many Standard BASIC programs use infinite loops to keep repeating an operation until the user aborts the program with CTRL-BREAK. In Turbo Basic this task should be handled by a control structure that repeats a loop until a special key is pressed.

Exiting Loops and Decision Structures

Loops have a well-defined entry point and exit point. However, sometimes you might like to have the option of exiting the loop in the middle of the sequence of statements. In Turbo Basic, you can have this option by using the **EXIT** statement. You use the statements **EXIT LOOP**, **EXIT WHILE**, and **EXIT FOR** to exit **DO**, **WHILE...WEND**, and **FOR...NEXT** loops, respectively, and to jump to the statement after the loop.

Program 5-13 does a sequential search of the 100 entries in the unordered string array **cities$( )** to determine if a particular city is in the array. Note that, when the program EXITS a **FOR...NEXT** loop prematurely, the program does not increment the value of the counter variable.

Turbo Basic uses the statements **EXIT IF** and **EXIT SELECT** to leave **IF** blocks and **SELECT CASE** blocks, respectively. Although these statements are never essential, the **EXIT IF** statement can lessen the number of levels of **IF** blocks.

```
REM Sequential search   [5-13]
INPUT "Enter name of city", city$
FOR j = 1 TO 100
   IF cities$(j) = city$ THEN EXIT FOR
NEXT j
IF j = 101 THEN
     PRINT "City not found."
  ELSE
     PRINT "City is element"; j; of the array."
END IF
```

Program 5-13. *Segment using an* **EXIT** *statement*

Indentation and Nesting

Turbo Basic will correctly compile a program even if it contains no indentation. However, indentation improves the readability of a program and, therefore, is good programming style. This chapter has consistently indented the contents of each block and loop to clarify its structure.

You should also use indentation to show that one block or loop is contained, or nested, within another. Doing so allows the reader to pair up each **DO** statement with its associated **LOOP** statement

```
DO UNTIL condition
    FOR j = 1 TO 3
LOOP
    NEXT j
FOR j = 1 TO 5
    FOR k = 3 TO 9
NEXT j
    NEXT k
Improperly
nested loops


DO UNTIL condition
    FOR j = 1 TO 3
    NEXT j
LOOP
FOR j = 1 TO 5
    FOR k = 3 TO 9
    NEXT j
Properly
nested loops
```

Figure 5-8. Nested loops

```
REM Shell sort of array$(), an array of N elements    [5-14]
gap = INT(N/2)
DO WHILE gap > 0
  sorted$ = "no"
  DO WHILE sorted$ = "no"
    sorted$ = "yes"    'Innocent until proven guilty
    FOR j = 1 TO N - gap
      IF array$(j) > array$(j + gap) THEN
        SWAP array$(j), array$(j + gap)
        sorted$ = "no"
      END IF
    NEXT j
  LOOP
  gap = INT(gap/2)
LOOP
```

Program 5-14. *Segment including a Shell sort*

and each **FOR** statement with its associated **NEXT** statement. Indentation also helps to prevent improper nesting, as shown in Figure 5-8. When you nest loops properly, the *entire* inner loop is inside the outer loop.

Program 5-14 uses nested loops to rearrange the elements of an array into increasing order. The program uses a process called a *Shell sort*. It systematically compares distant elements and interchanges pairs that are out of order. (The statement **SWAP array$(j), array$(j + gap)** exchanges the values of the two subscripted variables.) The program sets the distance over which pairs are compared, called the *gap*, to half the number of elements and successively divides the distance in half until the entire array is ordered.

6 Functions and Procedures

Stepwise Refinement

A programmer is a person who solves problems with the aid of a computer. The problem-solving process consists of the following four steps:

1. Understand the problem.
2. Devise a plan for solving the problem.
3. Code the solution as a program.
4. Test the program.

The first step requires that the programmer have a clear idea of what data (input) will be given, what results (output) will be produced, and what relationships exist between them. The difficulty of the third step depends on the quality of the plan devised in the second step.

There is a consensus among computer scientists that the most effective method of solving a problem is *stepwise refinement.* This key problem-solving method is also known as *top-down design, iterative multilevel modeling, hierarchical programming,* or *divide-and-conquer programming.* Stepwise refinement is the process of breaking a problem into smaller problems that consist of manageable chunks. (A *manageable chunk* is a small problem that is easy to solve or is similar to a problem that the programmer has already solved.) If any of these are not manageable chunks, the programmer breaks them down into yet-smaller subproblems. The programmer repeats the process until all subproblems are manageable. After breaking down the original problem, the programmer solves the manageable chunks one at a time and puts them together to produce a solution to the original problem.

Standard BASIC has two devices for coding subproblems and manageable chunks: subroutines and single-line user-defined functions. Turbo Basic not only has these two devices, but has upgraded them into two of the most important structures of modern programming: procedures and multiline functions. This chapter briefly discusses the devices from standard BASIC in order to explain their enhancements in Turbo Basic.

Single-line Functions

Turbo Basic has many predefined functions. Table 6-1 presents some of these functions that you have already encountered. Although the input can involve several values, the output always consists of a single value. You can determine the type of output by looking at the name of the function. If a dollar sign follows the name, then the output is a string; if not, then the output is a number.

In addition to these predefined functions, you can define functions of your own. These new functions, called *user-defined functions,* are referred to by names preceded by the letters **FN**. The names must conform to the rules of naming variables. Like variable

Functions and Procedures

Function	Example	Input	Output
INT	INT(2.6) is 2	number	number
CHR$	CHR$(65) is "A"	number	string
LEN	LEN("perhaps") is 7	string	number
MID$	MID$("perhaps",4,2) is "ha"	string,number,number	string
INSTR	INSTR("to be"," ") is 3	string,string	number

Table 6-1. *Some Predefined Functions*

names, these names should be suggestive of the role performed. You can define these functions in programs by writing **DEF** followed by the function definition. Here are two examples:

DEF FNFirstName$(n$) = LEFT$(n$,INSTR(n$," ") − 1)
DEF FNDoublingTime(x) = 72/x

The function **FNFirstName$** takes the first name from a person's full name. The function **FNDoublingTime** estimates the number of years required for an investment to double in value when the investment earns interest at a rate of **x** percent. (The formula used is commonly known as the *Rule of 72*.) For instance, **FNDoublingTime(8)** is 9; that is, an investment that earns 8% interest will double in value in about 9 years. Programs 6-1 and 6-2 illustrate the use of the two functions just discussed.

```
REM  Determine a person's first name  [6-1]
DEF FNFirstName$(n$) = LEFT$(n$,INSTR(n$," ") - 1)
INPUT "Person's name"; nom$
PRINT "The person's first name is "; FNFirstName$(nom$)
END

Run
Person's name? Thomas Woodrow Wilson
The person's first name is Thomas
```

Program 6-1. *A single-line user-defined function*

```
REM Calculate doubling time for an investment   [6-2]
DEF FNDoublingTime(x) = 72/x
INPUT "Percent interest rate earned"; p
PRINT "Your investment will double in about";_
  FNDoublingTime(p); "years."
END

Run
Percent interest rate earned? 8
Your investment will double in about 9 years.
```

Program 6-2. *Another example of a user-defined function*

The variables **x** and **n$** that appear in the function definitions just given are called *formal parameters, arguments,* or *dummy variables*. They have meaning only within the definition of the function. When you actually use or *invoke* a user-defined function in a program, constants, variables, or expressions appear in place of the formal parameters. These constants, variables, or expressions are called *actual parameters*. For example, in Program 6-2, the formal parameter is **x** and the actual parameter is **8**. As with predefined functions, the only restrictions on the actual parameters used when you invoke a user-defined function are that there should be the proper number of them, and that each parameter should be of the appropriate type—numeric or string. For example, **FNDoublingTime(5.5)**, **FNDoublingTime(rate)**, and **FNDoublingTime(net/7)** are all proper invocations of **FNDoublingTime** since Program 6-2 defined **FNDoublingTime** with a single numeric formal parameter. However, **FNDoublingTime(rate,net/7)** and **FNDoublingTime (rate$)** are not proper invocations of **FNDoublingTime**.

Like a predefined function, a user-defined function has a single output that is either a number or a string. A dollar sign must follow the name of the function if the output is a string. In addition, you can use one of the numeric type declaration tags at the end of the name to specify a specific numeric type. (A **DEFtype** statement can also specify the type of the output.) The input of a user-defined

Functions and Procedures

```
REM Find length of the hypotenuse of a right triangle   [6-3]
DEF FNHypotenuse(a,b) = SQR(a^2 + b^2)
INPUT "Enter lengths of two legs of a right triangle: ",a,b
PRINT "The hypotenuse has length"; FNHypotenuse(a,b)
End

Run
Enter lengths of two legs of a right triangle: 3,4
The hypotenuse has length 5
```

Program 6-3. *An example using the function FNHypotenuse*

function can consist of one or more parameters. Two examples of user-defined functions with several parameters are as follows:

FNHypotenuse(a,b) = SQR(a^2 + b^2)
FNFutureValue(p,n,r) = p*(1 + r)^n

The function **FNHypotenuse** gives the length of the hypotenuse of a right triangle that has sides of lengths **a** and **b**. The function **FNFutureValue** gives the balance in a savings account after **n** interest periods when **p** dollars is deposited at an interest rate **r** per period. Program 6-3 uses the hypotenuse function.

Program 6-4 uses the future-value function. With the responses shown, the program computes the balance in a savings account when $100 is deposited for 5 years at 8% interest, compounded quarterly. Interest is earned 4 times per year at the rate of 2% per interest period. There will be 4*5, or 20, interest periods.

Logical expressions can be used to define functions that perform some of the same tasks as **IF__THEN** statements. Logical expressions are either **true** or **false**. However, rather than utilize the values true and false, the computer evaluates false logical expressions to 0 and true logical expressions to −1. Program 6-5 illustrates the numeric evaluation of logical expressions. In the fourth line of the program, the true expressions evaluate to the number −1, and are used as part of a numeric expression.

```
REM Find the future value of a bank deposit    [6-4]
DEF FNFutureValue(p,n,r) = p*(1 + r)^n
INPUT "Amount of bank deposit"; p
INPUT "Number of interest periods"; n
INPUT "Interest rate per period"; r
PRINT USING "The balance is $####.##"; FNFutureValue(p,n,r)
END

Run
Amount of bank deposit? 100
Number of interest periods? 20
Interest rate per period? .02
The balance is $ 148.59
```

Program 6-4. *An example using the function FNFutureValue*

```
REM Numeric evaluation of logical expressions    [6-5]
PRINT 2 = 1
PRINT 1 < 2
PRINT (1 < 2)*3 + (4 < 5)*6
END

Run
 0
-1
-9
```

Program 6-5. *Numeric evaluation of logical expressions*

Program 6-6 uses logical expressions to define the function **FNMax**, which determines the larger of two numbers. If **x** is greater than **y**, then (**x** >= **y**) is true and has the value −1, while (**y** > **x**) is false and has the value 0. Thus, in this case, the value of **FNMax(x,y)** will be

$$-(x >= y)*x - (y > x)*y$$
$$= -(-1)*x - (0)*y$$
$$= x$$

Functions and Procedures

```
REM Find maximum of two numbers  [6-6]
DEF FNMax(x,y) = -(x >= y)*x - (y > x)*y
INPUT "Two numbers"; x, y
PRINT "The larger number is"; FNMax(x,y)
END

Run
Two numbers? 3,7
The larger number is 7
```

Program 6-6. *A function using logical expressions*

A similar analysis shows that the function evaluates to **y** when **y** is greater than **x**, and to **x** when **x** and **y** are equal.

Since Turbo Basic treats false as 0 and true as −1, you can define numeric functions whose possible values are thought of as true and false, even though these values are really −1 and 0. As an example of how such a function might be useful, consider the problem of determining whether a character is an uppercase letter. If **a$** holds a single character, then the statement

IF (a$ >= "A") AND (a$ <= "Z") THEN *action*

causes the *action* to be performed when **a$** is an uppercase letter. To make the decision being made in this statement more obvious, you can define a function **FNIsUppercase** by using the statement

DEF FNIsUppercase(c$) = (c$ >= "A") AND (c$ <= "Z")

and then write the **IF** statement as

IF FNIsUppercase(a$) THEN *action*

It cannot be overemphasized that the formal parameters used to define a function are just placeholders, and have no meaning outside of the definition of the function. You can change the names of the parameters to any other name of the same type without affecting the definition. Actually, the compiler creates special memory locations for the formal parameters that it only uses when the function is invoked. The names that the compiler gives to these locations have nothing whatsoever to do with the variable names used in the program. Therefore, in the event that a user-defined function uses as a formal parameter a variable that appears in the program, the value of the variable does not change as the result of invoking the function. Program 6-7 demonstrates this feature. If you think that the second number in the output should have been 5, consider the fact that the definition of the function is, in effect, simply

FNTriple(*numericValue*) = 3∗*numericValue*

Some of Turbo Basic's predefined functions, such as **TIME$** and **ERR**, have no parameters. (**TIME$** gives the current time and **ERR** gives the error code of the most recent error.) User-defined functions also do not have to have parameters. For instance, the function

FNStateTime$ = "The time is now " + TIME$

gives the time preceded by a phrase. You can invoke this function by executing a statement such as **PRINT FNStateTime$**.

```
REM Triple a number    [6-7]
x = 2
DEF FNTriple(x) = 3*x
PRINT FNTriple(5)
PRINT x
END

Run
 15
  2
```

Program 6-7. *Demonstrate the fact that parameters are dummy variables*

Multiline Functions

In Turbo Basic, a block of several statements can also define a function. This capability both simplifies the definition of certain functions, and opens up the opportunity to define some new and more powerful functions.

The block of statements that defines a multiline function begins with a statement of the form

DEF FN*FunctionName*(list of formal parameters)

and ends with the statement **END DEF**. Commas separate the formal parameters in the list. When a function is invoked, the computer assigns values of actual parameters to these formal parameters, and the statements within the block use the values to determine the function value. Normally, the statement immediately preceding the **END DEF** statement has the form

FN*FunctionName* = value

and actually carries out the assignment of the function value.

The block of statements that defines a function does not have to precede the first use of the function. This book places all definitions of multiline functions after the main program's **END** statement, and separates the definitions from each other and the main body of the program by using a blank line.

Program 6-8 contains a simple multiline user-defined function. Notice that when the program uses the statement **FNTriple = 3∗x** to assign a value to the function name, no parameters follow the function name. It would also be an error to begin this statement with the keyword **LET**.

Program 6-9 is the same as Program 6-6, except that this program uses a multiline block of statements to define the function. The meaning of the function is clearer and easier to figure out in this multiline definition.

```
REM Triple a number   [6-8]
number = 5
PRINT FNTriple(number)
END

DEF FNTriple(x)
   FNTriple = 3*x
END DEF
```

Program 6-8. *A simple multiline user-defined function*

```
REM Find maximum of two numbers   [6-9]
INPUT "Two numbers"; x, y
PRINT "The larger number is"; FNMax(x,y)
END

DEF FNMax(x,y)
   IF x >= y THEN FNMax = x ELSE FNMax = y
END DEF
```

Program 6-9. *A multiline version of the function from Program 6-6*

Program 6-10 includes the definition of the true or false function **FNIsALeapYear**. To make the function definition clearer, the program assigns numeric variables named **true** and **false** appropriate values at the beginning of the definition. Note also that you may assign a value to the function name in more than one statement within the function definition.

Program 6-11 uses a multiline block to define a function that cannot be defined in a single line. The function determines the number of words in a sentence by counting the number of spaces and adding one. Note: the increment statement **INCR** *numvar* adds one to the value of *numvar*.

There is one potential problem with Program 6-11 if the variables **i%** or **n%** appear elsewhere in the program. Whenever the function is invoked, the computer will change the values of these

Functions and Procedures

```
REM Determine number of days in a given year    [6-10]
INPUT "What year are you interested in";year
PRINT "The year"; year; "has ";
IF FNIsALeapYear(year) THEN PRINT "366 days." _
                       ELSE PRINT "365 days."
END

DEF FNIsALeapYear(y)
   true = -1
   false = 0
   IF y MOD 4 <> 0 THEN
     FNIsALeapYear = false
   ELSEIF (y MOD 100 = 0) AND (y MOD 400 <> 0) THEN
     FNIsALeapYear = false
   ELSE
     FNIsALeapYear = true
   END IF
END DEF

Run
What year are you interested in? 1900
The year 1900 has 365 days.
```

Program 6-10. *A user-defined function evaluating to true and false*

```
REM Count the number of words in a sentence    [6-11]
INPUT "Enter a sentence: ", sentence$
PRINT "The sentence contains";
PRINT FNNumberOfWords%(sentence$); "words."
END

DEF FNNumberOfWords%(a$)
   n% = 0         'Number of spaces
   FOR i% = 1 TO LEN(a$)
     IF MID$(a$,i%,1) = " " THEN INCR n%
   NEXT i%
   FNNumberOfWords% = n% + 1
END DEF

Run
Enter a sentence: Inch by inch is a cinch; yard by yard is hard.
The sentence contains 11 words.
```

Program 6-11. *A user-defined function containing a loop*

variables with unpredictable consequences. One solution to this problem is to be careful to avoid using these variables in the main body of the program. However, Turbo Basic has a better solution. Recognizing that these variables are intended for use only locally inside the function-definition block and should have no relationship to any variables outside of the block, Turbo Basic allows these variables to be declared as *local* variables through the statement

LOCAL i%, n%

which is placed immediately after the **DEF FN** statement. Then, each time that the function is invoked, Turbo Basic sets aside new locations in memory to hold their values. The situation is the same as if Turbo Basic added the name of the function to these two variables inside the block—treating them as **iNumberOfWords%** and **nNumberOfWords%**. When the program exits the block, Turbo Basic forgets these memory locations. This process not only uses memory efficiently, but also sets local numeric variables to zero and local string variables to the null string whenever the function is invoked.

    A variable that appears in the definition of a multiline function can also be declared as a *static* variable. Like local variables, static variables have no relationship to any variables outside of the block of statements that defines the function. However, they retain their values from one evaluation of the function to the next evaluation. Therefore, you can use or alter these values each time that the function is invoked. The statement **STATIC** *list of variables* declares each variable in the list to be static.

    Variables that appear in the definition of a multiline function and are recognized by the rest of the program are called *global* or *shared* variables. In the block of statements that defines a function, Turbo Basic assumes any variable that is not declared as local or static and is not a formal parameter to be a shared variable. Thus, Turbo Basic treats **true** and **false** in Program 6-10 as shared variables. To make programs easier to decipher, Turbo Basic allows you to declare variables explicitly as shared via a statement of the form **SHARED** *list of variables*. Like the **LOCAL** and **STATIC** dec-

Functions and Procedures

larations, **SHARED** declarations must follow the **DEF FN** statement and must precede every other executable statement in the definition block. Only **REM** statements can precede the declaration statements.

Good programming practice dictates that, other than the formal parameters, you declare all variables appearing in the statements that define a function to be either LOCAL, STATIC, or SHARED. This text will follow this practice from this point on. The outputs of the three programs in Figure 6-1 illustrate the effects of the three different declarations of the variable **n** in the definition of the function **FNTriple**.

There are many reasons for using user-defined functions. You can easily do each of the following due to Turbo Basic's capability of declaring variables as local, static, or shared.

1. The use of user-defined functions is consistent with the stepwise-refinement approach to program design. Once you realize that you need a particular function, you can give it a name but save the task of figuring out the computational details until later.

```
REM n shared              REM n local               REM n static
n = 2                     n = 2                     n = 2
PRINT FNTriple(5);        PRINT FNTriple(5);        PRINT FNTriple(5);
PRINT n;                  PRINT n;                  PRINT n;
PRINT FNTriple(6);        PRINT FNTriple(6);        PRINT FNTriple(6);
PRINT a                   PRINT a                   PRINT a
END                       END                       END

DEF FNTriple(x)           DEF FNTriple(x)           DEF FNTriple(x)
   SHARED a, n               SHARED a                  SHARED a
   a = n                     LOCAL n                   STATIC n
   n = 3*x                   a = n                     a = n
   FNTriple = n              n = 3*x                   n = 3*x
END DEF                      FNTriple = n              FNTriple = n
Run                       END DEF                   END DEF
   15   15   18   15
                          Run                       Run
                             15   2   18   0           15   2   18   15
```

Figure 6-1. *Programs that distinguish between* **SHARED**, **LOCAL**, *and* **STATIC**

2. Sometimes, a single algorithm must be performed several times in a program. Specifying the algorithm as a function saves repeated typing of the same formula, improves readability, and simplifies debugging.

3. You can use functions that are derived for one program in other programs. As a programmer, you can maintain a collection, or library, of functions that might be needed.

Subroutines

A subroutine is a portion of a program that lies outside of the main body of the program, ends with a **RETURN** statement, and is reached by a **GOSUB** statement. The first line of a subroutine must have either a line number or a preceding line label. (A *line label* is a name, terminated with a colon, that is inserted into a program on a line by itself. Then statements such as **GOTO** *labelName* cause control to jump to the line after the named label.) Whenever the statement **GOSUB** *labelName* (or **GOSUB** *lineNumber*) is executed, a program branches to the specified line. When Turbo Basic reaches a **RETURN** statement, control branches back to the statement that immediately follows the **GOSUB** statement. You usually place subroutines at the end of the program, and separate them from the main body of the program by using an **END** statement to prevent Turbo Basic from executing the subroutine inadvertently.

Program 6-12 uses a subroutine to make change for a customer. The program first converts the amount of money due to cents, and then determines the number of bills and coins of each denomination. (To simplify matters, the program uses only dollar bills, quarters, dimes, nickels, and pennies.) The subroutine has the named label **reportNumberOfUnits**.

The subroutine is Standard BASIC's principal device for dividing a program into small pieces that you can write one at a time. In

```
REM Make change  [6-12]
INPUT "Total cost of purchase"; cost
INPUT "Amount tendered by customer"; paid
changeDue% = 100*(paid - cost)    'Change due in cents
PRINT " Change:"
unit% = 100              '100 cents is 1 dollar
unitName$ = "dollar"
GOSUB reportNumberOfUnits
unit% = 25         '25 cents is 1 quarter
unitName$ = "quarter"
GOSUB reportNumberOfUnits
unit% = 10         '10 cents is 1 dime
unitName$ = "dime"
GOSUB reportNumberOfUnits
unit% = 5          '5 cents is 1 nickel
unitName$ = "nickel"
GOSUB reportNumberOfUnits
unit% = 1
unitName$ = "cent"
GOSUB reportNumberOfUnits
END

reportNumberOfUnits:
  number% = changeDue%\unit%
  IF number% > 0 THEN
    IF number% > 1 THEN unitName$ = unitName$ + "s"
    PRINT number%; unitName$
  END IF
  changeDue% = changeDue% - (number%*unit%)
RETURN

Run
Total cost of purchase? 1.65
Amount tendered by customer? 5.00
 Change:
 3 dollars
 1 quarter
 1 dime
```

Program 6-12. *Using GOSUB to make change*

addition to supporting subroutines, Turbo Basic has a device called a *procedure* that serves the same purpose as a subroutine, but is vastly improved. Procedures are regarded as the single most important enhancement of Standard BASIC by Turbo Basic.

Procedures

A procedure is a hybrid of a subroutine and a function. Like a subroutine, a procedure is branched to and from the main program, and performs a specific task. Like a function, a procedure has parameters and can pass values to these parameters when the procedure is invoked. Also, you can declare variables that appear in a procedure as **LOCAL**, **STATIC**, or **SHARED**. However, procedures have some features that go beyond the capabilities of functions. First, you can pass entire arrays to a procedure. Second, you can use parameters to pass data back to the main program from the procedure.

Each procedure is defined by a block that begins with a statement of the form

SUB *ProcedureName*(*list of formal parameters*)

and that ends with the statement **END SUB**. A procedure is invoked, or called, with the statement

CALL *ProcedureName*(*list of actual parameters*)

where the number and types of the actual parameters in the list are the same as those of the formal variables in the parameter list. As with functions, you can give each value as a constant, variable, or expression. When a procedure is called, the values of the actual parameters are passed to the formal parameters and used by the inner portion of the block. After Turbo Basic has executed all of the statements in the block, or when Turbo Basic encounters an **EXIT SUB** statement, program execution continues with the statement that follows the **CALL** statement.

Program 6-13 is another version of Program 6-12, which uses a procedure instead of the subroutine. The new program passes values to the procedure when the procedure is called, whereas the original program had to assign these values to variables before **GOSUB**ing to the subroutine.

Functions and Procedures

```
REM Make change  [6-13]
INPUT "Total cost of items purchased"; cost
INPUT "Amount tendered by customer"; paid
changeDue% = 100*(paid - cost)
PRINT " Change:"
CALL ReportNumberOfUnits(100,"dollar")
CALL ReportNumberOfUnits( 25,"quarter")
CALL ReportNumberOfUnits( 10,"dime")
CALL ReportNumberOfUnits(  5,"nickel")
CALL ReportNumberOfUnits(  1,"cent")
END

SUB ReportNumberOfUnits(unit%,unitName$)
  LOCAL number%
  SHARED changeDue%
  number% = changeDue%\unit%
  IF number% > 0 THEN
    IF number% > 1 THEN unitName$ = unitName$ + "s"
    PRINT number%; unitName$
  END IF
  changeDue% = changeDue% - (number%*unit%)
END SUB
```

Program 6-13. *A rewrite of Program 6-12 using procedures*

On the surface, **CALL**ing a procedure and doing a **GOSUB** to a subroutine appear to be equivalent. Both statements cause a jump to a new section of the program, perform a task, and then jump back to the same location in the program. However, the similarity between the statements ends there. The following considerations reveal the important differences between them. The remainder of this book uses procedures exclusively.

1. A **GOSUB** statement is simply a glorified **GOTO** statement to a new section of the main program. Turbo Basic can accidentally enter the statements that compose the subroutine without the use of a **GOSUB**, which can cause unpredictable results. However, **CALL** invokes a protected section of statements that Turbo Basic can never accidentally fall into. (No harm would have been done if you omitted the **END** statement in Program 6-13. The same cannot be said for Program 6-12.)

2. Subroutines cannot have local variables. All variables are equivalent to SHARED variables in procedures. Thus, when you are writing a subroutine, the question always arises as to whether you will be using the temporary variable being considered elsewhere and therefore should not use it in the subroutine.

3. GOSUB does not allow the task to be defined with generic variables (formal parameters). Before each use of a GOSUB statement, you must assign the values needed for the current invocation to the appropriate variables hidden away in the subroutine. The programmer must answer the question, "What names did I use for the variables when I wrote that subroutine?" However, procedures allow you to define a task with generic variables, and execute it later by using the actual variables, values, or expressions that appear in the program at that time.

4. All variables in subroutines stay in memory throughout the program. Therefore, valuable memory can be used up by temporary variables that have no use outside of the subroutine. However, procedures allow all temporary variables to be declared as LOCAL and, therefore, only use memory for these LOCAL variables when the procedure is called.

5. Although Turbo Basic allows you to use labels that are words and, therefore, have meaning, GOSUBing to one of these labels does not make it clear what variables will be affected by the subroutine. Thus, you will find it harder to read through the main program, especially at a later date, and recall exactly what is happening during each of its steps. Procedures, with their parameter lists, do not suffer this shortcoming.

Pass-by-Reference Versus Pass-by-Value

Programs 6-14 and 6-15 make assignments to the variables **state$** and **pop&**, and make no reassignments to these variables. Yet, when the values of the variables are displayed at the end of Program 6-14, the values have changed.

Functions and Procedures

```
REM Display population of the golden state   [6-14]
state$ = "CALIFORNIA"
pop& = 24000000
CALL DisplayInfo(state$,pop&)
PRINT state$; pop&
END

SUB DisplayInfo(a$,b&)
  a$ = LEFT$(a$,2)
  b& = b&/1000000
  PRINT b&; "million people live in "; a$
END SUB

Run
 24 million people live in CA
CA 24
```

Program 6-14. *Demonstrate pass-by-reference*

As in Program 6-14, when the **CALL** of a procedure uses a variable as an actual parameter, Turbo Basic makes a pass-by-reference. Turbo Basic uses (or references) the variable in the **CALL** statement in place of the formal parameter that appears in the procedure

```
REM Display population of the golden state   [6-15]
state$ = "CALIFORNIA"
pop& = 24000000
CALL DisplayInfo(state$ + "",pop& + 0)
PRINT state$; pop&
END

SUB DisplayInfo(a$,b&)
  a$ = LEFT$(a$,2)
  b& = b&/1000000
  PRINT b&; "million people live in "; a$
END SUB

Run
 24 million people live in CA
CALIFORNIA 24000000
```

Program 6-15. *Demonstrate pass-by-value*

definition. In Program 6-14, for example, the statement **CALL DisplayInfo(state$,pop&)** effectively executes the following statements:

```
state$ = LEFT$(state$,2)
pop& = pop&/1000000
PRINT pop&; "million people live in "; state$
```

One immediate consequence of pass-by-reference is that, within the procedure, you can give new values to the actual parameters used in the **CALL** of the procedure—thus, explaining the output of Program 6-14.

When you use a constant or expression in the **CALL** of a procedure, as in Program 6-15, Turbo Basic makes a pass-by-value: Turbo Basic places the constant or the value of the expression in a memory location created for the associated formal parameter. The effect is the same as if the formal parameter is assigned the value of the constant or expression at the beginning of the procedure. For example, in Program 6-15, the statement **CALL DisplayInfo(state$ + "",pop& + 0)** effectively executes the following statements:

```
a$ = state$ + ""
b& = pop& + 0
a$ = LEFT$(a$,2)
b& = b&/1000000
PRINT b&; "million people live in "; a$
```

From these statements, you can see why Program 6-15 did not change the values of **state$** and **pop&**: In a pass-by-value situation, since only the values of the actual parameters are made available to replace the formal parameters, Turbo Basic does not give to the procedure the actual variables to use and change.

As a further example, consider Program 6-16, which **CALL**s the procedure **Insert** with a constant as the first actual parameter. The procedure displays the string **Jonathan Livingston Sea Gull**, but the string is not available for use in the main body of the program. However, if the **CALL** statement in Program 6-16 is replaced by the two statements

```
item$ = "Jonathan Sea Gull"
CALL Insert(item$,"Livingston ",10)
```

Functions and Procedures

```
REM Add in Jonathan's middle name
CALL Insert("Jonathan Sea Gull","Livingston ",10)
END

SUB Insert(first$,second$,position)
  REM Insert second$ into first$, starting at position
  first$ = LEFT$(first$,position-1) + second$ + _
      MID$(first$,position)
  PRINT first$
END SUB

Run
Jonathan Livingston Sea Gull
```

Program 6-16. *Pass-by-value versus pass-by-reference*

so that the program uses a variable as the first actual parameter, then the procedure **Insert** not only displays the string **Jonathan Livingston Sea Gull**, but also passes this string back as the new value of the variable **item$**. Subsequent statements in the main program can then use the string in **item$**.

Occasionally, you may have data stored in a variable that you wish to pass to a procedure, and yet you do not want the procedure to change the value of the variable. Program 6-15 achieved this result for the variables **state$** and **pop&** by using the expressions **state$+""** and **pop&+0** as actual parameters, thus causing a pass-by-value. Turbo Basic provides a cleaner solution: If you enclose a variable in an extra pair of parentheses when a procedure is called, then Turbo Basic will pass-by-value the value of the variable to the procedure. After executing the procedure, Turbo Basic guarantees the variable to have its original value. For example, if you replace the **CALL** statement in Program 6-16 by the three statements

```
item$ = "Jonathan Sea Gull"
CALL Insert((item$),"Livingston ",10)
PRINT item$
```

then the program will display

```
Jonathan Livingston Sea Gull
Jonathan Sea Gull
```

Passing Arrays to Procedures

You have seen many examples of simple numeric and string variables being used as procedure parameters. Turbo Basic also supports the passing of an entire array to a procedure. To define a procedure so that you can pass an array, the formal parameter used in the **SUB** statement must contain the formal name for the array followed by a pair of parentheses that contain the number of dimensions of the array. The **CALL** statement must contain first the actual name of the array to be passed and then an empty pair of parentheses.

In Program 6-17, the procedure **MergeLists** merges two sorted lists of words into one sorted list. The formal parameters **listA$(1)**, **listB$(1)**, and **newList$(1)** in the procedure definition tell Turbo Basic that string arrays of one dimension each (and not one entry) will be used whenever **MergeLists** is called. In the **CALL** statement, a set of empty parentheses follows each array name. This order allows Turbo Basic to distinguish between actual parameters like **oldNames$**, **oldNames$( )**, and **oldNames$(8)**, which Turbo Basic interprets as a regular string variable, an entire string array, and the eighth element in the string array **oldNames$( )**, respectively.

Declaring Arrays

Although only procedures can have arrays passed to them, both functions and procedures can utilize arrays within their definitions. To use an array within a procedure or function definition, first declare the array as either LOCAL, STATIC, or SHARED. In making this declaration, you specify the array by giving its name followed by an empty pair of parentheses. Second, for LOCAL, STATIC, and not-yet-dimensioned SHARED arrays, include the appropriate **DIM** statement after the declaration statement. Figure 6-2 shows the beginning of a procedure that declares and dimensions several arrays.

An array declared in a **LOCAL** statement is always dynamic. To help emphasize this fact, it is best to include the keyword **DYNAMIC** in the dimension statement of local arrays, as shown in

Functions and Procedures

```
REM Merge two sorted lists [6-17]
DIM oldNames$(1:5),newNames$(1:7),combinedList$(1:12)
FOR index = 1 TO 5
   READ oldNames$(index)
NEXT index
FOR index = 1 TO 7
   READ newNames$(index)
NEXT index
CALL MergeLists(oldNames$(),newNames$(),combinedList$())
CLS
FOR index = 1 to 12
   PRINT combinedList$(index);" ";
NEXT index
PRINT
DATA Alan, Bill, Jim, Sue, Tina
DATA Adam, Bob, Chris, Gail, Kim, Mike, Steve
END

SUB MergeLists(listA$(1),listB$(1),newList$(1))
   LOCAL sizeA, sizeB, sizeNew, aNow, bNow, newNow, index
   REM Each array must have been dimensioned by a
   REM statement of the form DIM arrayName(1:m),
   REM where m is a positive whole number
   sizeA   = UBOUND(listA$(1))
   sizeB   = UBOUND(listB$(1))
   sizeNew = UBOUND(newList$(1))
   REM If array newList$() is not large enough
   REM for combined lists, do not try to merge.
   IF sizeNew < sizeA + sizeB THEN
      PRINT "Result array not large enough for merge"
      EXIT SUB
   END IF
   aNow    = 1
   bNow    = 1
   newNow = 1
   DO WHILE (aNow <= sizeA) AND  (bNow <= sizeB)
      IF listA$(aNow) < listB$(bNow) THEN
         newList$(newNow) = listA$(aNow)
         INCR aNow
      ELSE
         newList$(newNow) = listB$(bNow)
         INCR bNow
      END IF
      INCR newNow
   LOOP
   REM Logically, one of the arrays, listA$() or listB$(),
   REM has been exhausted, and so, of the following two
   REM loops, only one will actually have work to do.
   FOR index = aNow TO sizeA
      newList$(newNow) = listA$(index)
      INCR newNow
   NEXT index
   FOR index = bNow TO sizeB
      newList$(newNow) = listB$(index)
      INCR newNow
   NEXT index
END SUB

Run
Adam Alan Bill Bob Chris Gail Jim Kim Mike Steve Sue Tina
```

Program 6-17. *Passing arrays to a procedure*

```
SUB UseManyArrays
  LOCAL count(),totals()
  STATIC lastCounts()
  SHARED letters$()
  DIM DYNAMIC count(1:20),totals(1:10)
  DIM STATIC lastCounts(1:20)
  :
END SUB
```

Figure 6-2. *Declaring arrays in a procedure*

Figure 6-2. As with any other local variable, Turbo Basic initializes a local array to zero or the null string each time that the procedure or function is invoked, and removes the array from memory when execution of the procedure or function is complete.

You should also dimension an array declared in a **STATIC** statement by using the keyword **STATIC** to emphasize its permanent nature. However, note that, even though such a static array continues to occupy memory after execution of the procedure or function is complete, a program cannot access the array from outside the declaring procedure or function. Also recall that you must dimension a static array using integer constants to specify the lower and upper bounds; Turbo Basic does not allow you to use variables for this purpose.

An array declared in a **SHARED** statement may be dimensioned by using the keywords **DYNAMIC** or **STATIC**, as appropriate. Generally, you do not dimension shared arrays within procedures unless you design the procedure to be called just once for the purpose of initializing a number of variables.

Although you can dimension all three types of arrays inside the procedure block, you should usually dimension SHARED arrays in the main body of the program to avoid having the **DIM** statement produce an error message when it is executed a second time. However, Turbo Basic can execute the **DIM** statements for LOCAL and STATIC arrays repeatedly without causing an error message.

The procedure of Program 6-18 declares the array **count( )** as a LOCAL array. Since empty parentheses follow the array name, Turbo Basic can recognize it as an array rather than as a simple

Functions and Procedures

```
REM Count occurrences of various letters in a string   [6-18]
INPUT "String to analyze> ", a$
CALL LetterCount(a$)
END

SUB LetterCount(info$)
  LOCAL A,Z,place,char,count()
  'A       holds the ASCII value of "A"
  'Z       holds the ASCII value of "Z"
  'place   keeps track of our current position in info$
  'char    stores the ASCII value of the character found at place
  '        in info$, and serves as the index into the count array
  'count() is an array to hold the count of the number of times
  '        a letter occurs in info$ (case of letters is ignored)
  A = ASC("A")
  Z = ASC("Z")
  DIM DYNAMIC count(A:Z)
  REM The array count should initially be filled with zeros.
  REM Turbo Basic does this automatically for DYNAMIC arrays.
  'Scan across info$, count occurrences of each letter
  FOR place = 1 to LEN(info$)
    char = ASC(UCASE$(MID$(info$,place,1)))
    'If the character is a letter, count it, otherwise ignore it.
    IF char >= A AND char <= Z THEN INCR count(char)
  NEXT place
  REM Print results, putting letter on
  REM first line and count on second
  FOR char = A TO Z
    PRINT USING "  !"; chr$(char);
  NEXT char
  PRINT
  FOR char = A TO Z
    PRINT USING " #";count(char);
  NEXT char
  PRINT
END SUB

Run
String to analyze> Don't count time; make time count.
A B C D E F G H I J K L M N O P Q R S T U V W X Y Z
1 0 2 1 3 0 0 0 2 0 1 0 3 3 3 0 0 0 0 5 2 0 0 0 0 0
```

Program 6-18. *A procedure utilizing a local array*

numeric variable. The word **DYNAMIC** in the **DIM** statement emphasizes the fact that the array is of a temporary nature, like the other local variables.

Program 6-19 shows a simple mechanism called a *last-in-first-out*, or *LIFO*, stack. This stack permits the program to store values in the order received and then to bring them back for processing in reverse order. In the procedure **LifoStackControl**, the array **stack()**

```
REM Demonstrate a Last-In-First-Out stack    [6-19]
CALL LifoStackControl("push",5,status$)
PRINT status$;" ";
CALL LifoStackControl("push",8,status$)
PRINT status$;" ";
CALL LifoStackControl("pop",num,status$)
PRINT status$;num;
CALL LifoStackControl("pop",x,status$)
PRINT status$;x;
'All pushed values have been popped, so status$
'will report an error for calling pop again
CALL LifoStackControl("pop",wrong,status$)
PRINT status$;wrong
END

SUB LifoStackControl(operation$,value,status$)
REM Implementation of a simple Last In First Out (LIFO) stack
  STATIC top%, stack()
  'operation$ is the action to be taken, either PUSH or POP
  'value      is the data to be PUSHed onto the stack or
  '           the data that has been POPped off the stack
  'status$    passes back "OK" if operation$ is successful
  '           or an error message if not
  'top%       records the last location into which data
  '           has been placed
  'stack      is a STATIC array to hold the values being
  '           PUSHed & POPped
  DIM STATIC stack(1:256)
  SELECT CASE UCASE$(operation$)
    CASE "PUSH"
      IF top% < 256 THEN
         INCR top%
         stack(top%) = value
         status$ = "OK"
      ELSE
         status$ = "Stack is Full"
      END IF
    CASE "POP"
      IF top% > 0 THEN
         value = stack(top%)
         DECR top%
         status$ = "OK"
      ELSE
         status$ = "Stack is Empty"
      END IF
    CASE ELSE
      status$ = "Stack Operation Error"
  END SELECT
END SUB

Run
OK OK OK 8 OK 5 Stack is Empty 0
```

Program 6-19. *A procedure with a static memory allocation of an array*

and the variable **top** must be allocated permanent memory, and not be created and initialized each time that **FifoStackControl** is called. The declaration of **stack( )** and **top%** as STATIC tells Turbo Basic to make the desired permanent allocation of memory. Turbo Basic initializes STATIC variables declared in this way only once. You can think of this initialization of numeric variables to zero and string variables to null as occurring when the procedure is first called. Note that the decrement statement **DECR** *numvar* subtracts one from the value of *numvar*.

The Differences Between Functions and Procedures

All tasks that are performed by functions can also be performed by procedures. However, when your objective is solely to calculate a single value, functions are more natural to work with. There are four main differences between procedures and functions:

1. While you invoke procedures by using **CALL** statements, you invoke functions by using the function in a place that Turbo Basic would otherwise expect to find a constant or expression.

2. While a procedure name serves only to identify the procedure and to describe its task, a function name identifies the function, describes the task, *and* is assigned a value by the statements within its definition. When a function is invoked, it *returns* a value. That value can be a string or any of the four numeric types, according to the type indicated by the name of the function.

3. A procedure allows pass-by-reference parameters whose values can be altered by the procedure. However, all parameters passed to a function are treated as passed-by-value. In other words, a function will never change the values of the parameters passed to it, even if some of those parameters are simple variables. As a consequence of this pass-by-value rule, you cannot pass entire arrays to a function — you can only pass individual elements of arrays.

4. Good programming practice dictates that all variables used in a function or procedure definition either appear in the parameter list or be declared as LOCAL, STATIC, or SHARED. However, if undeclared variables do appear, then Turbo Basic treats them as SHARED in function definitions and as STATIC in procedure definitions.

The first two differences are illustrated by Program 6-20, which uses both a string function and a procedure to reverse the order of the characters in a sentence input by the user.

The two programs in Figure 6-3, which calculate the factorial of a number, illustrate the third difference. (Note that the factorial

```
REM Show the difference in using a function and a procedure [6-20]
REM to reverse the order of the characters in a string
INPUT "> ", phrase$
PRINT "   "; FNReverseLine$(phrase$)
CALL ReverseLine(phrase$,answer$)
PRINT "   "; answer$
END

DEF FNReverseLine$(info$)
   LOCAL index,temp$
   FOR index = LEN(info$) to 1 STEP -1
     temp$ = temp$ + mid$(info$,index,1)
   NEXT index
   FNReverseLine$ = temp$
END DEF

SUB ReverseLine(info$,result$)
   LOCAL index
   FOR index = LEN(info$) to 1 STEP -1
     result$ = result$ + mid$(info$,index,1)
   NEXT index
END SUB

Run
> LEVEL is a palindrome
    emordnilap a si LEVEL
    emordnilap a si LEVEL
```

Program 6-20. *A program showing some differences between functions and procedures*

Functions and Procedures

of a positive integer is the product of the numbers from 1 to the integer.) In the program on the left, the value of **n%** remains unchanged since Turbo Basic always passes parameters by value to functions. However, in the program on the right, the variable **n%** is passed by reference to the procedure and the procedure alters the value of **n%**.

Procedures and Functions That Invoke Each Other: Stepwise Refinement

As discussed at the beginning of this chapter, a programmer's key problem-solving strategy is stepwise refinement. As a programmer, you break down a large problem into a sequence of smaller problems. You then deal with each subproblem in a procedure or function. If the task assigned to a subproblem is still complicated, you

```
REM Calculate a factorial              REM Calculate a factorial
n% = 5                                  n% = 5
result& = FNFactorial&(n%)              CALL Factorial(n%,result&)
PRINT n%;"factorial is";result&         PRINT n%;"factorial is";result&
END                                     END

DEF FNFactorial&(num%)                  SUB Factorial(num%,answer&)
   LOCAL answer&                           answer& = 1
   answer& = 1                             DO WHILE num% > 0
   DO WHILE num% > 0                          answer& = answer&*num%
      answer& = answer&*num%                  DECR num%
      DECR num%                            LOOP
   LOOP                                 END SUB
   FNFactorial& = answer&
END DEF                                 Run
                                        0 factorial is 120
Run
 5 factorial is 120
```

Figure 6-3. *The same task performed by a function and a procedure*

should break the subproblem into a sequence of still-smaller subproblems. Since Turbo Basic allows procedures and functions to call other procedures and functions, it is easy to code this type of solution. Let's illustrate this process by using stepwise refinement to solve a specific problem.

The current calendar, known as the Gregorian calendar, was introduced in 1582. Imagine that you want to convert any numeric date after the year 1582 into an improved form that gives the day of the week and spells out the month. Figure 6-4 gives a breakdown of the problem into subproblems. Each rectangle except the top one

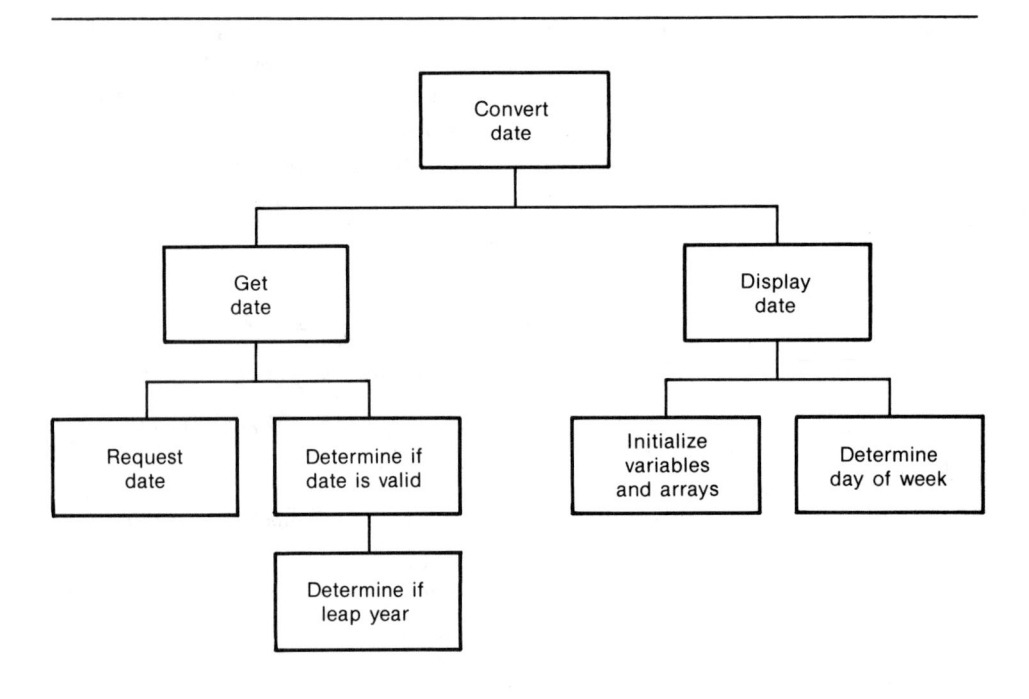

Figure 6-4. *A stepwise-refinement chart*

Functions and Procedures

corresponds to a procedure or a function. This diagram is called a *stepwise-refinement chart*.

By solving the problem in pieces rather than in its entirety, the main body of Program 6-21 is short and easily understood. The procedure **GetDate** not only requests the month, day, and year, but also checks that the input is valid. The names for procedures and functions invoked in **GetDate** readily reflect these tasks. Note that, by definition, **FNDateIsValid** is assigned the result of a logical expression that is **true** or **false**. The value of the function **FNDateIsValid** is best thought of as **true** or **false**, even though Turbo Basic actually considers the value as either −1 or 0. The function **FNDateIsValid** also invokes the **true**-or-**false**-valued function **FNIsALeapYear** that Program 6-10 introduced earlier. Further,

```
REM Convert numeric date to day-of-week, month, day, year   [6-21]
DEFINT a-z
CALL GetDate(month,day,year)
CALL PrintFancyDate(month,day,year)
END

SUB GetDate(month,day,year)
   DO
      CALL RequestDate(month,day,year)
   LOOP UNTIL FNDateIsValid(month,day,year)
END SUB

SUB PrintFancyDate(m,d,y)
   LOCAL day$(),month$(),f$
   DIM day$(0:6),month$(1:12)
   CALL Initialize(day$(),month$())
   IF d < 10 THEN f$="&_, & #_, ####" ELSE f$="&_, & ##_, ####"
   PRINT USING f$;day$(FNDayOfWeek(m,d,y)),month$(m),d,y
END SUB

SUB RequestDate(month,day,year)
   CLS
   INPUT "Month (1-12)";month
   INPUT "Day (1-31)";day
   INPUT "Year (1582->)";year
END SUB

DEF FNDateIsValid(month,day,year)
   LOCAL yearOk,monthOk,dayOk,temp$
   yearOk = (year >= 1582)
```

Program 6-21. *A program written with stepwise refinement*

```
    monthOk = (month >= 1) AND (month <= 12)
    SELECT CASE month
      CASE 2
        IF FNThisIsALeapYear(year) THEN
            dayOk = (day >= 1) AND (day <= 29)
          ELSE
            dayOk = (day >= 1) AND (day <= 28)
        END IF
      CASE 4,6,9,11
        dayOk = (day >= 1) AND (day <= 30)
      CASE ELSE
        dayOk = (day >= 1) AND (day <= 31)
    END SELECT
    FNDateIsValid = yearOk AND monthOk AND dayOk
    IF NOT (yearOk AND monthOk AND dayOk) THEN
      PRINT "Date is not valid. Press any key to continue."
      temp$=INPUT$(1)
    END IF
END DEF

DEF FNThisIsALeapYear(year)
  LOCAL true,false
  true = -1 :  false = 0
  IF year MOD 4 <> 0 THEN
    FNThisIsALeapYear = false
  ELSEIF (year MOD 100 = 0) AND (year MOD 400 <> 0) THEN
    FNThisIsALeapYear = false
  ELSE
    FNThisIsALeapYear = true
  END IF
END DEF

SUB Initialize(d$(1),m$(1))
  m$(1) = "January"     :  m$(2) = "February"
  m$(3) = "March"       :  m$(4) = "April"
  m$(5) = "May"         :  m$(6) = "June"
  m$(7) = "July"        :  m$(8) = "August"
  m$(9) = "September"   :  m$(10) = "October"
  m$(11) = "November"   :  m$(12) = "December"
  d$(0) = "Saturday"    :  d$(1) = "Sunday"
  d$(2) = "Monday"      :  d$(3) = "Tuesday"
  d$(4) = "Wednesday"   :  d$(5) = "Thursday"
  d$(6) = "Friday"
END SUB

DEF FNDayOfWeek(month,day,year)
  IF month <= 2 THEN
    month = month + 12
    year = year - 1
  END IF
  FNDayOfWeek = (day + 2*month + 3*(month+1)\5 + year + _
                year\4 - year\100 +year\400 + 2) MOD 7
END DEF

Run
Month (1-12)? 7
Day (1-31)? 4
Year (1582- ?)? 1776
Thursday, July 4, 1776
```

Program 6-21. *A program written with stepwise refinement* (continued)

Functions and Procedures

FNDateIsValid demonstrates the fact that a function can do more than just compute a value: part of **FNDateIsValid**'s job is to print an error message when the given date is not valid.

The procedure **PrintFancyDate** first dimensions two local arrays—one for holding the names of the days of the week, and the other for holding the names of the months—and then calls the procedure **Initialize** to assign values to the arrays. By putting these assignments in a procedure by themselves, the program avoids cluttering up the procedure **PrintFancyDate**. Note also the compact yet readable way in which **PrintFancyDate** calls upon the function **FNDayOfWeek**. Since Turbo Basic allows you to use a function any place where you can use a constant value, it is perfectly legitimate to obtain the subscript for the array **day$** by invoking the function **FNDayOfWeek**. The function **FNDayOfWeek** itself makes use of a strange-looking but effective formula for determining the day of the week that corresponds to a given month, day, and year. Note that, in order for the formula to work, the program considers January and February as months 13 and 14 of the previous year.

If you have written programs in languages that allow you to nest procedure definitions and function definitions, note that Turbo Basic does not allow this style of program construction—you must define each procedure or function separately.

Recursion

Not only can a function or procedure invoke other functions and procedures, but also it can invoke itself. This process is called *recursion*. There are some functions that have a recursive flavor and, therefore, are most naturally defined recursively. For example, suppose that a country of 6 million people is experiencing an annual population growth rate of 2% and a steady immigration of 20000 people each year. You can use this simple formula that gives the population at the beginning of any year in terms of the population at the beginning of the previous year:

(pop. at beg. of year) = 1.02**(pop. at beg. of previous year)* + 20000

(Since 2% is 0.02, you can think of the number 1.02 as 1.00 + 0.02, or 1 plus 2%. Therefore, multiplying the population by 1.02 is the same as adding 2% to the current population.) Next, you can define a function, **FNPopulation**(n), that will give the population at the beginning of any year. The parameter **n** will assume values such as 0, 1, 2, and so on, that correspond to the present year, 1 year hence, 2 years hence, and so on, respectively. **FNPopulation(0)** has the value 6000000. You can use the formula just given to compute population sizes for successive years, as follows:

FNPopulation(1) = 1.02*FNPopulation(0) + 20000
FNPopulation(2) = 1.02*FNPopulation(1) + 20000
.
.
.
FNPopulation(n) = 1.02*FNPopulation(n−1) + 20000

Suppose that you wanted to know the value of **FNPopulation(3)**. You could use the following calculations:

FNPopulation(3) = 1.02*FNPopulation(2) + 20000

Now,

FNPopulation(2) = 1.02*FNPopulation(1) + 20000
FNPopulation(1) = 1.02*FNPopulation(0) + 20000

But **FNPopulation(0)** is known to be 6000000. You can now trace through the equations one at a time until you obtain the value of **FNPopulation(3)**:

FNPopulation(1) = 1.02*6000000 + 20000 = 6140000
FNPopulation(2) = 1.02*6140000 + 20000 = 6282800
FNPopulation(3) = 1.02*6282800 + 20000 = 6428456

Program 6-22 follows this process. Each time that the function is invoked, the program decreases the value of **n%** by 1 and, therefore, the value of **n%** will eventually reach 0. At this point, the recursion

Functions and Procedures

```
REM Compute future populations [6-22]
INPUT "Number of years in future"; numberOfYears%
PRINT "The population will be"; FNPopulation&(numberOfYears%)
END

DEF FNPopulation&(n%)
   IF n% = 0 THEN
       FNPopulation& = 6000000
     ELSE
       FNPopulation& = 1.02*FNPopulation&(n%-1) + 20000
   END IF
END DEF

Run
Number of years in future? 3
The population will be 6428456
```

Program 6-22. *A recursively defined function*

will terminate. Whenever you use recursion in a function or procedure, you must provide a way to stop the recursion. If you do not, Turbo Basic will display an **Out of memory** error message.

Program 6-23 uses a recursively defined procedure to guess the number that a person is thinking of. The main body of the program gives directions to the user and then calls the procedure **Guess** to begin making guesses. The main program also provides for repeated play.

The procedure **Guess** makes and displays a guess halfway between the lowest value and the highest value that the player could possibly be thinking of. Initially, this value is between 1 and 1000. The procedure **Guess** then asks the player to indicate whether the displayed guess is high, low, or correct. If the current guess is high, then a value that is one less than the current guess becomes the new value for the highest number that the player can be thinking of. The procedure **Guess** is called again with this new highest possible value. Similarly, if the current guess is low, the procedure **Guess** is called again with a value that is one more than the current guess used as the new lowest possible value. The program maintains a count of the number of guesses made, which allows the program to report the number of guesses made before a correct answer is given.

```
REM Guess my number [6-23]
REM User thinks of number, computer does guessing
DO 'until response$ = "N"
  PRINT "Think of a number between 1 and 1000, ";
  PRINT "but don't tell me what it is."
  PRINT "I will guess your number in 10 tries or less."
  PRINT "Press any key when you've decided on your number."
  response$ = INPUT$(1)
  tries% = 1
  CALL Guess(1,1000,tries%)
  PRINT "Want to play again (Y,N)?"
  response$ = UCASE$(INPUT$(1))
  CLS
LOOP UNTIL response$ = "N"
END

SUB Guess(low,high,tries%)
  LOCAL currentGuess,response$
  currentGuess = INT((low + high)/2)
  PRINT
  PRINT USING "My guess is ####!"; currentGuess,".";
  PRINT "  Is my guess High, Low, or Correct (H,L,C)?"
  DO
     response$ = UCASE$(INPUT$(1))
  LOOP UNTIL (response$ = "H") OR (response$ = "L") OR _
             (response$ = "C")
  SELECT CASE response$
    CASE "H"
      high = currentGuess - 1
      CALL Guess(low,high,tries%+1)
    CASE "L"
      low = currentGuess + 1
      CALL Guess(low,high,tries%+1)
    CASE "C"
      PRINT "I guessed your number in"; tries%; "tries."
  END SELECT
END SUB

Run
Think of a number between 1 and 1000
but don't tell me what it is.
I will guess your number in 10 tries or less.
Press any key when you've decided on your number.

My guess is  500.
Is my guess High, Low, or Correct (H,L,C)? H

My guess is  250.
Is my guess High, Low, or Correct (H,L,C)? L

My guess is  375.
Is my guess High, Low, or Correct (H,L,C)? C

I guessed your number in 3 tries.
Want to play again (Y,N)? N
```

Program 6-23. *A recursively defined procedure*

7 Data Files

The Three Types of Data Files

In previous chapters, data that a program processed was either assigned by **LET** statements, stored in **DATA** statements, or supplied by the user in response to an **INPUT** statement. These methods are sufficient for small quantities of data that you will use in only one program. However, large amounts of data, data that many programs will access, or data that users will update (such as stock prices and employee payroll information) must be kept on a disk.

Turbo Basic offers three different ways to organize a data file. The resulting three types of files are called *sequential, random,* and *binary.* Each type of file has advantages and disadvantages. Sequential files use space efficiently, but are not easily updated and are difficult to search for a single piece of information. Random files provide rapid access to individual pieces of information, but require considerable effort to program and maintain. Binary files offer the greatest flexibility, but have no structure and, therefore, place considerable responsibility on the programmer.

This chapter creates and uses all three types of data files. The creation process physically records data onto a disk. The computer can then read this data from the disk and assign it to variables in much the same way that the computer can read from **DATA** statements.

Sequential Files

The ASCII table in Appendix A contains 256 characters. While not all of these characters can be displayed on the screen or printed on the printer, you can use all of them in files. The characters with ASCII values that range from 0 through 31 are referred to as *control characters*. Of special importance for sequential files are the control characters numbered 10, 13, and 26, which are the linefeed, carriage-return, and end-of-file characters. This text will denote character 26 by <EOF>. The pair of characters that consists of a carriage-return character followed by a linefeed character is called a carriage-return/linefeed pair, and is written <CR/LF>. (The carriage-return/linefeed is a standard way of denoting the end of a line. For example, you indicate the end of a line of a BASIC program by pressing ENTER. Doing this sends a carriage-return/linefeed instruction to the screen, which causes the cursor to move to the beginning of the next row on screen.)

A sequential file can be thought of as a long sequence of characters that is terminated with an end-of-file character. Sequential files normally contain a number of carriage-return/linefeed pairs that subdivide the file into blocks called *records*. In most of the sequential files discussed in this section, each record consists of several pieces of related data, called *fields*, that are separated by commas. The sequential file in Figure 7-1 holds employee-payroll data for a company. The record for each employee contains four fields: a name field, a Social Security number field, an hourly wage field, and an earnings-to-date for the current-year field. Each string appears in quotation marks, and each amount of money is given in cents as an integer or long integer.

"Smith,John","123-45-6789",17000,19091000<CR/LF>"Johnson,Robert",
"456-98-7654",1350,1537650<CR/LF>"Williams,David","238-91-2355",
825,934725<CR/LF><EOF>

Figure 7-1. *An employee payroll file*

Creating a Sequential File

There are many ways to organize and place data into a sequential file. The technique presented here is easy to visualize and apply. This text discusses other techniques later.

1. Choose a *file name*. A file name is a string that consists of two parts—a name of at most 8 characters followed by an optional extension that consists of a period and at most 3 characters. You can use letters, digits, and a few other characters (& ! _ @ ' ' ~ ( ) { } - # % $) in either the name or the extension. Some examples of file names are INC&EXP.87, CUSTOMER.DAT, and FORT500.

2. Choose a number from 1 through 15 to be the *reference number* of the file. While in use, the file will be identified by this number.

3. Execute the statement

OPEN *filename* FOR OUTPUT AS #n

where n is the reference number. This is referred to as *opening a file for output*. The procedure opens a communications line between the computer and the disk drive for storing data *onto* the disk. The statement allows the computer to output data and record it in the specified file. (You should execute this statement only once when you first create a file. If you open an already existing sequential file for output, the computer will erase the existing data.)

4. Record data into the file with the **WRITE#** statement. If $a\$$ is a string, then the statement

WRITE #n, a$

writes the string *a$* in quotation marks into the file. (Remember that *n* is the reference number of the file.) If *c* is a number, then

WRITE #*n*, *c*

writes the number *c*, without any leading or trailing spaces, into file number *n*. The statement

WRITE #*n*, *a$*, *c*

enters *a$* and *c* as before, but uses a comma to separate them. Similarly, if several strings, or numbers, or a combination of these, which are separated by commas, follow the statement **WRITE** #*n*, all of the strings and numbers appear as before, with commas separating them. After executing each **WRITE#** statement, Turbo Basic places the pair <CR/LF> into the file.

5. After you have recorded all of the data into the file, execute

CLOSE #*n*

where *n* is the reference number of the file. This places the character <EOF> at the end of the file and then disassociates the number *n* from the file. This procedure is referred to as *closing the file*.

Program 7-1 creates the file that was given in Figure 7-1. The values in the last **DATA** statement are known as *sentinel values*. They signal that the computer has read all of the data.

Adding Items to a Sequential File

You can add data to the end of an existing sequential file by following these steps:

1. Choose a number from 1 through 15 to be the reference number for the file. You do not have to use the same number that you used when creating the file.

2. Execute the statement

OPEN *filename* FOR APPEND AS #*n*

where *n* is the reference number. This procedure is referred to as *opening a file for append*. The statement allows the computer to

```
REM Create the file PAYROLL.87 and record some data in it. [7-1]
OPEN "PAYROLL.87" FOR OUTPUT AS #1  'Name file and assign a number
READ nom$,ssn$,hourlyWage%,yearToDate&
DO UNTIL nom$ = "EOD"                  'Loop until End of Data
  WRITE #1,nom$,ssn$,hourlyWage%,yearToDate&
  READ nom$,ssn$,hourlyWage%,yearToDate&  'Read next group of data
LOOP
CLOSE #1
REM Data:name,soc. sec. number,hourly wage,year-to-date earnings
DATA "Smith,John",123-45-6789,17000,19091000
DATA "Johnson,Robert",456-98-7654,1350,1537650
DATA "Williams,David",238-91-2355,825,934725
DATA EOD,"",0,0
END
```

Program 7-1. *Create the sequential file PAYROLL.87*

output data and record it at the end of the specified file. (If the specified file does not exist, the computer will create a new file.)

3. Record data into the file by using the **WRITE#** statement.

4. After you have has recorded all of the data into the file, close the file with the statement **CLOSE** #*n*.

Program 7-2 adds new records to the end of the PAYROLL.87 file. Figure 7-2 shows the contents of PAYROLL.87 after the computer has executed the program and been given the underlined input.

Reading Information from a Sequential File

You can direct Turbo Basic to read in order (sequentially) data stored in a sequential file and assign the data to variables by using the following steps:

1. Choose a number from 1 through 15 to be the reference number for the file. You do not have to use the same number that you used when recording the file.

```
REM Place an additional record into the file PAYROLL.87    [7-2]
OPEN "PAYROLL.87" FOR APPEND AS #1
CLS
INPUT "First name"; firstName$
INPUT "Last name"; lastName$
INPUT "Social security number"; ssn$
INPUT "Hourly wage (in cents)"; hourlyWage%
INPUT "Year to date earnings (in cents)"; yearToDate&
nom$ = lastName$ + "," + firstName$
WRITE #1,nom$,ssn$,hourlyWage%,yearToDate&
CLOSE #1
END

Run
First name? Al
Last name? Jones
Social security number? 450-21-3678
Hourly wage (in cents)? 1325
Year to date earnings (in cents)? 1275975
```

Program 7-2.   *Add a new record to the end of PAYROLL.87*

2. Execute the statement

OPEN *filename* **FOR INPUT AS** #*n*

where *n* is the reference number. This procedure is referred to as *opening a file for input*. The statement opens a communications line between the computer and the disk drive for copying data *from* the diskette. You can then input data from the specified file to the computer.

"Smith,John","123-45-6789",17000,19091000<CR/LF>"Johnson,Robert","456-98-7654",1350,<CR/LF>"Williams,David","238-91-2355",825,934725<CR/LF>"Jones,Al",450-21-3678,1325,1275975<CR/LF><EOF>

Figure 7-2.   *The contents of the appended file PAYROLL.87*

3. Read data from the file by using the **INPUT#** statement. The **INPUT#** statement assigns data from a file to variables in much the same way that **INPUT** assigns data from the keyboard. Correct use of the **INPUT#** statement requires that you know how the **WRITE#** statement recorded the data on the disk. The statement

INPUT #n, var1, var2,...

assigns to each of the variables (*var1, var2,* and so on) one of the items of the file. (Commas or the pair of characters carriage-return/linefeed separate the items in the file.) The number and type of the variables in the **INPUT#** statement should be the same as those of the variables in the **WRITE#** statement that created each record.

4. After the computer has found the items that it was searching for or after it has read all of the data from the file, close the file with the statement **CLOSE #n.**

Turbo Basic has a useful function, **EOF**, that tells you if you have reached the end of a file. At any time, the condition

EOF(n)

will be true if you have reached the end of file *n*, and false if you have not.

Program 7-3 gives the number of hours worked by each employee in PAYROLL.87. By using the **DO UNTIL EOF(1)** statement, you do not have to know the number of records in the file. The **PRINT USING** format prevents the computer from displaying fractional parts of hours.

The **EOF** function serves the same role for a file that a sentinel value (such as EOD or −1) does for a set of **DATA** statements. However, there are some important differences. A typical program segment for **READ**ing **DATA** statements must read a record both before entering a loop and at the bottom of the loop, as in Figure 7-3a. This construction is necessary because Turbo Basic detects the

```
REM Process data from PAYROLL.87
REM to find hours worked in 1987   [7-3]
OPEN "PAYROLL.87" FOR INPUT AS #1
CLS
PRINT "Name";                TAB(20); "Hours Worked"
PRINT "---------------";     TAB(20); "------------"
DO UNTIL EOF(1)                'Process the entire file
   INPUT #1,nom$,ssn$,hourlyWage%,yearToDate&
   PRINT nom$; TAB(20);
   PRINT USING "     #####"; yearToDate&/hourlyWage%
LOOP
CLOSE #1
END

Run
Name                 Hours Worked
---------------      ------------
Smith,John              1123
Johnson,Robert          1139
Williams,David          1133
Jones,Al                 963
```

Program 7-3. *Calculate hours worked by each employee*

```
READ info$, etc.                    DO UNTIL EOF(1)
DO UNTIL info$ = "EOD"                 INPUT #1,info$, etc.
   'process info$, etc.                'process info$, etc.
              ⋮                                   ⋮
   READ info$, etc.                 LOOP
LOOP

   a.                                  b.
```

Figure 7-3. *Typical READ/DATA and file INPUT# loops*

Data Files

end-of-data condition by reading an extraneous sentinel value that should not be processed. In contrast, a typical program segment for **INPUT**ting from a file must check for the end-of-file condition first, and then input a record as the first action inside the loop, as in Figure 7-3*b*. This construction is necessary because the end-of-file condition is true as soon as Turbo Basic sees that no more data exists in the file. Executing **INPUT#** when no more records are available results in an error.

Program 7-4 illustrates a common error when reading a sequential file. Turbo Basic will not process the last item in the file. In addition, if the file contains no data, then the third line will produce the error message **Input past end**.

Sequential files can be quite large. Rather than list the entire contents, you often search the file for a specific piece of information. Program 7-5 allows a user to input a Social Security number, and finds the corresponding person in PAYROLL.87 by examining each record until it finds the desired one. Since a particular Social Security number may not be in the file, the **DO UNTIL** statement must check the function **EOF(1)** to determine if Turbo Basic reached the end-of-file without finding a match.

Other Methods of Outputting and Inputting Data to Sequential Files

You can use statements other than **WRITE#** and **INPUT#** to place data into and retrieve data from sequential files.

The statements **PRINT#** and **PRINT# USING** place data into files in much the same way that their counterparts **PRINT** and **PRINT USING** display information on screen. With **PRINT#**, Turbo Basic records numbers with trailing and possibly leading spaces; semicolons cause subsequent data to be displayed in the next position, and commas cause subsequent data to be recorded in the next 14-character zone. Unless you terminate **PRINT#** and **PRINT# USING** statements with a comma or semicolon, Turbo Basic automatically records a carriage-return and a linefeed.

```
REM Display names of employees
REM earning more than $10 per hour    [7.4]
OPEN "PAYROLL.87" FOR INPUT AS #1
CLS
INPUT #1,nom$,ssn$,hourlyWage%,yearToDate&
DO UNTIL EOF(1)
   IF hourlyWage% > 1000   THEN PRINT nom$
   INPUT #1,nom$,ssn$,hourlyWage%,yearToDate&
LOOP
CLOSE #1
END
```

Program 7-4. *A flawed file-reading program*

```
REM Process data from PAYROLL.87 file
REM for individual years of birth.   [7.5]
OPEN "PAYROLL.87" FOR INPUT AS #1
CLS
INPUT "Social Security Number"; a$
DO UNTIL (ssn$ = a$) OR EOF(1)   'Examine names until person found
   INPUT #1,nom$,ssn$,hourlyWage%,yearToDate&
LOOP
IF ssn$ = a$ THEN
     PRINT nom$; " has the number "; a$
   ELSE
     PRINT a$; " is not in the file PAYROLL.87"
END IF
CLOSE #1
END

Run
Social Security Number? 238-91-2355
Williams,David has the number 238-91-2355

Run
Social Security Number? 222-33-4444
222-33-4444 is not in the file PAYROLL.78
```

Program 7-5. *A sequential search of a sequential file*

The statements **LINE INPUT#** and **INPUT$** can be used to read data from a sequential file. The statement

LINE INPUT #*n*, a$

Data Files

reads all characters to the next carriage-return/linefeed in file n and assigns this string of characters to the variable $a\$$. The statement

a$ = INPUT$(m,n)

reads the next m characters from file number n, and assigns them to the string variable $a\$$. (The statement reads all characters, including commas and carriage-returns.) You usually use **LINE INPUT#** to retrieve data that you recorded with **PRINT#**.

Sorting a Sequential File

In addition to accessing sequential files for information, you regularly update them by modifying certain pieces of data, removing some records, and adding new records. You can perform these tasks most efficiently if you first sort the files. Turbo Basic can sort the records of a sequential file on any field, by first reading the data into parallel arrays and then sorting on a specific array. Program 7-6 uses this technique to sort the sequential file PAYROLL.87 by employee name.

Program 7-6 provides a good example of top-down design. The main body of the program is short and consists primarily of calls to procedures whose names describe the different tasks to be performed. The procedure **CountRecords** determines the number of records in the payroll file so that it can dimension sufficiently large parallel arrays. (There will be an array for each field, and arrays with the same subscript will hold fields from the same record.) The program gives the user the opportunity to save processing time by entering the number of records in the payroll file, if known. If the user does not know the number, the program uses the **LINE INPUT#** statement to read everything up to the next <CR/LF> pair—thus, the program can read an entire record without regard for fields. Counting the number of **LINE INPUT#** statements executed before Turbo Basic reaches the end-of-file gives the number of records in the payroll files.

```
REM Sort records in PAYROLL.87 file by employee names   [7-6]
DEFINT a-z      'cause all tagless variables to be of type integer
CLS
CALL CountRecords(total)
DIM nom$(total),ssn$(total),hourlyWage%(total),yearToDate&(total)
CALL LoadArrays(total,nom$(),ssn$(),hourlyWage%(),yearToDate&())
CALL SortByName(total,nom$(),ssn$(),hourlyWage%(),yearToDate&())
CALL WriteArrays(total,nom$(),ssn$(),hourlyWage%(),yearToDate&())
PRINT "Sort complete"
END

SUB CountRecords(number)
  LOCAL temp$
  PRINT "How many records are in PAYROLL.87?"
  INPUT "(Enter 0 to have me count them.) ", number
  IF number = 0 THEN
    OPEN "PAYROLL.87" FOR INPUT AS #1
    PRINT "Counting records"
    number = 0
    DO UNTIL EOF(1)
      LINE INPUT #1,temp$
      number = number + 1
    LOOP
    CLOSE #1
  END IF
END SUB

SUB LoadArrays(count,n$(1),s$(1),hw%(1),ytd&(1))
  LOCAL j
  OPEN "PAYROLL.87" FOR INPUT AS #1
  PRINT "Reading from file"
  FOR j = 1 to count
    INPUT #1,n$(j),s$(j),hw%(j),ytd&(j)
  NEXT j
  CLOSE #1
END SUB

SUB SortByName(count,n$(1),s$(1),hw%(1),ytd&(1))
  LOCAL j, k, swapped
  PRINT "Sorting"
  FOR j = 1 TO count              'at most count loops needed for sort
    swapped = 0                   'set flag indicating no swaps yet
    FOR k = 1 TO count-j
      IF n$(k) > n$(k+1) THEN     'swap successive elements
        SWAP n$(k),   n$(k+1)     'in all arrays whenever
        SWAP s$(k),   s$(k+1)     'sucessive elements in the
        SWAP hw%(k),  hw%(k+1)    'nom$ array are out of order
        SWAP ytd&(k),ytd&(k+1)
        swapped = 1               'swap occured, set a flag
      END IF
    NEXT k
    IF swapped = 0 then EXIT FOR  'if no swaps made in the
  NEXT j                          'FOR k loop, then arrays
END SUB                           'are sorted, so EXIT
```

Program 7-6. *Sort the file PAYROLL.87*

Data Files

```
SUB WriteArrays(count,n$(1),s$(1),hw%(1),ytd&(1))
  LOCAL j
  PRINT "Writing sorted file"
  OPEN "PAYROLL.87" FOR OUTPUT AS #1
  FOR j = 1 TO count
    WRITE #1,n$(j),s$(j),hw%(j),ytd&(j)
  NEXT j
  CLOSE #1
END SUB
```

Program 7-6. *Sort the file PAYROLL.87* (continued)

The procedure **LoadArrays** uses the **INPUT#** statement to read the four fields of each record of the payroll file directly into the appropriate array elements. The program uses the loop **FOR j = 1 TO count ... NEXT j** rather than the loop **DO UNTIL EOF(1) ... LOOP** since the program already knows the number of records to be processed. In addition, if the user gave an incorrect count and the program used a **DO UNTIL** loop, there would be the danger of trying to read more data than the arrays were dimensioned to hold.

The procedure **SortByName** uses a modified bubble sort to put the **nom$** array in order. Whenever the program interchanges the values of two elements of the **nom$** array, it also interchanges the values of the corresponding elements of the other three arrays. Doing so assures that array elements with the same subscript continue to hold information from the same record.

The procedure **WriteArrays** does the opposite of **LoadArrays**. **WriteArrays** uses the **WRITE#** statement to put the sorted data from the arrays back into a new version of the payroll file. Like each of the other procedures, **WriteArrays** prints a message before starting to process. This message reassures the user that the sort is proceeding properly.

There is another method of sorting a file by the first field. DOS has a command called **SORT** that orders the records of a sequential file. The command

SORT <*filename1* >*filename2*

```
REM Sort records in PAYROLL.87 file by employee names   [7-7]
NAME "PAYROLL.87" AS "TEMPFILE"
SHELL "SORT <TEMPFILE >PAYROLL.87"
KILL "TEMPFILE"
END
```

Program 7-7. *Sort PAYROLL.87 with DOS's SORT command*

sorts the records of *filename1* in ascending order by the first field, and places them into a new file called *filename2*. The DOS command

SORT <*filename1* >*filename2* /R

produces a descending-order sort.

Program 7-7 produces the same result as Program 7-6 did. The second line changes the name of the file PAYROLL.87. The **SHELL** statement invokes DOS, which carries out the indicated **SORT** command.

Suppose that the sorted file PAYROLL.87 is quite large and that the company has hired new employees. Also suppose that the payroll data for the new people is in the sorted sequential file NEWEMP. Program 7-8 merges these two files into one sorted file, by copying the records of the file PAYROLL.87 into another file while inserting each record from NEWEMP in the proper place. You can modify this program to perform similar tasks, such as deleting the records of employees who leave the company and changing the hourly wages of some employees.

Comments About Sequential Files

You can use a string variable for the *file name* in an **OPEN** statement. Doing this is advantageous for programs that process data from several different data files. In response to an **INPUT** statement, the user can identify the data file to be processed.

Data Files

```
REM Update the file PAYROLL.87 by inserting new employees    [7-8]
REM Merge NEWEMP into PAYROLL.87 (both files sorted by name)
CALL OpenFiles
CLS
PRINT "Merging NEWEMP into PAYROLL.87"
nom1$ = ""        'Null value indicates next record needs to be read
nom2$ = ""
DO UNTIL EOF(1) OR EOF(2)
  'Read next record if required
  IF nom1$ = "" THEN _
    INPUT #1,nom1$,ssn1$,hourlyWage1%,yearToDate1&
  IF nom2$ = "" THEN _
    INPUT #2,nom2$,ssn2$,hourlyWage2%,yearToDate2&
  'Write out the record having the "lesser" name
  'and indicate that the next record needs to be read
  IF nom1$ < nom2$ THEN
      WRITE #3,nom1$,ssn1$,hourlyWage1%,yearToDate1&
      nom1$ = ""
    ELSE  'nom2$ <= nom1$
      WRITE #3,nom2$,ssn2$,hourlyWage2%,yearToDate2&
      nom2$ = ""
  END IF
LOOP
'Either tempfile or newemp has now been completely processed.
'Any additional data from the other file must now be written out.
IF nom1$ <> "" THEN _
  WRITE #3,nom1$,ssn1$,hourlyWage1%,yearToDate1&
DO UNTIL EOF(1)
  INPUT #1,nom1$,ssn1$,hourlyWage1%,yearToDate1&
  WRITE #3,nom1$,ssn1$,hourlyWage1%,yearToDate1&
LOOP
IF nom2$ <> "" THEN _
  WRITE #3,nom2$,ssn2$,hourlyWage2%,yearToDate2&
DO UNTIL EOF(2)
  INPUT #2,nom2$,ssn2$,hourlyWage2%,yearToDate2&
  WRITE #3,nom2$,ssn2$,hourlyWage2%,yearToDate2&
LOOP
CLOSE
KILL "TEMPFILE"
PRINT "Merge complete"
END

SUB OpenFiles
  'Tempfile must not exist in order for renaming to succeed,
  'but tempfile must exist in order that KILL not cause an error.
  'Create tempfile in case it doesn't exist, then KILL it for sure
  OPEN "TEMPFILE" FOR OUTPUT AS 1
  CLOSE #1
  KILL "TEMPFILE"
  NAME "PAYROLL.87" AS "TEMPFILE"
  OPEN "TEMPFILE" FOR INPUT AS #1
  OPEN "NEWEMP" FOR INPUT AS #2
  OPEN "PAYROLL.87" FOR OUTPUT AS #3
END SUB
```

Program 7-8. *Merge two files*

So far, this chapter has assumed that you will be storing files on the disk in the default drive, the current drive at the time that you invoked Turbo Basic. To work with a file from another disk drive, place the letter of the drive and a colon before the name of the file. For instance, if the file PAYROLL.87 is on a disk in drive B, then the statement

OPEN "B:PAYROLL.87" FOR INPUT AS #1

gives you access to the file. A file name or a file name preceded by a drive letter and a colon is referred to as a *filespec*. If you are using subdirectories, the filespec should also contain the path to the subdirectory.

Normally, a maximum of 15 files can be open at any one time. The following steps will allow you to increase this number.

1. Execute the following program with the disk that you used to boot the computer in the default drive. Replace the number 15 by the number of files that you would like to use. This program adds a command to the file that DOS uses to configure the system when you first turn the computer on.

```
REM Alter the maximum number of files allowed
OPEN "\CONFIG.SYS" FOR APPEND AS #1
PRINT #1, "FILES=15"
CLOSE #1
END
```

2. Reboot the system by pressing CTRL-ALT-DEL.

Sequential files make efficient use of disk space and are easy to create and use. Their disadvantages are as follows:

■ Often a large portion of the file must be read in order to find one specific item.

■ You cannot easily change or delete an individual item of the file. You must create a new file by reading each item from the original file and recording it, with the single item changed or deleted, into the new file.

Data Files   **149**

Another type of file, known as a *random file*, has neither of the disadvantages of sequential files. However, random files tend to use more disk space and require greater effort to program.

Random Files

Information that resides in a random file is comparable to data that is organized on an accountant's pad in rows numbered 1, 2, 3, and so on. You can read or write on any row without first looking through every row of the pad. In Figure 7-4, each row is partitioned into four regions. Each row is called a *record* and each region is called a *field*. Of the four fields in Figure 7-4, two contain string data and two contain numeric data. (The numeric data has been encoded into two-character and four-character strings.) By adding up the spaces allocated to the fields, you can see that the total number of characters that you can place in each record is 44 (27 + 11 + 2 + 4 = 44). Thus each record has *length* 44.

For a random file, one statement is sufficient to open the file for any purpose: creating, appending, or reading. Suppose that each

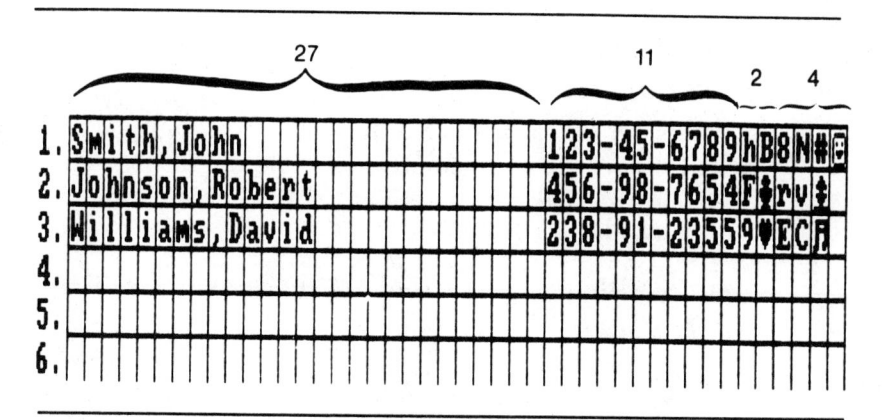

Figure 7-4. *An accountant's pad*

record will have length *g* and the reference number chosen for the file is *n*. Then executing the statement

OPEN *filename* AS #*n* LEN=*g*

permits Turbo Basic to write, read, add, or change records in the specified file.

Every time that you open a random file, you must also specify the format of the records; that is, you must specify the number of characters in each field and a string variable name for each field. The **FIELD** statement defines the record format. For the records that were shown in Figure 7-4, an appropriate statement is

FIELD #*n*, 27 AS nomf$, 11 AS ssnf$, 2 AS hourlyWagef$, —
4 AS yearToDatef$

The variables **nomf$**, **ssnf$**, **hourlyWagef$**, and **yearToDatef$** are referred to as field variables of *widths* 27, 11, 2, and 4, respectively.

Suppose that you have opened a random file and executed a field statement. The two-step procedure for entering data into a record is as follows:

1. Assign a string to each variable in the **FIELD** statement. This assignment must be carried out with a variation of the **LET** statement, called **LSET**. Suppose that *af$* is a field variable of width *w* and that *d$* is any string. Then the statement

LSET *af$* = *d$*

assigns to the variable *af$* a string of length *w*. If the length of *d$* is *w* or more, the statement assigns to *af$* the first *w* characters of *d$*. If not, the statement assigns to *af$* the string that consists of *d$* followed by spaces.

2. Place the data into record *r* of file number *n* with the statement
PUT #*n*, *r*

Note that Turbo Basic stores all data in random files by using string format. Thus, numeric values must be converted into string format before they can be stored. Turbo Basic provides four functions for making such conversions. The functions **MKI$**, **MKL$**,

```
REM Create the random file PAYROLL.87R   [7-9]
OPEN "PAYROLL.87R" AS #1 LEN = 44
FIELD #1, 27 AS nomf$, 11 AS ssnf$, 2 AS hourlyWagef$, _
          4 AS yearToDatef$
recordNumber% = 1
READ a$, b$, c%, d&
DO UNTIL a$="EOD"
  LSET nomf$ = a$:   LSET ssnf$ = b$
  LSET hourlyWagef$ = MKI$(c%):   LSET yearToDatef$ = MKL$(d&)
  PUT #1,recordNumber%
  recordNumber% = recordNumber% + 1
  READ a$, b$, c%, d&
LOOP
CLOSE #1
REM Data:name,soc. sec. number,hourly wage,year-to-date earnings
DATA "Smith,John",123-45-6789,17000,19091000
DATA "Johnson,Robert",456-98-7654,1350,1537650
DATA "Williams,David",238-91-2355,825,934725
DATA EOD,"",0,0
END
```

Program 7-9. *Create the random file PAYROLL.87R*

MKS$**, and **MKD$ convert integers, long integers, single-precision numbers, and double-precision numbers into strings of length 2, 4, 4, and 8, respectively. The method that Turbo Basic uses involves writing the number in binary notation and then breaking up the zeros and ones into 8-tuples each of which corresponds to an ASCII character. You do not need to be concerned about this method; Turbo Basic has the functions **CVI**, **CVL**, **CVS**, and **CVD** that convert these strings back to numbers.

Program 7-9 uses **MKI$** and **MKL$** to produce the random file that was shown in Figure 7-4. Note that a sentinel value controls the processing loop within the program, even though the number of data records is easily determined. This design has the advantage that you do not need to make changes to the body of the program if you add new data statements to the end of the program.

Suppose that you have opened a random file and executed a field statement. The two-step procedure for reading data from a record is as follows:

1. Execute the statement

GET #*n*, *r*

to read record *r* of file number *n* and associate each field variable with the appropriate portion of the record.

2. Use the field variables — perhaps converted by **CVI**, **CVL**, and so on — either to display their values with **PRINT** or to transfer their values to other variables with **LET**.

The value of the function

LOF(*n*)

is the total number of characters in the file of reference number *n*. Dividing the value of the **LOF** function by the record length *g* gives the number of records in a random file. Program 7-10 uses this technique to display the complete contents of the random file PAYROLL.87R.

```
REM Access the random file PAYROLL.87R   [7-10]
OPEN "PAYROLL.87R" AS #1 LEN = 44
FIELD #1, 27 AS nomf$, 11 AS ssnf$, 2 AS hourlyWagef$, _
         4 AS yearToDatef$
CLS
PRINT "                            Social                      Year to"
PRINT "                            Security        Hourly         Date"
PRINT "Name                        Number          Wage          Wages"
PRINT "••••••••••••••••••••••      ••••••••••      ••••••      •••••••••"
f$ = "\                        \   \         \     ###.##    ######.##"
FOR i% = 1 TO LOF(1)\44
   GET #1, i%                           'Bring forward record i
   PRINT USING f$; nomf$, ssnf$, _
      CVI(hourlyWagef$)/100, CVL(yearToDatef$)/100
NEXT i%
CLOSE #1
END

Run
                            Social                      Year to
                            Security        Hourly         Date
Name                        Number          Wage          Wages
••••••••••••••••••••••      ••••••••••      ••••••      •••••••••
Smith,John                  123-45-6789     170.00      190910.00
Johnson,Robert              456-98-7654      13.50       15376.50
Williams,David              238-91-2355       8.25        9347.25
```

Program 7-10. *Exhibit the contents of PAYROLL.87R*

Data Files

Comments About Random Files

Random files are also known as *random access files, direct access files,* or *relative files.* Since each record has the same number of characters, the computer can calculate where to find a specified record and, therefore, does not have to search for it.

Unlike with sequential files, you do not need to close random files after you place information into them in order to read from them.

Records do not have to be filled in order. For instance, you can open a file and use **PUT #n, 9** as the first **PUT** statement.

Never assign a value to a field variable by using a **LET** statement. To avoid this type of error, this text uses the letter f as the last character in the name of each field variable to distinguish it from an ordinary variable.

A field variable retains its current value unless a **GET** or **LSET** statement alters the value.

If you omit the record number r from a **PUT** or **GET** statement, then the record number used will be the one that follows the number most recently used in a **PUT** or **GET** statement. For example, if you add the statement **PUT #1** to Program 7-9 just before the program closes the file, then the program will duplicate the information on **David Williams** in record 4 of the file PAYROLL.87R.

Users often enter records into a random file without keeping track of the record numbers. If file number n is open, then the value of the function

LOC(n)

is the number of the record that the computer has most recently copied into or out of file n through the use of a **PUT** or **GET** statement.

The record length g specified in the **OPEN** statement can routinely be any number from 1 to 32767. If you do not specify a record length, Turbo Basic uses a default length of 128.

The L in **LSET** stands for *left.* If $af\$$ is a field variable of width w, then the statement

LSET $af\$ = d\$$

left-justifies the string *d$* into *w* spaces. **RSET** also assigns strings to field variables, but right-justifies the string into *w* spaces. If the length of *d$* is *w* or more, then **RSET** has the same effect as **LSET**: **RSET** assigns the leftmost *w* characters of *d$* to *af$*.

Binary Files

A binary file is the most rudimentary type of file. It offers the greatest flexibility of any type of file, but makes the most demands on the programmer. A binary file can be thought of as a sequence of characters without having any structure imposed by delimiters or records. The characters are said to occupy positions 0, 1, 2, and so on. You can jump to any position, and read or write any number of characters. Turbo Basic overwrites characters that occupy positions being written to.

Like random files, binary files have just one all-purpose **OPEN** statement. The statement

OPEN *filespec* FOR BINARY AS *#n*

assigns reference number *n* to the specified binary file, which then may be both written to and read. At any time, there is a location in the file called the *current file position*. Initially, the current file position is 0. The primary tasks of accessing a binary file are accomplished by the three statements **SEEK**, **PUT$**, and **GET$**, with help from the functions **LOC** and **LOF**.

For a file with reference number *n*, the statement

SEEK *#n, r*

changes the current file position to *r*. The statement

PUT$ *#n, a$*

begins at the current file position, writes the value of the string *a$* in successive positions, and moves the current file position to the

Data Files

position that follows the last character written. The statement

GET$ #*n*, *m*, *a$*

begins at the current file position, assigns the string that consists of *m* consecutive characters to the variable *a$*, and moves the current file position to the position that follows the last character read.

At any time, the value of the function

LOC(*n*)

is the current file position in the binary file with reference number *n*, while the value of

LOF(*n*)

is the length of the file. Program 7-11 shows several examples of the use of these functions. Each comment after a **PUT$** statement shows the contents of the file at that point.

Any file can be **OPEN**ed as a binary file, and accessed with **SEEK**, **GET$**, and **PUT$**. For example, you can open a sequential

```
REM Demonstrate the use of a binary file  [7-11]
OPEN "DEMOFILE" FOR BINARY AS #1
PUT$ #1,"abcde"          'abcde
PUT$ #1,"fgh"            'abcdefgh
SEEK #1,3                'Move to position 3
GET$ #1,2,a$             'Read 2 characters; the value of a$ is "de"
PRINT LOC(1)             'Display the current file position, 5
PUT$ #1,"FGHIJ"          'abcdeFGHIJ
SEEK #1,0                'Move to beginning of file
PUT$ #1,"A"              'AbcdeFGHIJ
SEEK #1,LOF(1)           'Move to end of file
b$ = "kl"
PUT$ #1,b$               'AbcdeFGHIJkl
SEEK #1,LOC(1)-5         'Move current file position 5 to the left
PUT$ #1,"done"           'AbcdeFGdonel
CLOSE #1                 'Close the file
END
```

Program 7-11. *Working with a binary file*

file as a binary file and change certain pieces of data without recopying the entire file. Program 7-12 alters the sequential file PAYROLL.87 that appeared in Figure 7-1. Note that Figure 7-1 gave the pay rate for John Smith, $170.00, beginning at the twenty-eighth character in the file.

Files created outside of Turbo Basic will have their own special formats. This case exists for those files that you create with popular spreadsheet and database programs. You can open such files as binary files, and examine or change them. Program 7-13 uses the binary file mode to display the contents of an arbitrary file. Each line of this display consists of two parts. The left side displays the ASCII values of 15 characters from the file. The right side shows the 15 characters themselves, with a period in the place of each character that is not one of the 96 standard keyboard characters.

Program 7-14 not only allows the user to see the contents of an arbitrary file, but also allows the user to change characters. The program displays characters vertically, one per line, with their position in the file. The user can view a maximum of 19 characters from the file at one time. The user can then alter the most recently displayed character.

The procedure **DisplayCommands** lists in the lower portion of the screen the five commands that this file-editing program understands. To prevent this command menu from being erased, the program restricts any other items that it displays to the first 19 lines of the screen.

The procedure **AdvanceToNextByte** uses the **GET$** function to read the character at the current file position, after first checking

```
REM Give John Smith a $15.00 pay raise    [7-12]
OPEN "PAYROLL.87" FOR BINARY AS #1
SEEK #1,28              'move file pointer to 28th character
PUT$ #1,"18500"         'change 28th through 32nd character
CLOSE #1
END
```

Program 7-12. *Use the binary file mode to cheat*

Data Files

that the current file position is not past the last character of the file. The procedure then displays this character on screen. Since **GET$** automatically moves the current file position ahead by one position, any action that will affect the character just displayed must begin by using the **SEEK** statement to move the current file position back by one position.

The procedure **ReplaceCurrentByte** repositions the cursor on the line that contains the last character displayed, and prompts for a replacement character. After the user gives a new character, the procedure uses the **SEEK** statement to move the current file position back by one position to the point from which the **GET$** function read the old character. The **PUT$** statement then replaces the old character with the new one.

The procedure **GoToByteRelativeToStart** prompts the user to enter a new value for the current file position. The user should give this position in relation to the beginning of the file. The command

```
REM Decode any file into ASCII code and
REM standard characters   [7-13]
CLS
INPUT "Source File: ", filename$
OPEN filename$ FOR BINARY AS #1
text$ = ""
FOR index = 1 TO LOF(1)      'process entire file
  'Read a single character from the file
  GET$ #1,1,byte$
  'Print the ASCII value of the character
  PRINT USING "\   \"; STR$(ASC(byte$));
  'If character is not a regular character, change it to a period
  IF (ASC(byte$) < 32) OR (ASC(byte$) > 126) THEN byte$ = "."
  'Add the character in byte$ onto the string in text$
  text$ = text$ + byte$
  'After printing 15 ASCII values, print corresponding text
  IF index MOD 15 = 0 THEN
    PRINT "   "; text$
    text$ = ""
  END IF
NEXT index
PRINT TAB(63); text$      'Print out text for last (partial) line
CLOSE #1
END
```

Program 7-13. *Use the binary file mode to snoop*

```
REM Examine and change a file byte by byte    [7-14]
DEFINT a-z
bottomLine = 19
CLS
INPUT "Source File: ",filename$
OPEN filename$ FOR BINARY AS #1
CALL DisplayCommands
currentLine = 1
GET$ #1,1,byte$
CALL Display(byte$)
CALL ReadIn(action$)
DO UNTIL action$ = "Q"
  SELECT CASE action$
    CASE "N",CHR$(13)
      CALL AdvanceToNextByte
    CASE "R"
      CALL ReplaceCurrentByte
    CASE "G"
      CALL GoToByteRelativeToStart
    CASE "J"
      CALL JumpToByteFromHere
  END SELECT
  CALL ReadIn(action$)
LOOP
CLOSE #1
END

SUB DisplayCommands
  SHARED bottomLine
  CLS
  LOCATE bottomLine+2,1
  PRINT "N or [ENTER]   = move to next byte"
  PRINT "J              = jump forwards or backwards from here"
  PRINT "G              = go to specific byte (0 to";_
    STR$(LOF(1)-1); ")"
  PRINT "R              = replace this byte"
  PRINT "Q              = save file and quit";
END SUB

SUB AdvanceToNextByte
  SHARED currentLine
  IF LOC(1) < LOF(1) THEN              'if not at the end of the file
    GET$ #1,1,byte$                    'advance to next byte
    CALL Display(byte$)
  END IF
END SUB

SUB ReplaceCurrentByte
  SHARED currentLine, bottomLine
  currentLine = currentLine - 1        'back cursor up one line
  IF currentLine = 0 THEN _            'if this moves us off screen
    currentLine = bottomLine           'then loop to bottom of screen
  LOCATE currentLine,1                 'place cursor and
  PRINT "replace with --> ";           'print prompt
  text$ = INPUT$(1)                    'read in replacement character
  SEEK #1,LOC(1) - 1                   'Undo auto advance of current
                                       'file position due to last GET$
  PUT$ #1,text$                        'replace last byte displayed
```

Program 7-14. *A file editor*

Data Files

```
      CALL Display(text$)
   END SUB

   SUB GoToByteRelativeToStart
      SHARED currentLine
      INPUT "go to offset --> ",size
      IF (size >= 0) AND (size < LOF(1))  THEN
         SEEK #1,size                    'change current file position
         GET$ #1,1,byte$                 'to position given by user and
         CALL Display(byte$)             'display the byte read
      ELSE
         CALL ReportError
      END IF
   END SUB

   SUB JumpToByteFromHere
      SHARED currentLine
      INPUT "size of jump --> ",size
      IF (size+LOC(1) > 0) AND (size+LOC(1) < LOF(1))  THEN
         SEEK #1,size + LOC(1) - 1       'change current file position
         GET$ #1,1,byte$                 'relative to LOC(1)-1 which is
         CALL Display(byte$)             'position of last  byte read
      ELSE
         CALL ReportError
      END IF
   END SUB

   SUB ReadIn(action$)
      SHARED currentLine
      PRINT "action?";                      'display prompt then read
      action$ = UCASE$(INPUT$(1))           'one key and capitalize it
      LOCATE currentLine,1: PRINT "        ";  'erase prompt
      LOCATE currentLine,1
   END SUB

   SUB Display(byte$)
      SHARED currentLine, bottomLine
      LOCATE currentLine,1
      'Display positon of byte in file and its ASCII value
      PRINT USING "##########   \   \"; LOC(1)-1, STR$(ASC(byte$));
      'Display a 1 to 3 character description of byte
      SELECT CASE byte$
        CASE CHR$(0) TO CHR$(31)
          PRINT "^"; CHR$(ASC(byte$)+64);
        CASE CHR$(32) TO CHR$(127)
          PRINT byte$;
        CASE CHR$(128) TO CHR$(159)
          PRINT "*^"; CHR$(ASC(byte$)-64);
        CASE CHR$(160) TO CHR$(255)
          PRINT "*"; CHR$(ASC(byte$)-128);
      END SELECT
      PRINT "       ";
      'Advance to a new line and clear line below it
      currentLine = (currentLine MOD bottomLine) + 1
      LOCATE currentLine,1: PRINT SPACE$(30);
      LOCATE currentLine,1
   END SUB
```

Program 7-14. *A file editor* (continued)

```
SUB ReportError
  SHARED currentLine
  'Display error message on next line,
  'then erase it and current line
  LOCATE currentLine+1,1: PRINT "Not in file";
  DELAY 1
  LOCATE currentLine+1,1: PRINT SPACE$(30);
  LOCATE currentLine,  1: PRINT SPACE$(30);
  LOCATE currentLine,  1
END SUB
```

Program 7-14. *A file editor* (continued)

menu shows the allowed range of values, from 0 for the beginning of the file to LOF(1)−1 for the end of the file. If the user supplies a valid position, the procedure uses the **SEEK** statement to move the current file position and then displays the character at the new position.

The procedure **JumpToByteFromHere** prompts the user to enter a value that is used to move the current file position in relation to its current location. Negative values move the current file position toward the beginning of the file, and positive values move it toward the end of the file. The procedure tells the user if the newly specified position is not in the file. If the position is in the file, the procedure uses the **SEEK** statement to move the current file position and then displays the character at the new position.

The procedure **ReadIn** prompts the user to give one of the five commands listed in the lower portion of the screen. After the user presses a key, the procedure erases the prompt.

The procedure **DisplayByte** displays the current file position, the ASCII value of the character passed to it, and a description of the character, and then erases the "next line" on screen. (If the **currentLine** is 19, the "next line" is 1; if **currentLine** is any other number, the "next line" is one more than **currentLine**.) The description displayed for a character depends upon its ASCII value. The procedure displays the 96 standard keyboard characters (ASCII values 32 through 127) as themselves. The procedure displays each control character (ASCII values 0 through 31) as a caret (^) followed by the character whose ASCII value is 64 more than the ASCII value of the control character. For example, the character with ASCII value 7 displays as ^G (the character G has ASCII value 71). **DisplayByte** displays each high ASCII character (ASCII values 128 through 255) as an "at symbol" (**@**) followed by the description of the character whose ASCII value is 128 less than the ASCII value of the high ASCII character. For example, the character with ASCII value 135 displays as **@^G**, while the character with ASCII value 193 displays as **@A** (the character A has ASCII value 65).

The program uses the procedure **ReportError** to tell the user that the given **G** (**Go**) or **J** (**Jump**) command resulted in a position not in the file. **ReportError** displays an error message, waits one second, and then clears both the message and the user input that caused the error.

8 Graphics and Sound

Introduction

Turbo Basic has the capacity to produce dazzling graphics displays and a wide range of musical notes and sound effects. This chapter explains the way to create still and animated images on screen in both color and black-and-white. Later Chapter 11 shows the way to obtain mathematical graphs, and Chapter 12 explains the way to display business data in bar and pie charts.

Graphics can be produced with Turbo Basic on any type of monitor except for a monochrome display that is attached to a monochrome display adapter. (The monochrome display produces sharper text than other monitors, but will not produce color or graphics in Turbo Basic unless you attach it to an Enhanced Graphics Adapter.) This book will refer to all other monitors as *graphics monitors*. All discussions of graphics in this text assume that you are using a graphics monitor.

Graphics monitors that can be used with either an IBM PC or an IBM PC compatible are primarily of three types. These types are, in order of popularity, IRGB monitors, enhanced graphics monitors, and composite monitors. (Standard television sets are composite monitors.) A graphics monitor is plugged into either a *CGA (Color/Graphics Adapter) board* or an *EGA (Enhanced Graphics Adapter) board.* The most powerful of these configurations is an enhanced graphics monitor with an EGA board. This chapter initially discusses graphics techniques that work for every configuration, and then addresses the additional capabilities that the EGA board provides.

Graphics

The two graphics modes available on all graphics monitors are referred to as medium-resolution and high-resolution graphics modes. Medium-resolution graphics mode allows the use of up to four colors at any time, whereas high-resolution graphics mode permits only black and white. On the other hand, high-resolution graphics mode permits finer detail.

Specifying Points on Screen

The graphics screen is divided into an array of small rectangles, called *points* or *pixels.* Both modes contain 200 pixels vertically. Horizontally, there are 320 pixels in medium-resolution graphics mode and 640 pixels in high-resolution graphics mode, as shown in Figure 8-1.

A pair of numbers called *coordinates* identify each pixel. The upper-left point has coordinates (0,0). You reach the point with coordinates (x,y) by starting at the upper-left point, and then by moving x points to the right and y points down, as shown in Figure 8-2. For instance, the center of the screen has the coordinates (160,100) in medium-resolution graphics mode and (320,100) in high-resolution graphics mode.

The primary graphics statements available in Turbo Basic are **SCREEN**, **PSET**, **PRESET**, **LINE**, **CIRCLE**, **DRAW**, **PAINT**,

Graphics and Sound

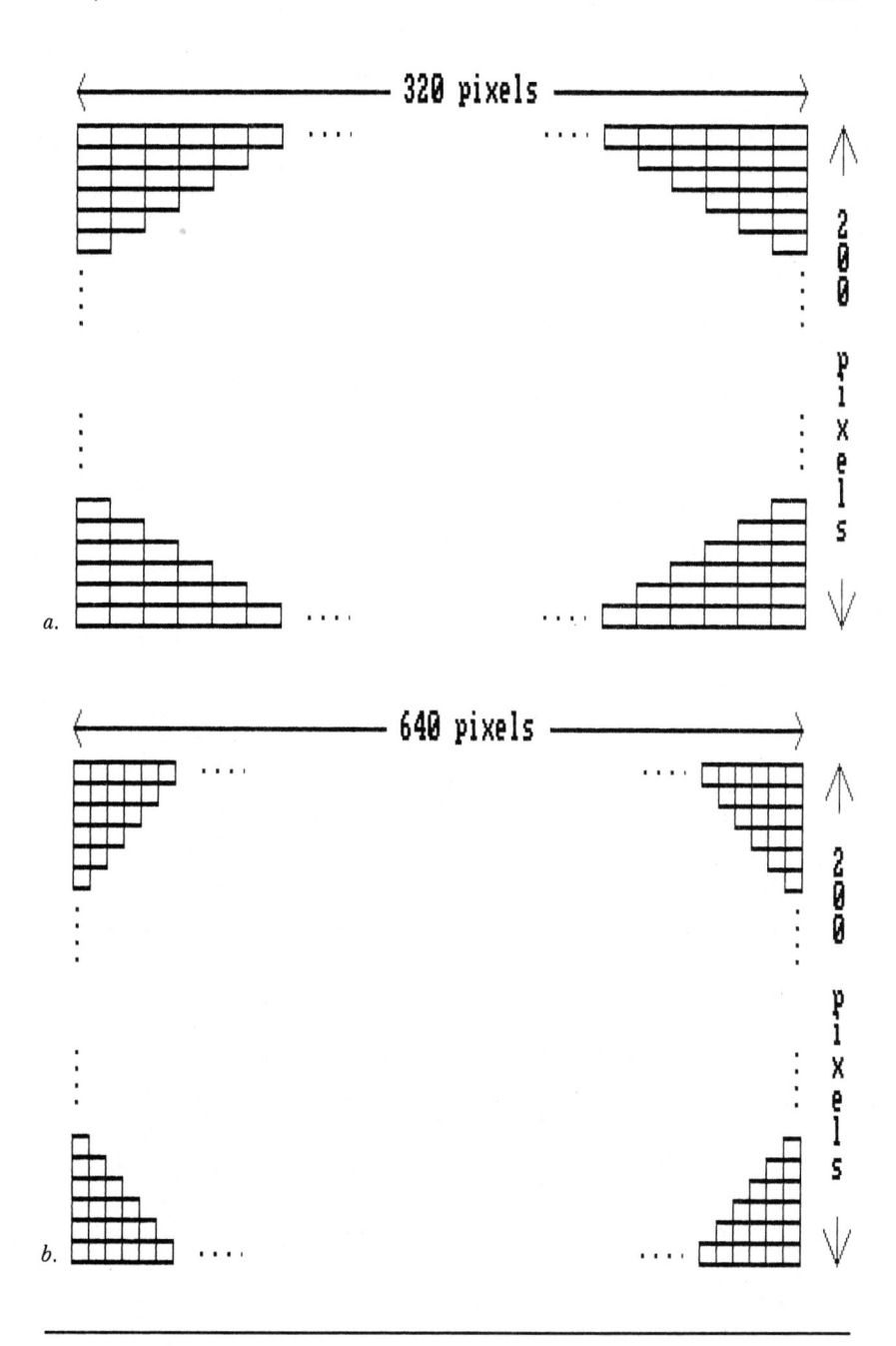

Figure 8-1. *The Graphics modes:* a, *medium-resolution, and* b, *high-resolution*

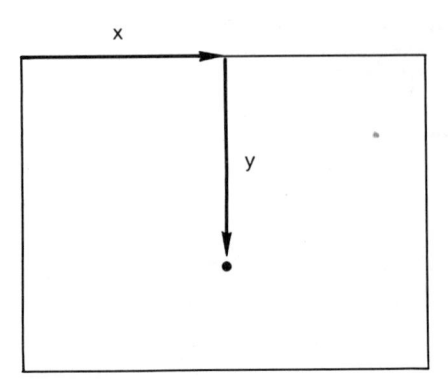

Figure 8-2. *The coordinates of a point*

COLOR, **GET**, **PUT**, **POINT**, **VIEW**, **WINDOW**, and **PMAP**. You use the **SCREEN** statement to specify one of the graphics modes. You can display points, lines, and circles with the statements **PSET**, **LINE**, and **CIRCLE**, respectively. The **DRAW** statement produces figures on screen in much the same way that you draw them on paper with a pencil. In medium-resolution graphics mode, you can use the **COLOR** statement to select colors for the displayed objects and for the background. You can animate a display by first storing a rectangular portion of the screen with **GET** and then placing it in different locations with **PUT**. With **VIEW**, you can limit graphics displays to a rectangular portion of the screen. The **WINDOW** statement allows you to customize the coordinate system used to specify points so that it suits the user. If you use **WINDOW** to do so, **PMAP** translates back and forth from one coordinate system to the other.

A number identifies each screen mode. Table 8-1 lists the numbers. The statement

SCREEN 0,1

Graphics and Sound

Number	Screen mode	Capabilities
0	text mode	text only
1	medium-resolution graphics mode	text and graphics
2	high-resolution graphics mode	text and graphics

Table 8-1. *The Screen Modes*

specifies text mode, while the statement

SCREEN *n*,0

specifies the graphics-screen mode that number *n* designates. Text characters are wider in mode 1 (40 characters per line) than in mode 2 (80 characters per line). The remainder of this chapter assumes that you have specified one of the graphics modes. (The second parameters in the **SCREEN** statement enable color when you use a composite monitor.)

Points, Lines, Rectangles, and Circles

The statement

PSET (*x,y*)

turns on the point with coordinates (*x,y*) and the statement

PRESET (*x,y*)

turns the point off. The statement

LINE (*x1,y1*) − (*x2,y2*)

draws a line from the point (*x1,y1*) to the point (*x2,y2*). The statement

LINE (*x1,y1*) − (*x2,y2*),,B

draws a rectangle that has the points (x1,y1) and (x2,y2) as opposite corners. The statement

LINE (x1,y1) — (x2,y2),,BF

draws the same rectangle, but as a solid. The statement

CIRCLE (x,y),r

draws the circle with center (x,y) and radius r. (The radius is measured in terms of the number of pixels from the center of the circle horizontally to the circumference.) Figures 8-3 through 8-7 show the effects that these statements produce in medium-resolution

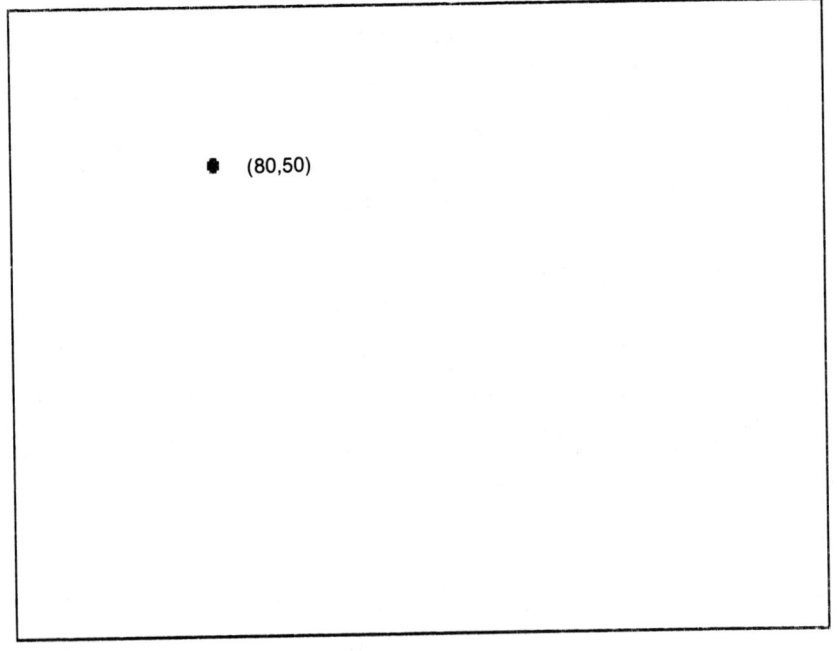

Figure 8-3. *The result of PSET (80,50)*

Graphics and Sound

graphics mode. Variations of the **CIRCLE** statement draw ellipses, and arcs of circles and ellipses. Chapter 12 discusses these features, by using them to create pie charts.

The Last Point Referenced and Relative Coordinates

After Turbo Basic executes each graphics statement, there is a special point on screen known as the *last point referenced*. This point is always the last point referred to in the statement. The *RUN*

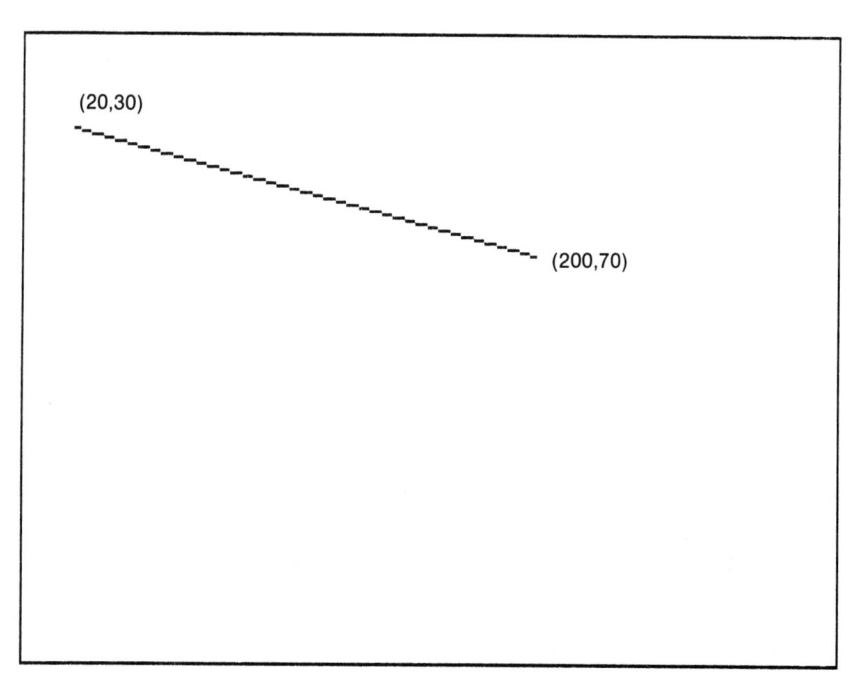

Figure 8-4. *The result of LINE (20,30) − (200,70)*

command and the *CLS* statement both set the last point referenced to the center of the screen.

A variation of the **LINE** statement allows you to omit one of the points. If so, Turbo Basic interprets the omitted point to be the last point referenced. For instance, the statements
CLS: LINE — (100,50)

draw a line from the center of the screen to the point (100,50).

The coordinates used to identify points in the examples given earlier are called *absolute coordinates*. You can also identify points by using *relative coordinates*. These coordinates are given in rela-

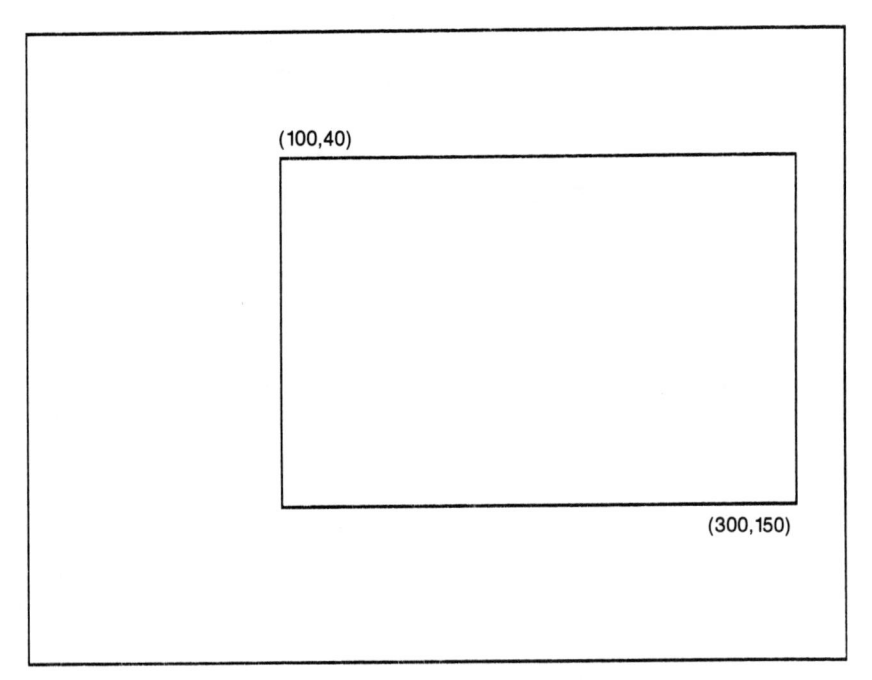

Figure 8-5. *The result of LINE (300,150) — (100,40),,B*

Graphics and Sound

tion to the last point referenced and are preceded by the word **STEP.** Turbo Basic obtains the point that
STEP (r,s)

specifies by starting at the last point referenced, moving r units horizontally (to the right if r is positive or to the left if r is negative), and then moving s units vertically (down if s is positive and up if s is negative). Therefore, if the last point referenced has absolute coordinates (a,b), then **STEP** (r,s) designates the point with coordinates $(a+r,b+s)$. Figure 8-8 gives some statements and the last point referenced after Turbo Basic executes the statement.

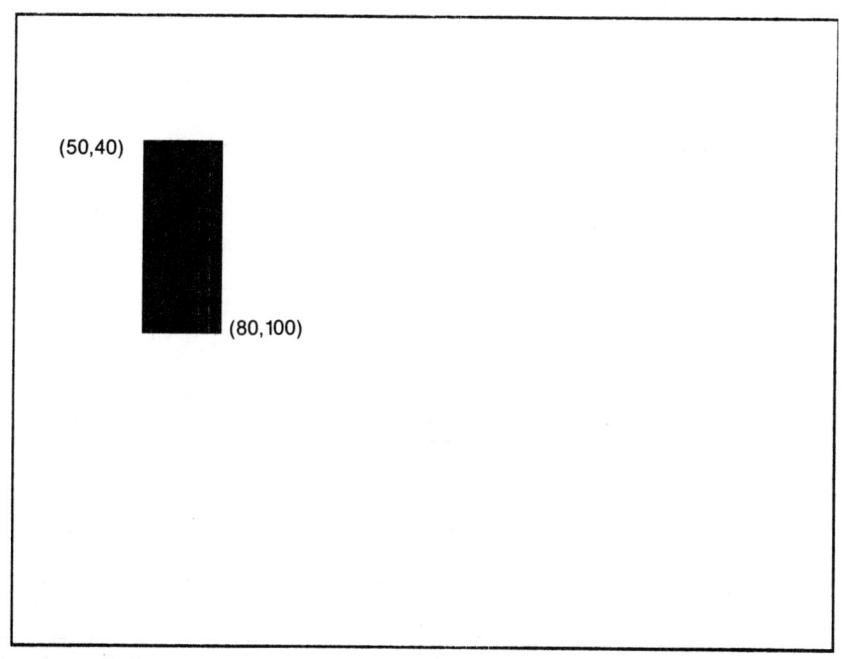

Figure 8-6. *The result of LINE (50,40) — (80,100),,BF*

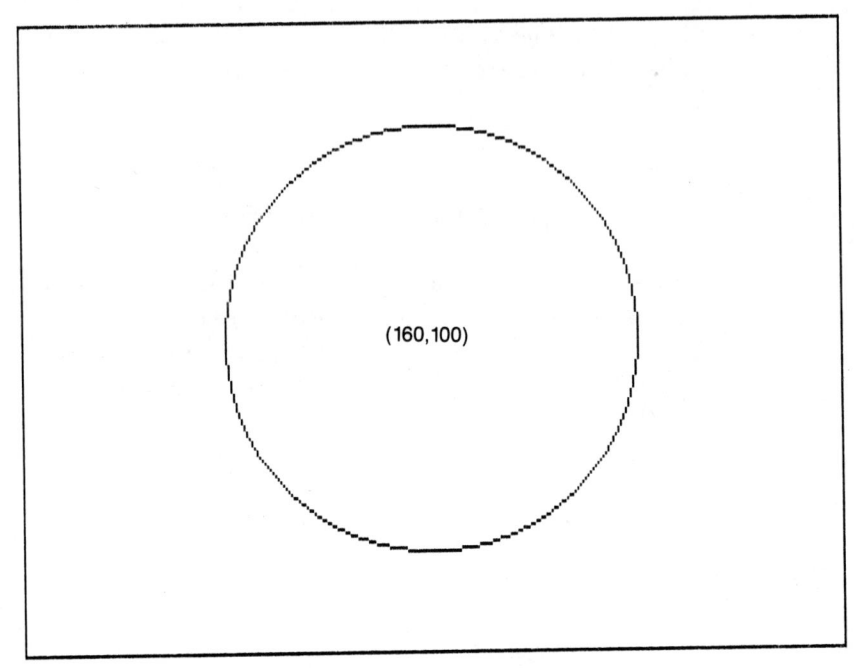

Figure 8-7. *The result of CIRCLE (160,100),80*

Statement	Last Point Referenced
CIRCLE (80,70), 30	(80,70)
LINE (0,0) − (40,50)	(40,50)
LINE (50,80) − STEP (20,10)	(70,90)
PSET (20,30)	(20,30)
PSET(10,20): CIRCLE STEP (30,40), 10	(40,60)

Figure 8-8. *Examples of the last point referenced and relative coordinates*

Graphics and Sound

The DRAW Statement

The **DRAW** statement provides a small graphics language that sketches figures by drawing a sequence of lines — each line emanating from the last point referenced to a specified point or in a specified direction. You can rotate, color, duplicate, and enlarge or reduce these figures.

The M Subcommand of the DRAW Statement The statement

DRAW "M x,y"

draws a straight line from the last point referenced to the point with coordinates (x,y). After Turbo Basic executes the statement, the point (x,y) becomes the new last point referenced. For instance, the statements

CLS: DRAW "M 200,50": DRAW "M 300,150"

produce both a line from the center of the screen to the point (200,50), and a line from (200,50) to (300,150). You can condense the last two statements into the single statement

DRAW "M 200,50 M 300,150"

If the letter **N** precedes the letter **M** in a **DRAW** statement, the last point referenced will be the same as it was before Turbo Basic drew the line. For example,

CLS: DRAW "NM 200,50 M 300,150"

draws a line from the center of the screen to the point (200,50) and then from the center of the screen to (300,150). (The point (300,150) will be the last point referenced for future **DRAW** statements.) Often, you may think of the lines as being drawn by a moving point, and say that the point drew the first line, and then returned to the original position before drawing the second line.

If the letter **B** precedes the letter **M** in a **DRAW** statement, the point moves without drawing the line; that is, the statement **DRAW "BM** x,y" merely makes (x,y) the new last point referenced. For example,

CLS: DRAW "BM 200,50 M 300,150"

draws a single line from the point (200,50) to the point (300,150). The statement **DRAW "BM** x,y" is used extensively to set the starting point before a program traces a figure with a **DRAW** statement.

You can also give the coordinates of the specified point in relative form. If r and s are nonnegative numbers, then the statement

DRAW "M +r,s"

draws a line from the last point referenced to the point that is r units to the right and s units down. For instance, in medium-resolution graphics mode,

CLS: DRAW "M +40,50"

draws a line from the point (160,100) to the point (200,150). The statements **DRAW "M** −r,s", **DRAW "M** +r,−s" and **DRAW "M** −r,−s" have similar interpretations. The presence of the + or − sign in front of the first coordinate provides a tip-off that tells you that the statement uses relative coordinates.

The following statements (in medium-resolution graphics) all draw the large letter **X** shown in Figure 8-9:

CLS: DRAW "NM 210,50 NM 210,150 NM 110,150 M 110,50"
CLS: DRAW "BM 110,50 M 210,150 BM 210,50 M 110,150"
CLS: DRAW "BM 110,50 M +100,100 BM +0,−100 M −100,100"

Graphics and Sound

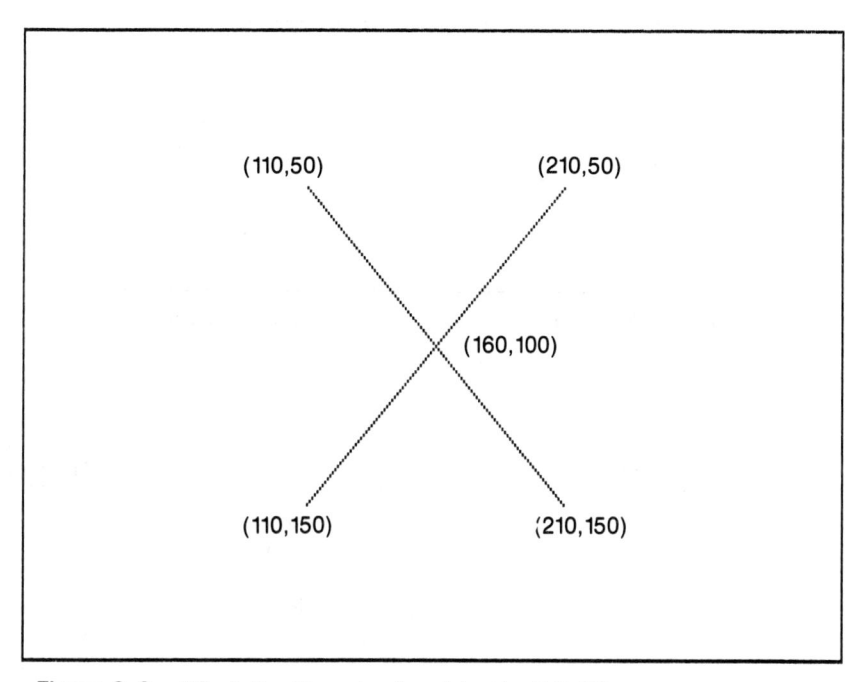

```
            (110,50)           (210,50)
                  \           /
                   \         /
                    \       /
                     \     /
                      \   /
                       \ /
                        X (160,100)
                       / \
                      /   \
                     /     \
                    /       \
                   /         \
                  /           \
            (110,150)          (210,150)
```

Figure 8-9. *The letter X, as produced by the DRAW statement*

The DRAW Direction Subcommands U, D, L, R, E, F, G, and H

A statement of the form

DRAW "U *n*"

where *n* is a positive integer, draws a line by starting at the last point referenced and moving *n* units up. The statement is equivalent to the statement **DRAW "M +0,−*n*"**. The other direction subcommands operate as shown in Figure 8-10 and Table 8-2.

Figure 8-10. *Eight directions used by the DRAW statement*

Subcommand	Moves	Equivalent to
U n	n units up	M $+0,-n$
D n	n units down	M $+0,n$
L n	n units left	M $-n,0$
R n	n units right	M $+n,0$
E n	n units NE	M $+n,-n$
F n	n units SE	M $+n,n$
G n	n units SW	M $-n,n$
H n	n units NW	M $-n,-n$

Table 8-2. *The DRAW Direction Subcommands*

Whenever the number 1 follows the subcommands **U, D, L, R, E, F, G,** or **H** you can omit the 1. The parameter n in the subcommands **U, D, L, R, E, F, G,** and **H** can also assume negative integer values. The results are as you probably would expect: for instance, **DRAW "U −9"** has the same effect as **DRAW "D 9"**, and **DRAW "E −9"** has the same effect as **DRAW "G 9"**.

Program 8-1 turns the computer into an electronic Etch A Sketch. While the program is running, you can control a moving dot by typing the eight letters **U, D, L, R, E, F, G,** or **H**, and holding them down for as long as you like. To terminate the program, type **Q**. Typing a letter other than one of those mentioned pro-

```
REM Convert the screen into a drawing pad   [8-1]
SCREEN 1,0
CLS
PRINT "Draw using U D L R E F G H."
PRINT "To quit press Q."
a$=""
DO UNTIL a$ = "Q"
   SELECT CASE a$
      CASE "U","D","L","R","E","F","G","H",""
         DRAW a$
      CASE ELSE
         PRINT CHR$(7);
   END SELECT
   a$ = UCASE$(INPUT$(1))
Loop
END
```

Program 8-1. *An electronic Etch A Sketch*

```
REM Draw a sailboat   [8-2]
SCREEN 1,0
CLS
DRAW "L60 E60 D80 L60 F20 R40 E20 L20"
END
```

Program 8-2. *DRAW a sailboat*

duces a beep. Program 8-2 produces the sailboat shown in Figure 8-11.

Using the prefixes **N** and **B** with the direction subcommands produces the same results as before. For example, the statement **DRAW "BU20"** moves the last point referenced up 20 units without drawing a line. The following statements can also draw the letter **X** that was shown in Figure 8-9:

CLS: DRAW "E50 G100 E50 H50 F100"
CLS: DRAW "NE50 NF50 NG50 H50"
CLS: DRAW "BE50 G100 BU100 F100"

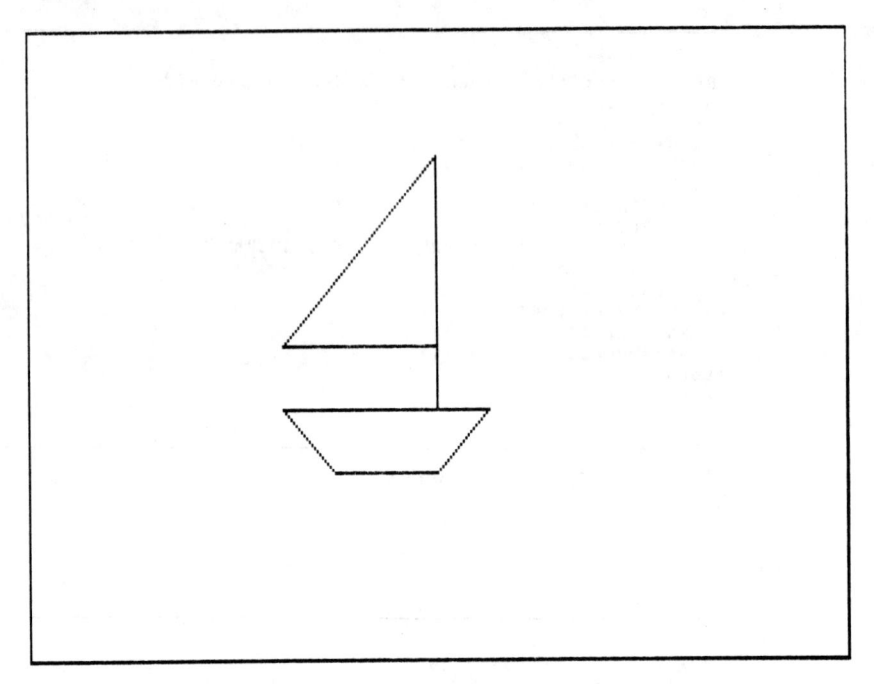

Figure 8-11. *The sailboat drawn by Program 8-2*

The **DRAW** statements given so far have consistently used uppercase letters and have included spaces to improve readability. Neither of these conventions is necessary. For instance, you can write the statement that drew the sailboat in Program 8-2 as

DRAW "l60e60d80l60f20r40e20l20"

The Angle Subcommands The statement

DRAW "A *n*"

tells Turbo Basic to draw all subsequent figures rotated counter-clockwise through *n*∗90 degrees, where *n* is 0, 1, 2, or 3. The statement

DRAW "TA *n*"

Graphics and Sound **179**

```
REM Draw a sailboat on an angle  [8-3]
SCREEN 1,0
A$ = "L60 E60 D80 L60 F20 R40 E20 L20"
DRAW "TA45" + A$
END
```

Program 8-3. *Illustrate the angle subcommand of DRAW*

tells Turbo Basic to draw all subsequent figures rotated through *n* degrees, where *n* is between -360 and 360.

Program 8-3 draws the sailboat given earlier in Figure 8-12. The boat has been rotated through a counterclockwise angle of 45 degrees.

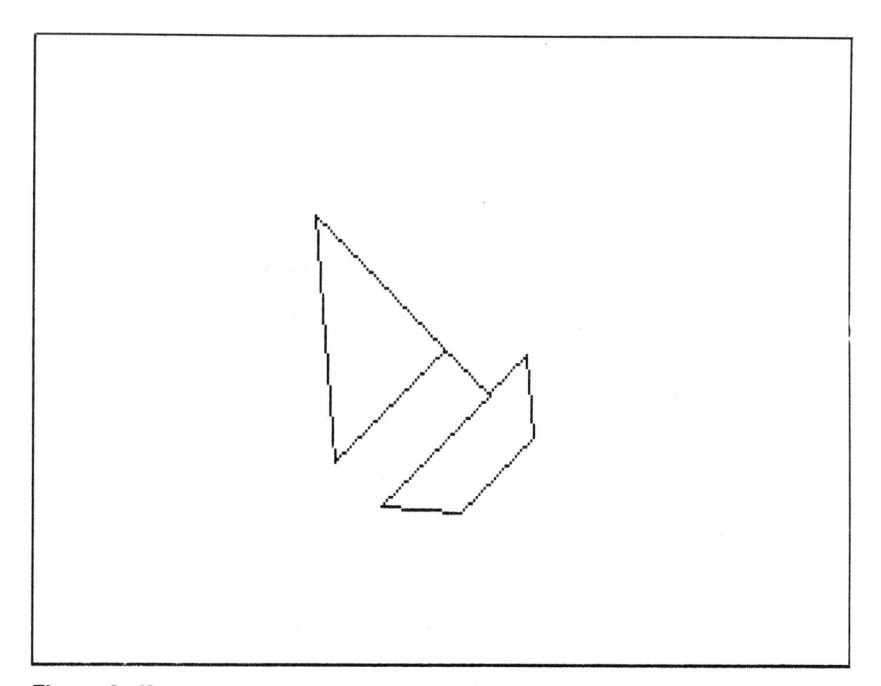

Figure 8-12. *The sailboat produced by Program 8-3*

The Scale Subcommand You can enlarge figures created with **DRAW** statements by using the Scale subcommand. The statement

DRAW "S *n*"

specifies that Turbo Basic should draw all subsequent segments at $n/4$ times their stated size until you specify another scale. The number n can range from 1 to 255. For instance, the statement **DRAW "S8 U10 L15 D10 R15"** is equivalent to the statement **DRAW "U20 L30 D20 R30"**. Both statements draw a rectangle of height 20 and width 30.

Using Variables and Substrings in DRAW Until now, the numbers that appeared in **DRAW** strings were all numeric constants. You can also use numeric variables; however, the command letter must be followed by an equal sign and a string that gives the location of the variable in memory. The **VARPTR$** function determines this location. Figure 8-13 shows several **DRAW** statements and their equivalent forms that use a variable.

Program 8-4 uses the **Scale** subcommand to draw sailboats of various sizes. (The sailboat will not completely fit in the screen if the scale is greater than about 140.)

Statement	Equivalent form using variables
DRAW "U 20"	a=20: DRAW "U =" + VARPTR$(a)
DRAW "TA 45"	angle = 45: DRAW "TA ="+VARPTR$ (angle)
DRAW "NL5 D2"	a=5: b=2: DRAW "NL ="+VARPTR$(a)+ "D="+VARPTR$(b)
DRAW "M 200,50"	a=200: b=50: DRAW "M="+VARPTR$(a) +",="+VARPTR$(b)
DRAW "M +40,50"	a=40: b=50: DRAW "M+="+VARPTR$(a) +",="+VARPTR$(b)

Figure 8-13. *Examples of DRAW statements with variables*

You can assign the string in a **DRAW** statement to a string variable, and then use the string variable to represent the string. For example, the statement **DRAW "U20 L30 D20 R30"** is equivalent to

a$ = "U20 L30 D20 R30": DRAW a$

You can also incorporate the string variable as a *substring* within a **DRAW** statement by using an **X** subcommand and the location of the variable. For instance, the statement just given is equivalent to

a$ = "U2 L3 D2 R3": DRAW "S40 X" + VARPTR$(a$)

Substrings are cumbersome to code in Turbo Basic and are not necessary. For instance, you can replace the statement just given with

a$ = "U2 L3 D2 R3": DRAW "S40" + a$

Turbo Basic includes substrings since they occur in BASICA.

Color

Table 8-3 shows the 16 principal colors that are available on a color monitor. A number from 0 through 15 identifies each color. This section considers the use of color in medium-resolution graphics

```
REM Draw various size sailboats    [8-4]
SCREEN 1,0
INPUT "SCALE (1-255) "; scale
DRAW "S =" + VARPTR$(scale)
DRAW "BM +1,0 L3 E3 D4 L3 F1 R2 E1 L1"
END
```

Program 8-4. *Illustration of the use of variables in a DRAW string*

0 Black	4 Red	8 Gray	12 Light red
1 Blue	5 Magenta	9 Light blue	13 Light magenta
2 Green	6 Brown	10 Light green	14 Yellow
3 Cyan	7 White	11 Light cyan	15 High-intensity white

Table 8-3. *The 16 Principal Colors*

Jar #	Palette 0 Assigned Color	Jar #	Palette 1 Assigned Color
0	*b* (background color)	0	*b* (background color)
1	2 (green)	1	3 (cyan)
2	4 (red)	2	5 (magenta)
3	6 (brown)	3	7 (white)

Table 8-4. *The Two Standard Palettes*

mode. Later this chapter presents the enhancements that are possible if you use the monitor with an Enhanced Graphics Adapter.

A *palette* can be thought of as a collection of four paint jars numbered 0, 1, 2, and 3, with each jar containing a color of paint. Medium-resolution graphics mode offers two palettes—palette 0 and palette 1—that you can use at any time. Table 8-4 gives the colors contained in the jars. Only four colors can appear on screen at one time, and all of these colors must be from the same palette.

The **COLOR** statement is used to select either palette 0 or palette 1 as the current palette, and assign a background color to the jars numbered 0. The statement

Graphics and Sound

COLOR b,p

where *b* is a number from 0 to 15 and *p* is either 0 or 1, makes *b* the new background color (the color in the 0 jars) and specifies that Turbo Basic should take the color of each point on screen from palette *p*. Text always appears in the color from jar 3 of the current palette. Any figure that one of the following statements produces will appear in the color from jar *m* of the current palette:

```
PSET (x,y),m
LINE (x1,y1) — (x2,y2),m
CIRCLE (x,y),r,m
DRAW "C m" + draw string
```

If you omit the parameter *m* in any of these statements, then Turbo Basic will draw the figure in the third color of the current palette.

Note: This text often refers to the color assigned to jar 3 of the current palette as the third color of the current palette, the color assigned to jar 2 as the second color, and the color assigned to jar *m* as the *m*th color. The *Turbo Basic Owner's Handbook* uses the word attribute to refer to the number *m*.

Program 8-5 produces figures and text in several different colors. Program 8-6 draws the sailboat given earlier in Figure 8-11 with a white background, cyan sail, and magenta boat.

Not only can Turbo Basic draw colored lines and curves, but also it can fill in, or paint, enclosed regions with a color that you selected from the current palette. A region to be painted is identified by giving both the coordinates of a point inside the region and the color of the boundary. If the point (x,y) is inside an enclosed region whose boundary has the *b*th color of the current palette, then the statement

PAINT (x,y),m,b

fills in the region with the *m*th color of the current palette. For example, Program 8-7 creates a dart board. The inner circle is black and the three rings are cyan, magenta, and white.

```
REM Demonstrate the use of colors   [8·5]
SCREEN 1,0
COLOR 8,0                    'Grey background, palette 0
PRINT "Hello"                'Brown greeting
PSET (50,50)                 'Brown point
PSET (100,100),1             'Green point
LINE (10,20) - (30,40),2     'Red line
CIRCLE (100,100),50,3        'Brown circle
DRAW "C1 R6 U5 L6 D5"        'Green square
END
```

Program 8-5. *Display text and figures in color*

```
REM Draw the sailboat of Figure 8·11 with different colors   [8·6]
SCREEN 1,0
COLOR 7,1
CLS
DRAW "C1 L60 E60 D80 C2 L60 F20 R40 E20 L20"
END
```

Program 8-6. *DRAWing in color*

```
REM  Create a dart board   [8-7]
SCREEN 1,0
COLOR 0,1
FOR n = 1 TO 4
   CIRCLE (160,100),20*n,3
NEXT n
FOR n = 1 TO 3
   PAINT (170 + 20*n,100),n,3
NEXT n
END
```

Program 8-7. *Illustration of the PAINT statement*

Graphics and Sound

The **DRAW** statement has a paint command that you can incorporate into its command string. The statement

DRAW "P *m,b*"

has the same effect as the statement **PAINT** (*x,y*),*m,b*, where the point (*x,y*) is the last point referenced.

Program 8-8 creates a solid red boat with a solid green sail, against a white background. The sixth line of the program uses **BD5** to set a point in the boat as the last point referenced.

There are actually six palettes available in medium-resolution graphics mode. The four undocumented palettes, which are shown in Table 8-5, are accessed in certain cases when the second parameter of the **SCREEN** statement or the first parameter of the **COLOR** statement is omitted. The last three palettes are high-intensity versions of the others. To obtain one of the two documented palettes, execute **SCREEN** and **COLOR** statement with both parameters present. In addition, after you obtain one of the low-intensity palettes, you must change the screen mode before acquiring a high-intensity palette. Program 8-9 displays the six different palettes.

```
REM Paint a sailboat   [8-8]
SCREEN 1,0
COLOR 7,0
A$ = "L60 E60 D80 L60 F20 R40 E20 L20"
DRAW A$
DRAW "BD5 P 2,3"
PSET(150,90),1
DRAW "P 1,3"
END
```

Program 8-8. *Illustrate painting with the DRAW statement*

Jar #	Palette U	Palette HI-0	Palette HI-1	Palette HI-U
0	background color	background color	background color	background color
1	cyan	light green	light cyan	light cyan
2	red	light red	light magenta	light red
3	white	yellow	high-intensity white	high-intensity white
Invoked by	SCREEN 1 COLOR b,p	SCREEN 1,0 COLOR ,0	SCREEN 1,0 COLOR ,1	SCREEN 1 COLOR ,p

Table 8-5. *The Four Undocumented Palettes*

```
REM Show all six palettes available in SCREEN 1 [8-9]
'Standard palette 0
SCREEN 1,0
COLOR 0,0
CALL DisplayPalette
LOCATE 1,12
PRINT "Standard Palette 0";
CALL WaitForKey
'High intensity palette 0
SCREEN 0
SCREEN 1,0
COLOR ,0
CALL DisplayPalette
LOCATE 1,9
PRINT "High Intensity Palette 0";
CALL WaitForKey
'Standard palette 1
SCREEN 1,0
COLOR 0,1
CALL DisplayPalette
LOCATE 1,12
PRINT "Standard Palette 1";
CALL WaitForKey
'High intensity palette 1
SCREEN 0
SCREEN 1,0
COLOR ,1
CALL DisplayPalette
```

Program 8-9. *The six palettes*

```
        LOCATE 1,9
        PRINT "High Intensity Palette 1";
        CALL WaitForKey
        'Standard undocumented palette
        SCREEN 1
        COLOR 0
        CALL DisplayPalette
        LOCATE 1,6
        PRINT "Standard Undocumented Palette";
        CALL WaitForKey
        'High intensity undocumented palette
        SCREEN 0
        SCREEN 1
        CALL DisplayPalette
        LOCATE 1,3
        PRINT "High Intensity Undocumented Palette";
        CALL WaitForKey
        END

        SUB DisplayPalette
          CLS
          LINE (0,30)-(99,180),1,BF
          LINE (110,30)-(209,180),2,BF
          LINE (220,30)-(319,180),3,BF
          LOCATE 3, 3: PRINT "1st Color";
          LOCATE 3,17: PRINT "2nd Color";
          LOCATE 3,30: PRINT "3rd Color";
        END SUB

        SUB WaitForKey
          LOCATE 25,6
          PRINT "Press any key for next palette";
          WHILE INKEY$="": WEND
        END SUB
```

Program 8-9. *The six palettes* (continued)

Styling and Tiling

Turbo Basic has two graphics enhancements that substitute for and complement colors. A *styled line* is a line made up of a repeating pattern of dots and dashes. A *tiled region* is an enclosed region of the screen that is filled in with a repeating rectangular pattern, which resembles a tiled floor.

0000 0	0100 4	1000 8	1100 C
0001 1	0101 5	1001 9	1101 D
0010 2	0110 6	1010 A	1110 E
0011 3	0111 7	1011 B	1111 F

Table 8-6. *Binary Numbers and Their Hexadecimal Equivalents*

Line styling requires the ability to convert a binary number (a sequence of 0's and 1's) to hexadecimal form (which begins with **&H** and uses the digits 0 through 9 and the letters A through F). In every situation that arises in line styling, the binary number is given as a 16-tuple of zeros and ones. The following process will determine the hexadecimal form:

1. Partition the 16-tuple into four 4-tuples.

2. Replace each 4-tuple with the digit or letter shown in Table 8-6.

3. Place **&H** at the front of the derived string of four characters.

For example, with this method, you would partition the 16-tuple 0101111110100010 so that it appears as 0101 1111 1010 0010, and then write **&H5FA2**.

Figure 8-14 shows four styled lines. The style of each line is a 16-point pattern that is repeated as many times as necessary. To draw a styled line from (a,b) to (c,d), consider the pixels that lie on the straight line between the two specified points, and turn on some of these pixels. Suppose that you begin with the point (c,d) and, of the first 16 pixels, you turn on the first, fifth, tenth, and fourteenth pixels. You can represent this pattern by using the 16-tuple

1000100001000100

If you count from left to right, this 16-tuple has 1's in its first, fifth, tenth, and fourteenth positions and 0's in all other positions. The 16-tuple is the binary representation of the hexadecimal number **&H8844**. The statement

LINE $(a,b)-(c,d)$,,,&H8844

Graphics and Sound

```
. . . . . . . . . . . . . . . . . . . . . . . . . . . . . . . . . . . . . . . . . . .
      0000000100000001           &H0101


    . . . . . . . . . . . . . . . . . . . . . . . . . . . . . . . . . . . . . . . . .
      0001000100010001           &H1111


    - - - - - - - - - - - - - - - - - - - - - - - - - - - - - - - - - -
      0000111100001111           &H0F0F


    - - . . - - . . - - . . - - . . - - . . - - . . - - . . - - . .
      0001111100010001           &H1F11
```

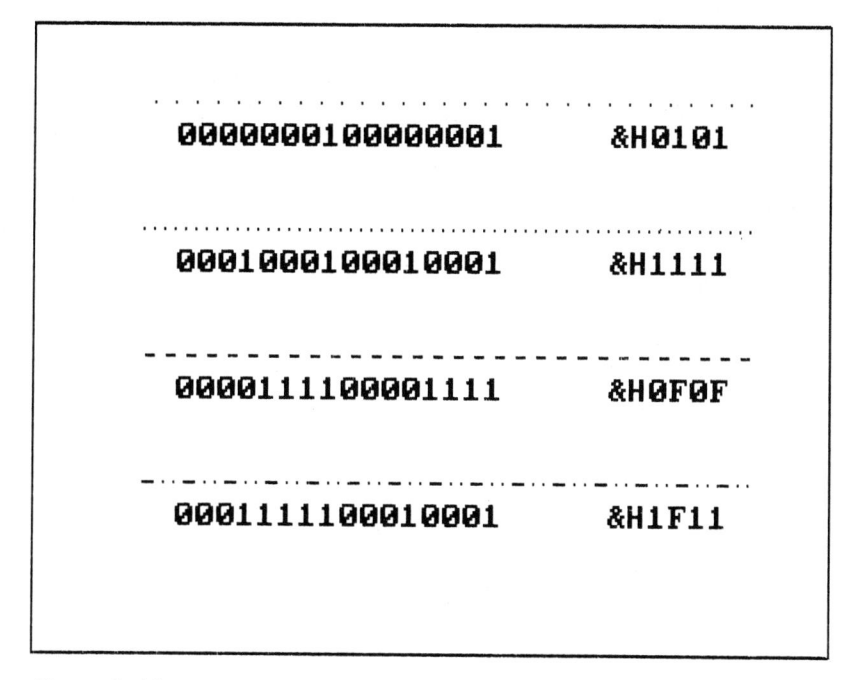

Figure 8-14. *Styled lines*

draws the line from (*a,b*) to (*c,d*), by beginning at (*c,d*) with the first 16 pixels as just described, and then repeating the same pattern in each successive 16-tuple until reaching the point (*a,b*). In general, if *s* is the hexadecimal representation of a 16-tuple of zeros and ones, then the statement

LINE (*a,b*)−(*c,d*),,,*s*

draws the line from (*a,b*) to (*c,d*) with the pattern that the 16-tuple determines. The number *s* is referred to as the *style* of the line. Figure 8-14 showed each pattern with its associated 16-tuple and style. The parameters *m*, **B**, or both may be inserted between the appropriate commas to obtain color, a styled rectangle, or both.

Program 8-10 draws the last styled line shown in Figure 8-14 and displays descriptive numbers. The **POINT** function has the value 3 if the indicated pixel is on and the value 0 if it is off. The

Using Turbo Basic

```
REM Determine the pattern of a styled line    [8-10]
SCREEN 1,0
LINE (20,170)-(300,170),,,&H1F11
FOR n = 0 TO 15
  PRINT POINT(300-n,170);
NEXT n
END

Run
 0  0  0  3  3  3  3  3  0  0  0  3  0
 0  0  3
```

Program 8-10. *Illustrate the effect of the style parameter*

The pattern of 0's and 3's is the same as the pattern of 0's and 1's that appears in the binary representation of **&H1F11**.

Figure 8-15 shows two examples of enclosed regions **PAINT**ed with tile patterns. The method for designing patterns is different

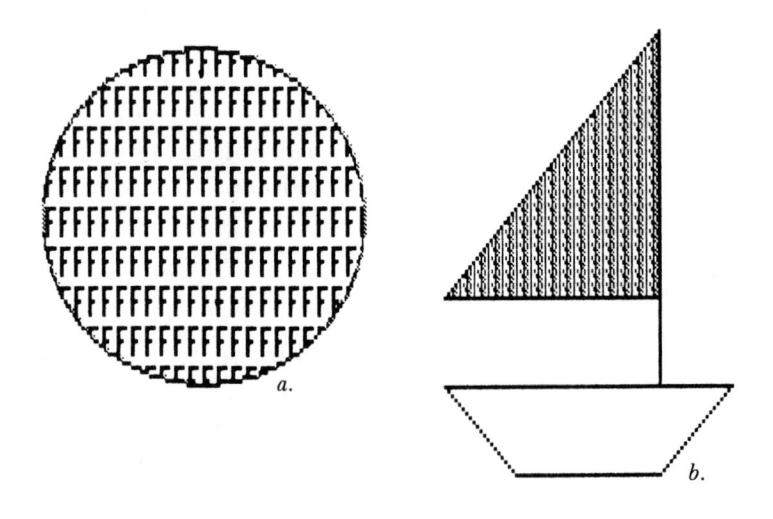

Figure 8-15. *Examples of tiling*

Graphics and Sound

for high-resolution graphics than the method for medium-resolution graphics. This section will discuss each case separately.

In high-resolution graphics, each tile is 8 pixels horizontally, and from 1 to 64 pixels vertically. You specify a tile by identifying each pixel as on or off. You can associate each row of the tile with an 8-tuple of 0's and 1's, where the 1's correspond to the pixels to be turned on and the 0's correspond to the pixels to be turned off. Each 8-tuple is the binary representation of a decimal integer from 0 to 255.

Figure 8-16 shows the tiling used in Figure 8-15a, along with the binary 8-tuples and integers that are associated with each row. The tile in Figure 8-16 is specified by the string

$t\$ $ = CHR\$(0) + CHR\$(63) + CHR\$(48) + CHR\$(48) + CHR\$(60) + CHR\$(48) + CHR\$(48) + CHR\$(48) +CHR\$(0)

where $t\$ $ is the tile specifier. Program 8-11 uses the tile in Figure 8-16 to obtain the tiling that was shown in Figure 8-15a.

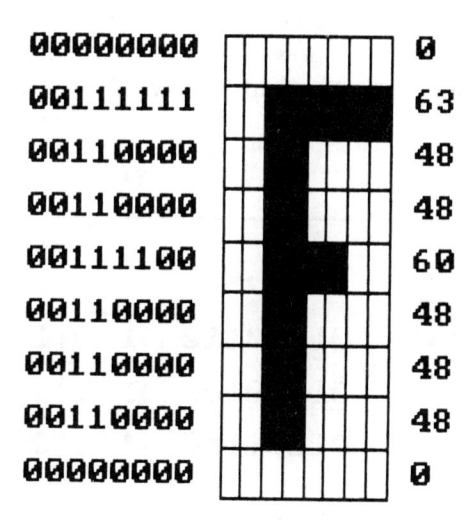

```
00000000                0
00111111               63
00110000               48
00110000               48
00111100               60
00110000               48
00110000               48
00110000               48
00000000                0
```

Figure 8-16. *The tile used in Figure 8-15*a

```
REM Produce a circle filled with Fs  [8-11]
SCREEN 2,0
CIRCLE (100,75),90
t$ = CHR$(0) + CHR$(63) + CHR$(48) + CHR$(48) + CHR$(60) _
       + CHR$(48) + CHR$(48) + CHR$(48) +CHR$(0)
PAINT (100,75),t$
END
```

Program 8-11. *Produce the tiling shown in Figure 8-15a*

In medium-resolution graphics, each tile is 4 pixels horizontally, and from 1 to 64 pixels vertically. You specify a tile by giving the number of the jar (0, 1, 2, or 3) to be used to color each pixel. Then, you translate each of the four numbers into binary notation: 0 is 00, 1 is 01, 2 is 10, and 3 is 11. You can then associate each row of the tile with an 8-tuple of 0's and 1's, by stringing together the 4 binary numbers in the row. Each of the 8-tuples is the binary representation of a decimal integer from 0 to 255. (Note: You can use a simple Turbo Basic program to find the decimal number that is associated with the binary 8-tuple. The statement **PRINT &B***8-tuple* displays the decimal form of the binary 8-tuple.)

Figure 8-17 shows the tiling used in Figure 8-15*b*, along with the binary 8-tuples and integers associated with each row.

```
01000110   | 1 | 0 | 1 | 2 |   70
01010101   | 1 | 1 | 1 | 1 |   85
01001110   | 1 | 0 | 3 | 2 |   78
```

Figure 8-17. *The tile used in Figure 815b*

Graphics and Sound

You specify the tile that was given in Figure 8-17 by using the string

t$ = CHR$(70) + CHR$(85) + CHR$(78)

In either high-resolution or medium-resolution graphics, suppose that a tile has r rows with associated integers $n_1, n_2, \ldots, n_r$. Then the string

t$ = CHR$($n_1$) + CHR$(n_2) + ... + CHR$($n_r$)

specifies the tile. If an enclosed region contains the point (x,y) in its interior and has a boundary drawn in the bth color of the current palette, then the statement

PAINT (x,y),t$,b

fills in the region by tiling it with the tile $t\$$.

Program 8-12 uses the tile that was given in Figure 8-17 to obtain the tiling that was shown in Figure 8-15b.

In medium-resolution graphics, the statement **PAINT** $(x,y),t\$,b$ is not always able to tile over a region that you have already **PAINT**ed with a tile pattern or color. A general solution to this problem is possible as long as the border of the region does not have the background color (that is, b is not 0). In this case, the statement **PAINT** $(x,y),0,b$ should precede the **PAINT** statement given earlier. The first **PAINT** statement clears the region to the background color—thereby allowing the next **PAINT** statement to execute its tiling properly.

```
REM Sailboat with tiled sail  [8-12]
SCREEN 1,0
COLOR 0,0
DRAW "L60 E60 D80 L60 F20 R40 E20 L20"
t$ = CHR$(70) + CHR$(85) + CHR$(78)
PAINT (150,90),t$
END
```

Program 8-12. *Produce the tiling shown in Figure 8-15*b

```
REM Draw a red rectangle and then paint it with stripes   [8-13]
SCREEN 1,0
COLOR 0,0
LINE (10,10) - (50,90),,B
PAINT (30,50),2
t$ = CHR$(255) + CHR$(255) + CHR$(0) + CHR$(0) + _
      CHR$(170) + CHR$(170) + CHR$(0) + CHR$(0)
PAINT (30,50),t$
END
```

Program 8-13. *A tiling problem*

Program 8-13 presents an example of the retiling problem. To solve the problem, you should place the statement **PAINT (30,50),0** before **PAINT (30,50),t$**.

The tile specifier *t$* is just a string. Hence, you can use any string of length at most 64 for *t$*. Program 8-14 tiles the entire screen in a pattern that the user-supplied string determines.

Animation

Animation is accomplished by using the **GET** statement to take a snapshot of a rectangular portion of the screen, and then repeatedly using the **PUT** statement to place the snapshot at a nearby location.

```
REM Experiment with different tile patterns   [8-14]
SCREEN 1,0
COLOR 0,0
INPUT "Type in any string of characters: ",t$
PAINT (5,5),t$
END

Run
Type in any string of characters: FUN
     [The pattern produced is the same one that appears in the
      sailboat in Figure 8-15 (b).]
```

Program 8-14. *The patterns generated by strings*

Graphics and Sound

The graphics **GET** statement stores a copy of a rectangular portion of the screen in memory. The rectangular portion of the screen is designated by giving the coordinates of its upper-left corner *(x1,y1)* and its lower-right *(x2,y2)*, as shown in Figure 8-18. The saved information consists of the jar number that is associated with each point of the region. (Remember that your palette choice and the jar number determine the point color.) The statement

GET (x1,y1)-(x2,y2), arrayName

stores a description of the specified rectangle in the named array. You may use any numeric array type. For simplicity, the rest of this section discusses only integer arrays.

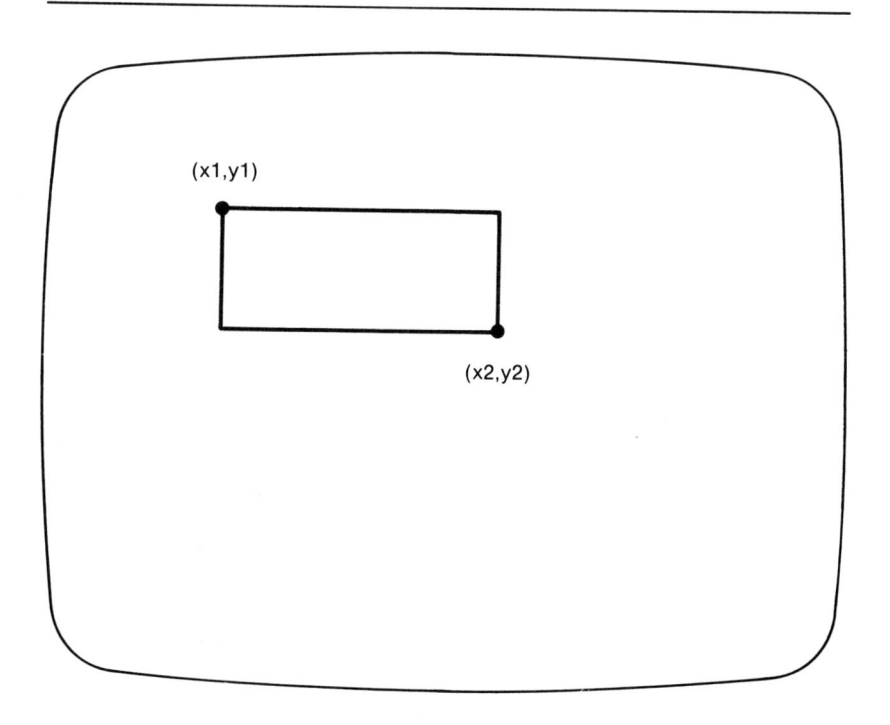

Figure 8-18. *A rectangular region captured by a GET statement*

You must first dimension the array. (Normally, arrays with a size n less than 11 do not have to be specifically dimensioned. However, this is not the case if you will use the array with a **GET** statement.) In medium-resolution graphics mode, the size n of the integer array is determined in the following manner:

1. Assume that h is the number of points in a horizontal side of the rectangle, and v is the number of points in a vertical side. Thus,
$$h = x2 - x1 + 1$$
and
$$v = y2 - y1 + 1$$

2. Calculate the number $(2*h + 7)/8$, multiply its integer part by v, and then add 4. Call the result b.

3. The value of n must be at least $(b/2) - 1$.

In high-resolution graphics mode, the procedure for determining the value of n is the same, except that you replace the number 2 in step 2 with the number 1.

The number n in Program 8-15 is determined as follows:

1. Using the same assumptions as those in step 1,
$$h = 25 - 4 + 1 = 22$$
$$v = 60 - 20 + 1 = 41$$

```
REM Capture a rectangular region of the screen    [8-15]
SCREEN 1,0
n = 124
DIM a%(n)
GET (4,20)-(25,60), a%
END
```

Program 8-15. *Illustrate the dimensioning of an array to be used with GET*

Graphics and Sound

2. $2*h + 7 = 2*22 + 7 = 51$
$51/8 = 6.375$, which has integer part 6
$b = 6*v + 4 = 6*41 + 4 = 250$

3. $n = (250/2) - 1 = 124$

The graphics **PUT** statement usually is used in conjunction with the graphics **GET** statement. Suppose that a **GET** statement has recorded a rectangular portion of the screen into an integer array. Then, the statement

PUT (x,y), *arrayName*, PSET

will place an exact image of the rectangular region on the screen, positioned with its upper left corner at the point (x,y). In Program 8-16, **H₂O** is displayed on screen. The number **2** will appear as a subscript of **H**.

Program 8-17 draws a truck, as shown in Figure 8-19, and then moves it across the screen. The rectangular region chosen is a little larger than necessary to include the truck. On the left, the region has a small blank border, which erases the overhanging part of the previous truck drawing each time that the program places a new picture of the truck on the screen.

The word **PSET**, which appears at the end of the **PUT** state-

---

```
REM Display the formula for water   [8-16]
SCREEN 1,0
LOCATE 1,1
PRINT "2"
DIM two%(9)
GET (0,0)-(7,7),two%
CLS
LOCATE 1,1
PRINT "H O"
PUT (8,4),two%,PSET
END
```

Program 8-16. *Use PUT to display a subscript*

```
REM Move a truck across the screen   [8-17]
SCREEN 1,0
CALL DrawTruck
DIM truck%(629)
GET (20,21)-(119,70),truck%
CLS
FOR n = 1 TO 200
  PUT (n,100),truck%,PSET
  DELAY .01
NEXT n
END

SUB DrawTruck
   CIRCLE (105,60),10            'Draw front tire
   PAINT (105,60),3              'Paint front tire
   CIRCLE (35,60),10             'Draw rear tire
   PAINT (35,60),3               'Paint rear tire
   LINE (21,21)-(101,40),,BF     'Draw back of truck
   LINE (21,40)-(119,60),,BF     'Draw hood
END SUB
```

Program 8-17. *A demonstration of animation*

ment just given is referred to as the *action* of the statement. There are four other possible actions: **PRESET, AND, OR,** and **XOR**. We first consider the effects of these actions for high-resolution graphics mode.

In high-resolution graphics mode, each point is colored either black or white. Suppose that a **GET** statement has recorded a rectangular portion of the screen into an array. Then, each of the four actions of the **PUT** statement affect the rectangular region that has the point (*x,y*) as its upper-left corner and has the same size as the original rectangle.

The statement

PUT (*x,y*), *arrayName*, PRESET

displays a reversed image of the original rectangular region. Every point that was originally white will be black, and vice versa.

The remaining three actions of the **PUT** statement interact with whatever images are already in the rectangular part of the screen

Graphics and Sound

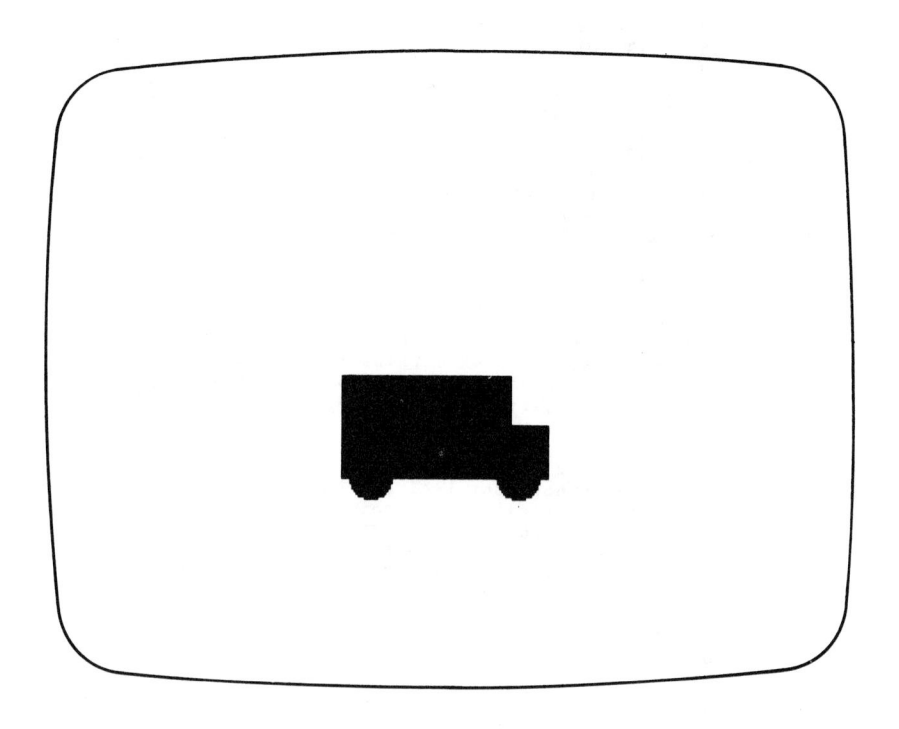

Program 8-19. *A truck created by Program 8-17*

that will be **PUT** upon. The action **AND** results in a point being white if it is already white, and is also white in the image that is transferred. The action **OR** results in a point being white if it is already white or if it is white in the image that is transferred. The action **XOR** results in a point being white either if it is already white or if it is white in the image that is being transferred, but not both. If you do not specify an action in a **PUT** statement, then Turbo Basic will automatically invoke **XOR**.

XOR is commonly used in animation. **PUT**ting an image on top of itself with **XOR** has the effect of erasing the image and restor-

```
REM Move a ball around the screen    [8-18]
DIM ball%(10)
SCREEN 2,0
'Get an image of the ball
CIRCLE (20,20),4
PAINT (20,20),3
GET (16,16)-(24,24),ball%
'Specify initial position of ball
'and increments for finding new position
horizontal = 16
vertical   = 16
hIncrement = 1
vIncrement = 1
PRINT " Press any key to quit."
DO WHILE INKEY$=""
   'If ball is at edge of screen, reverse the value of increment
   IF vertical>190   OR vertical<1   THEN vIncrement = -1*vIncrement
   IF horizontal>630 OR horizontal<1 THEN hIncrement = -1*hIncrement
   'Save old position for later PUT that erases ball
   oldHorizontal = horizontal
   oldVertical   = vertical
   'Compute new position
   horizontal=horizontal+hIncrement
   vertical=vertical+vIncrement
   'Erase ball from old position
   PUT (oldHorizontal,oldVertical),ball%,XOR
   'Place ball at new position
   PUT (horizontal,vertical),ball%,XOR
   'Control speed of ball
   DELAY .01
LOOP
END
```

Program 8-18. *Illustrate the use of XOR*

ing the original background. Program 8-18 moves a ball around the screen and bounces it off the sides. Press any key to terminate the program.

To create a variation of Program 8-18, add the following line before the **DO WHILE** loop:

LINE (320,0)−(410,199),,BF

The program will then draw a solid vertical rectangle in the middle of the screen. After the ball passes through the rectangle, the rectangle will still be intact.

In medium-resolution graphics mode, the action **PSET** causes an exact copy of the original rectangle to be displayed (unless you

		Stored jar number		
		0 1 2 3	0 1 2 3	0 1 2 3
Old Jar Number	0	0 0 0 0	0 1 2 3	0 1 2 3
	1	0 1 0 1	1 1 3 3	1 0 3 2
	2	0 0 2 2	2 3 2 3	2 3 0 1
	3	0 1 2 3	3 3 3 3	3 2 1 0
		AND	OR	XOR

Table 8-7. *Jar Numbers That Result from the Actions AND, OR, and XOR*

have changed the current palette, in which case, points colored from jar m of the old palette will now be colored from jar m of the new palette). The action **PRESET** displays a reverse image: points that were colored from jar 3 are now colored from jar 0 of the current palette, and vice versa. Similarly, points colored from jar 1 are now colored from jar 2, and vice versa.

Every point of the screen has an associated jar number. This number is 0 until the point is affected by a graphics or **PRINT** statement. The remaining three **PUT** actions interact with the colors that are already in the rectangular part of the screen that will be **PUT** upon. The new jar number of each point is determined by using its old jar number, the jar number of the corresponding point in the stored rectangle, and the action. The resulting jar numbers (which determine the colors) are given in Table 8-7.

You can also obtain the resulting jar numbers if you understand logical operators and the binary representation of numbers. For example, to determine the result of combining jars 2 and 3 with respect to the action **XOR**, you would write the two jar numbers in binary notation and apply the logical operator **XOR** to the components. The numbers 2 and 3 are 10 and 11 in binary notation, respectively. Since **10 XOR 11** is 01 or 1, the action **XOR** combines jars 2 and 3 to produce jar 1.

You can use the **POINT** function in animation to determine if two objects are about to collide. The value of

POINT (*x,y*)

```
REM Move a ball across a screen with a barrier   [8-19]
DEFINT d, x
SCREEN 1,0
'Get the image of a ball
DIM ball%(9)
CIRCLE (3,100),2
PAINT (3,100),3
GET (0,97)-(6,103),ball%
'Get size and location of barrier then draw it
INPUT "Enter a position from 10 to 300: ",position
INPUT "Enter a length from 1 to 199: ",length
CLS
LINE (position,0)-(position+20,length),,BF
'Move ball across screen. If ball hits barrier, reverse it direction
d = 1            '1=right, -1=left
x = 3            'x-coordinate of center of ball
DO UNTIL x>315 OR (x<4 AND d=-1)
   IF POINT(x+4,99)<>0 THEN d = -1
   x = x + d
   PUT (x-3,97),ball%,PSET
   DELAY .01
LOOP
END
```

Program 8-19. *Illustrate the use of POINT to detect a collision*

is the jar number of the point with coordinates (x,y). (In high-resolution graphics mode, points that are black (off) have a jar number of 0, while points that are white (on) have a jar number of 1.)

In Program 8-19, a barrier of position and length that the user specifies appears, and a ball moves from left to right across the screen. Figure 8-20 shows the barrier and the ball. If the ball hits the barrier, the ball's direction will be reversed. The program repeats the **DO** loop until the ball either reaches the right side of the screen or reaches the left side of the screen while moving to the left. The **POINT** function detects objects in the path of the ball and tells the program whether it should reverse the direction of the ball. The upper-left corner of the rectangle that contains the ball is 3 pixels to the left and 3 pixels above the center of the ball. If the length of the barrier is less than 100, then the ball will cross the entire screen. If the length is more than 100, the ball will appear to bounce off the barrier.

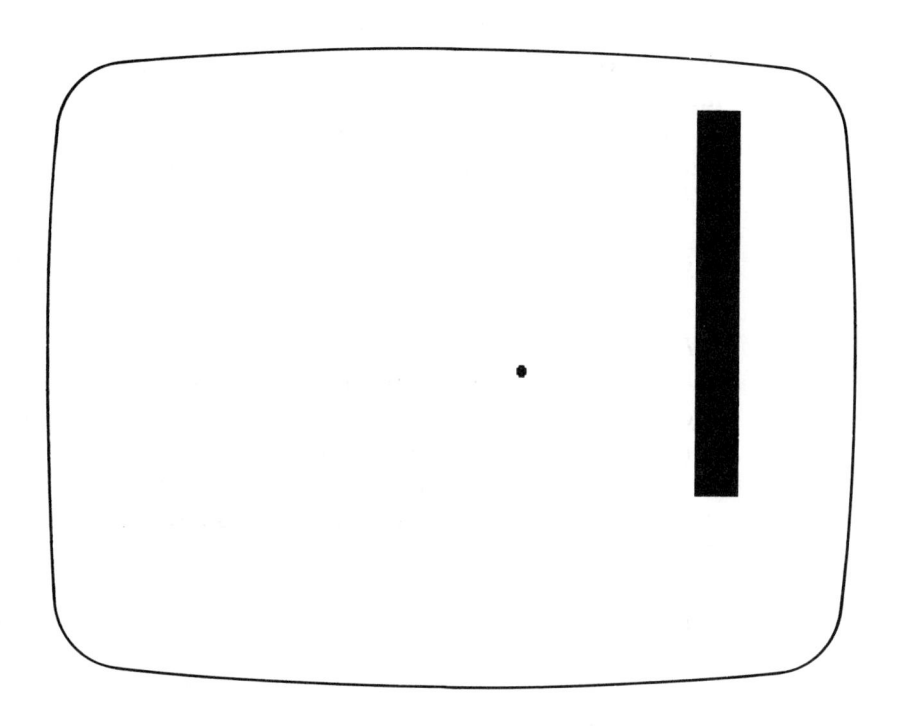

Figure 8-20. *The ball and the barrier*

The Use of an EGA Board

You can attach three types of monitors to an EGA (Enhanced Graphics Adapter) board: an EGM (Enhanced Graphics Monitor), an IRGB monitor (an ordinary color monitor, whose letters stand for *Intensity Red Green Blue*), and a Monochrome Display.

You can realize the full power of the EGA if you use an EGM. Sixty-four colors and three additional screen modes are available. (Chapter 4 presents a discussion of the 64 colors available on an

EGM.) With an IRGB monitor, you can change the colors assigned to the jars in the two medium-resolution graphics mode palettes to any four of the sixteen standard colors; in high-resolution graphics mode, you can specify the foreground and background colors. With a Monochrome Display, you can display graphics in a special screen mode. Each screen mode supported by Turbo Basic is described below:

■ **SCREEN** mode 1 (320 × 200 graphics resolution, 40 characters per line)

IRGB. The situation is the same as with a CGA board, except that you may now use the **PALETTE** statement to change the colors assigned to the palettes. If m is a number from 0 to 3 and c is a number from 0 to 15, then the statement **PALETTE** m,c changes the color in jar m of the current palette to color c as was shown in Table 8-3. Note that selecting a palette with a **COLOR** statement restores the default color assignments of that palette. Program 8-20 prepares to work in **SCREEN** mode 1 with a light blue background, and the colors yellow, magenta, and light green for the foreground.

EGM. The situation is the same as with an IRGB monitor, except that there are 64 colors available to the **COLOR** statement for the background color, b, and to the **PALETTE** statement for the assigned color, c.

```
REM   New colors for palette 0 on an IRGB Monitor with an EGA   [8-20]
SCREEN 1,0
COLOR ,0            'Select palette 0
PALETTE 0,9         'Put light blue in jar 0 (as background color)
PALETTE 1,14        'Put yellow in jar 1
PALETTE 2,5         'Put magenta in jar 2
PALETTE 3,10        'Put light green in jar 3
```

Program 13-20. *Setting up a new palette in SCREEN mode 1*

Graphics and Sound **205**

- **SCREEN** mode 2 (640 × 200 graphics resolution, 80 characters per line)

    IRGB. The situation is the same as with a CGA board, except that you can use the **PALETTE** statement to change both the foreground and background colors to any one of the 16 standard colors. If c is a number from 0 to 15, then the statement **PALETTE 0,**c selects color c as the background color and the statement **PALETTE 1,**c selects color c as the foreground color. Program 8-21 sets up **SCREEN** mode 2 to have a light blue background with all text and graphics appearing in black.

    EGM. Any two of the 64 EGA colors are available as foreground or background. If c is a number from 0 to 63, then the statement **PALETTE 0,**c selects color c as the background color and the statement **PALETTE 1,**c selects color c as the foreground color.

- **SCREEN** mode 7 (320 × 200 graphics resolution, 40 characters per line)

    IRGB. A single palette with 16 jars, numbered 0 to 15, is available. Initially, jar m is assigned color m from Table 8-3. However, you can use the **PALETTE** statement to assign any of the 16 principal colors to any of the 16 jars. The statement **COLOR** f,b specifies that Turbo Basic should use the color in jar f of the palette as foreground, and the color in jar b of the palette for background. The parameter m in the graphics statements **PSET**, **LINE**, **CIRCLE**, **DRAW**, and **PAINT** can range from 0 to 15. When you use a **GET** statement to capture a rectangular region of the screen in an integer array, the number 2 in step 2 of the

```
REM New colors in SCREEN 2 on an IRGB Monitor with an EGA    [8-21]
SCREEN 2,0
PALETTE 0,9      'Make the background light blue
PALETTE 1,0      'Make the foreground black
```

Program 8-21. *Changing colors in SCREEN 2 when using an EGA*

procedure for determining the size of the array should be changed to 4.

EGM. The situation is the same as for the IRGB, with the exception that the **PALETTE** statement can assign any of the 64 EGM colors to each of the 16 jars in the palette.

- **SCREEN** mode 8 (640 × 200 graphics resolution, 80 characters per line)

With either an IRGB or an EGM, the **COLOR, PALETTE,** and **GET** statements perform the same as in **SCREEN** mode 7.

- **SCREEN** mode 9 (640 × 350 graphics resolution, 80 characters per line)

EGM. The **COLOR** and **PALETTE** statements perform the same as they do in **SCREEN** modes 7 and 8. However, if only 64K of memory exists on the EGA board, the palette will consist of just the four jars numbered 0 to 3.

- **SCREEN** mode 10 (640 × 350 graphics resolution, 80 characters per line)

Monochrome Display. A single palette with four jars is available. You can assign nine pseudocolors, listed in Table 8-8, to these jars by using the **PALETTE** statment. If m is a number from 0 to 3 and c is a number from 0 to 8, then the statement **PALETTE**

0	black
1	blinking (black to white)
3	blinking (black to high-intensity white)
4	white
5	blinking (white to high-intensity white)
6	blinking (high-intensity white to black)
7	blinking (high-intensity white to white)
8	high-intensity white

Table 8-8. *Pseudocolors Available on the Monochrome Display*

m,c assigns pseudocolor *c* to jar *m* of the palette. The statement **COLOR** *f,b* specifies that Turbo Basic should use the pseudocolor in jar *f* of the palette for foreground, and the pseudocolor in jar *b* of the palette for background.

Special IBM PS/2 Graphics Modes Turbo Basic supports two special graphics modes on IBM PS/2 computers. The statement **SCREEN 11** selects the 640-by-480 black-and-white graphics screen mode. The statement **SCREEN 12** selects the 640-by-480 color graphics screen mode. In **SCREEN 12**, you may use the **PALETTE** statement to assign any of the 256000 available colors to the 16 palette jars for use by Turbo Basic's graphics statements.

User-defined Coordinate Systems

The coordinates discussed in the beginning of this chapter are known as *physical coordinates*. The use of physical coordinates has two disadvantages. First, the coordinates of an actual point on the physical screen depend on the screen mode. For example, the center of the screen has coordinates (160,100) in screen mode 1, (320,100) in screen mode 2, and (320,175) in screen mode 9. Second, the coordinate systems are difficult to use in many applications, such as displaying data in bar graphs or graphing mathematical functions. You can eliminate these limitations by using the **WINDOW** statement, which allows you to design your own coordinate system. The statement

WINDOW (x1,y1)−(x2,y2)

embeds the screen in a standard *x-y* coordinate system. The points of the plane have *x*-coordinates that range from *x1* rightward to *x2*, and *y*-coordinates that range from *y1* up to *y2*, as shown in Figure 8-21a. The statement

WINDOW SCREEN (x1,y1)−(x2,y2)

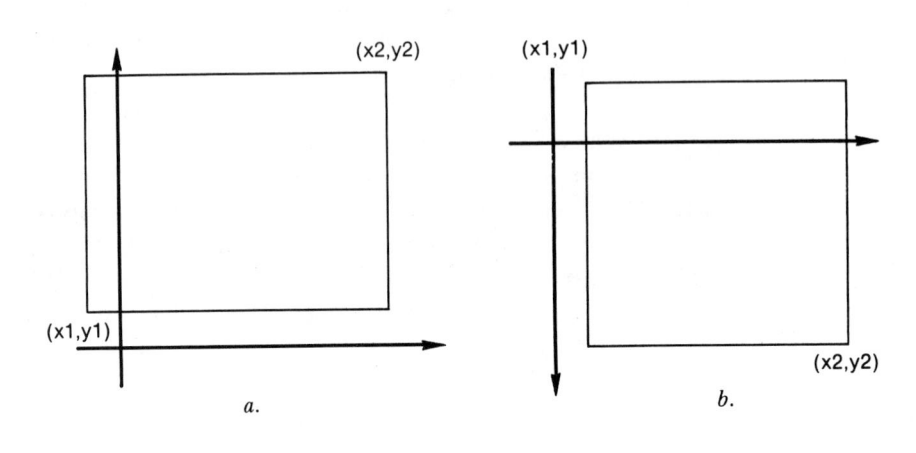

Figure 8-21. *The coordinate systems specified by the WINDOW statement*

embeds the screen in a nonstandard *x-y* coordinate system. The points of the plane have *x*-coordinates that range from *x1* rightward to *x2*, and *y*-coordinates that range from *y1* down to *y2*, as shown in Figure 8-21*b*. These user-defined coordinate systems are referred to as *world coordinate systems*. After Turbo Basic executes either of these statements, the graphics statements **PSET**, **PRESET**, **LINE**, **CIRCLE**, **GET**, and **PUT** will use the new world coordinates. After having specified world coordinates with a **WINDOW** statement, you can return to physical coordinates by executing a **WINDOW** statement without the word **SCREEN** and without specifying coordinates. You will also return to physical coordinates if you change the screen mode.

The **WINDOW** statement does not affect the size and location of text characters, the **DRAW** statement, or the scale of a **LINE** style or a **PAINT** tile. Also, the **WINDOW** statement sets the last point referenced to the center of the screen. The **PMAP** function (described in Appendix B) can be used to convert from physical coordinates to world coordinates, and vice versa.

Graphics and Sound

```
REM  Using the WINDOW Statement  [8-22]
SCREEN 2,0
WINDOW (-5,-5)-(5,100)
'Draw y axis and arrow
LINE (0,-5)-(0,100)
LINE (0,100)-( .3,95)
LINE (0,100)-(-.3,95)
'Draw x axis and arrow
LINE (-5,0)-(5,0)
LINE (5,0)-(4.7,5)
LINE (5,0)-(4.7,-5)
'Draw an example circle and rectangle
CIRCLE (1,60),2
LINE (-4,8)-(1,20),,B
END
```

Program 8-22. *Illustrate the use of the WINDOW statement*

Program 8-22 specifies a standard *x-y* coordinate system in which the *x* coordinates range from −5 to 5, and the *y* coordinates range from −5 to 100. The outcome of this program appears in Figure 8-22.

Program 8-23 specifies a nonstandard *x-y* coordinate system in which the *x* coordinates range from −200 to 2000, and the *y* coordinates range from −500 to 500. The outcome of this program appears in Figure 8-23.

Each time you specify a world-coordinate system in a program, the coordinate system determines how the program will place points until Turbo Basic executes another **WINDOW** statement. By varying the coordinate system, you can enlarge, shrink, and move figures to different parts of the screen. Program 8-24 produces Figure 8-24.

Viewports

Turbo Basic provides the capability of setting aside a rectangular portion of the screen and specifying that Turbo Basic display all subsequent graphics only in this region. Such a rectangular region is called a *viewport*.

Using Turbo Basic

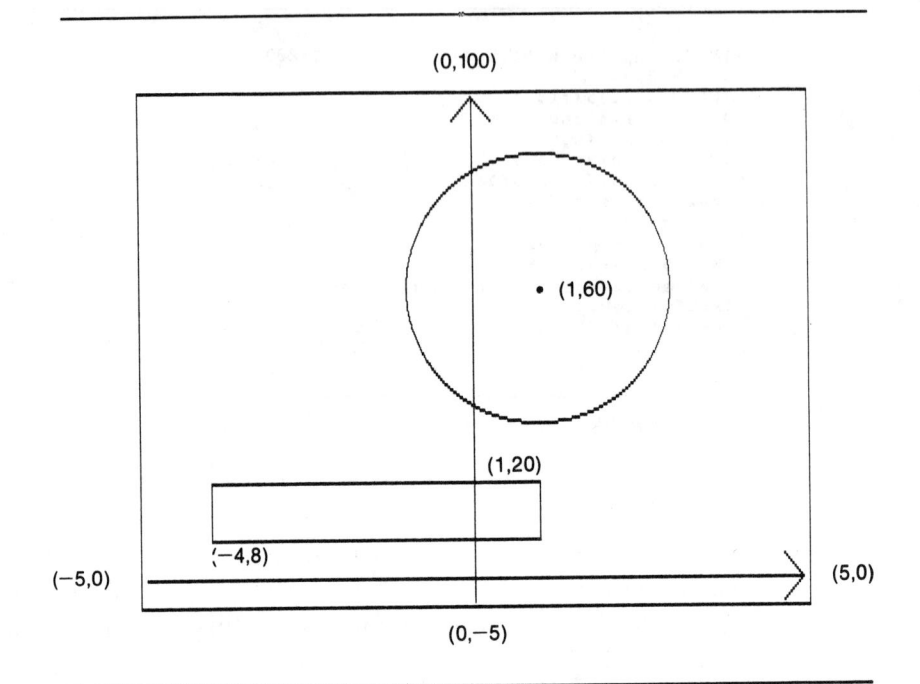

Figure 8-22. *The result of Program 8-22*

```
REM  Using the WINDOW SCREEN statement   [8-23]
SCREEN 2,0
WINDOW SCREEN (-200,-500)-(2000,500)
'Draw y axis and arrow
LINE (0,-500)-(0,500)
LINE (0,500)-( 70,450)
LINE (0,500)-(-70,450)
'Draw x axis and arrow
LINE (-200,0)-(2000,0)
LINE (2000,0)-(1930,50)
LINE (2000,0)-(1930,-50)
'Draw an example circle and line
CIRCLE (1100,100),400
LINE (100,-100)-(900,-400)
END
```

Program 8-23. *Illustrate the use of the WINDOW SCREEN statement*

Graphics and Sound

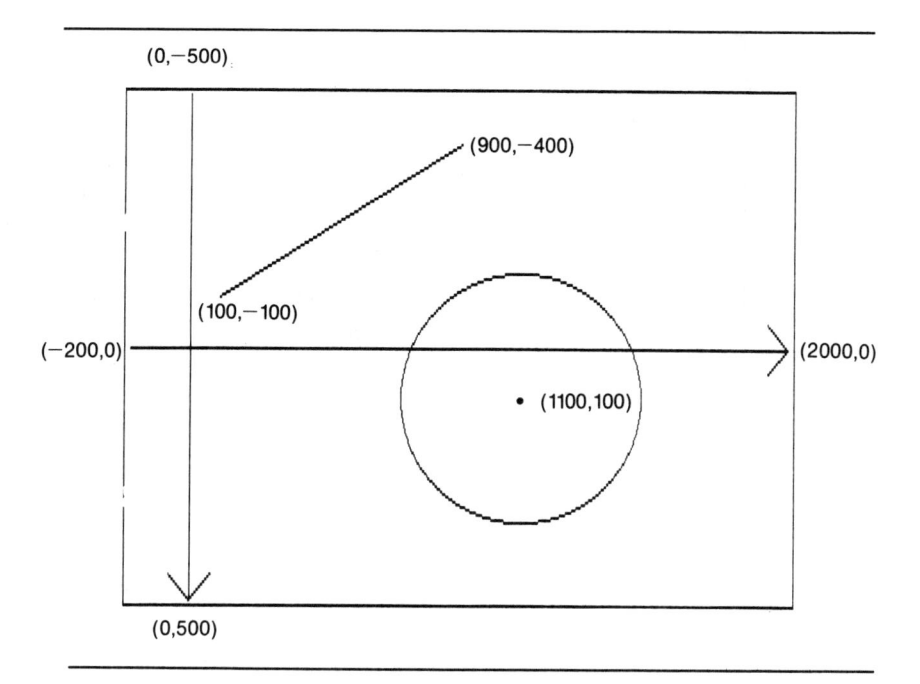

```
                    (0,−500)
          ┌─────────────────────────────────────┐
          │                                     │
          │                        (900,−400)   │
          │                      ╱              │
          │                    ╱                │
          │                  ╱                  │
          │                ╱                    │
          │      (100,−100)                     │
(−200,0) ─┼─────────────────────────────────────┼──▶ (2000,0)
          │                   ⌒                 │
          │                 ⌒   ⌒               │
          │                │ •(1100,100)│       │
          │                 ⌒   ⌒               │
          │                   ⌒                 │
          │                                     │
          │           ▼                         │
          └─────────────────────────────────────┘
                    (0,500)
```

Figure 8-23. *The result of Program 8-23*

```
REM Draw a stick figure in different sizes and locations  [8-24]
SCREEN 1,0
CALL DrawFigure
WINDOW SCREEN (0,0)-(900,600)
CALL DrawFigure
WINDOW SCREEN (-50,50)-(190,190)
CALL DrawFigure
END

SUB DrawFigure
   CIRCLE (160,80),20
   PAINT (160,80),2,3
   LINE (160,97)-(160,150)
   LINE (160,120)-(190,110)
   LINE (160,120)-(130,110)
   LINE (160,150)-(190,180)
   LINE (160,150)-(130,180)
END SUB
```

Program 8-24. *Illustrate the use of WINDOW to enlarge, shrink, and move figures*

Figure 8-24. *The result of Program 8-24*

Consider the rectangular portion of the medium-resolution graphics screen having $(x1,y1)$ as its upper-left corner and $(x2,y2)$ as its lower-right corner. Then, after Turbo Basic executes the two statements

```
WINDOW SCREEN (0,0)-(319,199)
VIEW (x1,y1)-(x2,y2),v,b
```

all graphics that **PSET**, **PRESET**, **LINE**, and **CIRCLE** specify will be scaled and displayed inside the specified rectangular region. The viewport will be filled with the vth color of the current palette, and the boundary will appear in the bth color of the palette. If you omit either v or b, Turbo Basic uses the background color. Similar results hold for the other graphics screen modes. In these cases, you must replace the coordinates (319,199) by the coordinates of the point in the lower-right corner of the screen.

Graphics and Sound

```
REM Draw a circle in a viewport   [8-25]
SCREEN 1,0
COLOR 1,1
CIRCLE (80,100),40
WINDOW SCREEN (0,0)-(319,199)  'Project future graphics into upper
VIEW (160,1)-(318,100),,2      'right-hand quarter of screen
CIRCLE (80,100),40
END
```

Program 8-25. *Project graphics into a viewpoint*

Program 8-25 produces Figure 8-25. The viewport consists of the upper-right corner of the screen, and has a blue background and a red boundary. The second circle drawn is scaled to fit into the viewport by using the same proportions as used for the original circle fit into the entire screen.

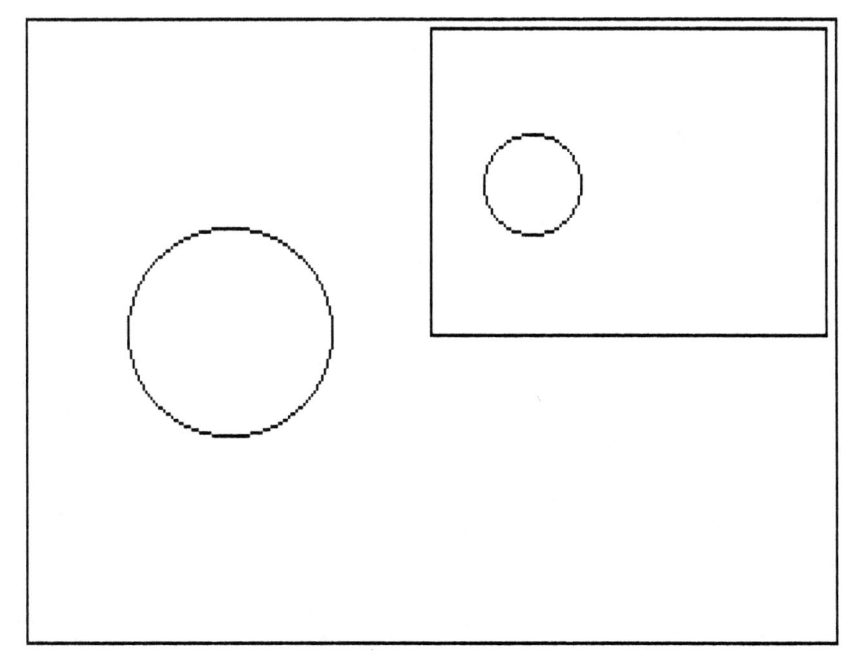

Figure 8-25. *The result of Program 8-25*

You can replace the **WINDOW SCREEN** statement just used with a more general **WINDOW** statement that specifies world coordinates. If you do so, then the graphics projected into the viewport will be a scaled version of the graphics that Turbo Basic would have drawn (by using world coordinates) onto the entire screen in the absence of the **VIEW** statement. Note, however, that the world coordinates that the **WINDOW** or **WINDOW SCREEN** statements establish do not affect the creation of the viewport by the **VIEW** statement. Turbo Basic always interprets the coordinates that appear in the **VIEW** statement as physical coordinates, as Program 8-26 shows.

When a **VIEW** statement follows another **VIEW** statement, only the second viewport will be active. Thus, subsequent graphics statements address themselves to the second viewport. Program 8-26 uses the **VIEW** statement with the **WINDOW** statement to vary the size of a star. The output is shown in Figure 8-26.

If a **WINDOW** statement is not active at the time that Turbo Basic executes the **VIEW** statement, then no scaling takes place.

```
REM Draw four graphs of a star    [8-26]
SCREEN 1,0
COLOR ,1
WINDOW (-8,-8)-(8,8)
VIEW (1,1)-(159,99),,3
CALL DrawStar(1)
VIEW (161,101)-(240,149),,1
CALL DrawStar(2)
VIEW (242,151)-(282,176),,2
CALL DrawStar(3)
VIEW (284,178)-(304,190),,3
CALL DrawStar(1)
END

SUB DrawStar(starColor)
    PSET   ( 0, 8)
    LINE - ( 5,-8),starColor
    LINE - (-7, 2),starColor
    LINE - ( 7, 2),starColor
    LINE - (-5,-8),starColor
    LINE - ( 0, 8),starColor
END SUB
```

Program 8-26. *Illustrate the use of the VIEW statement*

However, Turbo Basic will translate points that were specified to be drawn by graphics statements *x1* points to the right and *y1* points down, and will draw the points only if the new location is within the viewport. (Think of the viewport as taking a picture of the upper-left part of the screen.) For example, if you delete the fifth line of Program 8-25, the result will be the portion of the circle shown in Figure 8-27.

If you replace the statement **VIEW** (*x1,y1*)−(*x2,y2*),**v,b** with the statement

VIEW SCREEN (x1,y1)−(x2,y2),v,b

then no scaling or relocation occurs. Instead, when Turbo Basic draws a figure, only the portion of the figure inside the viewport

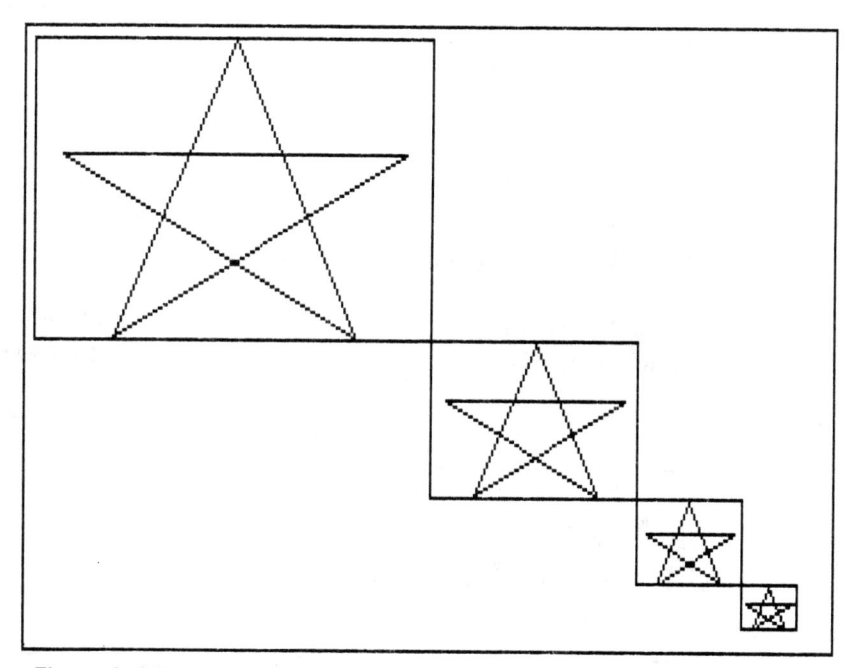

Figure 8-26. *The result of Program 8-26*

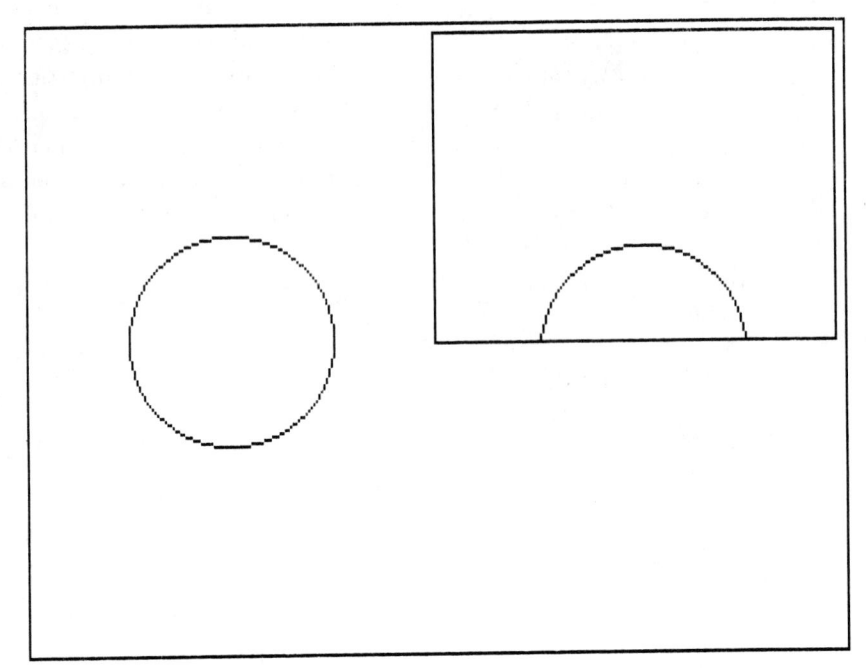

Figure 8-27. *The result of Program 8-25 with the fifth line deleted*

will be visible. Consider the sailboat that was drawn in Program 8-2. Program 8-27 draws a portion of the sailboat by executing a **VIEW SCREEN** statement before drawing. The output of the program is shown in Figure 8-28.

The **VIEW** statement does not affect the size and location of text characters, the **DRAW** statement, or the scale of a **LINE** style or a

```
REM Crop a picture of a sailboat   [8-27]
SCREEN 1,0
VIEW SCREEN (140,80)-(200,150),,3
DRAW "L60 E60 D80 L60 F20 R40 E20 L20"
END
```

Program 8-27. *Illustrate the use of VIEW*

Graphics and Sound

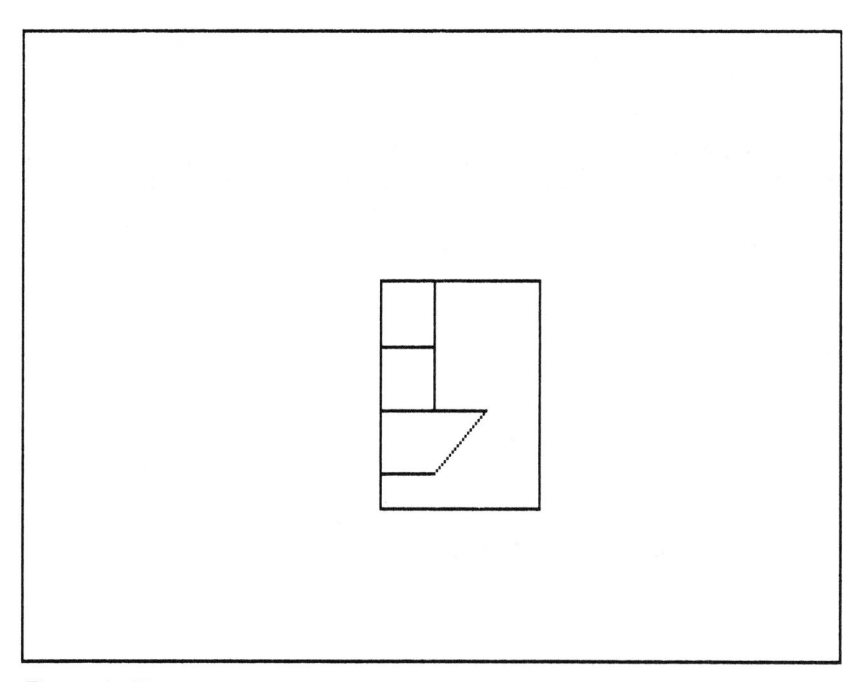

Figure 8-28. *The result of Program 8-27*

PAINT tile. If Turbo Basic executes a **CLS** statement while a **VIEW** statement is active, only the contents of the viewport will be cleared. This applies to text as well as to graphics. To clear the entire screen without altering active **WINDOW** and **VIEW** statements, execute **PRINT CHR$(12)**. To clear the entire screen and also to deactivate the viewport, use the statements **VIEW:CLS**.

Sound

The computer can play musical compositions by using the **PLAY** statement. You designate the notes and their lengths, the tempo of the composition, and whether or not the program should pause until the computer plays all of the notes.

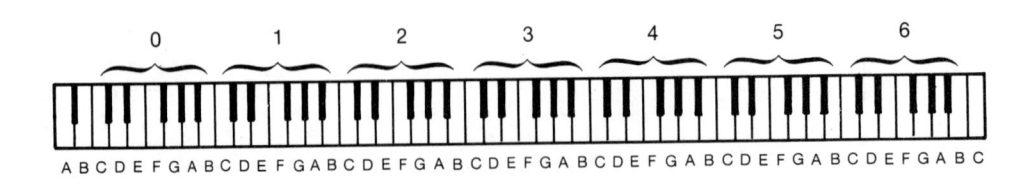

```
                    0          1          2          3          4          5          6
                   ___        ___        ___        ___        ___        ___        ___
[keyboard diagram]
    A B C D E F G A B C D E F G A B C D E F G A B C D E F G A B C D E F G A B C D E F G A B C
```

Figure 8-29. *A piano keyboard*

The piano keyboard consists of 88 keys. You can play 84 of these keys on the computer. Figure 8-29 groups these 84 keys into 7 octaves labeled 0 to 6.

You identify each note by its octave (0 to 6) and its letter (A to G). Sharps and flats are denoted by following the letter with # or + for a sharp, and − for a flat. **PLAY** statements gives the word **PLAY** followed by a string that contains information about the notes to be played. A typical statement is

PLAY "O3 C"

which results in middle C being played. The statement

PLAY "O2 DE O4 E+B−"

results in Turbo Basic playing 4 notes in succession: the first 2 being from octave 2 and the second 2 from octave 4. In general, the letter **O** and one of the numbers 0 to 6 determine that all subsequent notes will be from the designated octave, until you specify another octave. The designated octave will even affect subsequent **PLAY** statements. If you do not specify an octave before the computer **PLAY**s the first note, the computer will take the note from octave 4. You can increase or decrease the octave at any time by inserting either > or <, respectively, into the **PLAY** string.

Graphics and Sound

```
REM Convert the screen into an electronic piano   [8-28]
CLS
PRINT "I can play A B C D E F and G. Use < or > to ";
PRINT "change octaves. Press Q to quit."
a$ = ""
DO UNTIL  a$ = "Q"
  SELECT CASE a$
    CASE "A","B","C","D","E","F","G",">","<",""
      PLAY a$
    CASE ELSE
      LOCATE 3,1: PRINT "I Can't play that!";
  END SELECT
  a$ = UCASE$(INPUT$(1))
  LOCATE 3,1: PRINT "                         ";
LOOP
END
```

Program 8-28. *An electronic piano*

Program 8-28 turns the computer into an electronic piano. While the program is running, you can play notes by typing any of the keys **A** through **G**, and holding their keys down for as long as you like. You can change the octave by typing > or < an appropriate number of times. To terminate the program, type **Q**.

Program 8-29 plays a few notes. Since the program does not specify an octave before the first **PLAY** statement, the first two notes—E and F sharp—will be from octave 4, which is the default octave. All of the remaining five notes (C, D flat, E, E, and F sharp) are from octave 1. The octave designation O1 continues to affect

```
REM Play 7 notes  [8-29]
PLAY "EF+"
PLAY "O1 CD-E"
PLAY "EF#"
END
```

Program 8-29. *Specifying pitch*

```
REM Scale of D Minor   [8-30]
PLAY "D E F G A B- O5 C+ D"
END
```

Program 8-30. *PLAY the scale of D minor*

future **PLAY** statements until you designate another octave. You could condense the three **PLAY** statements into the single statement **PLAY "EF+ O1 CD-EEF#"**. Program 8-30 plays the D-minor scale.

The **PLAY** statement can choose one of two execution modes. In the Music Foreground (MF) mode, whenever Turbo Basic encounters a **PLAY** statement during the running of a program, the computer plays the designated notes before the next statement of the program is executed. In the Music Background (MB) mode, the computer stores up to 32 notes in a buffer, and plays them while continuing to execute the program. You invoke these modes with the statements **PLAY "MF"** and **PLAY "MB"**. The default mode is Music Foreground. You can enlarge the music buffer with the metastatement **$SOUND**. The statement

$SOUND n

where *n* is a numeric constant from 0 to 4096, sets aside a portion of memory for the music buffer that can hold up to 4096 notes. (Turbo Basic counts the pause between successive notes as a note.)

When you run Program 8-31, the words appear as soon as the tune begins playing. If you replace the MB in the second line with MF, the words would not appear until the tune finished playing.

The standard musical notes are whole notes (1/1), half notes (1/2), quarter notes (1/4), eighth notes (1/8), sixteenth notes (1/16), thirty-second notes (1/32), and sixty-fourth notes (1/64). The computer not only can produce all of these lengths, but also can produce 1/*n*th notes for any *n* from 1 to 64.

```
REM Play beginning of Happy Birthday  [8-31]
CLS
PLAY "MB"
PLAY "CCDCFE"
PRINT "Happy Birthday to You"
END
```

Program 8-31. *Demonstration of Music Background mode*

When the number *n* follows one of the letters **A** to **G** in a **PLAY** statement, that note will have the length of a 1/*n*th note. For example, the statement

PLAY "C2 C1 C25"

results in the key of C (above middle C) being played three times — first as a half note, then as a whole note, and finally as a twenty-fifth note.

You can also specify lengths of notes by following the letter L with a number from 1 to 64, which ensures that (until you specify another length) all subsequent notes that do not carry their own trailing length designation will have that length. The specified length will affect even subsequent **PLAY** statements. If you do not specify a length before the computer **PLAY**s the first note, the computer will play notes as quarter notes until you specify otherwise. For example, the statement

PLAY "CC8 L16 CCC L1 CCC2"

results in the key of C being played eight times — first as a quarter note, then as an eighth note, three times as a sixteenth note, twice as a whole note, and finally once as a half note.

You can also use numeric variables in place of constants to specify lengths; however, the note or the letter **L** must be followed by both an equal sign and a string that gives the location of the vari-

Statement	Equivalent form using a variable
PLAY "C4"	a=4: PLAY "C =" + VARPTR$(a)
PLAY "L2 D"	length = 2: PLAY "L =" + VARPTR$(length) + "D"

Figure 8-30. *Using variables to specify lengths*

able in memory. The **VARPTR$** function determines this location. Figure 8-30 shows several **PLAY** statements and their equivalent forms that use a variable. You can use variables with the other **PLAY** command parameters in an analogous way. Program 8-32 uses the variable from a **FOR/NEXT** loop to play middle C in 64 different lengths.

Following the letter **P** with a number n from 1 to 64 produces a pause (or rest) of duration $1/n$. For instance, the statement

PLAY "C P2 C P16 C"

plays the key C three times, separated by half and sixteenth note pauses.

In standard musical notation, a small dot after a note or rest means it should last one and a half times its normal length. Fol-

```
REM Vary the lengths of notes
CLS
LOCATE 12,1
PRINT "This is a whole note."
PLAY "MF O3 C1"
FOR n = 2 TO 64
   LOCATE 12,11
   PRINT " 1 /"; n
   PLAY "L="+VARPTR$(n)+" O3 C"
NEXT n
END
```

Program 8-32. *Demonstrate the different lengths of notes*

Graphics and Sound

lowing a note or pause in a **PLAY** statement with a period produces the same effect. For instance, the statement

PLAY "C C. C8. C.. L15 P4. C2. C."

plays C six times with lengths 1/4, 3/8, 3/16, 9/16, 3/4, and 1/10. There is a pause of length 3/8 between the fourth and fifth notes.

In standard musical notation, a small dot over or under a note means that the note should be short and sharp, with a pause between each note and the next one. This is called *staccato*. A curved line over or under several notes means that they should be played smoothly with no pause between each note and the next. This is called *legato*. You can induce staccato and legato within **PLAY** statements by using the pairs of letters **MS** and **ML**. The pair **MN** refers to *normal music*. The pair of letters **MS** within a **PLAY** statement ensures that the computer plays all subsequent notes staccato until Turbo Basic encounters one of the pairs of letters **MN** and **ML**. Similar considerations apply to **ML**.

Program 8-33 plays the first part of the song "Happy Birthday" with staccato mode, then with normal mode, and finally with legato mode. Notice that, in the legato mode, the first two Cs blend into a single long note. Program 8-34 plays the beginning of the song "Frère Jacques" by using the length of notes that the user designates.

The speed or tempo of a composition is usually given in Italian. Some common tempos are shown in Table 8-9. In the **PLAY** statement, you can specify the tempo of a composition by following the

```
REM    Happy Birthday in three styles    [8-33]
b$ = "CCDCFE"
PLAY "MS" + b$
PLAY "MN" + b$
PLAY "ML" + b$
END
```

Program 8-33. *Staccato versus legato*

```
REM Play the beginning of Frère Jacques   [8-34]
CLS
INPUT "Length of notes (1-64)"; n
f$ = "CDEC"
PLAY "L =" + VARPTR$(n) + f$ + f$ + "EFGPEFG"
END
```

Program 8-34. *Demonstrate different lengths of notes*

letter **T** with a number *n* from 32 to 255, which ensures that Turbo Basic will play all subsequent notes at the speed of *n* quarter notes per minute until you specify another tempo. If you do not specify a tempo before the computer **PLAY**s the first note, the tempo will be 120 quarter notes per minute until you specify otherwise. For instance, the statement

PLAY "C T60 C"

plays C twice—first for 1/2 second and then for 1 second. Program 8-35 plays the scale of C major at each of the tempos in Table 8-9.

Tempo	Translation	Approximate number of quarter notes per minute
Largo	Very slow	50
Adagio	Slow	70
Andante	Slow and flowing	90
Moderato	Medium	110
Allegro	Fast	130
Vivace	Lively	150
Presto	Very fast	170

Table 8-9. *Music Tempos*

Graphics and Sound

```
REM Scale of C  [8-35]
CLS
PLAY "MF"
FOR n = 50 TO 170 STEP 20
  PRINT n; "quarter notes per minute"
  PLAY "T =" + VARPTR$(n) + "O3 CDEFGAB O4 C"
NEXT n
END
```

Program 8-35. *Demonstrate different tempos*

In this discussion, each of the 84 keys available to the **PLAY** statement has been identified by a combination of octave (0 to 6) and letter (**A** to **G** with possible + or −). These keys can also be identified by the letter N followed by one of the numbers from 1 to 84, as shown in Table 8-10.

Octave 0 Key Number	Octave 1 Key Number	Octave 2 Key Number	Octave 3 Key Number	Octave 4 Key Number	Octave 5 Key Number	Octave 6 Key Number
C 1	C 13	C 25	C 37	C 49	C 61	C 73
C+ 2	C+ 14	C+ 26	C+ 38	C+ 50	C+ 62	C+ 74
D 3	D 15	D 27	D 39	D 51	D 63	D 75
D+ 4	D+ 16	D+ 28	D+ 40	D+ 52	D+ 64	D+ 76
E 5	E 17	E 29	E 41	E 53	E 65	E 77
F 6	F 18	F 30	F 42	F 54	F 66	F 78
F+ 7	F+ 19	F+ 31	F+ 43	F+ 55	F+ 67	F+ 79
G 8	G 20	G 32	G 44	G 56	G 68	G 80
G+ 9	G+ 21	G+ 33	G+ 45	G+ 57	G+ 69	G+ 81
A 10	A 22	A 34	A 46	A 58	A 70	A 82
A+ 11	A+ 23	A+ 35	A+ 47	A+ 59	A+ 71	A+ 83
B 12	B 24	B 36	B 48	B 60	B 72	B 84

Table 8-10. *The Number Associated with Each Key*

```
REM Jingle Bells  [8-36]
CLS
PRINT "Jingle bells, Jingle bells"
PLAY "MF L8 N41 N41 L4 N41 L8 N41 N41 L4 N41"
PRINT "Jingle all the way"
PLAY "L8 N41 N44 N37. L16 N39 L4 N41 N0"
PRINT "Oh what fun it is to ride in a"
PLAY "L8 N42 N42 N42. L16 N42 L8 N42 N41 N41 L16 N41 N41"
PRINT "One horse open"
PLAY "L4 N44 N44 N42 N39"
PRINT "Sleigh"
PLAY "L1 N37"
END
```

Program 8-36. *PLAY a tune by numbers*

You use the combination **N0** to identify a pause. For instance, the statement

PLAY "N37 N0 N38"

plays middle C, a pause, and then C sharp. Program 8-36 uses numbers to identify keys.

Turbo Basic has another statement for producing tones. The statement

SOUND *f,d*

produces a sound of pitch *f* hertz with a duration of *d*∗0.055 seconds. Although the frequency can range from 37 to 32767 hertz, the human ear can hear only up to about 20000 hertz. You use the **SOUND** statement to create special effects, such as falling bombs, sirens, and clock ticks, as shown in Program 8-37.

```
REM Falling bomb, clock, and siren  [8-37]
CLS
'Bomb
PRINT "Falling Bomb"
FOR n=1000 TO 700 step -5
   SOUND n,1
NEXT n
FOR n=1 TO 700
   SOUND 50*RND+37,.0015
NEXT n
DELAY 1
'Clock
PRINT "Clock"
FOR n=1 TO 5
   SOUND 500,.01
   DELAY .4
   SOUND 2000,.01
   DELAY .4
NEXT n
DELAY 1
'Siren
PRINT "Siren"
FOR n=1 TO 5
   SOUND 1700,5
   SOUND 1000,5
NEXT n
END
```

Program 8-37. *Special effects using the SOUND statement*

9 A Closer Look at the Turbo Environment

The File Menu Commands

Until now, the selections used from Turbo Basic's main menu have been primarily **Edit**, **Compile**, and **Run**. This chapter discusses the five remaining main menu selections and their pull-down menus.

Pressing **F** from the main menu (or ALT-F from any of the other menus or from inside the Edit window) pulls down the File menu, which contains the following nine command options.

Load

The **Load** command copies a program from a disk into the computer's memory so that the program can be edited, compiled, or run.

The **Load** command exhibits an input box titled Load File Name that displays ***.BAS**. The asterisk is referred to as a *wild-card* character or a *global file name character*. The other wild-card character is the question mark. You use wild-card characters to represent classes of file names. A question mark in a file name indicates that any character can occupy that position. An asterisk in either part of the file name—the first eight positions or the extension—indicates that any character can occupy that position and all remaining positions in the part.

Pressing ENTER with *.**BAS** displayed produces a list of all programs on the disk that have the extension .BAS. You can then select the file name that you want to load by using the cursor-movement keys and ENTER. You can list other classes of files by typing other file names that contain wild-card characters.

Another way to load a specific file is to type the file name over *.**BAS**. If the file name has the standard extension of .BAS, you need not include the extension. (To specify a file whose name has no extension, include the period at the end of the file name.) If the file that you request is not present, Turbo Basic assumes that you want to work on a new program that you will later save in a file with this new name.

Pay attention to the following when you use **Load**:

- You can also use **Load** while editing by pressing F3.

- The first time that the file input box appears, it contains *.**BAS**. On subsequent appearances, it contains whatever string that you typed into the box during your last load command.

- If a recently edited program is in memory when you give the **Load** command, Turbo Basic gives you an opportunity to save the edited program before loading the newly specified file.

New

The **New** command clears any current program from the editor's memory, so that you can write a new program.

A Closer Look at the Turbo Environment 231

Turbo Basic gives the new program the default name NONAME.BAS. If you give the **New** command when a recently edited program is in memory, Turbo Basic offers you the opportunity to save this edited program before clearing the editor's memory.

Save

The **Save** command copies the program currently in memory onto a disk.

If the program in memory has not been named (that is, if its current name display is **NONAME.BAS** in the Edit window), Turbo Basic presents an input box titled Rename NONAME that allows you to give the file a meaningful name. If the file name ends with a period, then Turbo Basic will save it with no extension. If the file name does not have a period or an extension, Turbo Basic will automatically add the extension .BAS.

Note that you can also give the **SAVE** command from the Edit window by pressing F2.

Write to

The **Write to** command saves the program currently in memory in a disk file with a name other than the current program name.

If the requested name is the same as that of a file already on the disk, then Turbo Basic warns you and asks you whether it should overwrite the old file or cancel the **Write to** command. As with the **Save** command, Turbo Basic adds the extension .BAS to any file name that has no extension and no period. This command is equivalent to using the editor to mark the entire program as a block, and then writing the program to a disk with the Block Write command, which you invoke by pressing CTRL-KW.

Main File

The **Main File** command prompts you for the name of the disk file, or *main file*, with which Turbo Basic should begin compiling a program.

A **Main File** must be specified when the statements for a program have been placed in more than one file. Chapter 10 discusses in detail the method for splitting a program into several files and the concept of a main file.

Directory

The **Directory** command displays a list of all or a specified set of file names in any subdirectory.

A directory is a list of file names that are on a disk. With the introduction of hard disks, the subdirectory structure was developed to facilitate the tracking of large numbers of files. Essentially, in addition to holding file names, a directory can contain the names of other lists called subdirectories. When you first format a disk, it contains one directory called the *root directory*. You create subdirectories by using the DOS command **MD** *dirname* or the Turbo Basic command **MKDIR** *dirname*, where *dirname* is a string of up to eight characters. (The allowable characters for a subdirectory name are the same as those permitted for a file name.) You can place files, other subdirectories, or both in each of these subdirectories. A subdirectory is specified by using a string that consists of the sequence of successive subdirectories leading to it from the root directory. A backslash (\ ) precedes the sequence of subdirectories, called a *path*, and backslashes separate successive subdirectories. At any time, you can specify one subdirectory as the current subdirectory by using the DOS command **CD** *path* or the Turbo Basic command **CHDIR** *path*, where *path* is the path from the root directory to the selected subdirectory.

The current disk drive is the drive from which you invoked Turbo Basic. The **filespec** of a file on the current drive consists of the path that leads from the root directory to the subdirectory containing the file, followed by a backslash and the file name. For files not on the current drive, the letter of the drive and a colon must precede the path and file name.

The **Directory** command gives the names of selected files and subdirectories in the current subdirectory of the current disk. In the input box, you can either enter the name of a single file to find out if it is in the current subdirectory, or use wild-card characters to request selected names. The default entry, *.*, requests all of the items in the current subdirectory.

Change Dir

The **Change Dir** command alters the current drive, the current subdirectory, or both.

You may respond to the prompt by entering a new drive, path, or both. Unlike DOS's **CD** command, **Change Dir** allows you to change both the current drive and the current directory at once. Turbo Basic uses the current drive and directory for all of its default **Load**, **Save**, and **Directory** displays.

OS Shell

The **OS Shell** command allows you to execute DOS commands without quitting Turbo Basic.

After you give the **OS Shell** command, the DOS prompt appears and you can execute one or more DOS commands (such as **COPY**, **FORMAT**, and **ERASE**). Entering **EXIT** at the DOS prompt returns you to Turbo Basic with all of your work intact in memory.

Be careful: Do not return to Turbo Basic by typing **TB**. In addition, be certain that the boot disk containing COMMAND.COM is in the default drive.

Quit

The **Quit** command abandons Turbo Basic and returns to DOS.

This command has the same effect as pressing ALT-X from anywhere in Turbo Basic. If you give the **Quit** command when you have not saved the program in memory in its current form, **Quit** gives you the opportunity to do so before abandoning Turbo Basic.

The Options Menu Commands

Pressing **O** from the main menu (or ALT-O from any of the other menus or from inside the Edit window) pulls down the Options menu, which in turn presents the following eight command options.

Compile to

The **Compile to** command specifies the type of compiled program that the compiler will produce.

So far, all of the compiled programs produced in this book reside in memory and can be run only from within Turbo Basic. However, Turbo Basic can also compile to two other types of files—executable files and chain files. You can run executable files (referred to as .EXE files) directly from DOS without any help from Turbo Basic. Chain files reside on a disk with the extension .TBC and can be chained to by using an executable file or another chain file. Chapter 10 discusses chaining in detail.

The **Compile to** command produces a pop-up menu with the three choices **Memory file**, **EXE file**, and **Chain file**. The **Memory file** selection causes the compiler to create only a standard compiled program in memory. The other two selections produce the specified type of disk file, in addition to a memory file.

8087 required

The **8087 required** command toggles the **8087 required** status from OFF to ON, and vice versa.

Some computers have an 8087 math-coprocessor chip that can speed up number crunching. When the **8087 required** status is OFF, Turbo Basic checks to see whether or not an 8087 chip is present. If so, Turbo Basic utilizes it; if not, Turbo Basic emulates it. When the **8087 required** status is ON, the program will run only if the computer has an 8087 chip. Programs compiled with the ON status are shorter and more efficient than those compiled with the OFF status. The default status of **8087 required** is OFF.

Keyboard break

The **Keyboard break** command toggles the **Keyboard break** status from OFF to ON, and vice versa.

In order for CTRL-BREAK to cause the early termination of a program, the **Keyboard break** status must be ON. However, note that just having the **Keyboard break** status ON is not enough to guarantee that a program is stoppable. Pressing CTRL-BREAK can stop a program only at a point where the program either outputs text to the screen or printer or performs keyboard input. Figures 9-1 and 9-2 present unstoppable and stoppable program segments, respectively.

```
100 GOTO 100                        aLabel:
                                    GOTO aLabel
```

Figure 9-1. Program segments that cannot be terminated by pressing CTRL-BREAK

```
100 PRINT "";: GOTO 100          aLabel:
                                  PRINT "";: GOTO aLabel
```

Figure 9-2. *Program segments that can be terminated by pressing CTRL-BREAK*

Turbo Basic generates the most efficient compiled programs when the **Keyboard break** status is OFF. However, in this case, the only way to terminate a program prematurely is to restart the computer by pressing CTRL-ALT-DEL. Programs should be written and debugged with the **Keyboard break** status ON, and then compiled in their final form with the status OFF. The default status of **Keyboard break** is OFF.

Bounds

The **Bounds** command toggles the **Bounds checking** status from OFF to ON, and vice versa.

After dimensioning an array, the compiler checks to see that constants used as subscripts are in the proper range. However, the compiler does not check for the proper range when the subscript is given by a variable as in the program segment shown below:

```
DIM month$(1:12)
month = 13
month$(month)="Holiday"
```

However, Turbo Basic will catch such **subscript out of range** errors at run-time, as long as the **Bounds checking** status is ON. When these errors occur with the OFF status, the program is likely to perform incorrectly. The default status of **Bounds checking** is OFF.

Overflow

The **Overflow** command toggles the **Overflow checking** status from OFF to ON, and vice versa.

When **Overflow checking** is ON, Turbo Basic inserts extra code into the compiled program to check that values assigned to integer and long integer variables are not too large. If they are, such an error terminates the execution of the program and displays an **Overflow** run-time error message. With **Overflow checking** OFF, Turbo Basic generates more efficient compiled programs, but will ignore overflow assignments, which can lead to bizarre program operation. The default status of **Overflow checking** is OFF. Note that Turbo Basic always checks overflow for single-precision and double-precision numbers. Figure 9-3 shows the results of running a program both with and without overflow checking.

Stack test

The **Stack test** command toggles the **Stack test** status from OFF to ON, and vice versa.

```
REM "Overflow checking" ON          REM "Overflow checking" OFF
count% = 20000                      count% = 20000
count% = 2 * count%                 count% = 2 * count%
PRINT count%                        PRINT count%
END                                 END

Run                                 Run
Error 6 Overflow                    -25536
```

Figure 9-3. *Two different ways that integer overflow is handled*

Turbo Basic uses a fixed area, or stack, in memory, to hold special information needed when invoking procedures or functions. When **Stack test** is ON, Turbo Basic inserts extra code into the compiled program so that it can report a run-time **Out of memory** error when the stack lacks sufficient space to store new information. This type of error often occurs in programs that use recursive procedures and functions. If the **Stack test** option is ON and Turbo Basic displays **Out of Memory**, place a **$STACK** metastatement, such as **$STACK 2048**, in your program to request a larger stack.

With **Stack test** OFF, Turbo Basic generates more efficient compiled programs, but may end up placing new information on the stack by using memory that does not belong to the stack. Such "Stack overflow" errors will likely cause system hang-up or other catastrophic results. The default status of **Stack test** is OFF.

Parameter line

The **Parameter line** command prompts you to enter the value for the string that the function **COMMAND$** will return.

When you execute a standalone program from DOS, you can often pass parameters to the program by typing them immediately after the program name. (For instance, you can type the DOS command **TYPE** followed by a parameter that consists of the name of the file that you want to display on screen.) When you are debugging such a program in Turbo Basic, you use the **Parameter line** command to simulate the passing of parameters to the program. Chapter 10 discusses further the passing of parameters.

Metastatements

The **Metastatements** command produces a pop-up menu that allows you to specify the amounts of memory that will be allocated to the stack, the music buffer, and the communications buffers.

The stack holds information such as the location in the program that Turbo Basic should return to after a subroutine, function, or procedure call. The default stack size is 1024 bytes. The stack can be increased to as many as 32767 bytes.

When the computer generates music or sound in the **music background** mode, Turbo Basic stores the pitches and durations in the music buffer, and plays them as the program executes. The default buffer size is 32 notes, but you can reset the size to anywhere from 0 to 4096 notes. When music is played *legato* — with no pause between notes — this size gives the true maximum number of notes that the buffer can hold. If you play music in any other manner, you should count the pauses between notes as notes.

Turbo Basic first holds information passing to and from a serial communications port in a buffer before sending or receiving it. The two ports available in Turbo Basic are COM1 and COM2; each have a buffer with a default size of 256 bytes. You can specify a new size for the communications buffers by pressing **C** and then **1** for COM1 or **2** for COM2, and then giving a value from 0 to 32767 bytes.

The metastatements **$STACK**, **$SOUND**, **$COM1**, and **$COM2** can be used within a program to tell the compiler the amount of memory to allocate to the stack, the music buffer, the COM1 buffer, and the COM2 buffer, respectively.

The Setup Menu Commands

Pressing **S** from the main menu (or pressing ALT-S from any of the other menus or from inside the Edit window) pulls down the Setup menu, which presents the following five command options.

Colors

The **Color** command generates a series of pop-up menus that can be used to custom-color windows, menus, and system boxes. Figures 9-4, 9-5, and 9-6 show the different parts of the windows, menus, and system boxes, respectively, that can be custom-colored.

240 Using Turbo Basic

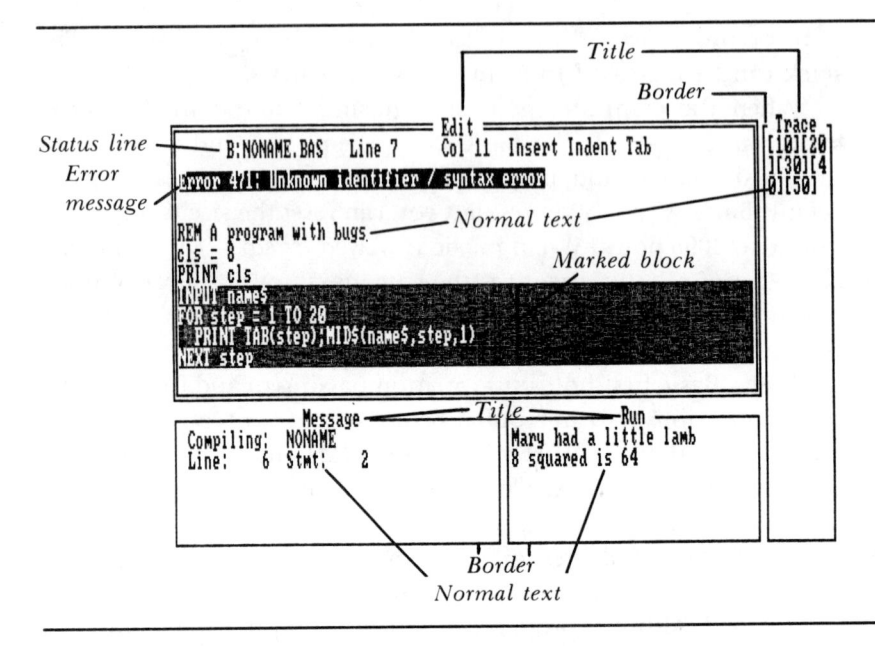

Figure 9-4. *Windows*

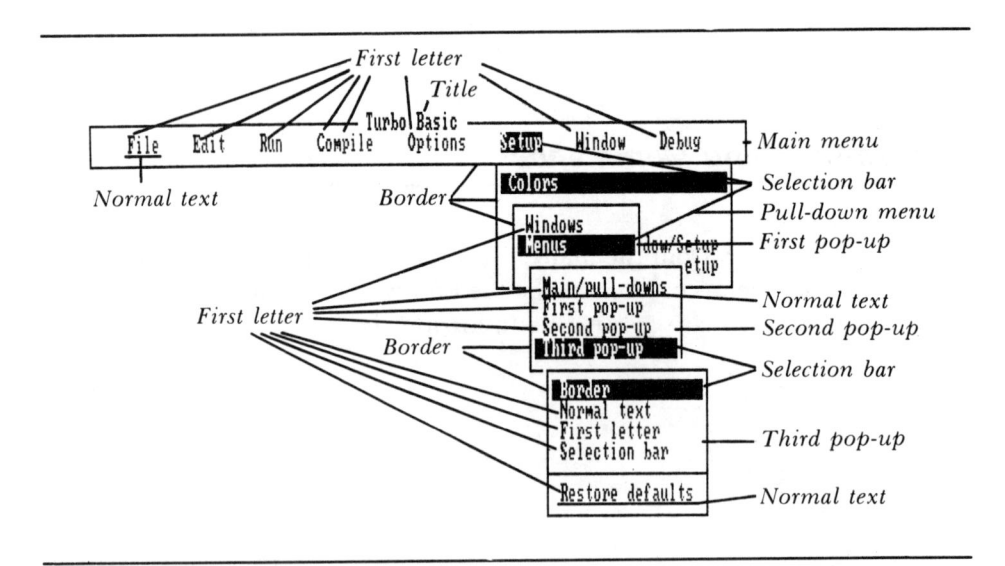

Figure 9-5. *Menus*

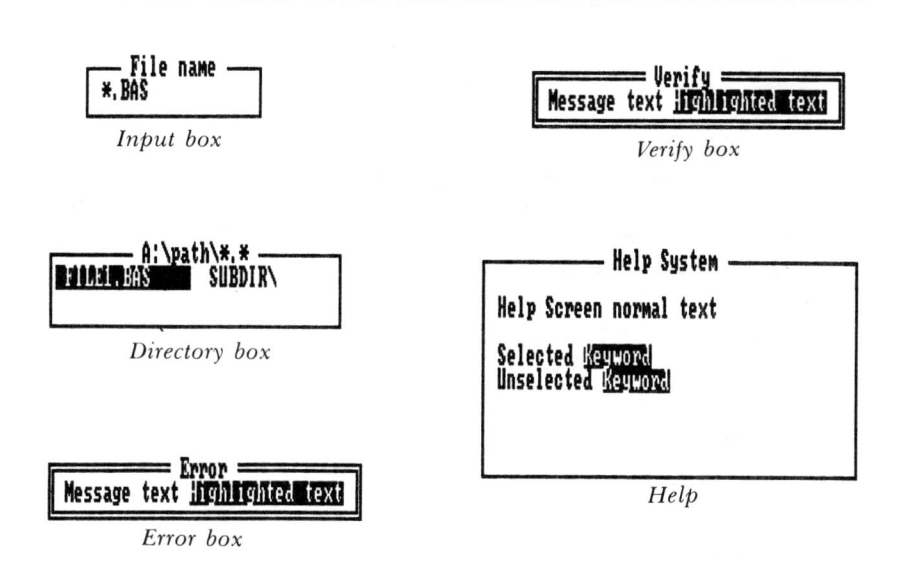

```
        ┌─ File name ─┐              ═══ Verify ═══
        │ *.BAS       │              │Message text highlighted text│
        └─────────────┘              
           Input box                       Verify box


       ┌── A:\path\*.* ──┐         ┌──── Help System ────┐
       │ FILE1.BAS  SUBDIR\│       │ Help Screen normal text │
       └─────────────────┘         │                     │
          Directory box            │ Selected keyword    │
                                   │ Unselected keyword  │
                                   │                     │
                                   └─────────────────────┘
                                            Help

       ══ Error ══
       │Message text highlighted text│
          Error box


   F1-Help F2-Save F3-New F5-Zoom F6-Next F7-Beg Blk F8-End Blk SCROLL-Size/move
                              Status line
```

Figure 9-6. *System boxes*

Figure 9-7 shows the choices presented in the Windows pop-up menu. **Normal text** is the text that appears as you write your program in the editor, the text produced by INPUT and PRINT when a program is run, or the text that appears within the message and trace windows. **Marked block** refers to text that has been marked in the editor with F7, F8, CTRL-KB, CTRL-KK, or CTRL-KT. **Status line** refers to the informational text in the top line of the edit window. **Error message** refers to text displayed at the top of the edit window when a compile-time or run-time error is detected.

Figure 9-8 shows the choices presented in the Menus pop-up menu. **Main/pull-downs** refers to the main menu and the five pull-down menus File, Options, Setup, Window, and Debug. **Normal**

Using Turbo Basic

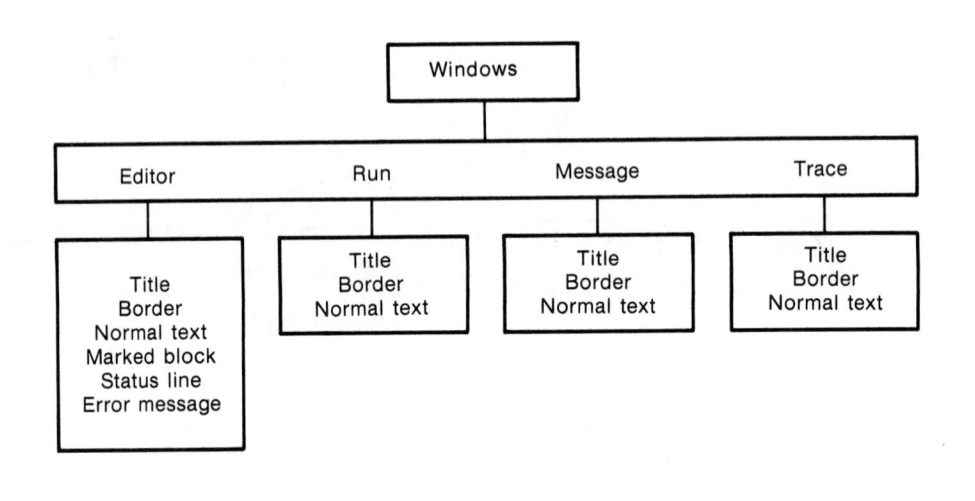

```
                        ┌─────────┐
                        │ Windows │
                        └────┬────┘
    ┌──────────┬────────────┼──────────────┬──────────┐
  Editor      Run         Message        Trace
    │          │             │              │
┌─────────┐ ┌─────────┐  ┌─────────┐   ┌─────────┐
│ Title   │ │ Title   │  │ Title   │   │ Title   │
│ Border  │ │ Border  │  │ Border  │   │ Border  │
│ Normal  │ │ Normal  │  │ Normal  │   │ Normal  │
│  text   │ │  text   │  │  text   │   │  text   │
│ Marked  │ └─────────┘  └─────────┘   └─────────┘
│  block  │
│ Status  │
│  line   │
│ Error   │
│ message │
└─────────┘
```

Figure 9-7. *The second and third pop-up menus for coloring Windows*

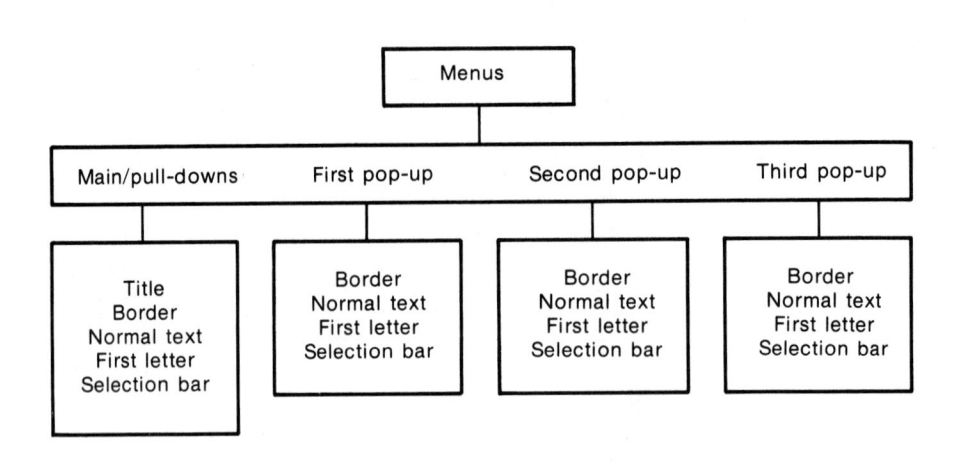

```
                              ┌───────┐
                              │ Menus │
                              └───┬───┘
      ┌────────────────┬──────────┼──────────────┬──────────────┐
  Main/pull-downs  First pop-up  Second pop-up  Third pop-up
        │              │              │              │
  ┌──────────┐   ┌──────────┐   ┌──────────┐   ┌──────────┐
  │ Title    │   │ Border   │   │ Border   │   │ Border   │
  │ Border   │   │ Normal   │   │ Normal   │   │ Normal   │
  │ Normal   │   │  text    │   │  text    │   │  text    │
  │  text    │   │ First    │   │ First    │   │ First    │
  │ First    │   │  letter  │   │  letter  │   │  letter  │
  │  letter  │   │Selection │   │Selection │   │Selection │
  │Selection │   │   bar    │   │   bar    │   │   bar    │
  │   bar    │   └──────────┘   └──────────┘   └──────────┘
  └──────────┘
```

Figure 9-8. *The second and third pop-up menus for coloring Menus*

A Closer Look at the Turbo Environment 243

```
System boxes
    ├── Input box
    │       Title
    │       Border
    │       Normal text
    │
    ├── Directory box
    │       Title
    │       Border
    │       Normal text
    │       Highlighted text
    │
    ├── Error box
    │       Title
    │       Border
    │       Normal text
    │       Highlighted text
    │
    ├── Verify box
    │       Title
    │       Border
    │       Normal text
    │       Highlighted text
    │
    ├── Help
    │       Title
    │       Border
    │       Normal text
    │       Keywords
    │       Selected keyword
    │
    └── Status line
            Normal text
            Highlighted text
            Lock keys
```

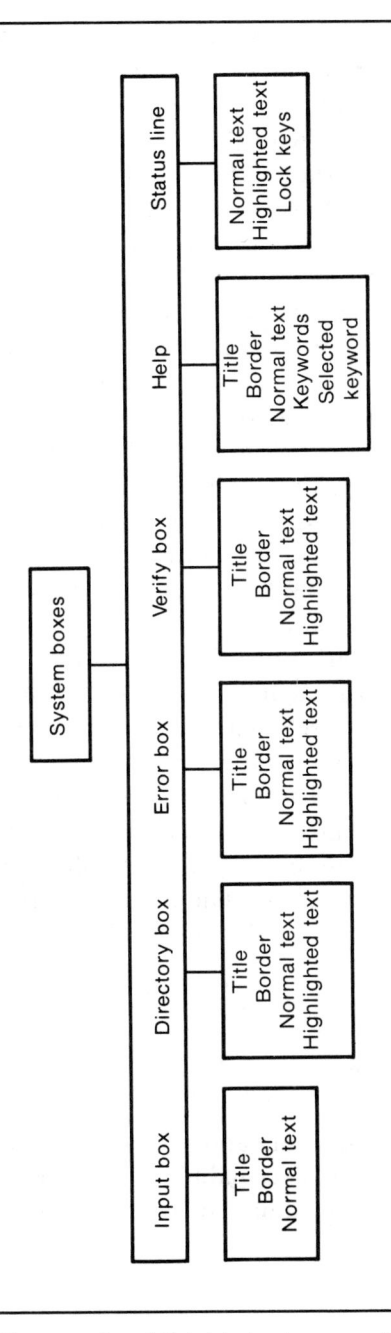

Figure 9-9. *The second and third pop-up menus for coloring System boxes*

text is the text of a command name in a menu, except for the first letter. **First letter** refers to the first letter in a command name. The **Selection bar** is the highlighted rectangle that can be moved up or down in a menu with the cursor-movement keys.

Figure 9-9 shows the choices presented in the System boxes pop-up menu. **Normal text** refers to the text that you type into a box or the general descriptive text in a help screen. **Status line** refers to the help line across the bottom of the screen. **Input box** refers to the box that appears when input, such as a file name, is needed. **Directory box** refers to the box showing the directory for choosing a file. **Error box** refers to the general error reporting box. **Verify box** refers to the box that appears when Turbo Basic requests a yes or no response; for example, to inquire about saving a modified program before quitting. **Keywords** refers to those words in a help description for which additional help is available. The **Selected keyword** is the keyword for which additional information can be displayed by pressing the ENTER key. **Lock keys** refers to the indication of Caps Lock, Num Lock, and Scroll Lock that appears in the help line.

After an item is specified in the third pop-up menu, an array of 8-by-16 foreground/background combinations is displayed. A sample of the item selected changes color as the cursor control keys move a small box around the array. Pressing the ENTER key selects the foreground/background combination specified by the box. Pressing ESC cancels color selection, leaving the display as it was. A considerable number of different color combinations are available with a color monitor. The number of possibilities is much more limited with a monochrome display.

Directories

The **Directories** command produces a pop-up menu that is used to specify Include, Executable, and Turbo directories where Turbo Basic places and looks for certain special types of files. A drive, path, or both identifies each directory. As a default, these directories are set to the directory from which you invoked Turbo Basic.

Turbo Basic looks in the Include directories for files named in **$INCLUDE** metastatements. When you specify more than one Include directory, you must separate successive directories by using a semicolon.

Turbo Basic places in the Executable directory all .EXE and Chain files that the compiler creates. You may specify only one directory.

Turbo Basic looks for the files normally present on the program disk, such as configuration files (that have the extension .TB) and the help file TBHELP.HLP, in the Turbo directory. Specifying a Turbo directory is particularly important when you use a DOS path statement to allow Turbo Basic to be invoked from any directory on a hard disk.

Miscellaneous

The **Miscellaneous** command produces a pop-up menu that allows you to specify whether or not Turbo Basic should save certain programs on disk.

The **Auto save edit** command toggles the **Auto save edit** status from OFF to ON, and vice versa. When **Auto save edit** is ON, Turbo Basic automatically saves the program in memory to disk as soon as you give the **Run** command. This feature protects you from losing a program during a system hangup or an unbreakable infinite loop in the program.

The **Backup source files** command toggles the **Backup source files** status from OFF to ON, and vice versa. With **Backup source files** ON, each time you save a revised version of a program with the same name as the original version of the program, Turbo Basic does not erase the original program, but rather changes its extension to .BAK.

Load Options/Window/Setup

The **Load Options/Window/Setup** command allows you to load a configuration file that sets custom-designed window layouts, color assignments, and specific Options and Setup values.

Normally, Turbo Basic automatically loads the configuration file TBCONFIG.TB when invoked from DOS. However, in the event that you have created other configuration files with the **Save Options/Window/Setup** command discussed next, you can type the name of one of these files into the input box and use it to reset the configuration values.

Save Options/Window/Setup

The **Save Options/Window/Setup** command allows you to create a configuration file (with extension .TB) to save the current window layout, color assignments, and all of the current Options and Setup.

You can create different configuration files to serve several needs. If you give the name TBCONFIG.TB to a configuration file created with this command, Turbo Basic will use it to specify the configuration values whenever you invoke Turbo Basic from DOS.

The Window Menu Commands

Pressing **W** from the main menu (or pressing ALT-W from any of the other menus or from inside the Edit window) pulls down the Window menu, which presents the following seven command options.

Open

The **Open** command produces a pop-up menu from which you can choose one of the four windows to open and be made the active window.

At any time, Turbo Basic encloses one of the four windows in a double border. This window is called the **active window**. The **Open** command makes the newly appointed active window reappear if you "closed" it, and brings it to the top if the windows are overlapping. Note that Turbo Basic automatically reopens a closed window whenever you write information to the window.

Close

The **Close** command makes the active window invisible.

When executed, the command brings into view any other windows or parts of windows that were hidden beneath the active window. The command preserves the contents of closed windows. The "Next" open window, if any, becomes the active window. A closed window is automatically reopened and made active whenever Turbo Basic needs to write information to the window. The **Tile** and **Stack** commands described later ignore closed windows.

Next

Next changes the active window to the next open window.

Turbo Basic considers the windows to be in the order Edit-Trace-Run-Message and then back to Edit again.

The **Next** command has the same effect as the pressing of F6 when the Help Line displays the key's meaning as **Next**.

Goto

The **Goto** command causes Turbo Basic to leave the Window menu and go to the active window.

When the Edit window is active, the effect of **Goto** is the same as pressing **E** from the main menu. When the Run, Trace, or Message window is active, there is no reason to use the **Goto** command.

Tile

The **Tile** command causes Turbo Basic to allot an equal, nonoverlapping portion of the screen to each open window.

For example, if the Trace and Message windows are closed when you give the **Tile** command, it allocates the top half of the screen (excluding the main menu) to the Edit window and the bottom half of the screen (excluding the Help Line) to the Run window. A window that is closed when you give a **Tile** command but subsequently opened will have the size and position that it had at the time that you closed it.

Stack

The **Stack** command causes Turbo Basic to stack the open windows, one on top of the other.

Turbo Basic always displays the active window on top of the stack. Only a piece of the border of each open but nonactive window is visible. A window that is closed when you give a Stack command but is subsequently opened will continue to have the size and position that it had at the time that you closed it.

Zoom

The **Zoom** command zooms the active window in or out when the active window is the Edit or Run window.

The Debug Menu Commands

Pressing **D** from the main menu (or pressing ALT-D from any of the other menus or from inside the Edit window) pulls down the Debug menu, which presents the following two command options.

Trace

The **Trace** command shows the current status of the Trace toggle.
   The **Trace** command toggles the Trace status from OFF to ON, and vice versa. When **Trace** is ON and you run a program, Turbo Basic displays in the Trace window all line numbers and labels in the program as they are encountered during the program's execution.

Run-time error

You use the **Run-time error** command to find errors that occur when Turbo Basic executes .EXE or Chain files.
   A program counter is a four-digit hexadecimal number that identifies a location in a compiled program. The command

requests the program counter (abbreviated *pgm-ctr*) that Turbo Basic reports when a run-time error occurs in a standalone program. Turbo Basic then recompiles the program and uses the program counter to determine the line in which the run-time error occurred.

Adjusting Windows with SCROLL LOCK

In the default screen layout, the Edit window occupies nearly half of the screen, and the Run, Trace, and Message windows almost equally divide the remaining space. This default layout is easily modified to suit individual tastes. You can adjust the size and location of windows so that each fills as little or as much of the screen as desired. When two or more windows are displayed so that they overlap, the active window (the window with a double-line border) will always be visible on top of the other windows.

To adjust the location and size of the active window, press SCROLL LOCK. The help line at the bottom of the screen will then display the highlighted word **Scroll**, and indicate that you may use the cursor-movement keys to move the active window around the screen. If you press SHIFT for a second or two, the help line will indicate that you can use the cursor-movement keys with SHIFT to enlarge or shrink the active window. Pressing SCROLL LOCK again exits the window-moving and window-sizing modes. You can save the new window layout in a configuration file by using the **Save Options/Window/Setup** command in the Setup menu, and restore the layout at any time with the **Load Options/Window/Setup** command.

10 Compiler Directives and System-Level Tools

Directives

Directives are instructions that influence the compilation process. They are essential when the program being developed is too large to fit in memory, or when the program makes excessive demands on certain specialized parts of memory. However, you also can use directives to make compiled programs more efficient and your programming job easier.

A program written with the Turbo Basic editor is referred to as *source code*. When source code for a program is compiled, the compiler converts the source code to *object code*. The object code of a program is the version that the computer executes. There are three different types of object code: *standard memory-resident object code, standalone code,* and *Chain code.* Standard memory-resident object code can only be run from inside Turbo Basic, while standalone code is executed directly from DOS, and Chain code is executed from standalone programs. You determine the type of code that the compiler produces by making a selection from the Options pull-down menu.

Standalone Programs

Standalone Turbo Basic programs reside on a disk and have the extension .EXE (EXEcutable file). The compiler creates them when you select **Compile to EXE file** from the Options pull-down menu. This selection is made by going to the main menu, pressing O to obtain the Options pull-down menu, pressing C to access the **Compile to** command, and finally pressing E to choose .EXE file.

When you give the **Compile** command with the **Compile to EXE file** directive, Turbo Basic will create two compilations of the source code currently in memory—a standard memory-resident compiled program and an .EXE disk file. The computer will execute the standard memory-resident compiled program if you give the **RUN** command. You can execute the standalone .EXE file only by entering its name from DOS.

The .EXE file will be about 28K larger than the memory-resident compiled code because .EXE files contain not only a compilation of the statements in the source code, but also a piece of code known as the *nucleus* of the .EXE file. The nucleus contains all of the details needed to carry out certain operations, such as displaying data on screen and accepting input from the keyboard.

Using Command-Line Information

Many standalone programs, including most DOS routines, allow or require the user to type in additional information after the program name when invoking the program. Some examples of these routines are the DOS command **ERASE**, which must be followed by the name of a file, and the DOS command **COPY**, which can be followed by two pieces of information. The DOS command **FORMAT** can be executed alone or followed by information that gives the disk to be formatted and certain specifications for the formatting process. In each case, the information following the command is called the *command-line parameter.*

The function **COMMAND$** provides the ability to create standalone Turbo Basic programs that process command-line information. The value of the function **COMMAND$** is the string that consists of the command-line parameter that the user types when the program is executed. (Turbo Basic ignores spaces preceding the parameter.)

For example, if you invoke a program with a command line of the form

PROGRAMNAME *item1 item2 ... itemN*

then the value of the function **COMMAND$** is the string

"item1 item2 ... itemN"

This string can contain up to 127 characters. Program 10-1 looks for an optional command-line parameter that consists of a single item of information.

```
REM Greet the user   [10-1]
REM This program will be compiled as "GREETING.EXE"
IF COMMAND$ <> "" THEN
    nom$ = COMMAND$
  ELSE
    INPUT "What is your name"; nom$
END IF
PRINT "Hello "; nom$
END

C> GREETING.EXE Gabriel
Hello Gabriel

C> GREETING.EXE
What is your name? Gabriel
Hello Gabriel
```

Program 10-1. *A standalone program with command-line information*

During the developmental stage of writing and debugging a program, you execute the program from inside Turbo Basic by using the **Run** command; thus, you do not have a command-line parameter to serve as a value for **COMMAND$**. Turbo Basic provides for this circumstance with the **Parameter line** command in the Options pull-down menu. This command produces an input box with the title "Command line parameter" into which you may type the parameter. Turbo Basic will then use this string during runtime as the value of **COMMAND$**.

Before Program 10-2 was executed in Turbo Basic, the user typed the information **Gabriel 1980** into the Command line parameter input box. The program chopped the string into two items of information by using **INSTR** to locate the space, and the functions **LEFT$** and **MID$** to capture the characters to the left and right of the space. The program then converted the string that contained the year of birth to a number by using the **VAL** function.

Chain Programs

A standalone program created with Turbo Basic can pass control to another program. The program being chained to must reside on a disk and have been compiled as either a .TBC (Turbo Basic Chain)

```
REM Find age at turn of century   [10-2]
'Locate first space in the string
spaceLoc = INSTR(COMMAND$," ")
nom$ = LEFT$(COMMAND$,spaceLoc-1)
yearOfBirth = VAL(MID$(COMMAND$,spaceLoc+1))
PRINT "In the year 2000, "; nom$; _
" will be"; 2000 - yearOfBirth
END

Run
In the year 2000, Gabriel will be 20
```

Program 10-2. *Using the* **Parameter line command** *to specify a trailer*

Compiler Directives and System-Level Tools **255**

file or an .EXE file. The compiler creates .TBC files when you select **Compile to Chain file** from the Options pull-down menu. You make this selection by going to the main menu, pressing O to obtain the Options pull-down menu, pressing C to access the **Compile to** command, and finally pressing C to choose **Chain file**.

.TBC files can chain to other .TBC (or .EXE) files, and so on. There is no limit to the number of levels of chaining. The first program must be an .EXE file since .TBC files do not have the nucleus code that the .EXE file supplies.

The **CHAIN** statement invokes chaining. When Turbo Basic encounters

CHAIN *filespec*

it stops execution of the current program (as if it encountered an **END** statement) and executes the specified program.

Turbo Basic standalone programs must have the extension .EXE. Programs being chained to may also have this extension, but to emphasize their role as chained-to programs, Turbo Basic usually gives them the extension .TBC. For this reason, if you give *filespec* with no extension, then Turbo Basic assumes the extension .TBC.

When one program chains to another, the computer deletes all of the variables from the first program. However, Turbo Basic allows you to pass the values of specified variables to variables of the same type in the second program. If the statement

COMMON *var1, var2,...varn*

appears in the first program and the statement

COMMON *newVar1, newVar2,...newVarn*

appears in the second program—where *var1* has the same type as *newVar1*, *var2* has the same type as *newVar2*, and so on—then the value of *var1* will be passed to *newVar1*, the value of *var2* will be passed to *newVar2*, and so on. The actual names of the new variables are not important. The only important consideration is that the new variables match the variables of the first **COMMON** statement in number, type, and order. Although you can place **COMMON** statements, like **DATA** statements, almost anywhere in a program, errors in matching the variables between the two programs are easier to avoid if each program has only one **COMMON** statement or if all of a program's **COMMON** statements are together. While it is usually best to place **DATA** statements at the end of the main program, it is best to place **COMMON** statements at the beginning.

Procedures and functions that you define in one program will not be available to a chained-to program. Also, when executing the **CHAIN** command, the computer closes all files opened in the original program before the chaining occurs.

As an example of chaining, consider Programs 10-3 through 10-5. Program 10-3 obtains some standard information from the user, and then invokes one of the other two programs, as appropriate. Suppose that Program 10-3 has been compiled as an .EXE file and that the other two programs have been compiled as Chain files.

```
REM An EXE program named HELLO.EXE    [10-3]
COMMON firstName$,lastName$,gender$
INPUT "What is your year of birth"; year%
INPUT "What is your first name"; firstName$
INPUT "What is your last name"; lastName$
INPUT "Are you male or female (M/F)"; gender$
gender$ = UCASE$(gender$)
IF year% > 1970 THEN
      CHAIN "YOUTH.TBC"       'See Program 10-4
   ELSE
      CHAIN "ADULT.TBC"       'See Program 10-5
END IF
END

C> HELLO.EXE
What is your year of birth? 1980
What is your first name? Gabriel
What is your last name? Schneider
Are you male or female (M/F)? M
Greetings Gabriel
```

Program 10-3. *An .EXE program that chains to another program*

Compiler Directives and System-Level Tools

```
REM A Chain program named YOUTH.TBC   [10-4]
COMMON first$,last$,sex$
'greet youth using first name only
PRINT "Greetings " + first$
END
```

Program 10-4. *A chain program that is chained to by Program 10-3*

```
REM A Chain program named ADULT.TBC   [10-5]
COMMON f$, l$, g$
'Greet adult using title and last name
IF g$="F" THEN title$="Ms. " ELSE title$="Mr. "
PRINT "Greetings "; title$; l$
END
```

Program 10-5. *Another chain program that is chained to by Program 10-3*

Although Program 10-4 only needs to have the first name passed and Program 10-5 only needs to have the last name and gender passed, each of the **COMMON** statements must involve all three variables so that each paired set of **COMMON** statements will match.

Tracing Run-time Errors in Standalone Programs

If an error occurs while a standalone program is running, Turbo Basic cannot transfer to the Turbo Basic editor at the point of the error since Turbo Basic is not running. However, the standalone program will issue an error message of the form

Error *errnum* at pgm-ctr: *pcnum*

which you can use later from within Turbo Basic to find the point of the error.

The error number, *errnum*, can be used to look up an explanation of the error in Appendix E of the *Turbo Basic Owner's Handbook*. In addition, you can use the program-counter number, *pcnum*, to locate the point in the program at which the run-time error occurred. To do this, note the program-counter number, invoke Turbo Basic, and **LOAD** the source (.BAS) version of the program. Then, from the main menu, press D to see the Debug pull-down menu, press R to obtain the Run-time error input box, and enter the program-counter number. Turbo Basic will then recompile the source code, invoke the editor, and place the cursor at the location of the error. If an error occurs in a program that an .EXE program chained to, then the cursor will appear at the **CHAIN** statement in the first program.

Special Instructions for the Compiler: Metastatements

The task of the compiler is to translate a Turbo Basic program into a form that the computer's microprocessor can understand directly. You can control certain aspects of how the compiler translates by placing *metastatements* within a program. Each metastatement must appear on a line by itself, and begin with a dollar sign ($) so that the compiler can spot it and treat it as a *compiler directive*, rather than a statement to be translated. This section discusses the 13 metastatements understood by the Turbo Basic compiler in detail and presents an explanation of named constants.

Named Constants

A *named constant* is a name given to an integer constant. A percent character (%) must precede this name, which can consist of any letter followed by any number of letters and digits. The statement *namedConstant* = *integer constant*

assigns the *integer constant* to the *namedConstant*. After such a statement, you may use *namedConstant* anywhere that you would use the *integer constant*. Two examples of this statement are **%year = 1987** and **%pop1980 = 32000**. The assignment statement is not a **LET** statement. (Actually, the statement **LET %year = 1987** produces the message **Error 424: Variable expected**.) This statement differs from a **LET** statement in two ways. First, the value on the right must be a whole number. (The assignment statement will not round a noninteger to the nearest integer, but instead will produce the message **Error 425: Integer constant expected**.) Second, a particular named constant cannot appear on the left side of two different assignment statements. (Using the statements **%year = 1987** and **%year = 1988** in the same program produces the message **Error 459: Duplicate named constant**.)

Some of Turbo Basic's metastatements require the use of an integer value. Often, integer constants are all that is needed. However, for some metastatements—$IF particularly—you should use a named constant in place of a given integer constant. Since integer variables are not permitted in metastatements, named constants play a role in metastatements similar to the role that integer variables play in conventional statements.

To Compile or Not to Compile: $IF, $ELSE, and $ENDIF

Turbo Basic provides a simple mechanism that allows designated sections of a program to be either skipped or processed by the compiler. When the compiler encounters a block of the form

$IF *namedConstant*
  statement(s)
$ENDIF

the compiler processes *statement(s)* as part of the program whenever *namedConstant* is not zero, or skips over *statement(s)* as if they were **REM**arks whenever *namedConstant* is zero. The metastatements $IF and $ENDIF are said to allow the *conditional compilation* of sections of a program. *Note:* There is no space between $END and IF in $ENDIF.

Conditional compilation is a useful debugging aid. Often, you insert **PRINT** statements in a program to check the values of certain variables during the debugging process. Once you write and debug the program completely, you no longer need these **PRINT** statements and should not compile them with the rest of the program. You have at least three options for handling these unwanted **PRINT** statements: you can delete them, convert them to **REM** statements, or conditionally compile them with $IF. The disadvantage of deleting these statements or changing them to **REM**s is that any future need for debugging will require you to retype each deleted statement or change back each new **REM** statement, which are potentially tedious steps. However, you can reinstate statements that you used the $IF metastatement to conditionally exclude from compilation by simply changing the value of a named constant in one statement at the beginning of the program.

Program 10-6 is a segment that contains two **PRINT** statements used for debugging. Since the second line of the program segment assigns the value **0** to the named constant **%debug**, the compiler will skip the two debugging **PRINT** statements as if the program segment had been written as shown in the segment of Program 10-7. If you changed the second line of Program 10-6 so that it

```
REM A demonstration program    [10-6]
%debug = 0              'Set to 1 for debugging
CALL GetAge(age%)
$IF %debug
   PRINT "After calling GetAge, age% is"; age%
$ENDIF
CALL GetCommand(action$)
$IF %debug
   PRINT "After calling GetCommand, action$ is "; action$
$ENDIF
```

Program 10-6. *An illustration of the $IF metastatement*

```
REM A demonstration program    [10-7]
CALL GetAge(age%)
CALL GetCommand(action$)
```

Program 10-7. *An equivalent of Program 10-6*

assigned any nonzero value to **%debug**—for example, **%debug = 1**—then the compiler would press the debugging **PRINT** statements as if the program segment had been written as shown in the segment of Program 10-8.

A variation of the **$IF** metastatement selects one of two blocks of statements for compilation. When the compiler encounters

```
$IF namedConstant
    block1 statement(s)
 $ELSE
    block2 statement(s)
$ENDIF
```

the compiler processes either *block1 statement(s)* or *block2 statement(s)*, but not both. When *namedConstant* is zero, the compiler processes *block2 statement(s)*. All other values for *namedConstant* cause the compiler to process *block1 statement(s)*.

Program 10-9 uses **$IF** and **$ELSE** metastatements to place two versions of a program in the same source file. If you set the named constant **%CtoF** to **1** prior to compilation, the resulting program

```
REM A demonstration program    [10-8]
CALL GetAge(age%)
PRINT "After calling GetAge, age% is";age%
CALL GetCommand(action$)
PRINT "After calling GetCommand, action$ is "; action$
```

Program 10-8. *An equivalent of Program 10-6 with %debug=1*

```
REM Convert between temperature scales    [10-9]
%CtoF=0  'set to 1 for a program to convert celsius to Fahrenheit
         'set to 0 for a program to convert Fahrenheit to celsius
$IF %CtoF
  INPUT "What is the temperature in degrees celsius"; celsius
  PRINT "The corresponding temperature in degrees Fahrenheit is ";
  PRINT USING "###.#"; celsius*9/5 + 32
$ELSE
  INPUT "What is the temperature in degrees Fahrenheit";Fahrenheit
  PRINT "The corresponding temperature in degrees celsius is ";
  PRINT USING "###.#"; (Fahrenheit-32)*5/9c
$ENDIF
END
```

Program 10-9. *An illustration of $IF...$ELSE*

will request temperatures in degrees Celsius and convert them to degrees Fahrenheit. You can create a program to do the opposite conversion by setting **%CtoF** to **0** before compilation.

Event Trapping: $EVENT

Turbo Basic provides a number of statements that permit you to interrupt regular program execution at any point and execute a special subroutine when an *event* occurs. Executing a statement of the form

ON *eventName* GOSUB *label*

specifies that the subroutine that begins at *label* should be executed whenever the event that corresponds to *eventname* is *trapped*. Turbo Basic will trap an event if it occurs after a statement of the form

eventName ON

Compiler Directives and System-Level Tools

Event causing program interruption	Trap defining statement
Arrival of a character at a serial port *n*	ON COM(*n*) GOSUB *label*
Pressing of function key *n*	ON KEY(*n*) GOSUB *label*
Activation of the light pen	ON PEN GOSUB *label*
Note count in music buffer dropping below *n*	ON PLAY(*n*) GOSUB *label*
Pressing of joystick button *n*	ON STRIG(*n*) GOSUB *label*
Elapsed time reaching *n* seconds	ON TIMER(*n*) GOSUB *label*
Occurrence of a run-time error	ON ERROR GOTO *label*

Table 10-1. *Trappable Events*

has been executed. Table 10-1 lists each event that you can trap in this way, with the statement that specifies the subroutine to be executed whenever the event is trapped. You can terminate trapping of a given event by using a statement of the form

eventName OFF

or you can suspend trapping by a statement of the form

eventName STOP

If an event occurs while trapping is **OFF**, the event is forgotten about. However, if an event occurs while trapping is **STOP**ped, Turbo Basic remembers that the event occurred and executes a **GOSUB** as soon as event trapping is turned **ON** again.

Turbo Basic traps the last event described in Table 10-1 — the occurrence of a run-time error — as soon as the **ON ERROR** statement is executed; there is no such thing as **ERROR ON**. To turn run-time error trapping off requires the use of the statement **ON ERROR GOTO 0**. Note that run-time error trapping can only **GOTO** a set of error-handling statements; Turbo Basic does not allow **GOSUB**ing to a subroutine. Placing a **RESUME** statement at the end of the error-handling statements passes control back to the statement in which the error occurred.

If a program contains any event-trapping statements, the compiler places event-checking code between every pair of statements of the program. This process can result in a great deal of excess code in portions of the program that do not need to do trapping. The metastatement

$EVENT OFF

tells the compiler not to place the extra code between statements until the point in the program that contains the metastatement

$EVENT ON

The **$EVENT** metastatements are different than the conventional statements *eventName* **ON** and *eventName* **OFF**. The metastatements eliminate *all* event-checking code. The conventional statements have no effect on code produced by the compiler, but only suppress the checking that is done between statements.

Importing Machine-Language Programs into Turbo Basic Programs: $INLINE

Turbo Basic provides a general but powerful means of incorporating machine-language subroutines created outside of Turbo Basic into Turbo Basic programs. If *filespec* specifies a file that contains a machine-language subroutine, then the statements

```
SUB procName INLINE
    $INLINE filespec
END SUB
```

cause the compiler to read the machine-language code from *filespec* as is, and place the code within the compiled Turbo Basic program.

You can then execute the machine-language code by making a **CALL** of the procedure *procName*.

Instead of specifying the name of a file that contains machine-language code, you may use the **$INLINE** metastatement to give a list of values explicitly that constitute a machine-language subroutine. For example, Program 10-10 contains an **$INLINE** procedure definition that has the same effect as pressing SHIFT-PRTSC.

Machine-language subroutines must follow certain guidelines when used in **$INLINE** procedures. First, the subroutines must preserve the values in the DS, BP, SS, and SP registers. You can do this by pushing the values on the stack at the beginning of the subroutine, and then popping the values back off the stack and into the appropriate registers at the end of the subroutine. Second, the subroutines cannot have any return instructions. You should use an instruction to jump to an assembly language label at the end of the routine in order to terminate a subroutine early.

Controlling Stack and Buffer Sizes: $COM1, $COM2, $SOUND, and $STACK

The metastatements **$COM1**, **$COM2**, **$SOUND**, and **$STACK** alter the size of special sections of memory that are set aside for specific purposes. The most important of these metastatements is **$STACK**,

```
REM Print the contents of the screen    [10-10]
CALL PrintScreen
END

SUB PrintScreen INLINE
   $INLINE &HCD
   $INLINE &H05
END SUB
```

Program 10-10. *Calling a machine-language routine*

which controls the amount of memory reserved for Turbo Basic's stack. Turbo Basic uses the stack extensively whenever a program invokes procedures or functions, particularly if you use recursion. The stack holds the values or addresses of variables being passed to procedures and functions, and contains an indication of where the program should continue executing after a procedure, function, or subroutine concludes. By default, Turbo Basic allocates 1024 bytes for the stack. You can increase this size by placing a metastatement of the form

$STACK *stackSize*

at any point in the program, where *stackSize* is any whole-number constant in the range of 1024 to 32768. The current stack size is shown in the Message window after **Stack:**.

The metastatements **$COM1** and **$COM2** specify the size of the communications buffers of the two ports COM1 and COM2. The metastatement **$SOUND** specifies the size of the music buffer that the **PLAY** and **SOUND** statements use in music-background mode. The default size of all of these buffers is 256 bytes.

Controlling Array-Memory Allocation: $DYNAMIC and $STATIC

Turbo Basic has two allocation methods for setting aside memory for an array—*static allocation* and *dynamic allocation*. When you use static allocation for an array, the compiler reserves a specific portion of memory exclusively for that array. Regardless of where the **DIM** statement for the array occurs in the program, the memory allocated to the array is never available for any other purpose. When you use dynamic allocation for an array, the compiler does not reserve a portion of memory for the array. Instead, Turbo Basic grabs memory for the array from the pool of free memory (if available) when encountering the **DIM** statement during the execution of the program. When you no longer need a dynamically allocated array, you can release its memory to the free pool by using an **ERASE** statement.

Table 10-2 gives the conditions under which Turbo Basic predefines the memory allocation for an array. When none of these conditions apply to the dimensioning of an array, then the type of memory allocation will be the *default allocation type,* which the metastatements **$DYNAMIC** and **$STATIC** control. Initially, the default-allocation type is static. When the compiler encounters the metastatement **$DYNAMIC**, it changes the default allocation type to dynamic. Then, until Turbo Basic encounters a **$STATIC** metastatement, all arrays not meeting one of the conditions in Table 10-2 will be allocated dynamically.

Managing the Development of Large Programs: $INCLUDE

Eventually, when creating Turbo Basic programs, you will find yourself faced with one or both of the following situations:

- You want to use sections of an old program within the program that you are currently creating.

Condition	Allocation
Array is dimensioned using variables or expressions to specify subscript range	Dynamic
DIM statement for array includes the keyword DYNAMIC	Dynamic
Array is declared LOCAL to a procedure or function	Dynamic
Array is dimensioned two or more times, not counting the dimensionings for LOCAL and STATIC declarations	Dynamic
DIM statement for array includes the keyword STATIC (Constants must be used to specify the subscript range or an error occurs)	Static
Array is declared STATIC to a procedure or function (Constants must be used to specify the subscript range or an error occurs)	Static

Table 10-2. *Rules for Array-Memory Allocation*

■ The program that you are creating is very large and the Turbo Basic editor reports that it has run out of space; you cannot enter any new text.

You can resolve both of these problems by using the metastatement **$INCLUDE**. When the compiler encounters a metastatement of the form

$INCLUDE *filespec*

where the specified file *filespec* contains Turbo Basic source code, then the compiler inserts those lines into the program at the location of the **$INCLUDE** statement. Although you may use any file name extension desired for the specified file, this text always uses the extension .INC for files that will be **$INCLUDE**d into programs. *Note:* A variable cannot be used for **filespec**.

When the compiler encounters an **$INCLUDE** metastatement, it suspends processing the current program file and instead processes the statements in the specified file. After compiling all statements in *filespec,* the compiler resumes processing statements in the original program file by starting with the first statement after the **$INCLUDE** metastatement.

Program 10-11 contains a **$INCLUDE** metastatement that specifies the source code in the segment of Program 10-12. Compiling Program 10-11 is equivalent to compiling Program 10-13.

```
REM Display the current date in the form
REM "month name, day, year"   [10-11]
month = VAL(LEFT$(DATE$,2))
day = VAL(MID$(DATE$,4,2))
year = VAL(RIGHT$(DATE$,4))
$INCLUDE "MONTHS.INC"
PRINT USING "& ##_, ####"; month$(month),day,year
END
```

Program 10-11. *Using the $INCLUDE metastatement*

Compiler Directives and System-Level Tools

```
REM These statements are contained in the file MONTHS.INC [10-12]
DIM month$(1:12)
FOR index = 1 TO 12
   READ month$(index)
NEXT index
DATA January, February, March, April, May, June,
     July, August, September, October, November, December
```

Program 10-12. *The include file for Program 10-11*

```
REM Display the current date in the form
REM "month name, day, year"   [10-13]
month = VAL(LEFT$(DATE$,2))
day = VAL(MID$(DATE$,4,2))
year = VAL(RIGHT$(DATE$,4))
DIM month$(1:12)
FOR index = 1 TO 12
   READ month$(index)
NEXT index
DATA January, February, March, April, May, June,
     July, August, September, October, November, December
PRINT USING "& ##_, ####"; month$(month),day,year
END
```

Program 10-13. *A program equivalent of Program 10-11*

A solution to the problem of handling a program that is too large for Turbo Basic's editor memory is to do the following: save one or more blocks of statements from the original program in disk files, and then shorten the original program file by replacing each block with an appropriate **$INCLUDE** metastatement. Program 10-14 carries out this technique to an extreme. Each .INC file in Program 10-14 must be small enough to be loaded and edited by the editor, but no prior limit exists for the combined size of the files.

Even when the size of the program is not an issue, **$INCLUDE** statements serve a valuable purpose. Since good programming

```
REM A program that carries $INCLUDE to an extreme   [10-14]
$INCLUDE "PART1.INC"
$INCLUDE "PART2.INC"
$INCLUDE "PART3.INC"
$INCLUDE "PART4.INC"
$INCLUDE "PART5.INC"
END
```

Program 10-14. *A program that consists entirely of $INCLUDE metastatements*

practice dictates that the main body of a program be kept to a maximum of 50 lines, a major portion of most programs consists of procedure definitions and function definitions. Rather than having these definitions clutter up the main-program file, it is quite natural to group related procedure definitions and function definitions together, and place them in separate disk files that you then **$INCLUDE** into the main program.

Important procedures and functions (in particular, those that do not use SHARED variables) are often useful in more than one programming situation. If you keep commonly used procedures and functions in separate disk files, then all that you need to do to use these procedures or functions in later programs is to place the appropriate **$INCLUDE** metastatements at the beginnings of the program.

A good organizational device is to create one or more special directories to hold .INC files, with each of these *Include directories* holding related files. Often, a collection of related .INC files is referred to as a *library* of include files. Normally, Turbo Basic looks in the default directory—that is, the directory from which you invoked Turbo Basic—for all files to be processed. Therefore, you must make Turbo Basic aware of the Include directories that contain the files needed by the program. You can do this from the Directories pop-up menu of the Setup pull-down menu. The command **Include directories:** produces an input box called "Include directory" into which you should type all of the needed directories. When you specify more than one directory, you must use semicolons to separate successive directory names. The input box will hold up to 67 characters. Once you specify the Include directories, Turbo Basic not only will look in its default directory for a file specified in a **$INCLUDE** metastatement, but also will look through each of the Include directories.

The Main File

Whenever you divide the statements constituting a program into more than one file, it becomes necessary to speak in terms of the *main file* and the **$INCLUDE** files. Each program has exactly one main file, but may have zero, one, or many **$INCLUDE** files. The main file is the file with which the compiler must start the processing of the program. The main file is also the place that usually contains the main body of the program. The **$INCLUDE** files generally consist of groups of related procedure and function definitions.

The program currently in memory is called the *work file*. At certain times during the writing of a program, the main file will be the work file but, at other times, one of the **$INCLUDE** files will be the work file. Normally, compilation begins with the current work file. You can override this choice by using the **Main file** command of the Files pull-down menu to specify a main file. The command **Main file** produces an input box with the title "Main file," into which you should type the name of the main file. After you designate a main file, compilation will always begin with the main file, no matter what file is the current work file.

Breaking a Large Program into Segments: $SEGMENT

Although breaking a program down into manageable (and editable) pieces through the use of **$INCLUDE** files solves the problem of editing a large program, a second size-related problem may develop at compile-time. Even though the source code for a program is split into many small pieces, the compiled form of the program will be a single and potentially very large piece.

A *segment* of memory is a block of 64K consecutive memory locations. Medium-sized programs compiled to memory or compiled as Chain files usually fit into a single segment of memory. However, large-sized or medium-sized programs compiled as .EXE files may require more than 64K of memory. If so, attempts to compile them are unsuccessful and produce the error message **Segment exceeds 64K**. In some versions of BASIC that would be the end of the story: You would have to rewrite the program to make it smaller. However, Turbo Basic permits a program to grow until its compiled code fills available memory. This is possible because Turbo Basic can use as many as 16 different memory segments for the machine code of a program. Turbo Basic displays the number of bytes used in the various segments by using hexadecimal notation, separated by slashes, in the Message window after **Code:**.

Although Turbo Basic can use as many as 16 segments when compiling a program, it does not automatically start a new segment when the current segment becomes full. Instead, Turbo Basic requires you as the programmer to place a **$SEGMENT** metastatement in the program to indicate the point at which the compiler should begin using a new memory segment to hold the machine-language code. The reason for requiring this is that you can make a judicious choice that can help a program run faster. To understand how to make a judicious choice, you only need to realize that program execution is slowed down whenever execution must move from one segment to another. Thus, for example, it is best to group together in a single segment those functions and procedures that are used together and invoke each other. Note that you cannot place the metastatement **$SEGMENT** inside a procedure definition or function definition.

11 Mathematical and Scientific Programming

Predefined Mathematical Functions

Chapter 4 discussed the predefined arithmetic functions **ABS**, **CEIL**, **FIX**, **INT**, and **SGN**. This chapter explores the predefined square-root function (**SQR**), trigonometric functions (**ATN**, **COS**, **SIN**, and **TAN**), exponential functions (**EXP**, **EXP2**, and **EXP10**), and logarithmic functions (**LOG**, **LOG2**, and **LOG10**). For each of these new functions, the chapter gives its definition and some applications.

The Square-root Function

For any nonnegative number x, the value of

SQR(*x*)

is the nonnegative number whose square is x. For example, **SQR(25)** is 5 and **SQR(1)** is 1.

Quadratic Formula   The roots of the quadratic equation $ax^2 + bx + c = 0$ are $(-b + \textbf{SQR}(b\wedge 2 - 4*a*c))/2*a$.

Hypotenuse of a Right Triangle   The length of the hypotenuse of a right triangle that has sides of lengths a and b is **SQR**$(a*a + b*b)$.

Trigonometric Functions

A circle of radius 1 is called a *unit circle*. The circumference of a unit circle is 2*pi, where pi is approximately 3.141592653589793. Figure 11-1 shows a unit circle with an angle having one leg along the positive side of the X-axis. You can measure angles either in degrees or in radians. When you measure in radians, the size of the angle is the length of the arc of the unit circle that the angle *subtends* (or sweeps out). For example, since a right angle subtends one-quarter of the unit circle, a right angle consists of (2*pi)/4, or pi/2 radians. Another way to obtain the radian measure of an angle is to multiply the number of degrees of the angle by pi/180. For example, since a right angle has 90 degrees, its radian measure is 90*(pi/180), or pi/2.

Each of the trigonometric functions assigns a number to an angle. Consider an angle of r radians that is placed in the unit circle like the one in Figure 11-1, and that intersects the circle at the point P. The value of **COS**(r) is the first coordinate of the point P and the value of **SIN**(r) is the second coordinate of P. The value of **TAN**(r) is **SIN**$(r)/$**COS**(r). These three functions are called the *sine*, *cosine*, and *tangent* functions. If x is any number, then the value of **ATN**(x) is an angle (in radians) whose tangent is x. You can make a good approximation of the transcendental number pi by using 4*ATN(1).

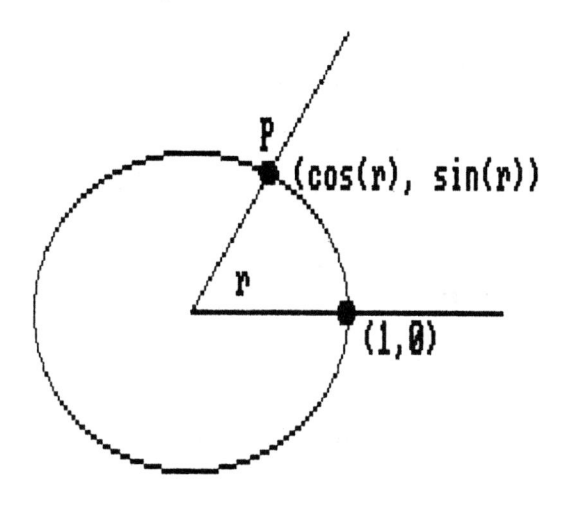

Figure 11-1. *An angle drawn in a unit circle*

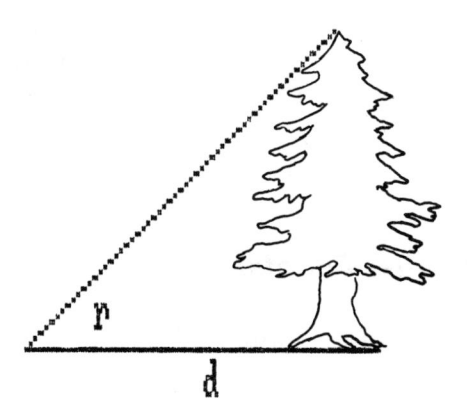

Figure 11-2. *Finding the height of a tree*

Surveying The height of the tree shown in Figure 11-2 is $d*\mathbf{TAN}(r)$.

```
REM Predict tap water temperature in Dallas   [11-1]
INPUT "Day of the year (1-365)";day%
pi = 4*ATN(1)
PRINT USING "The tap water temperature will be ### degrees"; _
  59 + 14*COS((day%-208)*pi/183)
END

Run
Day of the year (1-365)? 180
The tap water temperature will be  71 degrees
```

Program 11-1. *An example using the cosine and arctangent functions*

Periodic Phenomena The trigonometric functions can help to model certain cyclical natural occurrences. For example, the temperature of the tap water in Dallas, Texas, on the nth day of the year is approximately $59 + 14*COS((n-208)*pi/183)$. Program 11-1 uses this formula.

Projectile Motion If you hit a golf ball at an angle of r radians with the ground at a speed of s feet per second, then the distance that the ball travels is $s\wedge2*COS(r)*SIN(r)/16$. (Note: This formula assumes minimum wind resistance.) Program 11-2 employs a respectable speed of 170 feet per second in this formula to give the driving range for a pro golfer.

Exponential Functions

Any function of the form

b^x

is called an *exponential function*. The number b is called the *base* and the number x is called the *exponent*. There are three bases that occur so frequently in applications that Turbo Basic has defined

Mathematical and Scientific Programming

```
REM Give horizontal distance traveled by a golf ball   [11-2]
REM starting off with a speed of 170 feet per second
PRINT "At what angle (in degrees) with respect to the ground"
INPUT "was the golf ball hit (0-90)";degrees
pi = 4*ATN(1)
radians = degrees*pi/180
PRINT "A ball starting off at a speed of 170 feet per second"
PRINT "at an angle of"; degrees; "degrees will travel a distance"
PRINT USING "of ### feet";170^2*COS(radians)*SIN(radians)/16
END

Run
At what angle (in degrees) with respect to the ground
was the golf ball hit (0-90)? 45
A ball starting off at a speed of 170 feet per second
at an angle of 45 degrees will travel a distance
of 903 feet
```

Program 11-2. *Using trigonometric functions with angles given in degrees*

functions to evaluate the power of these bases. These bases are 2, 10, and e, where e is approximately 2.718281828459045. (The number e is similar to the number pi. You cannot write its exact value completely, but you can approximate it to any degree of accuracy.) The three functions are defined in Table 11-1.

Radioactive Decay Radioactive elements are unstable and disintegrate over time. The half-life of a specific radioactive element is the time required for one-half of the initial amount of the element to disintegrate. For example, the half-life of uranium 238 is 4.5×10^9

Function	Meaning	Example
EXP2(x)	2^x	EXP2(3) is 8
EXP10(x)	10^x	EXP10(3) is 1000
EXP(x)	e^x	EXP(3) is 20.0855369232

Table 11-1. *The Exponential Functions*

```
REM Show the effect of radioactive decay [11-3]
PRINT "Elapsed time (in days) since starting"
INPUT "with 100 grams of each material"; days
PRINT USING "###.## grams of Uranium 238 now remain";_
    FNRemaining(days,100,365*4.5E+9)
PRINT USING "###.## grams of Strontium 90 now remain";_
    FNRemaining(days,100,365*28)
PRINT USING "###.## grams of Iodine 131 now remain";_
    FNRemaining(days,100,8)
END

DEF FNRemaining(t,amount,halflife) = amount*EXP2(-t/halflife)

Run
Elapsed time (in days) since starting
with 100 grams of each material? 100
100.00 grams of Uranium 238 now remain
 99.32 grams of Strontium 90 now remain
  0.02 grams of Iodine 131 now remain
```

Program 11-3. *Applications of EXP2*

years, the half-life of strontium 90 is 28 years, and the half-life of iodine 131 is 8 days. If you begin with A units of a radioactive substance with half-life H, the amount that remains after t units of time is $A*\mathbf{EXP2}(-t/H)$. Program 11-3 shows how much of various radioactive elements will be left after a given number of days if originally there are 100 grams of each element.

Normal Curve The normal curve of statistics is used to estimate the likelihood of a measurement appearing in a certain range. For a population with mean m and standard distribution s, the normal curve is the graph of the function $(1/(s*\mathbf{SQR}(2*\mathbf{pi})))*\mathbf{EXP}(-.5*((x-m)/s)\wedge 2)$. For normally distributed measurements, the percentage of the measurements that lie between the values a and b is the area under the normal curve from $x=a$ to $x=b$. Given the mean and standard deviation of a population, Program 11-4 does a numeric integration of the area under the normal curve to estimate the probability that an event occurs within a given range of values.

```
REM  Find the area of a region under a normal curve  [11-4]
INPUT "Mean and standard deviation of data"; mean, sd
INPUT "Range of data over which to compute probability";xLow,xHigh
pi = 4*ATN(1)
sum = 0
FOR index = xLow TO xHigh STEP sd/100
   sum = sum + FNNormalCurve(index)
NEXT index
PRINT "The probability of an event occurring in the given range is"
PRINT USING "approximately ###.## percent or  1 in #####";_
   sum*sd, 100/(sum*sd)
END

DEF FNNormalCurve(x)
   SHARED mean, sd, pi
   FNNormalCurve = (1/(sd*SQR(2*pi)))*EXP(-.5*((x-mean)/sd)^2)
END DEF

Run
Mean and standard deviation of data? 80,10
Range of data over which to compute probability? 95,100
The probability of an event occurring in the given range is
    4.50 percent or  1 in    22
```

Program 11-4. *Application of EXP to probability*

Continuous Interest Most banks pay interest that is compounded either quarterly, monthly, or daily. However, many banks compound their interest continuously. If you deposit P dollars in a bank that pays interest rate r compounded continuously, then the balance in the account after t years is **P*EXP**($r*t$). For example, if you deposit 1000 dollars at 5% interest compounded continuously, then the balance after t years is **1000*EXP(.05*t)**. Program 11-5 further illustrates the use of **EXP** in continuous interest problems.

Quality Control Suppose that you have a large quantity of light bulbs and that the average lifetime of a light bulb is a hours. Then the percentage of light bulbs still remaining after t hours is approximately **EXP**($-t/a$). Program 11-6 shows how many light

```
REM  Calculate the balance in a savings account    [11-5]
INPUT "Amount originally deposited"; amount
INPUT "Annual rate of continuously compounded interest"; interest
INPUT "Number of years that have elapsed"; years
'Compensate for interest that was given as a percent
IF interest > 1 THEN interest = interest/100
PRINT USING "The current balance is $$##,###.##";_
   amount*EXP(interest*years)
END

Run
Amount originally deposited? 2000
Annual rate of continuously compounded interest? 8
Number of years that have elapsed? 20
The current balance is    $9,906.06
```

Program 11-5. *Application of EXP to continuous interest*

```
REM How many bulbs will remain?    [11-6]
INPUT "Average lifetime (in hours) of a light bulb"; avgLife
PRINT "Starting with 100 light bulbs, you can expect to have"
FOR index = avgLife/2 TO 3*avgLife STEP avgLife/2
   PRINT USING "## left after ##### hours";_
       FNLeft(index,avgLife),index
NEXT index
END

DEF FNLeft(t,avgL) = 100*EXP(-t/avgL)

Run
Average lifetime (in hours) of a light bulb? 5000
Starting with 100 light bulbs, you can expect to have
61 left after   2500 hours
37 left after   5000 hours
22 left after   7500 hours
14 left after  10000 hours
 8 left after  12500 hours
 5 left after  15000 hours
```

Program 11-6. *Application of EXP to quality control*

bulbs out of 100 you can expect to shine after various multiples of the average lifetime.

Logarithmic Functions

There is a logarithmic function that corresponds to each exponential function. For any base b,

$\log_b(x)$

is the power to which b must be raised to get x. Turbo Basic has defined logarithmic functions for the bases 2, 10, and e, which are written as **LOG2**, **LOG10**, and **LOG**, respectively. Several values of the logarithmic functions are shown here:

LOG2(8) is 3   LOG10(100) is 2   LOG(e) is 1
LOG2(.5) is -1 LOG10 (.1) is -5 LOG(1) is 0

Continuous Interest An investment at interest rate r compounded continuously will increase n-fold in **LOG**(n)/r years. For instance, an investment that earns 8% interest compounded continuously will triple in **LOG(3)/.08**, or 13.7326536084, years.

Measures of Sound Intensity and loudness are two quantities that are used to describe sound. Intensity, denoted by I, roughly measures the energy per unit area that is associated with the sound. There is a minimum intensity I_o that is audible. The value of I_o has been determined approximately by experiment and was standardized by international agreement to be 10^{-16} watts per square centimeter. The loudness of a sound of intensity I is said to be **10*LOG10(I/I_o)** decibels.

Binary Search The amount of time required to search an ordered array of n items is proportional to **LOG2**(n). For example, since **LOG2(256)** is 8 and **LOG2(1024)** is 10, you need only 20% more time to search a list of 1024 items than you need to search a list of 256 items.

Evaluating a Sorting Algorithm The amount of time required to sort a list of n items by a slow algorithm, such as the bubble sort, is proportional to n^2. The time required by a fast sort, such as the Shell sort, is proportional to $\text{LOG2}(n)*n$. Since $\text{LOG2}(n)$ grows much more slowly than n does while n increases, the Shell sort becomes more efficient than the bubble sort as n grows larger.

Techniques for Graphing Functions

No program is guaranteed to produce a good graph for every conceivable function. No matter how carefully a program is written, a clever mathematician can devise a function that the program cannot do justice to. The main program presented in this section incorporates safeguards against several of the idiosyncrasies that you commonly encounter when graphing functions, and will produce an adequate graph for many types of functions.

Program 11-7 is a no-frills function-graphing program. You specify the *domain* (the interval on the X-axis over which the program will graph the function) and the *range* (the smallest and largest Y-coordinates of points that will appear on screen). Then the program gives the appropriate **WINDOW** statement, draws the coordinate axes, and then draws 640 points on the graph.

Program 11-7 has the following shortcomings:

1. The X-axes, Y-axes, or both might not appear on screen. For example, this will occur if either **xLow** or **yLow** is a positive number.

2. You might not be able to provide good values for **yLow** and **yHigh**. In the most extreme case, making a poor choice can result in a completely blank screen.

3. There might be certain points in the domain at which the function is undefined (such as **x**=0 for the function **1/x**), or has a value that is too large and causes an overflow (such as **x**=2000 for the

```
REM Sketch the graph of a function    [11-7]
DEF FNF(x) = 1/x
'Request the domain of the function
INPUT "Graphing should begin with x = ", startGraph
INPUT "Graphing should  end  with x = ", endGraph
'Request the range of function values to appear on the screen
INPUT "What is the lower bound"; yMin
INPUT "What is the upper bound"; yMax
'Initialize the screen
SCREEN 2
WINDOW (startGraph,yMin) - (endGraph,yMax)
LINE (startGraph,0) - (endGraph,0)       'Draw x-axis
LINE (0,yMin) - (0,yMax)                 'Draw y-axis
'Draw the graph
increment = (endGraph-startGraph)/639
FOR x = startGraph TO endGraph STEP increment
   y = FNF(x)
   PSET (x,y)
NEXT x
END
```

Program 11-7. *A rudimentary graphing program*

function **EXP(x)**). Either of these situations will terminate the program and may lock up the system.

4. If the graph increases rapidly, two successive points might be far apart on screen with a substantial gap between them.

Program 11-8 is a sophisticated function-graphing program that corrects the four shortcomings of Program 11-7 in the following ways:

1. To guarantee that the Y-axis appears on screen, the **WINDOW** statement in Program 11-8 uses **startGraph** and **endGraph** to set the horizontal limits only when **startGraph** is negative and **endGraph** is positive. In all other cases, the program replaces one of these values with a number that guarantees that the horizontal limits will have different signs. For example, if both of the values are positive, the program uses **−endGraph/20** for the lower limit. This step guarantees that about 5% of the visible X-axis will consist of negative values. The program applies similar considerations to **yLow** and **yHigh**.

```
REM Draw the graph of a function     [11-8]
%false = 0: %true = -1
DEFDBL a-z
ON ERROR GOTO skipOverflow
CALL Initialize(startGraph,endGraph,yLow,yHigh)
CALL DrawGraph(startGraph,endGraph,yLow,yHigh)
END

skipOverflow:
  drawLine% = %false
  overflow% = %true
  RESUME continue

DEF FNF(x)
  SHARED drawLine%, overflow%
  overflow% = %false
  FNF = (x/300)*(x*x-45)*(x*x-10)        'Define function here
  continue:
END DEF

SUB Initialize(startGraph,endGraph,yLow,yHigh)
  LOCAL xLow, xHigh
  SCREEN 2
  INPUT "Graphing should begin with x = ", startGraph
  INPUT "Graphing should  end  with x = ", endGraph
  IF startGraph < 0 AND endGraph > 0 THEN
      xLow = startGraph: xHigh = endGraph
    ELSEIF startGraph >= 0 THEN
      xLow = -endGraph/20: xHigh = endGraph
    ELSEIF endGraph <= 0 THEN
      xLow = startGraph: xHigh = -startGraph/20
  END IF
  CALL FindyRange(startGraph,endGraph,yLow,yHigh)
  WINDOW (xLow,yLow) - (xHigh,yHigh)
  LINE (xLow,0) - (xHigh,0)      'Draw x-axis
  LINE (0,yLow) - (0,yHigh)      'Draw y-axis
END SUB

SUB FindyRange(startGraph,endGraph,yMin,yMax)
  SHARED overflow%
  LOCAL answer$, increment, drawLine%, x, y
  PRINT "Do you wish to give lower and upper bounds ";
  PRINT "for the graph (Y/N)"
  PRINT "     (IF not, the minimum and maximum value"
  PRINT "     of the function on the given interval "
  PRINT "     will be computed and used.)"
  PRINT
  answer$ = UCASE$(INPUT$(1))
  IF answer$ = "Y" THEN
      INPUT "What is the lower bound"; yMin
      INPUT "What is the upper bound"; yMax
```

Program 11-8. *A generic curve sketching program (output shown in Figure 11-3)*

```
      ELSE
        PRINT "Please standby ..."
        increment = (endGraph-startGraph)/639
        yMin = 1E+38
        yMax = -1E+38
        FOR x = startGraph to endGraph STEP increment
          y = FNF(x)
          IF NOT overflow% THEN
            IF y < yMin THEN yMin = y
            IF y > yMax THEN yMax = y
          END IF
        NEXT x
      END IF
      IF yMin >= 0 THEN
          yMin = -yMax/20
        ELSEIF yMax <= 0 THEN
          yMax = -yMin/20
      END IF
      CLS
END SUB

SUB DrawGraph(startGraph,endGraph,yLow,yHigh)
   SHARED drawLine%, overflow%
   LOCAL increment, x, y
   drawLine% = %false
   increment = (endGraph-startGraph)/639
   FOR x = startGraph TO endGraph STEP increment
     y = FNF(x)
     IF NOT overflow% THEN
        IF drawLine% THEN
           LINE - (x,y)
         ELSE
           PSET (x,y)
           drawLine% = %true
        END IF
        IF y<yLow OR y>yHigh THEN drawLine% = %false
     END IF
   NEXT x
END SUB

Run
Graphing should begin with x = -7
Graphing should  end   with x = 7
Do you wish to give lower and upper bounds for the graph (Y/N)"
     (IF not, the minimum and maximum value
      of the function on the given interval
      will be computed and used.)"

User pressed N
Please standby ...
(graph is shown in Figure 11-3)
```

Program 11-8. *A generic curve sketching program (output shown in Figure 11-3) (continued)*

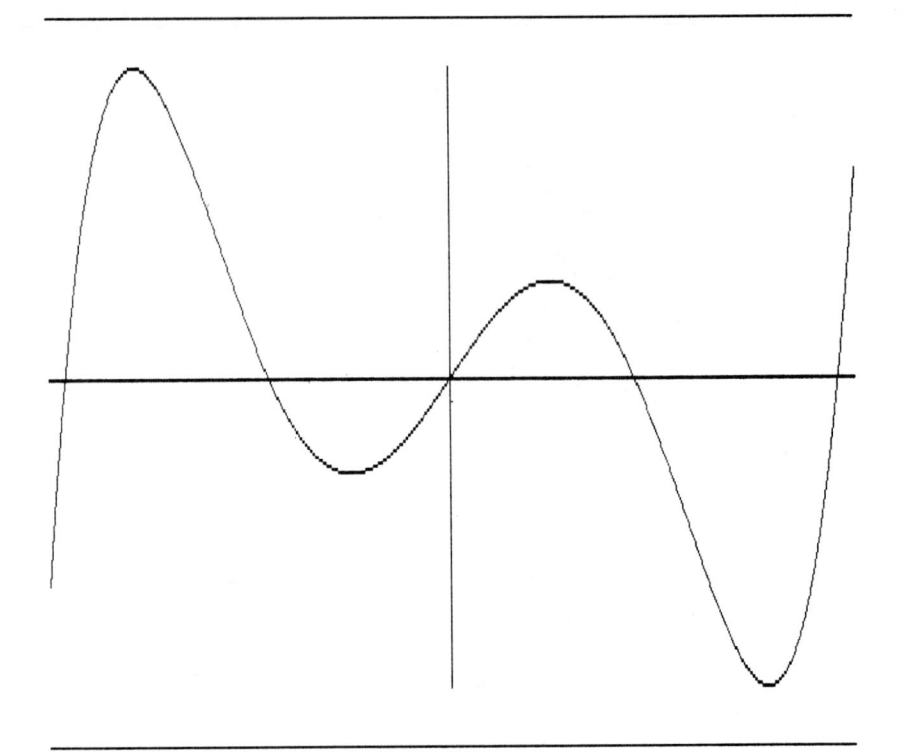

Figure 11-3. A graph of $f(x) = (x/300)(x^2-45)(x^2-10)$ as produced by Program 11-8

2. The program gives the user the option of supplying values for **yLow** and **yHigh**, or letting the program do it. The program accomplishes the task by examining all of the function values, and taking **yLow** and **yHigh** to be the least and greatest function values, respectively.

3. The program uses an error-trapping routine to handle undefined values. The statement **ON ERROR GOTO skipOverflow**

Mathematical and Scientific Programming   287

causes any error to transfer control to the error-handling routine that follows the label **skipOverflow**. When the program cannot compute the function for a certain value of **x**, an error occurs in the **DEF FN** block. Then, the program gives the value 0 to the variable **drawLine%** and the value −1 to the variable **overflow%**, and resumes execution at the end of the **DEF FN** block. The program uses the values assigned to the two variables in order to control the graphing.

4. To avoid gaps, Program 11-8 does not simply plot points, but draws lines between successive points on the graphs by using the statement **LINE − (x,y)**. This statement draws a line from the last point referenced to the point (**x**, **y**). However, there are certain exceptions to this action. The first point plotted must be displayed with **PSET**. If you define the Y-coordinate of a point but it is too large to appear on screen, then the program will not draw a line from this point to the next point; that is, the program should use **PSET** for the next point. If the Y-coordinate of a point is undefined or not computable, then the program will make no attempt to plot the point, and will begin graphing with **PSET** at the next displayable point of the graph. The values of **drawLine%** and **overflow%** recognize these three exceptions.

In Program 11-8, the source code had to be changed each time that the program considered a new function. Ideally, you would like the user to specify the function interactively during the execution of the program. You can do this easily in BASICA by using the **CHAIN MERGE** command. However, this task is formidable in a compiled language. The program must include a function interpreter that takes the function that the user inputs and keeps a symbolic representation of the function on a stack, a one-dimensional array. Evaluating the function at a point involves putting the actual parameters into a second stack, and then reading through the function representation in the first stack in order to decide what calculations to make.

Random Numbers

Consider a specific collection of numbers. You can say that a process selects a number at *random* from this collection if any number in the collection is just as likely to be selected as any other and if you cannot predict the number in advance. Some examples are shown in Table 11-2.

The function **RND**, which acts like the spinner in Figure 11-4, gives Turbo Basic the capability of selecting a number at random from any collection of numbers. The value of the function is a number from 0 up to, but not including, 1. Each time that **RND** appears in the program, it will be assigned a different number, and any number greater than or equal to 0 and less than 1 is just as likely to be generated as any other.

At this time, there is "good news" and "bad news." The good news is that thinking of the value that **RND** produces as the result of the spin of a spinner is exactly what you must think of to design applications of **RND**. The bad news is that successive repetitions of **RND** always generate the same sequence of numbers. (This feature of **RND** is intentional and is important in debugging programs that do simulations.) However, Turbo Basic has another function, **RANDOMIZE TIMER**, that uses the computer's built-in clock to

Collection	Process
1, 2, 3, 4, 5, 6	Toss a balanced die
0 or 1	Toss a coin: 0 = tails, 1 = heads
−1, 0, 1,..., 36	Spin a roulette wheel (interpret 00 as −1)
1, 2,..., N	Write numbers on slips of paper, and pull one from hat
Numbers from 0 to 1	Flip the spinner in Figure 11-4

Table 11-2. *Methods of Selecting Numbers at Random from Various Collections of Numbers*

Mathematical and Scientific Programming

change the sequence of numbers that **RND** generates. The sequence of numbers that **RND** generates is not truly random since, in practice, each number actually determines the next number. However, the sequence has the appearance of a randomly generated sequence. For any subinterval of the interval [0,1], the likelihood of **RND** generating a number in that subinterval is the same as for any other subinterval of the same length. The sequence of numbers that **RND** generates is said to be *pseudo-random*.

Program 11-9 uses the **RND** function to select a number at random from each collection of numbers in Table 11-2. Since the value of **RND** lies between 0 and 1 (exclusive of 1), **6∗RND** lies between 0 and 6 (excluding 6). Therefore, **INT(6∗RND)** is 0, 1, 2, 3, 4, or 5, while **INT(6∗RND) + 1** is 1, 2, 3, 4, 5, or 6. The program simulates the coin toss by finding an event that was likely to occur half of the time. During half of the time, the value of **RND** will lie in the left

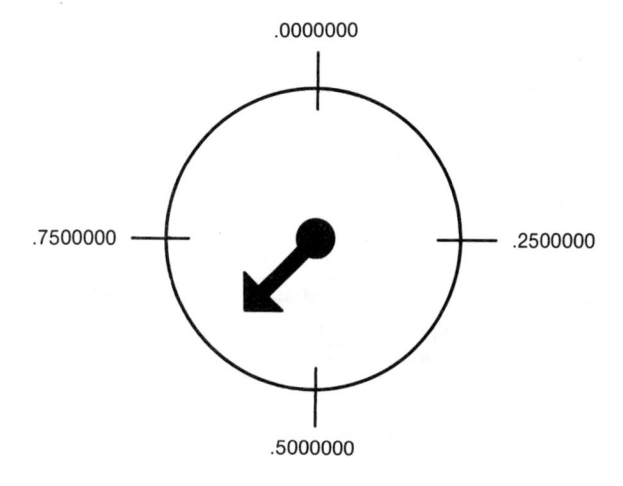

Figure 11-4. *A spinner to select a number between 0 and 1 randomly*

```
REM Select a number at random   [11-9]
RANDOMIZE TIMER
d% = INT(6*RND) + 1
PRINT "The number showing on the die is"; d%
IF RND < .5 THEN result$ = "heads" ELSE result$ = "tails"
PRINT "The coin landed "; result$
r% = INT(38*RND) - 1
PRINT "The roulette wheel shows the number";
IF r% = -1 THEN PRINT " 00" ELSE PRINT r%
PRINT "The spinner landed on the number"; RND
END

Run (results will vary)
The number showing on the die is 3
The coin landed tails
The roulette wheel shows the number 13
The spinner landed on the number .4247282003052533
```

Program 11-9. *Illustration of RND*

half of the interval from 0 to 1. The spin of the roulette wheel was handled analogously to the toss of the die. In general, the value of **INT($n*$RND)** will be one of the numbers 0, 1, 2, and so on to $n-1$, and the value of **INT($n*$RND)** $+ m$ will be one of the numbers m, $m+1$, and so on to $m+n-1$. Therefore, you can use this technique to select an integer from any consecutive set of integers.

Program 11-10 uses the **RND** function to shuffle a deck of cards and deal five cards from the top of the deck. The program places the 52 cards initially into a "fresh deck" array with all of the hearts first, followed by the diamonds, clubs, and spades. Therefore, cards 1 to 13 will be hearts, cards 14 to 26 will be diamonds, cards 27 to 39 will be clubs, and cards 40 to 52 will be spades. Each suit is in the order of ace, 2, 3, and so on to king. The program identifies each card by using a string that consists of the denomination and the suit. The symbols for heart, diamond, club, and spade have ASCII values 3, 4, 5, and 6, respectively, and can be generated as **CHR$(3)**, **CHR$(4)**, **CHR$(5)**, and **CHR$(6)**. The program shuffles the cards by successively interchanging the card at each position in the deck with a randomly selected card.

Program 11-10 presents a method for selecting a set of 5 cards from a deck of 52 cards. This situation is a special case of the prob-

Mathematical and Scientific Programming

```
REM   Shuffle a deck of cards   [11-10]
DIM   card$(1:52)
CALL  SetUpDeck(card$())        'Array to hold deck of cards
                                'Set up fresh deck
CALL  Shuffle(card$())          'Shuffle deck of cards
CALL  DisplayFive(card$())      'Display first five cards
REM ----------- Data for fresh deck: denomination
DATA  A, 2, 3, 4, 5, 6, 7, 8, 9, 10, J, Q, K
END

SUB SetUpDeck(card$(1))
  LOCAL hearts, spaces, ace, king
  LOCAL suit%, cardNumber, denomination%
  hearts = 3: spades = 6
  ace = 1: king = 13
  FOR suit% = hearts TO spades
    RESTORE
    FOR denomination% = ace TO king
      READ denom$
      cardNumber = 13*(suit%-hearts) + denomination%
      card$(cardNumber) = denom$ + CHR$(suit%)
    NEXT denomination%
  NEXT suit%
END SUB

SUB Shuffle(card$(1))
  LOCAL j%
  RANDOMIZE TIMER
  FOR j% = 1 TO 52
    SWAP card$(j%), card$(INT(52*RND)+1)
  NEXT j%
END SUB

SUB DisplayFive(card$(1))
  LOCAL j%
  CLS
  FOR j% = 1 TO 5
    PRINT card$(j%) + "  ";
  NEXT j%
END SUB

Run (results will vary)

8♣   9♣   6♥   K♣   4♣
```

Program 11-10. *Using RND to permute the elements of a set randomly*

lem of selecting *m* objects from a set of *n* objects or, equivalently, of selecting *m* integers from the integers 1 to *n*. A brilliant algorithm for accomplishing this task is shown in Program 11-11. (For details, see *The Art of Computer Programming* by D. E. Knuth [Volume 2,

```
REM Select m numbers between 1 and n  [11-11]
INPUT "Numbers are to lie between 1 and "; n
INPUT "Number of numbers to be selected"; m
RANDOMIZE TIMER
needed = m
remaining = n
FOR index% = 1 TO n
  IF RND < needed/remaining THEN PRINT index%;: needed = needed - 1
  remaining = remaining - 1
NEXT index%
PRINT
END

Run (results will vary)
Numbers are to lie between 1 and ? 10
Number of numbers to be selected? 3
    1  7  8
```

Program 11-11. *Using RND to select a subset of a set randomly*

p. 121, Addison-Wesley, 1969].) This algorithm has the additional feature of ordering the set of *m* numbers. Do a few pencil-and-paper walk-throughs that use small values of *m* and *n* to convince yourself that the algorithm does indeed produce the proper quantity of numbers.

You have seen the uses of the **RND** function in *sampling* (when you selected five cards from a deck) and *simulation* (when you created a model of the outcome of spinning a roulette wheel). Some other uses are as follows:

■ *Testing programs for correctness and efficiency* Selecting randomly chosen items of data avoids any bias of the tester.

■ *Numerical analysis* The areas under certain curves, such as the normal curves of statistics, have important interpretations. One method for determining the area under a curve consists of enclosing the area with a rectangle, selecting points at random from the rectangle, and counting the percentage that fall under the curve. You can then estimate the area to be this percentage of the area of the rectangle.

Mathematical and Scientific Programming **293**

- *Recreation* You can write programs that play games such as blackjack. In addition, you can use programs to simulate games of chance and to analyze various strategies.

- *Decision-making* In Game Theory, a branch of mathematics applied to economics, strategies involve using **RND** to make decisions.

Creating Custom-designed Mathematical Characters

In graphics mode, you can display only the first 128 characters of the ASCII table on screen. Executing a statement such as **PRINT CHR$(n)**, where n is greater than 127, produces garbage on screen. However, you can custom-design a character set for the upper ASCII values. Since Turbo Basic will store the character set in memory, you must first study the way that memory locations are specified.

Specifying Memory Locations

The letter K stands for 1024. Therefore, 64K is 65536, and K^2 is 1048576. You number memory locations from 0 to K^2-1, which is from 0 to 1048576. Certain 64K blocks of memory are called *segments,* and contain the following:

Segment 0 consists of memory locations 0, 1, 2, and so on to 65535
Segment 1 consists of memory locations 16, 17, 18, and so on to 65551
Segment 2 consists of memory locations 32, 33, 34, and so on to 65567
.
.
.

Segment m consists of memory locations 16*m, 16*m+1, 16*m+2, and so on to 16*m+65535

Within each segment, the locations are said to have *offsets* 0, 1, 2, and so on to 65535. You can specify any memory location by giving a segment number and an offset within that segment. These two numbers are usually written in the form *segment:offset*. In general, a specific memory location has several *segment:offset* representations. For example, you can specify memory location 35 as **0:35**, **1:19**, or **2:3**.

At any time, you can declare a certain segment of memory as the *current segment*. Statements and functions that read data from and write data to memory locations identify a location by using its offset in the current segment. The statement

DEF SEG = *m*

declares the *m*th segment to be the current segment.

Each memory location contains an 8-tuple of zeros and ones, which is called a *byte*. This 8-tuple is the binary representation of a number from 0 to 255. Therefore, you can say that each memory location holds a number from 0 to 255. The value of the function

PEEK(*n*)

is the number in the memory location of offset *n* in the current segment. The statement

POKE *n,r*

places the number *r* into the memory location with offset *n* in the current segment. You can give the number *r* in decimal, hexadecimal, or binary notation. You must place **&H** or **&B** before numbers written in hexadecimal notation or binary notation, respectively. The use of binary notation simplifies the task of placing a specific 8-tuple of zeros and ones into a memory location. You simply tack **&B** to the beginning of the 8-tuple and Turbo Basic will **POKE** the resulting binary number into memory. For example, the statement **POKE 3,&B10101010** places the 8-tuple 10101010 into the memory location of offset 3 in the current segment.

Mathematical and Scientific Programming

The memory locations in segment 0 give useful information about the hardware components of the computer, the status of the keyboard and the screen, and the whereabouts of special portions of memory. In particular, memory locations of offset 124, 125, 126, and 127 point to the offset and segment of the beginning of the portion of memory that generates the characters associated with the upper ASCII values. This portion of memory is called a *character table*. The offset and segment that are used for the beginning of the character table will be **PEEK(124)+256∗PEEK(125)** and **PEEK(126)+256∗PEEK(127)**, respectively.

Specifying Characters in Graphics Mode

In graphics screen modes 1 and 2, Turbo Basic displays each character in an eight-by-eight rectangular array of pixels. Figure 11-5 shows the user-defined character 1/3. To the right of each row of

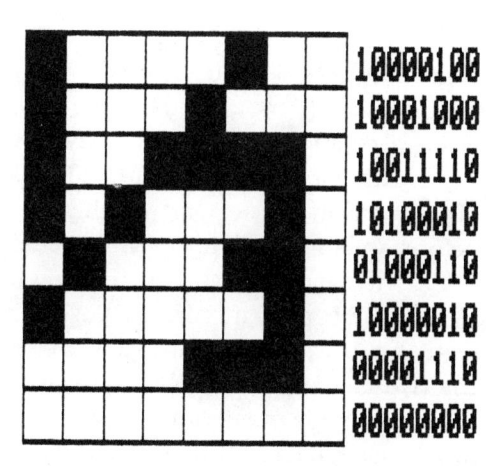

```
10000100
10001000
10011110
10100010
01000110
10000010
00001110
00000000
```

Figure 11-5. *How the character 1/3 will appear on screen*

the array is the 8-tuple of ones and zeros that describes the row. The ones denote pixels that are ON; the zeros denote pixels that are OFF. The sequence of eight binary numbers describes the character 1/3.

Here are the steps for specifying characters for the upper ASCII values:

1. Choose a place in memory to hold the character table. (Turbo Basic has two functions—**ENDMEM** and **MEMSET**—that help with this task.) Suppose that the location in *segment:offset* format is *s:f*.

2. Set the numbers in memory locations 124, 125, 126, and 127 of segment 0 to point to the first location of the character table. If the first location is *s:f*, in *segment:offset* form, then the values **POKE**d into memory locations 124, 125, 126, and 127 should be *f* **MOD 256**, *f* **\256**, *s* **MOD 256**, and *s* **\256**, respectively.

3. POKE the 8 binary numbers that describe character 128 into the first 8 locations of the character table. **POKE** the 8 binary numbers that describe character 129 into the next 8 locations of the character table. Continue in this manner to put into the table the descriptors for up to 128 characters.

Program 11-12 defines character 128 to be the fraction 1/3, and character 129 to be a solid right triangle. Although you only need 16 bytes of memory to describe these two characters, the program sets aside a character table of 1024 bytes that can potentially hold the descriptions of 128 characters. The value of **ENDMEM** is the memory location at the end of the available physical memory. Therefore, segment number (**ENDMEM**−1024)/16 has enough room for the character table in its first 1024 locations. The statement **MEMSET** prevents Turbo Basic from using these memory locations for any other purpose. The program stores the descriptors for the two characters in **DATA** statements and **POKE**s them into the character table. You can easily extend the program to define additional characters: all that is required to define a new character is first to type in the **DATA** statements that describe the character and then to **CALL** the procedure **DefineCharacter** with the number of the character as its actual parameter.

Mathematical and Scientific Programming

```
REM Define and display custom-designed
REM characters 128 and 129   [11-12]
SCREEN 1,0
CALL SetUpMemoryForHighAscii
CALL DefineCharacter(128)
CALL DefineCharacter(129)
PRINT CHR$(128);" ";CHR$(129)
END

SUB SetUpMemoryForHighAscii
  LOCAL segment%
  segment% = (ENDMEM-1024)/16
  MEMSET 16*CLNG(segment%)
  'Set pointers to beginning of character table
  DEF SEG = 0
  POKE 124, 0
  POKE 125, 0
  POKE 126, segment% MOD 256
  POKE 127, segment%\256
  'Change the current segment to the reserved segment,
  'in preparation for POKEing character patterns
  DEF SEG = segment%
END SUB

SUB DefineCharacter(n%)
  LOCAL index%, a%
  FOR index% = 0 TO 7
    READ a%
    POKE (n%-128)*8+index%,a%
  NEXT index%
END SUB

REM --- Data for character 128
DATA &B10000100
DATA &B10001000
DATA &B10011110
DATA &B10100010
DATA &B01000110
DATA &B10000010
DATA &B00001110
DATA &B00000000

REM --- Data for character 129
DATA &B00000010
DATA &B00000110
DATA &B00001110
DATA &B00011110
DATA &B00111110
DATA &B01111110
DATA &B11111110
DATA &B00000000

Run
```

Program 11-12. *A demonstration of the creation of a character table*

ASCII value	Description	ASCII value	Description
171	1/2	239	Intersection
172	1/4	241	Plus or minus sign
224-235	Greek letters	244—245	Integral sign
236	Infinity	251	Square root symbol
238	Is an element of	235	2 as a small exponent

Table 11-3. *Some Mathematical Characters of the ASCII Table*

Using the DOS Program GRAFTABL.COM

The upper 128 ASCII characters (shown in Appendix A) contain a number of mathematical characters. Some of these characters are described in Table 11-3.

DOS 3.0 and later versions contain a program called GRAFTABL.COM. When you execute this program, it creates a character table for graphics screen modes 1 and 2, and loads the table with the upper 128 characters from the ASCII table. Turbo Basic programs can then access these characters when you use the function **CHR$**. After executing GRAFTABL.COM, you can alter various characters by using Program 11-13.

Saving Graphs

Turbo Basic reserves a portion of memory that consists of 4000 locations for the Color/Graphics Adapter to hold the contents of the screen. After you draw a graph, you can save the contents of these memory locations in a disk file and then reload them to reproduce the graph. The statements

```
DEF SEG = &HB800
BSAVE filespec,0,4000
```

Mathematical and Scientific Programming

```
REM Modify character table loaded by GRAFTABL.COM  [11-13]
SCREEN 1,0
CALL SetUpMemoryForHighAscii(offset&)
CALL ModifyCharacter(offset&)
END

SUB SetUpMemoryForHighAscii(offset&)
  LOCAL segment&
  'Get pointers to beginning of character table
  DEF SEG = 0
  offset& = PEEK(124) + 256*PEEK(125)
  segment& = PEEK(126) + 256*PEEK(127)
  'Change the current segment to the character table segment
  'in preparation for POKEing character patterns
  DEF SEG = segment&
END SUB

SUB ModifyCharacter(offset&)
  LOCAL n%, index%, descriptor%
  CLS
  PRINT "Characters 128 - 255 may be modified."
  PRINT "New character is displayed on screen."
  PRINT "Enter 0 to terminate program."
  INPUT "Number of the character to alter: ", n%
  DO UNTIL n% = 0
    PRINT
    PRINT "Character is currently ";CHR$(n%)
    PRINT
    PRINT "Enter eight binary numbers"
    PRINT "that describe new character."
    PRINT
    FOR index% = 1 TO 8
      PRINT "Row"; index%;
      INPUT ": ", descriptor%
      POKE offset& + 8*(n%-128) + index% - 1, descriptor%
    NEXT index%
    PRINT "Character is now "; CHR$(n%)
    PRINT
    INPUT "Number of next character to alter: ", n%
  LOOP
END SUB
```

Program 11-13. *Modifying the character set specified by GRAFTABL.COM*

save the bytes in these memory locations into the specified file; you can use the statements

DEF SEG = &HB800
BLOAD filespec

at any time to restore the original screen.

Matrices

An $m \times n$ matrix is a two-dimensional array that is declared by a statement of the form

DIM *arrayName*(1:*m*,1:*n*)

The matrix will have m rows and n columns. Some versions of BASIC have predefined functions that add, multiply, and invert matrices. Although Turbo Basic does not have these functions, you can easily define them as procedures.

Matrix Addition

You must dimension all three of the matrices passed to the procedure in Program 11-14 — even the one that will eventually hold the sum — prior to calling the procedure. Inside the procedure, the two matrices to be added are named **first** and **second**, and their sum is named **sum**.

The twos in the first line of the procedure refer to the fact that each of the matrices has two dimensions. The procedure begins by verifying that all of the three matrices passed to it have the same number of rows and columns. After the verification, the procedure easily carries out the addition by using a pair of nested **FOR...NEXT** loops.

Matrix Multiplication

All three of the matrices passed to the procedure in Program 11-15 — even the one that will eventually hold the product — must be dimensioned prior to calling the procedure. Inside the procedure, the two matrices to be multiplied are **first** and **second**, and their product is **product**.

```
SUB MatrixAddition(first(2),second(2),sum(2))    '[11-14]
  LOCAL rowsFirst, columnsFirst, rowsSecond, columnsSecond,_
        rowsSum, columnsSum, index1%, index2%
  'the assumption is made that each matrix has been
  'dimensioned in the form arrayName(1:m,1:n)
  rowsFirst     = UBOUND(first(1))
  columnsFirst  = UBOUND(first(2))
  rowsSecond    = UBOUND(second(1))
  columnsSecond = UBOUND(second(2))
  rowsSum       = UBOUND(sum(1))
  columnsSum    = UBOUND(sum(2))
  'Verify that first two matrices have the same size
  IF (rowsFirst <> rowsSecond) OR _
     (columnsFirst <> columnsSecond) THEN
    PRINT "sizes not appropriate for addition"
    EXIT SUB
  END IF
  'Verify that the sum array has the correct size
  IF (rowsFirst <> rowsSum) OR _
     (columnsFirst <> columnsSum) THEN
    PRINT "Sum matrix not correct size."
    EXIT SUB
  END IF
  'Carry out the addition
  FOR index1% = 1 TO rowsSum
    FOR index2% = 1 TO columnsSum
      sum(index1%,index2%) = first(index1%,index2%) + _
                             second(index1%,index2%)
    NEXT index2%
  NEXT index1%
END SUB
```

Program 11-14. *A segment that forms the sum of two matrices*

The procedure begins by verifying that the three matrices passed to it have suitable sizes; that is, the number of columns of the **first** matrix must be the same as the number of rows of the **second** matrix, the number of rows of the **product** matrix must be the same as the number of rows of the **first** matrix, and the number of columns of the **product** matrix must be the same as the number of columns of the **second** matrix. After the verifications, the procedure obtains the entries in the **product** matrix one at a time. Each entry is a sum, accumulated in the variable **total**, of the products of numbers taken from the appropriate row of the **first** matrix and the appropriate column of the **second** matrix.

```
SUB MatrixMultiply(first(2),second(2),product(2))      '[11-15]
  LOCAL rowsFirst, columnsFirst
  LOCAL rowsSecond, columnsSecond
  LOCAL rowsProduct, columnsProduct
  LOCAL index1%, index2%, index3%, total
  'The assumption is made that each matrix has been
  'dimensioned in the form arrayName(1:m,1:n)
  rowsFirst       = UBOUND(first(1))
  columnsFirst    = UBOUND(first(2))
  rowsSecond      = UBOUND(second(1))
  columnsSecond   = UBOUND(second(2))
  rowsProduct     = UBOUND(product(1))
  columnsProduct  = UBOUND(product(2))
  'Verify that first and second matrices can be multiplied
  IF  columnsFirst <> rowsSecond THEN
    PRINT "Sizes not appropriate to multiply matrices"
    EXIT SUB
  END IF
  'Verify that product array is proper size
  IF (rowsFirst<>rowsProduct) OR _
     (columnsSecond<>columnsProduct) THEN
    PRINT "Product matrix not large enough"
    EXIT SUB
  END IF
  'Carry out the multiplication
  FOR index1% = 1 TO rowsProduct
    FOR index2% = 1 TO columnsProduct
      total = 0
      FOR index3% = 1 TO columnsFirst
        total=total+first(index1%,index3%)*second(index3%,index2%)
      NEXT index3%
      product(index1%,index2%) = total
    NEXT index2%
  NEXT index1%
END SUB
```

Program 11-15. *A segment that forms the product of two matrices*

Matrix Inversion

The two matrices passed to the procedure in Program 11-16—even the one that will eventually hold the inverse of the other—must be dimensioned prior to calling the procedure. Inside the procedure, the matrix to be inverted is **original#** and the matrix that will eventually hold its inverse is **inverse#**. The computation used to obtain

Mathematical and Scientific Programming

```
SUB MatrixInversion(original#(2),inverse#(2))       '[11-16]
  LOCAL size%, b#(), row%, column%
  LOCAL index%, switched%, testRow%, hold#, temp#
  'Arrays are assumed to be square with subscripts
  'that range from 1 to UBOUND(original#(1))
  'Verify that both matrices are square and of same size
  IF UBOUND(original#(1)) <> UBOUND(original#(2)) THEN PRINT _
      "Matrix to be inverted is not square.": EXIT SUB
  IF UBOUND(inverse#(1)) <> UBOUND(inverse#(2)) THEN PRINT _
      "Matrix to hold inverse is not square.": EXIT SUB
  IF UBOUND(original#(1)) <> UBOUND(inverse#(1)) THEN PRINT _
    "The matrix to hold the inverse has the wrong size.": EXIT SUB
  'Dimension an array that is twice as long as the given array,
  'copy the given array into the left half of this new array,
  'and make the right half an identity matrix
  size% = UBOUND(original#(1))
  DIM b#(size%,2*size%)
  FOR row% = 1 TO size%
    FOR column% = 1 TO size%
      b#(row%,column%) = original#(row%,column%)
    NEXT column%
    b#(row%,size%+row%) = 1
  NEXT row%
  'Use a modified Gauss-Jordan elimination to invert the matrix
  FOR index% = 1 TO size%
    'If diagonal element is zero, swap row with a later row
    'to obtain a non-zero diagonal element.
    IF b#(index%,index%) = 0 THEN
      switched% = 0
      FOR testRow% = index% + 1 TO size%
        IF b#(testRow%,index%) <> 0 THEN
          FOR column% = 1 TO 2*size%
            temp# = b#(index%,column%)
            b#(index%,column%) = b#(testRow%,column%)
            b#(testRow%,column%) = temp#
          NEXT column%
          switched% = -1
        END IF
      NEXT testRow%
      IF NOT switched% THEN
        PRINT "Matrix has no inverse."
        EXIT SUB
      END IF
    END IF
    'Reduce all non-diagonal elements in the index column to zero
    FOR row% = 1 to size%
      IF row% <> index% THEN
        hold# = b#(row%,index%)
        FOR column% = 1 TO 2*size%
          b#(row%,column%) = b#(index%,index%)*b#(row%,column%) _
                             - hold#*b#(index%,column%)
        NEXT column%
      END IF
    NEXT row%
  NEXT index%
```

Program 11-16. *A segment that obtains the inverse of a matrix*

```
'Divide each row by value on diagonal and
'assign values to inverse array
FOR row% = 1 TO size%
   FOR column% = 1 TO size%
      inverse#(row%,column%)=b#(row%,column%+size%)/b#(row%,row%)
   NEXT column%
NEXT row%
END SUB
```

Program 11-16. *A segment that obtains the inverse of a matrix* (continued)

the inverse of a matrix is very sensitive to round-off errors. Therefore, to avoid them the procedure uses double-precision throughout.

The procedure begins by verifying that the two matrices passed to it have proper sizes. Both matrices must be square matrices of the same size. The procedure carries out the inversion by using a variation of the Gauss-Jordan elimination algorithm: the procedure places the matrix to be inverted in the left half of a large matrix named **b#**, whose right half contains an identity matrix. The procedure then carries out elementary row operations on **b#** to transform the left half of **b#** into a diagonal matrix. In an attempt to minimize round-off errors, the algorithm postpones performing any divisions until the end. After appropriate divisions, the right half of **b#** will contain the inverse of the original matrix.

12 Business Programming

Financial Calculations

After justifying the value of long integers in financial calculations, this section gives a detailed analysis of the amortization of a loan.

The Value of Long Integers

Most financial calculations are best performed by writing all amounts in cents and by using long integer variables. Program 12-1 uses long integer variables to calculate interest earned, and then automatically rounds the interest to the nearest cent.

Program 12-2 uses double-precision variables to perform the same calculation as Program 12-1. The function **FNRound** is a standard function used to round numbers to two decimal places. While **FNRound** does its best, its effort is partly undone by the peculiarities of the way that Turbo Basic stores and displays double-precision numbers.

Using Turbo Basic

```
REM Calculate interest with long integers    [12-1]
p& = 123456
interestRate = .05
interestEarned& = interestRate*p&
PRINT "The interest earned is"; interestEarned&/100
END

Run
The interest earned is 61.73
```

Program 12-1. *Using long integers in financial computations*

```
REM Calculate interest with double-precision numbers   [12-2]
DEF FNRound(x#) = INT(100*x# + .5)/100
P# = 1234.56
interestRate = .05
interestEarned# = FNRound(interestRate*P#)
PRINT "The interest earned is"; interestEarned#
END

Run
The interest earned is 61.72999954223633
```

Program 12-2. *Rounding difficulties with double-precision numbers*

In Program 12-2, you can display the amount of interest correctly by using a **PRINT USING** statement. However, this is a cosmetic cure since the value of the variable is not exactly what you might want if you continued the program and performed further calculations with the earned interest.

Amortization of a Loan

The standard method of amortizing a loan is to make equal payments for a specified number of months, after which the loan is paid off. The following terms describe a specific amortization:

- *Amount* The amount of the loan, or the quantity of money borrowed

- *Rate* The annual rate of interest (given as a percentage), such as 12 or 10.5

- *Duration* The number of months over which loan is to be paid off

- *Payment* A monthly payment

Given the values of any three of these variables, you can determine the value of the fourth variable by using a mathematical formula. The most common situation is for you to know the amount, rate, and duration, and for you to determine the payment.

At any time, the *balance* of the loan is the amount outstanding on the loan — that is, the amount that you must pay at that time to retire the debt. The initial balance is the amount of the loan, and the balance decreases to 0 after you make all of the monthly payments. Part of each monthly payment consists of interest on the balance, and the remainder of the payment goes toward reducing the balance. Here are the equations that help to calculate the interest, reduction of the balance, and the balance for a given month.

interest paid for month = *monthly rate of interest* ∗ *balance at beginning of month*

reduction of debt for month = *payment* − *interest paid for month*

balance at end of month = *balance at beginning of month* − *reduction of debt for month*

Program 12-3 requests that the user input the terms of a loan — the amount, annual interest rate, duration, and monthly payment. If the user omits the amount, duration, or monthly payment, the program will automatically calculate it. (The calculation of the interest rate from the other terms is rather complex and has been omitted.) After all of the terms are known, the user can request an amortization schedule that shows a year's transactions.

Note that the formula used in the program to determine the monthly payment is accurate. However, since the smallest unit of currency is one cent, the currency system is inaccurate. Rounding the monthly payment to the nearest cent throws off the amortization schedule slightly. This inaccuracy is compensated for by adjusting the last payment so that it completely pays off the balance. Normally, the adjustment will be a small amount.

Pie Charts

Data achieves its greatest impact when you present it graphically. This section presents a generic program that creates a pie chart. This program has been designed both to present the essential programming techniques and to be flexible.

Pie charts are appropriate for showing the relative sizes of from three to ten quantities. (Displays that involve more than ten categories are usually more readable in the form of a bar chart. Bar charts

```
REM Calculate terms and display an amortization schedule   [12-3]
CLS
DEFDBL a - z
PRINT "Give a zero value for amount, duration, or payment"
PRINT "  in order to have that value computed."
INPUT "Amount of loan"; amount
INPUT "Annual interest rate (percent)"; rate
INPUT "Number of months over which loan will be paid off";duration%
INPUT "Amount of each payment"; payment
i = rate/1200     'Interest rate per month
IF amount = 0 THEN
    CALL FindAmount
  ELSEIF duration% = 0 THEN
    CALL FindDuration
    CALL FindPayment    'adjust payment for whole number duration
  ELSEIF payment = 0 THEN
    CALL FindPayment
END IF
PRINT "Display loan amortization schedule (Y/N)?"
answer$ = UCASE$(INPUT$(1))
IF answer$ = "Y" THEN CALL Amortize
END
```

Program 12-3. *Amortization of a loan (output shown in Figures 12-1 and 12-2)*

```
SUB FindAmount
   SHARED amount, i, duration%, payment
   amount = (payment/i)*(1-(1+i)^-duration%)
   PRINT USING "The amount of the loan is $$####,###.##"; amount
END SUB

SUB FindDuration
   SHARED amount, i, duration%, payment
   duration% = CEIL(LOG(payment/(payment-i*amount))/LOG(1+i))
   PRINT USING "The loan is paid off after ### months"; duration%
END SUB

SUB FindPayment
   SHARED amount, i, duration%, payment
   payment = (i*amount)/(1-(1+i)^-duration%)
   PRINT USING "Each payment will be $$,###.##";payment
END SUB

SUB Amortize
   SHARED amount, i, duration%, payment
   LOCAL balance&, payment&, interest&,
   LOCAL reductionOfLoan&, payNum%, a$
   CLS
   PRINT "PAY#    PAYMENT    INTEREST    RED. OF DEBT    BALANCE"
   balance& = 100*amount
   payment& = 100*payment
   FOR payNum% = 1 TO duration%
      interest& = i*balance&
      'If this is the last payment on loan, recompute payment
      IF payNum% = duration% THEN payment& = interest& + balance&
      reductionOfLoan& = payment& - interest&
      balance& = balance& - reductionOfLoan&
      PRINT USING
         "####    #####.##    #####.##    #####.##    #####,###.##";_
      payNum%, payment&/100, interest&/100, _
      reductionOfLoan&/100, balance&/100
      IF (payNum% MOD 12 = 0) AND (payNum% <> duration%) THEN
         PRINT
         PRINT "Press any key to continue."
         a$ = INPUT$(1)
         CLS
         PRINT "PAY#    PAYMENT    INTEREST    RED. OF DEBT    BALANCE"
      END IF
   NEXT payNum%
END SUB

Run
Give a zero value for amount, duration, or payment
   in order to have that value computed.
Amount of loan? 100000
Annual interest rate (percent)? 9.5
Number of months over which loan will be paid off? 360
Amount of each payment?
Each payment will be $840.85
Display loan amortization schedule (Y/N)? Y
(See Figures 12-1 and 12-2 for first and last year amortization.)
```

Program 12-3. *Amortization of a loan (output shown in Figures 12-1 and 12-2) (continued)*

PAY#	PAYMENT	INTEREST	RED. OF DEBT	BALANCE
1	840.85	791.67	49.18	99,950.82
2	840.85	791.28	49.57	99,901.25
3	840.85	790.88	49.97	99,851.28
4	840.85	790.49	50.36	99,800.92
5	840.85	790.09	50.76	99,750.16
6	840.85	789.69	51.16	99,699.00
7	840.85	789.28	51.57	99,647.43
8	840.85	788.88	51.97	99,595.46
9	840.85	788.46	52.39	99,543.07
10	840.85	788.05	52.80	99,490.27
11	840.85	787.63	53.22	99,437.05
12	840.85	787.21	53.64	99,383.41

Press any key to continue.

Figure 12-1. *Amortization of year 1 from Program 12-3*

PAY#	PAYMENT	INTEREST	RED. OF DEBT	BALANCE
349	840.85	75.99	764.86	8,833.35
350	840.85	69.93	770.92	8,062.43
351	840.85	63.83	777.02	7,285.41
352	840.85	57.68	783.17	6,502.24
353	840.85	51.48	789.37	5,712.87
354	840.85	45.23	795.62	4,917.25
355	840.85	38.93	801.92	4,115.33
356	840.85	32.58	808.27	3,307.06
357	840.85	26.18	814.67	2,492.39
358	840.85	19.73	821.12	1,671.27
359	840.85	13.23	827.62	843.65
360	850.33	6.68	843.65	0.00

Figure 12-2. *Amortization of year 30 from Program 12-3*

are discussed in the next section.) Program 12-4 is a special program that draws pie charts for up to ten categories. The only modification that you need to change the chart is to replace the numbers and their categories in the **DATA** statements at the top of the program. In the event that the names of the individual categories are

```
REM Illustrate the relative usages of the major languages    [12-4]
REM -- Data: number of people (in millions) that speak language
DATA 177, 171, 974, 420, 114, 300, 164, 285, 296, 2000, -1
REM -- Data: the major languages
DATA Arabic, Bengali, Chinese, English, French
DATA Hindi, Portuguese, Russian, Spanish, other
REM -- Data: title for pie chart
DATA Principal Languages of the World
scale = 1
'The size of the pie chart may be adjusted by varying the value
'of scale. The smaller the value of scale, the more room for the
'item descriptions. A scale of 1 gives the pie chart a diameter
'equal to half the width of the screen.
DIM tile$(1:10)
CALL AssignTilingPatterns(tile$())
CALL CountAndTotalData(itemCount,sumOfData)
CALL DrawChart(itemCount,sumOfData,tile$(),scale)
CALL DisplayLegend(itemCount,tile$(),scale)
END

SUB AssignTilingPatterns(tile$(1))
   'the following tiling patterns may be changed as desired
   tile$(1) = CHR$(136)+CHR$(136)+CHR$(170)
   tile$(2) = CHR$(85)+CHR$(0)
   tile$(3) = CHR$(128)+CHR$(32)+CHR$(8)+CHR$(2)
   tile$(4) = CHR$(3)+CHR$(12)+CHR$(48)+CHR$(192)
   tile$(5) = CHR$(170)+CHR$(170)+CHR$(0)+CHR$(0)
   tile$(6) = CHR$(17)
   tile$(7) = CHR$(168)+CHR$(168)+CHR$(0)
   tile$(8) = CHR$(1)+CHR$(16)
   tile$(9) = CHR$(255)
   tile$(10)= CHR$(5)
END SUB

SUB CountAndTotalData(count,total)
   LOCAL itemValue
   count = 0
   total = 0
   READ itemValue
   DO UNTIL itemValue < 0
      total = total + itemValue
      count = count + 1
      read itemValue
   LOOP
END SUB
```

Program 12-4. *A generic pie chart program*

```
SUB DrawChart(count,total,tile$(1),scale)
  LOCAL windowWidth, windowHeight, xcenter, ycenter, twoPi
  LOCAL index%, radius, startSector, endSector, itemValue, theta
  'Display results are independent of the values of
  'windowWidth and windowHeight. All that is important
  'is that these values be in the ratio of 4 to 3.
  windowWidth  = 4
  windowHeight = 3
  SCREEN 1,0
  COLOR ,0
  WINDOW (0,0) - (windowWidth,windowHeight)
  twoPi       = 8*ATN(1)            '2*pi
  radius      = scale*windowWidth/4
  xcenter     = radius
  ycenter     = windowHeight/2
  startSector = .00001
  RESTORE      'use first data statement again
  FOR index% = 1 TO count
    READ itemValue
    endSector = startSector + twoPi*(itemValue/total)
    CIRCLE (xcenter,ycenter),radius,,-startSector,-endSector
    theta = (startSector + endSector)/2
    PAINT (xcenter+radius*COS(theta)/2,_
          ycenter+radius*SIN(theta)/2),tile$(index%)
    startSector = endSector
  NEXT index%
  READ itemValue   'read the sentinel value
END SUB

SUB DisplayLegend(count,tile$(1),scale)
  LOCAL heightInRows, widthInColumns, boxWidth, boxHt, boxBottom
  LOCAL legendTop, leftEdge, index%, itemName$, title$
  heightInRows   = 25
  widthInColumns = 40
  WINDOW SCREEN (0,0)-(widthInColumns,heightInRows)
  boxWidth = 2
  boxHt = 1
  legendTop = (heightInRows-(boxHt+1)*count)\2
  leftEdge  = widthInColumns*(scale/2) + 2
  FOR index% = 1 TO count
    READ itemName$
    boxBottom = legendTop + (boxHt+1)*index%
    LINE (leftEdge, boxBottom-boxHt) -_
         (leftEdge+boxWidth,boxBottom),,B
    PAINT (leftEdge+boxWidth/2,boxBottom-boxHt/2),tile$(index%)
    LOCATE boxBottom,leftEdge + boxWidth + 2: PRINT itemName$
  NEXT index%
  'display title
  READ title$
  LOCATE heightInRows - 1,(widthInColumns-LEN(title$))/2
  PRINT title$;
END SUB
```

Program 12-4. *A generic pie chart program* (continued)

Business Programming   313

long, you can reduce the size of the pie chart by decreasing the value assigned to the variable **scale**.

Figure 12-3 contains the output from Program 12-4. The figure presents the percentages of the people in the world who speak each of the major languages. The sectors of the circle appear on screen in three different colors, and each sector has a different pattern. To change the patterns that appear in Figure 12-3, use the information presented in the discussion of tile patterns in Chapter 8, and change the characters to the right of the equal signs in the procedure **AssignTilingPatterns** in Program 12-4.

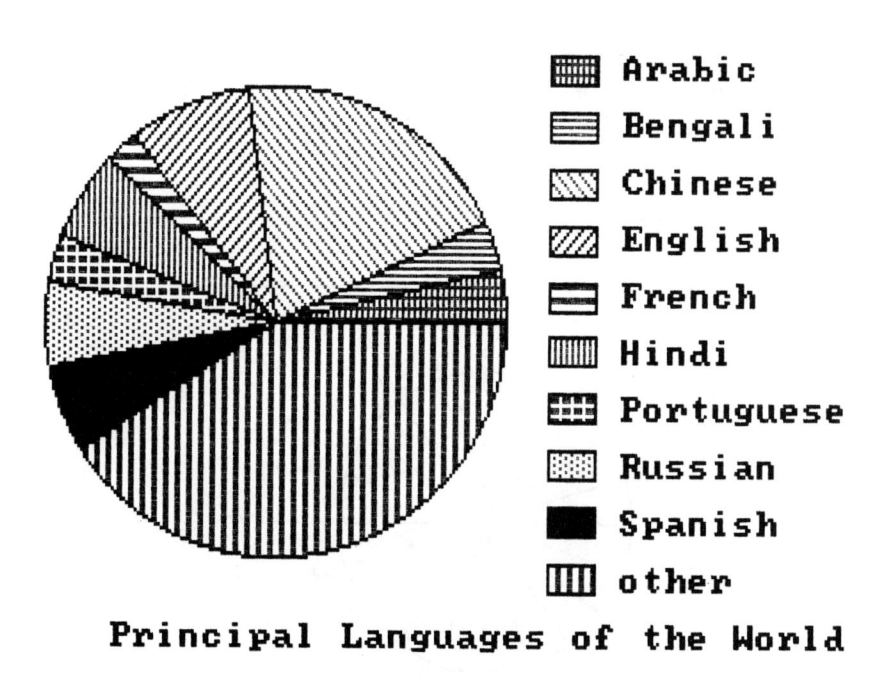

Figure 12-3. *A pie chart displayed by Program 12-4*

In a pie chart, each sector of the pie represents a percentage of the entire pie. Therefore, you must convert the numeric data into percentages. In Program 12-4, the procedure **CountAndTotalData** counts the number of different entries in the first **DATA** statement and totals these numbers. (Note: The last entry in this **DATA** statement, −1, serves as a sentinel to signal the end of the items.) The variable **count** gives the number of sectors that will appear in the pie chart, and the variable **total** will be used to convert each number from the **DATA** statement into percentages.

The procedure **DrawChart** draws and fills the sectors of the pie chart. An understanding of this procedure requires a further discussion of the **CIRCLE** statement. Figure 12-4 shows a circle that is segmented by several radius lines. The radius line that extends to the right from the center of the circle is called the *horizontal radius line*. Each radius line is assigned a number between 0 and 1 that gives the percentage of the circle that is found between the chosen line and the horizontal radius line. The radian measure of the angle from the horizontal radius line to any radius line is 2*pi

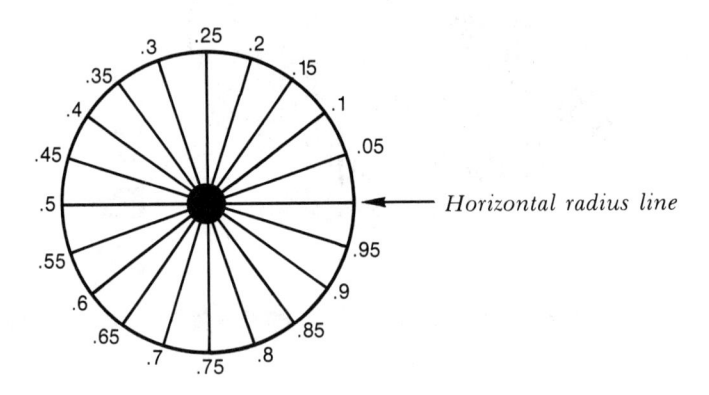

Figure 12-4. *The portions of a circle*

multiplied by the assigned number. The statement

CIRCLE (x,y),r,,−r1,−r2

draws the sector of the circle of radius r that is bounded by the radius lines that make angles of $r1$ and $r2$ radians with the horizontal radius line. The sector begins at the radius line that is associated with $r1$, and ends with the radius line that is associated with $r2$. This sector contains the portion $(r2-r1)/(2*pi)$ of the area of the entire circle. In other words, starting at $r1$, the portion p of the area of the circle is contained in the sector from $r1$ to $r2$, where $r2$ is $r1 + 2*pi*p$.

Program 12-4 creates a pie chart one sector at a time, beginning with the sector just above the horizontal radius line. For this sector, $r1$ is 0 and the **CIRCLE** statement involves −0. The computer cannot distinguish between −0 and 0, and, therefore, will not produce the intended result. You can remedy this situation by using a very small number, such as −.00001, instead of −0. The program will then draw the sectors of the pie chart one after the other. The program uses the ending radius line for each sector as the beginning radius line for the next.

In Program 12-4, the **PAINT** statement, which is used to fill a sector with a pattern, requires that the coordinates of a point inside the sector be determined. One way to find such a point is to select the midpoint of the radius line that bisects the sector. If the sector is bounded by the radius lines having radian measures $r1$ and $r2$, then the radian measure associated with the bisecting radius line is $t = (r1 + r2)/2$. You can then use the trigonometric functions to find the midpoint of this radius line. The coordinates of the point are $x + (r/2)*COS(t)$ and $y + (r/2)*SIN(t)$, where (x,y) is the center of the circle and r is the radius.

There is one more point to attend to. A **WINDOW** statement must be used to specify a coordinate system. After that, the circle drawn by the statement **CIRCLE** $(x,y),r$ will have a horizontal radius line of length r. The vertical radius line will appear on screen with the same length. However, the length in terms of the Y-scale that the **WINDOW** statement sets will most likely be different than *r*. In order for the trigonometric formulas just given to hold, these two lengths must agree. They will agree if the **WINDOW** statement specifies the lengths of the X-axis and Y-axis in a 4-to-3 ratio. (This is due to the fact that the lengths of the two sides of the screen are in a 4-to-3 ratio.) A suitable **WINDOW** statement is **WINDOW (0,0) — (4,3)**.

After Program 12-4 draws the pie chart, the procedure **DisplayLegend** draws legend boxes that give the identifying pattern to the left of each category name. The procedure draws each rectangular box by using the **LINE** statement, and the **PAINT** statement uses the center of the rectangle to fill the rectangle. The program centers the rectangles vertically on the right side of the screen. After displaying all of the legends, Program 12-4 displays the title of the pie chart centered at the bottom of the screen.

Bar Charts

The other primary graphical device for displaying data is the bar chart. This section develops a generic bar chart program that both displays a bar chart on screen and produces a high-quality printed version.

Figure 12-5 shows a printout obtained by using the bar chart program. Some of the features of this chart are as follows:

- The text looks like text produced by a printer in text mode, rather than text produced by a graphics screen dump.

- The tick marks on the Y-axis are evenly spaced and aligned with their labels. (Each of these labels can contain up to four digits.)

- The labels under the bars are vertical and centered. (On the screen display, each label is limited to a maximum of three characters. However, there is no limit to the number of characters for each label on the printed version.)

This section first analyzes each of the tasks that go into creating a bar chart, and then puts them together in a complete program.

Business Programming

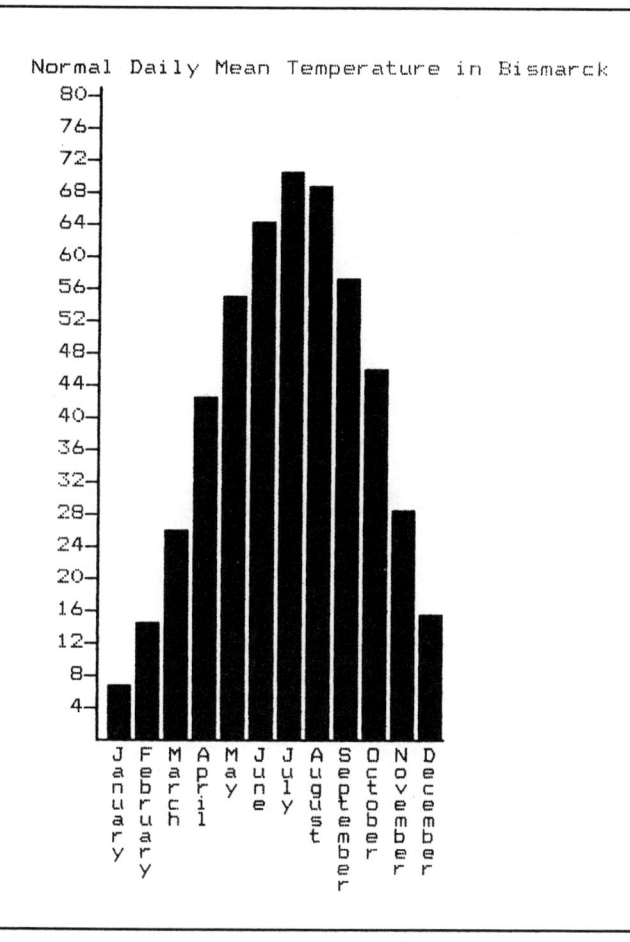

Figure 12-5. *A bar chart created with Program 12-8*

Setting Up a Coordinate System, Axes, and Tick Marks

The first step in designing any graphics program is to select a convenient screen mode and coordinate system. The high-resolution graphics mode is most appropriate for bar charts since it uses smaller text characters than does medium-resolution graphics mode. This minimizes the amount of space that labels require, which is one of the most important considerations in formatting bar charts. The statement

WINDOW (−40,−27) − (599,172)

establishes a well-suited coordinate system. Since the screen is divided into 640 × 200 pixels in high-resolution screen mode, each pixel corresponds to a point with integer coordinates; that is, a unit in this coordinate system is exactly one pixel wide or high.

Figure 12-6 shows the rationale for choosing the numbers −40 and −27 in the **WINDOW** statement. Since each character is eight pixels high and eight pixels wide, space exists for four digits and a tick mark to the left of the Y-axis, and space exists for three characters below the X-axis. By placing the X-axis at the twenty-eighth pixel from the bottom of the screen, the X-axis will be centered

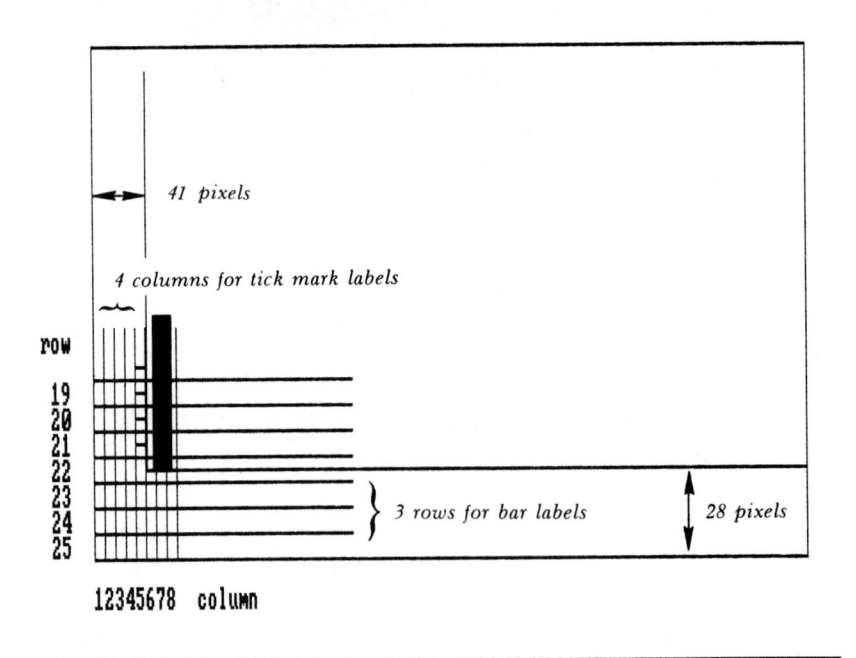

Figure 12-6. *Choosing coordinates for a bar chart*

Business Programming

vertically in the twenty-second text line. If you start from the X-axis, moving up eight pixels for successive tick marks guarantees that each tick mark will be centered vertically in a text line. Therefore, even though Turbo Basic draws the tick marks with graphics statements and displays the labels as text, the tick marks and labels will be perfectly aligned.

The statements

```
LINE (0,0) - (599,0)
LINE (0,0) - (0,164)
```

draw the axes. The Y-axis extends up only 164 pixels so that you can use the top 8 pixels, which form the top row, to display a title. Finally, the statements

```
FOR verticalPosition% = 8 TO 160 STEP 8
   LINE (0,verticalPosition%) - (-8,verticalPosition%)
NEXT verticalPosition%
```

place 20 tick marks—each pair of tick marks separated by 8 pixels—directly to the left of the Y-axis.

Determining a Scale for the Y-axis

The numbers used as labels for the tick marks on the Y-axis depend on the value that the highest bar represents. Here, let's refer to this value as **maximumDataValue**. One way to determine the scale is to label the top tick mark with this value, label the lowest tick mark with one-twentieth of this value, and so on. Another way is to label the lowest tick mark with a rounded up value of **maximumDataValue/20** and label the others accordingly. The first way can result in some strange labels. Although the second way is reasonable, graph makers prefer to have successive labels that differ by numbers such as 5, 10, or 100. Program 12-5 selects reasonable values for the tick labels by choosing a reasonable value for the interval between tick marks. The program segment also specifies a **PRINT USING** format string that will display the labels appropriately.

```
s = maximumDataValue/20
SELECT CASE s
  CASE >=100
    interval = CEIL(s/100)*100
    format$ = "####"
  CASE >=10
    interval = CEIL(s/10)*10
    format$ = "####"
  CASE >=1
    interval = CEIL(s/1)*1
    format$ = "####"
  CASE >=.1
    interval = CEIL(s*10)/10
    format$ = "##.#"
  CASE >=.01
    interval = CEIL(s*100)/100
    format$ = "#.##"
  CASE ELSE
    interval = CEIL(s*1000)/1000
    format$ = ".###"
END SELECT
FOR tick% = 1 TO 20
  LOCATE 22 - tick%, 1
  PRINT USING formatString$; tick%*interval
NEXT tick%
```

Program 12-5. *A segment that chooses a reasonable tick mark interval*

Displaying Vertical Bar Labels

The labels that are placed under the bars could be placed horizontally if the bars are sufficiently wide and the labels short. However, you gain more flexibility if you display the labels vertically under each bar. This format permits bars to be centered over every other character position and, in the printer version of the chart, allows labels of any length to be printed. As mentioned earlier, the program will display only the first three letters of each bar label on screen.

If the labels for each bar are held in the array **names$( )** and you place successive bars so that they are centered over character columns 7, 9, 11, and so on, then the bar labels can be displayed with the statements in the segment in Program 12-6. The segment

```
FOR bar% = 1 to barCount%
  FOR letter% = 1 TO 3
    LOCATE 22 + letter%, 7 + 2*(bar%-1)
    letter$ = MID$(names$(bar%),letter%,1)
    IF letter$ = "" THEN letter$ = " "
    PRINT letter$;
  NEXT letter%
NEXT bar%
```

Program 12-6. *A segment that displays vertical labels*

uses the **MID$** function to select the **letter%th** letter from each label. If there is no **letter%th** letter in a given label, **MID$** will give the null string. To preserve the spacing of the other labels, the segment converts this null value to a space.

Positioning and Displaying the Bars

The height of the bar reflects the value that each bar represents. Since the height of a single pixel is **interval/8**, the height of a bar (in pixels) should be

value represented by the bar/(interval/8)

Since only one space separates the labels under the bars, the maximum width that each bar could have is 16 pixels. For the moment, suppose that each bar is 16 pixels wide. Then the first bar would begin at the fourth pixel of the X-axis and extend to the twentieth pixel. The second bar would extend from the twentieth pixel to the thirty-sixth, and so on. The bars could then be drawn by the statements in Program 12-7, which assume that the labels and values of the bars are stored in the arrays **name$( )** and **values( )**, respectively. The **BF** parameter in the **LINE** statement draws a solid rectangle that has the two given points as opposite corners.

```
leftEdge% = 4
barWidth% = 16
FOR bar% = 1 TO barCount%
   height% = values(bar%)/(interval/8)
   LINE (leftEdge%,0) - (leftEdge%+barWidth%,height%),,BF
   leftEdge% = leftEdge% + barWidth%
NEXT bar%
```

Program 12-7. *A segment that draws the bars*

The bars drawn by Program 12-7 would be correct, but they would run together. The chart would be easier to read if space existed between successive bars. Therefore, you should replace the **LINE** statement with

LINE (leftEdge%+1,0) − (leftEdge%+barWidth%−1,height%),,BF

Printing the Bar Chart

The standard method to print the contents of the screen is to use a screen-dumping utility. Most DOS disks contain a program of this type called GRAPHICS.COM. You normally load the program from DOS before you run any programs; at any time thereafter, pressing SHIFT-PRTSC produces a screen dump. However, this method has some shortcomings. First, it is rather slow—particularly when a bar chart contains only a few bars and most of the screen is empty. Second, the printed image is distorted in comparison to the image on screen.

There is another method to print a bar chart that not only corrects the shortcomings of a screen dump, but also allows you to print all of the letters in the bar labels. This method involves writing a set of custom routines that use the original data to graph the bar chart directly on the printer, as opposed to using a screen dump to copy the image from the screen to the printer. The printing procedures presented in Program 12-8 form one example of such a

Business Programming

```
REM Display and print a barchart with up to 37 bars     [12-8]
%maxBars = 37    'Center over columns 7, 9, 11, ..., 79
DIM values(1:%maxBars), names$(1:%maxBars)
'These procedures share the variables values(),
'names$(), title$, interval, maxLength%, and barCount%
CALL GetInfo
CALL PrepareScreenAxisAndTickMarks
CALL DrawBars
CALL LabelBars
LOCATE 1,1: PRINT title$;
LOCATE 1,50: PRINT "Print chart on printer (Y/N)?"
IF UCASE$(INPUT$(1)) = "Y" THEN CALL PrintChart
END

SUB GetInfo
   SHARED values(), names$(), title$
   SHARED interval, maxLength%, barCount%
   LOCAL maxValue, newName$, newValue
   maxValue   = 0
   maxLength% = 0
   barCount%  = 0
   CLS
   CALL GiveInstructions
   INPUT "name"; newName$
   DO WHILE newName$ <> ""
      INPUT "value"; newValue
      IF LEN(newName$) > maxLength% THEN maxLength% = LEN(newName$)
      IF newValue     > maxValue   THEN maxValue    = newValue
      barCount% = barCount% + 1
      values(barCount%) = newValue
      names$(barCount%) = newName$
      IF barCount% = %maxBars THEN  EXIT LOOP
      'Redisplay instructions at bottom of screen
      'when they scroll off the top.
      IF barCount% MOD 10 = 0  THEN   CALL GiveInstructions
      INPUT "name"; newName$
   LOOP
   LINE INPUT "title? "; title$
   'Compute a nice value for the vertical interval between tick
   'marks that will accomodate the largest value given as data.
   CALL FindNiceInterval(maxValue/20)
END SUB

SUB GiveInstructions
   PRINT "Up to"; %maxBars;
   PRINT "names and corresponding values may be given."
   PRINT "When all desired names and values have been entered, "
   PRINT "respond to the prompt for a name by pressing ENTER"
   PRINT "without giving a name."
END SUB

SUB FindNiceInterval(s)
   SHARED interval, format$
   SELECT CASE s
      CASE >=100
         interval = CEIL(s/100)*100
         format$ = "####"
```

Program 12-8. *A generic bar chart program*

```
      CASE >=10
        interval = CEIL(s/10)*10
        format$ = "####"
      CASE >=1
        interval = CEIL(s/1)*1
        format$ = "####"
      CASE >=.1
        interval = CEIL(s*10)/10
        format$ = "##.#"
      CASE >=.01
        interval = CEIL(s*100)/100
        format$ = "#.##"
      CASE ELSE
        interval = CEIL(s*1000)/1000
        format$ = ".###"
    END SELECT
END SUB

SUB PrepareScreenAxisAndTickMarks
    SHARED interval, barCount%, format$
    LOCAL verticalPosition%, tick%
    SCREEN 2
    WINDOW (-40,-27) - (599,172)
    LINE (0,0) - (599,0)
    LINE (0,0) - (0,164)
    FOR verticalPosition% = 8 TO 160 STEP 8
      LINE (0,verticalPosition%) - (-8,verticalPosition%)
    NEXT verticalPosition%
    FOR tick% = 1 TO 20
      LOCATE 22 - tick%, 1
      PRINT USING format$;interval*tick%;
    NEXT tick%
END SUB

SUB DrawBars
    SHARED values(),interval, barCount%
    LOCAL leftEdge%, bar%, height%, barWidth%
    leftEdge% = 4
    barWidth% = 16
    FOR bar% = 1 TO barCount%
      height% = values(bar%)/(interval/8)
      LINE (leftEdge%+1, 0) - (leftEdge%+barWidth%-1,height%),,BF
      leftEdge% = leftEdge% + barWidth%
    NEXT bar%
END SUB

SUB LabelBars
    SHARED barCount%, names$()
    LOCAL bar%, letter%
    FOR bar% = 1 TO barCount%
      FOR letter% = 1 TO 3
        LOCATE 22 + letter%, 7 + 2*(bar%-1)
        letter$ = MID$(names$(bar%),letter%,1)
        IF letter$ = "" THEN letter$ = " "
        PRINT letter$;
      NEXT letter%
    NEXT bar%
END SUB
```

Program 12-8. *A generic bar chart program* (continued)

```
SUB PrintChart
  SHARED title$
  LOCAL index%
  CALL PrepareToPrint
  LPRINT title$
  LPRINT
  'Print two lines on printer for each row on screen
  FOR index% = 20 TO 1 STEP -1
    CALL PrintLine("tick",index%)
    CALL PrintLine("bar",index%)
  NEXT index%
  CALL PrintLastLine
  CALL PrintBarLabels
END SUB

SUB PrepareToPrint
  SHARED tick$, bar$, corner$
  WIDTH "LPT1:",1000
  'Set printer to graphic line spacing (8/72nds of an inch)
  'Both IBM and EPSON escape sequences given
  LPRINT CHR$(27);"@";CHR$(27);"A";CHR$(8);CHR$(2);
  LPRINT CHR$(27);"A";CHR$(8);
  'Define 18 dot wide characters used to form vertical axis
  tick$ = STRING$(10,CHR$(8)) + _
          STRING$( 2,CHR$(255)) + _
          STRING$( 6,CHR$(0))
  bar$  = STRING$(10,CHR$(0)) + _
          STRING$( 2,CHR$(255)) + _
          STRING$( 6,CHR$(0))
  corner$ = STRING$(10,CHR$(0)) + _
            STRING$( 2,CHR$(248)) + _
            STRING$( 6,CHR$(8))
END SUB

SUB PrintLine(mode$, index%)
  SHARED tick$, bar$, barCount%, interval, format$
  LOCAL info$, bar%
  IF mode$ = "tick" THEN
      LPRINT USING format$; interval*index%;
      info$ = tick$
    ELSE
      LPRINT "     ";
      info$ = bar$
  END IF
  FOR bar% = 1 TO barCount%
    info$ = info$ + CHR$(0) + CHR$(0) + _
            STRING$(20,CHR$(FNPattern%(mode$,index%,bar%))) + _
            CHR$(0) + CHR$(0)
  NEXT bar%
  CALL PrintGraphics(info$)
  LPRINT
END SUB

DEF FNPattern%(mode$,index%,bar%)
  SHARED values(), interval
  LOCAL adjustment%, extra%
  IF mode$ = "tick" THEN adjustment% = 4 _
                   ELSE adjustment% = 12
```

Program 12-8. *A generic bar chart program* (continued)

```
    extra% = values(bar%)/(interval/16) - 16*index% + adjustment%
    IF extra% < 0 THEN extra% = 0
    IF extra% >= 8 THEN   FNPattern% = 255
                  ELSE    FNPattern% = EXP2(extra%)-1
END DEF

SUB PrintLastLine
   SHARED corner$, values(), barCount%, interval
   LOCAL bar%, extra%, pattern%, info$
   info$ = corner$
   FOR bar% = 1 TO barCount%
      extra% = values(bar%)/(interval/16)
      IF extra% >= 4 THEN
         pattern% = 248
       ELSE
         pattern% = EXP2(extra%+4)-8
      END IF
      info$ = info$ + CHR$(8) + CHR$(8) + _
              STRING$(20,CHR$(pattern%)) + CHR$(8) + CHR$(8)
   NEXT bar%
   LPRINT "       ";
   CALL PrintGraphics(info$)
   LPRINT
END SUB

SUB PrintGraphics(graphicsString$)
   LOCAL low%, high%
   'Graphics escape sequence for IBM, Epson, and clone printers
   low% = LEN(graphicsString$) MOD 256
   high% = LEN(graphicsString$)\256
   LPRINT CHR$(27);"L";CHR$(low%);CHR$(high%);graphicsString$;
END SUB

SUB PrintBarLabels
   SHARED names$(), maxLength%, barCount%
   LOCAL letterCount%, bar%, letter$
   FOR letterCount% = 1 TO maxLength%
      LPRINT "       ";
      FOR bar% = 1 TO barCount%
         letter$ = MID$(names$(bar%),letterCount%,1)
         IF letter$ = "" THEN letter$ = " "
         LPRINT letter$; " ";
      NEXT bar%
      LPRINT
   NEXT letterCount%
END SUB
```

Program 12-8. *A generic bar chart program* (continued)

set of routines. The main print procedure, **PrintChart**, first invokes **PrepareToPrint** to set up the printer for graphics printing, then prints the bar chart title, and uses the procedure **PrintLine** to produce the body of the chart. The program then calls the procedure

PrintLastLine to print the horizontal axis and the pieces of bars just above this axis. Finally, the program calls the procedure **PrintBarLabels** to print, in a vertical column, the full label for each bar.

The printing procedures of Program 12-8 use a scale of **interval/16** to help the printed bar chart have the same shape as the displayed chart. As a result, each displayed row becomes two print lines. The procedures print the tick mark labels, tick marks, a portion of the vertical axis, and an appropriate portion of each bar as the first of the two lines. The second line prints just a portion of the vertical axis and an appropriate piece from each bar.

In standard printing, no more than 80 characters are printed on a line, and successive lines have a gap between them. For graphics printing, you may use nearly 1000 characters on a single line to form an 8-inch-wide image. Also, you must eliminate the gap between lines. In Program 12-8, the procedure **PrepareToPrint** sets the printing width to 1000 so that Turbo Basic will not insert a carriage return and a line feed before the procedure can send all of the graphics characters for a given line to the printer. **PrepareToPrint** also sets line spacing to eight seventy-seconds of an inch to cause successive lines to print without a gap between them. **PrepareToPrint** also gives the strings that define the three graphics characters used in printing the vertical axis.

The procedure **PrintLine** handles the printing of a given line. **PrintLine** first prints either a four-digit tick label or four spaces, and then prints a string of graphics data. The graphics data for a given line begins with either a tick mark and a portion of the vertical axis or only a portion of the vertical axis. This data is followed by appropriate sets of 24 patterns of dots, one set for each bar in the chart. (A standard printed character is 12 dots wide, so a 2-character-wide bar is 24 printed dots wide.)

The function **FNPattern%** determines the patterns to be printed for each bar, as well as how much of a given bar the current line of print contains. If a particular bar extends above the current line being printed, then the value of the function is 255, which results in a solid rectangle being printed as the print head moves over that bar's position. If a particular bar does not reach as high as the current line being printed, then the value of the function is 0, which results in nothing being printed as the print head moves over the bar's position. When a particular bar extends partially into the line being printed, the function returns a value between 1 and 127, which results in the appropriate portion of a rectangle being printed as the print head moves over the bar's position.

A Generic Bar Chart Program

Program 12-8 incorporates the various features discussed earlier in this section. The program allows the graphing of a maximum of 37 bars from values supplied interactively by the user during run-time. The program has been designed with four characters allocated for tick mark labels. This design does not actually limit the magnitude of the quantities that you can chart. For example, if the quantities are in the hundreds of thousands, then you can drop the last three digits from each quantity (in order to produce data between 1 and 999) and you can add **in thousands** to the title of the graph.

Database Management

Hypothetically, you can call any collection of data a *database*. However, the term *database* usually refers to a collection of data that is stored on a disk, and that can take on a variety of appearances depending on the requirements at the time. Thus, a database can serve as the data source for a variety of applications. A *database management program* is a program that can create and maintain a database.

Chapter 7 introduced random, sequential, and binary files. This section now uses the file-handling statements discussed there to create and maintain a database.

Opening a Generic Database

The primary data for the database will be stored in a random file. In order to create a random file, you must decide how many fields each record will have and how long each field will be. You need this information in order to write the appropriate **OPEN** and **FIELD** statements for the random file. Also, knowing the type of information that each field will contain will help you give meaningful names to the field variables. For example, suppose that a database will hold names and phone numbers. Each record might consist of first name, last name, and phone fields that have lengths 10, 15, and 12, respectively. With this information, appropriate statements to open the database are

```
OPEN "PHONEDIR.DB" AS #1 LEN = 37
FIELD #1, 10 AS firstNamef$, 15 AS lastNamef$, 12 AS phonef$
```

To produce a general database management program, you should generalize these statements by removing specific values and replacing them with variables. The statements in the segment in Program 12-9 carry out this generalization. Notice that the **OPEN** and **FIELD** statements no longer contain any constants that are specific to a particular database. These two statements can open any database with three fields. Since the generic field variables **item1f$**, **item2f$**, and **item3f$** no longer suggest the data that they hold, this segment creates three additional variables—**item1Name$**, **item2Name$**, and **item3Name$**—to hold this information.

You can carry the generalization in Program 12-9 one step further by introducing arrays to hold the field lengths and the field names, and to serve as field variables. In addition, you can place the

---

```
filename$ = "PHONEDIR.DB"
item1Len = 10
item1Name$ = "First Name"
item2Len = 15
item2Name$ = "Last Name"
item3Len = 12
item3Name$ = "Phone"
recordLength% = item1Len + item2Len + item3Len
OPEN filename$ AS #1 LEN = recordLength%
FIELD #1, item1Len AS item1f$, item2Len AS item2f$, _
          item3Len AS item3f$
```

Program 12-9. *A segment that obtains generalized OPEN and FIELD statements*

```
DATA "PHONEDIR.DB", 3
DATA "First Name",10
DATA "Last Name",15
DATA "Phone",12
READ filename$, fieldCount%
DIM itemName$(1:fieldCount%)     'description of field
DIM itemLen%(1:fieldCount%)      'length of field
DIM itemf$(1:fieldCount%)        'field variable for data
recordLength% = 0
FOR index% = 1 TO fieldCount%
   READ itemName$(index%),itemLen%(index%)
   recordLength% = recordLength% + itemLen%(index%)
NEXT index%
OPEN filename$ AS #1 LEN = recordLength%
FIELD #1, itemLen%(1) AS itemf$(1), itemLen%(2) AS itemf$(2), _
         itemLen%(3) AS itemf$(3)
```

Program 12-10. *A segment that opens a database by using DATA statements*

information specific to **PHONEDIR.DB** in **DATA** statements. The generalized database opening statements are those used in the segment of Program 12-10. These statements are so general that you only need to make two small changes to apply them to a database with 4, 5, or so on, up to 10 fields. You must change the **DATA** statements at the top of the program, and you must add more fields to the **FIELD** statement. You can execute the proper **FIELD** statement for a given number of fields automatically—up to some predefined maximum number of fields—by replacing the **FIELD** statement in Program 12-10 with a **CALL** to the procedure **Set-Fields** shown in Program 12-11. The procedure **SetFields** uses a **SELECT CASE** structure to choose the correct **FIELD** statement for the given number of fields, which is **fieldCount%**.

The final generalization consists of removing the **DATA** statements from the program, and placing the information that describes the structure of a database in a sequential file. For a given database, there then will be two files: a sequential file that holds the number, meanings, and lengths of the fields; and a random file that contains the actual records of the database. This section uses the conventions of placing the database structure in a file whose name has no extension and placing the database records in a file of the same name but with the extension .DB.

Business Programming

```
SUB SetFields(fieldCount%)
  SELECT CASE fieldCount%
    CASE 1
      FIELD #1, itemLen%(1) AS itemf$(1)
    CASE 2
      FIELD #1, itemLen%(1) AS itemf$(1),itemLen%(2) AS itemf$(2)
    CASE 3
      FIELD #1, itemLen%(1) AS itemf$(1),itemLen%(2) AS itemf$(2),_
                itemLen%(3) AS itemf$(3)
    CASE 4
      FIELD #1, itemLen%(1) AS itemf$(1),itemLen%(2) AS itemf$(2), _
                itemLen%(3) AS itemf$(3),itemLen%(4) AS itemf$(4)
    'Continue until there are as many CASE statements as the
    ' maximum number of field to be allowed in the database
  END SELECT
END SUB
```

Program 12-11. *A segment that chooses a FIELD statement when the field count is variable*

Suppose that you have created a sequential file with the entries

field count
first field name
first field length
second field name
second field length

and so on, in which delimiters separate the entries. This file describes a generic database. The statements of the segment in Program 12-12 will open this database.

After you open a generic database, you need a number of standard operations to maintain the database. Among these operations are the following:

- Creating a new database

- Appending a record to the end of a database

- Inserting a record in the middle of a database

- Deleting a record

- Listing the records

- Editing a record
- Sorting the records by one of the fields

The following sections discuss each of these operations in detail.

Creating a New Database

Not all records are required when you create a database—only the names and lengths of the fields. The interactive statements of the segment in Program 12-13 request the name of the new database and the names and lengths of the fields, and then produce a sequential file that contains the number of fields followed by the field names and lengths. (Note: The statements in Program 12-13 do not open the database.) The statements store the number of fields in the variable **count%**. Note the use of the named constant **%maxFields**: This constant will appear at the beginning of the master database management program. The value of this constant should be the number that appears in the last **CASE** statement in the **SELECT CASE** block of the **SetFields** procedure in the master program.

```
INPUT "Name of database"; datafile$
OPEN datafile$ FOR INPUT AS #1
INPUT #1, fieldCount%
DIM itemf$(1:fieldCount%), itemLen%(1:fieldCount%), _
    itemName$(1:fieldCount%)
recordLength% = 0
FOR index% = 1 TO fieldCount%
  INPUT #1, itemName$(index%), itemLen%(index%)
  recordLength% = recordLength% + itemLen%(index%)
NEXT index%
CLOSE #1
OPEN datafile$ + ".DB" AS #1 LEN = recordLength%
CALL SetFields(fieldCount%)
```

Program 12-12. *A segment that opens a database using a database description file*

```
%maxFields = 4
DIM DYNAMIC fieldName$(1:%maxFields), fieldLen%(1:%maxFields)
CLS
INPUT "Name for database (maximum of 8 letters)"; datafile$
PRINT
PRINT "Enter one field name and field length per line."
PRINT "Separate field name and field length by a comma."
PRINT "End list by entering   ,0"
count% = 0      'Count of number of fields specified
INPUT nom$,length%
DO UNTIL nom$="" OR length%=0
  INCR count%
  fieldName$(count%) = nom$
  fieldLen%(count%)  = length%
  IF count% = %maxFields THEN EXIT LOOP
  INPUT nom$,length%
LOOP
OPEN datafile$ FOR OUTPUT AS #1
WRITE #1, count%
FOR index% = 1 TO count%
  WRITE #1, fieldName$(index%), fieldLen%(index%)
NEXT index%
CLOSE #1
ERASE fieldName$, fieldLen%
```

Program 12-13. *A segment that creates a new database description file*

Appending a Record to the End of a Database

Adding, or appending, a blank record to the end of a database is one of the simplest tasks of managing a database. First, you must determine the record number for the last record currently in the database. You can do this by using the statement

lastRecord% = LOF(1)/recordLength%

The append process consists of assigning the null string to each field variable, and then placing this blank record after the last record. The statements of the segment in Program 12-14 append a blank record to a generic database.

```
lastRecord% = LOF(1)/recordLength%
FOR index% = 1 TO fieldCount%
  LSET itemf$(index%) = ""
NEXT index%
PUT #1, lastRecord% + 1
```

Program 12-14. *A segment that appends a blank record to a database*

Inserting a Record into the Middle of a Database

Inserting a record is similar to appending a record, but requires that you copy all records from a specified point on into the record that has the next higher record number. You can accomplish this task by using a **FOR** loop that **GET**s records and **PUT**s them at the next higher record number. Since shifting record r overwrites record $r+1$, the **FOR** loop starts with the current last record and steps backwards to the record that occupies the spot where you want to insert a new record. As in the append process, the final action is to **PUT** a blank record in the specified location. If a database has many records, an insertion near the beginning of the database may require a substantial amount of time while moving the necessary records. The statements of the segment in Program 12-15 insert a record into a generic database.

```
INPUT "Record number to insert before",n%
lastRecord% = LOF(1)/recordLength%
FOR index% = lastRecord% TO n% STEP -1
  GET #1, index%
  PUT #1, index% + 1
NEXT index%
FOR index% = 1 TO fieldCount%
  LSET itemf$(index%) = ""
NEXT index%
PUT #1, n%
```

Program 12-15. *A segment that inserts a record into a database*

Deleting a Record from a Database

One method of deleting a record from a database is to attempt to reverse the process of inserting a record. If you want to delete record **n%**, you might try to use statements such as

```
lastRecord% = LOF(1)/recordLength%
FOR index% = n% + 1 TO lastRecord%
   GET #1, index%
   PUT #1, index% - 1
NEXT index%
```

However, these statements have two drawbacks. First, as with inserting, deleting a record near the beginning of a large database will be time-consuming. Second—and equally important from a programming point of view—moving all of the records down by one record number does not remove the record with record number **lastRecord%**. In fact, this record now appears twice in the database. The standard solution to this problem is not to delete a record by moving records down, but by copying all records except the one to delete to a temporary file, erasing the old database, and renaming the temporary file with the name of the original database file. The segment in Program 12-16 deletes record **n%** in this manner.

Notice that the segment in Program 12-16 executes a new **FIELD** statement for the database file so that a single field variable can reference an entire record. Notice also that although Program 12-16 starts off by assuming that the database is already open, the segment closes the database after executing.

Since deleting a record requires the long process of copying the entire file, it is common practice not to delete a record physically whenever you no longer need it, but rather to mark it in a special way so that a program can ignore it. Later, after you mark many records for deletion, your program can copy the unmarked records to a new random file and erase the original file. This copying process is called *packing*. Marking records for deletion in anticipation of a later packing operation has the additional advantage that you can "undelete," or recover, a record at any time prior to the packing process.

To allow records to be marked as deleted, you should include an additional single-character field at the beginning of each database

```
lastRecord% = LOF(1)/recordLength%
FIELD #1, recordLength% AS file1f$
OPEN "temp" AS #2 LEN = recordLength%
FIELD #2, recordLength% AS file2f$
'Copy all records before n%
FOR index% = 1 TO n%-1
  GET #1, index%
  LSET file2f$ = file1f$
  PUT #2, index%
NEXT index%
Copy all records after n%
FOR index% = n% + 1 TO lastRecord%
  GET #1, index%
  LSET file2f$ = file1f$
  PUT #2, index% - 1
NEXT index%
CLOSE #1,#2
KILL datafile$ + ".DB"
NAME "temp" AS datafile$ + ".DB"
```

Program 12-16. *A segment that deletes a single record*

record. The database management program can produce this *status* field automatically when creating a database. If so, a generic **FIELD** statement will have the form

```
FIELD #1, 1 AS statusf$, _
  itemLen%(1) AS itemf$(1), itemLen%(2) AS itemf$(2), _
  etc.
```

The deletion process then becomes simply a matter of **GET**ting the specified record, setting **statusf$** to some special value—perhaps an asterisk (*)—and then **PUT**ting the record back. The statements of the segment in Program 12-17 toggle the status field of a record back and forth between **Removed** and **Restored**.

The packing process consists of copying to another file all records that are not marked by an asterisk in their status field. The statements of the segment in Program 12-18 will do the job. Note that, in the segment, **recordLength%** now includes the one-character length of **statusf$**. After the execution of this segment, the database will be closed.

```
INPUT "Record Number to be removed/restored",n%
GET #1, n%
IF statusf$ = "*" THEN
    LSET statusf$ = " "
    PRINT "Record Restored"
  ELSE
    LSET statusf$ = "*"
    PRINT "Record Removed"
END IF
PUT #1, n%
DELAY 1
```

Program 12-17. *A segment that marks records for removal*

Listing the Records of a Database

The volume of data listed from a database can vary from the entire database to only the records whose record numbers lie in a certain range. Also, the listings can consist of entire records or selected fields.

```
lastRecord% = LOF(1)/recordLength%
FIELD #1, 1 AS statusf$, recordLength%-1 AS file1f$
OPEN "temp" AS #2 LEN = recordLength%
FIELD #2, recordLength% AS file2f$
tempIndex% = 1
FOR index% = 1 TO lastRecord%
  GET #1, index%
  IF statusf$ = " " THEN
    LSET file2f$ = statusf$ + file1f$
    PUT #2, tempIndex%
    INCR tempIndex%
  END IF
NEXT index%
CLOSE #1, #2
KILL datafile$ + ".DB"
NAME "temp" AS datafile$ + ".DB"
```

Program 12-18. *A segment that packs a database*

```
lastRecord% = LOF(1)/recordLength%
FOR recordNumber% = 1 TO lastRecord%
  GET #1, recordNumber%
  PRINT USING "! #####"; statusf$, recordNumber%;
  FOR index% = 1 TO fieldCount%
    PRINT " "; itemf$(index%);
  NEXT index%
  PRINT
  IF (recordNumber% MOD 15 = 0) OR
     (recordNumber% = lastRecord%) THEN
    PRINT
    PRINT "Press any key to continue";
    a$ = INPUT$(1)
    PRINT
  END IF
NEXT recordNumber%
```

Program 12-19. *A segment that lists records from a database*

The statements of the segment in Program 12-19 display the record number and the contents of each field for every record in a database. After displaying each fifteenth record, the program pauses to let the user examine the records. After the user presses a key, the screen clears and the program displays the next 15 records.

Editing a Record

You can program the process of editing a record in a database in many ways. The simplest approach, which is illustrated by the segment in Program 12-20, displays the field name and current value of each field of a specified record. After displaying the data for a specific field, the segment prompts the user for a replacement value. If the user presses ENTER without giving a new value, the old value is retained.

More sophisticated editing routines display all of the field names and current values at one time, and allow you to move the cursor to any of the old values. Then you can modify any value as if you were using a word processor in overwrite mode.

```
INPUT "Record to be edited", n%
GET #1, n%
FOR index% = 1 TO fieldCount%
  PRINT itemName$(index%)
  PRINT itemf$(index%)
  INPUT "New Value",newItem$
  IF newItem$<>"" THEN LSET itemf$(index%) = newItem$
NEXT index%
PUT #1, n%
```

Program 12-20. *A segment that edits a database*

Sorting the Records by One Field

The technique for sorting a database is similar to the one used to sort a sequential file in Chapter 7. If your computer had sufficient memory available, you might read the entire database into **fieldCount%+1** parallel arrays and then sort these arrays as described in Chapter 7. However, for sorts on a single field of a database, there is a faster and more memory-efficient approach that requires only two parallel arrays. This approach assigns the values from the sort field of successive records to successive elements of the first array. The second array is a numeric array that contains the numbers 1 through **lastRecord%** in order. Therefore, each element of the second array holds the record number of the corresponding element of the first array. The approach then sorts these parallel arrays based on the values in the first array. Next, the approach copies the entire database to a temporary file in the order indicated by the now-shuffled record numbers held in the second array. The approach then completes the sort by erasing the old database file and renaming the temporary file. This technique, known as *sorting with pointers,* is illustrated in the segment of Program 12-21. After the segment sorts a database on a certain field, you can use a binary search to locate efficiently the record that contains a specified value in that field.

```
lastRecord% = LOF(1)/recordLength%
INPUT "Number of field on which sort is to be made",fieldNumber%
DIM recNum%(1:lastRecord%), value$(1:lastRecord%)
FOR index% = 1 TO lastRecord%
   GET #1, index%
   recNum%(index%) = index%
   value$(index%) = itemf$(fieldNumber%)
NEXT index%
CALL SortArrays(recNum%(),value$())
FIELD #1, 1 AS statusf$, recordLength%-1 AS file1f$
OPEN "temp" AS #2 LEN = recordLength%
FIELD #2, recordLength% AS file2f$
FOR index% = 1 TO lastRecord%
   GET #1, recNum%(index%)
   LSET file2f$ = statusf$ + file1f$
   PUT #2, index%
NEXT index%
CLOSE #1,#2
KILL datafile$ + ".DB"
NAME "temp" AS datafile$ + ".DB"
```

Program 12-21. *A segment that sorts a database*

A Master Generic Database Management Program

The discussions above have covered many aspects of writing a program to create and manage a general-purpose database. You can easily add other features once you understand these fundamental tasks. The following master program employs the techniques presented earlier and embellishes them with data-validation statements.

As indicated by the named constants at the top of the program, you may specify a maximum of ten fields in a database. (You can extend this number by adding more **CASE**s in the procedure **Set-Fields**.) Also, the program allows you to use a maximum of 15 characters when you name a field.

The program displays a menu of supported operations. As the user, you execute an operation by pressing the key enclosed in angle brackets, <>. All but two of the operations in the main menu were discussed previously. The two new operations are displaying the structure of a database—that is, field names and lengths—and displaying a listing of database files—that is, file names that end in .DB.

Many of the procedures share the variables **datafile$**, **fieldCount%**, **itemf$()**, **itemLen%()**, **itemName$()**, **statusf$**, **recordLength%**, and **lastRecord%**. These variables hold the following information about the database that is currently open:

- The **datafile$** variable holds the name of the database. If **datafile$** is the null string, then no database is open.

- The **fieldCount%** variable holds the number of fields in each record, and will be between 1 and **%maxFields**.

- The array **itemf$()** holds the field variables.

- The array **itemLen%()** holds the length of each field.

- The array **itemName$()** holds the names of each field. These names must contain no more than **%maxName** characters.

- The **statusf$** variable is the first field of each record. The character in this field is either a space or an asterisk. When the character is an asterisk, the current record is marked for deletion.

- The **recordLength%** variable is the length of the records in the database. The program calculates the length by adding up the values of **itemLen%()** and then adding 1 to account for **statusf$**.

- The **lastRecord%** variable is the record number of the last record in the database. Initially, the program computes **lastRecord%** by using the formula **LOF(1)/recordLength%**. At other times, such as during the append and insert procedures, the program computes a new value for **lastRecord%** by adding 1 to the old value.

The program could have listed these variables as procedure parameters and passed them as needed to the various procedures. This process is generally the preferred programming technique. However, since these variables appear throughout the entire program, it was decided to give them global status and simply **SHARE** them where needed.

Program 12-22 illustrates many aspects of top-down design, data validation, and formatting output. An examination of the various procedures reveals a wide variety of programming techniques—not all of which have been discussed in detail. Finally, to aid you in locating the procedures and functions, the program lists them alphabetically according to the procedure or function name.

```
REM A general database management system   [12-22]
%true = -1
%false = 0
%maxName = 15
%maxFields = 10
datafile$ = ""
DO
  CALL DisplayMenu
  action$ = UCASE$(INPUT$(1))
  PRINT
  SELECT CASE action$
    CASE "A" : CALL AppendRecord
    CASE "C" : CALL CreateDatabase
    CASE "D" : CALL DisplayStructure
    CASE "E" : CALL GetRecordNumber("Record Number",n%)
               CALL EditRecord(n%)
    CASE "F" : CALL DisplayDatabaseFiles
    CASE "I" : CALL InsertRecord
    CASE "L" : CALL ListRecords
    CASE "O" : CALL GetDatabaseName
               CALL OpenDatabase
    CASE "P" : CALL PackDatabase
    CASE "R" : CALL RemoveOrRestoreRecord(n%)
    CASE "S" : CALL SortDatabase
    CASE ELSE
  END SELECT
LOOP UNTIL action$ = "Q"
CLS
IF datafile$ <> "" THEN CALL CloseDatabase
PRINT "Database closed"
END

SUB AppendRecord
  SHARED fieldCount%, itemf$(), statusf$, lastRecord%
  LOCAL index%
  IF FNDatabaseIsOpen THEN
    INCR lastRecord%
    LSET statusf$ = " "
    FOR index% = 1 TO fieldCount%
      LSET itemf$(index%) = ""
    NEXT index%
```

Program 12-22. *A master database management program*

```
      PUT #1, lastRecord%
      CALL EditRecord(lastRecord%)
   END IF
END SUB

SUB CloseDatabase
   SHARED datafile$, itemf$(), itemLen%(), itemName$()
   CLOSE #1
   ERASE itemf$, itemLen%, itemName$
   datafile$ = ""
END SUB

SUB CreateDatabase
   SHARED datafile$
   LOCAL fieldName$(), fieldLen%(), count%, info$, comma, index%
   DIM fieldName$(1:%maxFields), fieldLen%(1:%maxFields)
   'If another database is already open, close it before proceeding
   IF datafile$ <> "" THEN CALL CloseDatabase
   CLS
   INPUT "Name for database (maximum of 8 letters)"; datafile$
   IF datafile$ = "" THEN EXIT SUB
   datafile$ = LEFT$(datafile$,8)
   count% = 0        'Count of number of fields specified
   PRINT
   PRINT "Enter one field name and field length per line."
   PRINT "Separate field name and field length by a comma."
   PRINT "Field name limited to";%maxName;"characters. "
   PRINT "A Maximum of";%maxFields;"fields may be specified."
   PRINT
   PRINT "> ";
   LINE INPUT info$
   DO UNTIL (info$ = "") OR (count% = %maxFields)
      comma = INSTR(info$,",")
      IF comma <> 0 THEN
         INCR count%
         fieldName$(count%) = LEFT$(LEFT$(info$,comma-1),%maxName)
         fieldLen%(count%)  = VAL(RIGHT$(info$,LEN(info$)-comma))
         IF fieldLen%(count%) = 0 THEN  DECR count%
      ELSE
         PRINT "Format error. Use name,length"
      END IF
      PRINT ">";
      LINE INPUT info$
   LOOP
   IF count% > 0 THEN
      OPEN datafile$ FOR OUTPUT AS #1
      WRITE #1, count%
      FOR index% = 1 TO count%
         WRITE #1, fieldName$(index%), fieldLen%(index%)
      NEXT index%
      CLOSE #1
      CALL OpenDatabase
   ELSE
      datafile$ = ""
   END IF
END SUB
```

Program 12-22. *A master database management program* (continued)

```
SUB DisplayDatabaseFiles
  LOCAL dd$, ch$, a$
  CLS
  INPUT "Drive/Directory to display"; dd$
  ch$ = RIGHT$(dd$,1)
  IF (ch$ <> ":") AND (ch$ <> "\") THEN dd$ = dd$ +"\"
  dd$ = dd$+"*.DB"
  ON ERROR GOTO noFiles
  PRINT
  FILES dd$
  PRINT
  PRINT "Press any key to continue"
  a$ = INPUT$(1)
  EXIT SUB
  noFiles:
    PRINT "No database files in ";dd$
    DELAY 2
END SUB

SUB DisplayFieldTitles
  SHARED fieldCount%, itemLen%(), itemName$()
  LOCAL index%, il%
  CLS
  PRINT "*   Rec#";
  FOR index% = 1 TO fieldCount%
    il% = itemLen%(index%)
    PRINT " ";LEFT$(itemName$(index%)+SPACE$(il%),il%);
  NEXT index%
  PRINT
  PRINT
END SUB

SUB DisplayMenu
  CLS
  PRINT "<A>ppend a record to database"
  PRINT "<C>reate a database"
  PRINT "<D>isplay structure of database"
  PRINT "<E>dit a specified record"
  PRINT "display list of database <F>iles"
  PRINT "<I>nsert blank record before specified record"
  PRINT "<L>ist records"
  PRINT "<O>pen an existing database"
  PRINT "<P>ack database"
  PRINT "<Q>uit"
  PRINT "<R>emove/recover a record"
  PRINT "<S>ort database on a given field"
  PRINT
  PRINT "action?";
END SUB

SUB DisplayRecordForEdit(n%)
  SHARED fieldCount%, itemf$(), itemName$(), statusf$
  LOCAL index%
  CLS
  PRINT USING "#####";n%;
  IF statusf$ = "*" THEN PRINT "      REMOVED";
```

Program 12-22. *A master database management program* (continued)

```
    PRINT
    FOR index% = 1 TO fieldCount%
      PRINT itemName$(index%); TAB(%maxName+1); ":"; itemf$(index%)
      PRINT
    NEXT index%
END SUB

SUB DisplayStructure
    SHARED fieldCount%, itemLen%(), itemName$()
    LOCAL index%, a$
    IF FNDatabaseIsOpen THEN
      CLS
      PRINT "Field Name"; TAB(%maxName+2); "Field Length"
      FOR index% = 1 TO fieldCount%
        PRINT itemName$(index%); TAB(%maxName+2); itemLen%(index%)
      NEXT index%
      PRINT
      PRINT "Press any key to continue."
      a$ = INPUT$(1)
    END IF
END SUB

SUB EditRecord(n%)
    SHARED fieldCount%, itemf$()
    LOCAL index%, newItem$
    IF n% = 0 THEN EXIT SUB
    GET #1, n%
    CALL DisplayRecordForEdit(n%)
    FOR index% = 1 TO fieldCount%
      LOCATE 2*index%+1, %maxName-9, 1
      LINE INPUT "New value> ",newItem$
      IF newItem$<>"" THEN LSET itemf$(index%) = newItem$
    NEXT index%
    PUT #1, n%
END SUB

DEF FNDatabaseIsOpen
    SHARED datafile$
    IF datafile$ = "" THEN
      PRINT "No database currently open"
      CALL GetDatabaseName
      CALL OpenDatabase
    END IF
    IF datafile$ = "" THEN
        FNDatabaseIsOpen = %false
      ELSE
        FNDatabaseIsOpen = %true
    END IF
END DEF

SUB GetDatabaseName
    SHARED datafile$
    IF datafile$<>"" THEN  CALL CloseDatabase
    PRINT
    INPUT "Database to open"; datafile$
END SUB
```

Program 12-22. *A master database management program* (continued)

```
SUB GetFieldNumber(n%)
  SHARED fieldCount%, itemName$()
  LOCAL index%
  CLS
  PRINT "Field    Field"
  PRINT "Number   Name"
  PRINT "------   ----------------"
  FOR index% = 1 TO fieldCount%
    PRINT USING " ##      &"; index%, itemName$(index%)
  NEXT index%
  PRINT
  DO
    INPUT "Number of field on which to perform sort"; n%
  LOOP UNTIL (n% >= 0) AND (n% <= fieldCount%)
END SUB

SUB GetRecordNumber(message$,n%)
  SHARED lastRecord%
  n% = 0
  IF FNDatabaseIsOpen THEN
    PRINT
    DO
      PRINT message$;
      INPUT n%
    LOOP UNTIL (n% >= 0) AND (n% <= lastRecord%)
  END IF
END SUB

SUB InsertRecord
  SHARED fieldCount%, itemf$(), statusf$, lastRecord%
  LOCAL index%, n%
  IF FNDatabaseIsOpen THEN
    CALL GetRecordNumber("Record Number to insert before",n%)
    IF n% <> 0 THEN
      FOR index% = lastRecord% TO n% STEP -1
        GET #1, index%
        PUT #1, index% + 1
      NEXT index%
      INCR lastRecord%
      LSET statusf$ = " "
      FOR index% = 1 TO fieldCount%
        LSET itemf$(index%) = ""
      NEXT index%
      PUT #1, n%
      CALL EditRecord(n%)
    END IF
  END IF
END SUB

SUB ListRecords   '15 records at a time
  SHARED fieldCount%, itemf$(), statusf$, lastRecord%
  LOCAL recordNumber%, a$, index%
  IF FNDatabaseIsOpen THEN
    CALL DisplayFieldTitles
    FOR recordNumber% = 1 TO lastRecord%
      GET #1, recordNumber%
      PRINT USING "! #####"; statusf$, recordNumber%;
```

Program 12-22. *A master database management program* (continued)

Business Programming

```
      FOR index% = 1 TO fieldCount%
        PRINT " "; itemf$(index%);
      NEXT index%
      PRINT
      IF (recordNumber% MOD 15 = 0) OR _
         (recordNumber% = lastRecord%) THEN
        PRINT
        PRINT "Press any key to continue";
        a$ = INPUT$(1)
        IF recordNumber% <> lastRecord% THEN _
          CALL DisplayFieldTitles
        PRINT
      END IF
    NEXT recordNumber%
  END IF
END SUB

SUB OpenDatabase
  SHARED datafile$, fieldCount%, itemf$(), itemLen%(), itemName$()
  SHARED recordLength%, lastRecord%
  LOCAL index%
  IF datafile$<>"" THEN
    OPEN datafile$ FOR INPUT AS #1
    INPUT #1, fieldCount%
    DIM itemf$(1:fieldCount%), itemLen%(1:fieldCount%), _
        itemName$(1:fieldCount%)
    FOR index% = 1 TO fieldCount%
      INPUT #1, itemName$(index%), itemLen%(index%)
    NEXT index%
    CLOSE #1
    recordLength% = 1
    FOR index% = 1 TO fieldCount%
      recordLength% = recordLength% + itemLen%(index%)
    NEXT index%
    OPEN datafile$ + ".DB" AS #1 LEN = recordLength%
    CALL SetFields
    lastRecord% = LOF(1)/recordLength%
  END IF
END SUB

SUB OpenAs2(filename$)
  SHARED recordLength%
  'any old version of filename$ must be erased to guarantee that
  'the temporary file opened below is empty. However, KILLing a
  'file that doesn't exists is an error. So, before KILLing
  'filename$, make sure that it exists by creating it.
  OPEN filename$ FOR OUTPUT AS 2
  CLOSE 2
  KILL filename$
  OPEN filename$ AS 2 LEN = recordLength%
END SUB

SUB PackDatabase
  SHARED datafile$, statusf$, recordLength%, lastRecord%
  LOCAL file1f$, file2f$, zindex%, rec%, holdName$
  IF FNDatabaseIsOpen THEN
    PRINT
```

Program 12-22. *A master database management program* (continued)

```
      PRINT "Packing " + datafile$ + ".DB"
      FIELD #1, 1 AS statusf$, recordLength%-1 AS file1f$
      CALL OpenAs2("zzzzzzzz.tmp")
      FIELD #2, recordLength% AS file2f$
      zindex% = 1
      FOR rec% = 1 TO lastRecord%
        GET #1, rec%
        IF statusf$ = " " THEN
          LSET file2f$ = statusf$ + file1f$
          PUT #2, zindex%
          INCR zindex%
        END IF
      NEXT rec%
      holdName$ = datafile$
      CLOSE #2
      CALL CloseDatabase
      KILL holdName$ + ".DB"
      NAME "zzzzzzzz.tmp" AS holdName$ + ".DB"
      datafile$ = holdName$
      CALL OpenDatabase
    END IF
END SUB

SUB RemoveOrRestoreRecord(n%)
  SHARED statusf$
  CALL GetRecordNumber("Record Number to be removed/restored",n%)
  IF n% <> 0 THEN
    GET #1, n%
    IF statusf$ = "*" THEN
        LSET statusf$ = " "
        PRINT "Record Restored"
      ELSE
        LSET statusf$ = "*"
        PRINT "Record Removed"
    END IF
    PUT #1, n%
    DELAY 1
  END IF
END SUB

SUB SetFields
  SHARED fieldCount%, itemf$(), itemLen%(), statusf$
  SELECT CASE fieldCount%
    CASE 1
      FIELD #1, 1 AS statusf$, _
        itemLen%(1) AS itemf$(1)
    CASE 2
      FIELD #1, 1 AS statusf$, _
        itemLen%(1) AS itemf$(1), itemLen%(2) AS itemf$(2)
    CASE 3
      FIELD #1, 1 AS statusf$, _
        itemLen%(1) AS itemf$(1), itemLen%(2) AS itemf$(2), _
        itemLen%(3) AS itemf$(3)
    CASE 4
      FIELD #1, 1 AS statusf$, _
        itemLen%(1) AS itemf$(1), itemLen%(2) AS itemf$(2), _
        itemLen%(3) AS itemf$(3), itemLen%(4) AS itemf$(4)
```

Program 12-22. *A master database management program* (continued)

Business Programming

```
      CASE 5
        FIELD #1, 1 AS statusf$, _
          itemLen%(1) AS itemf$(1), itemLen%(2) AS itemf$(2), _
          itemLen%(3) AS itemf$(3), itemLen%(4) AS itemf$(4), _
          itemLen%(5) AS itemf$(5)
      CASE 6
        FIELD #1, 1 AS statusf$, _
          itemLen%(1) AS itemf$(1), itemLen%(2) AS itemf$(2), _
          itemLen%(3) AS itemf$(3), itemLen%(4) AS itemf$(4), _
          itemLen%(5) AS itemf$(5), itemLen%(6) AS itemf$(6)
      CASE 7
        FIELD #1, 1 AS statusf$, _
          itemLen%(1) AS itemf$(1), itemLen%(2) AS itemf$(2), _
          itemLen%(3) AS itemf$(3), itemLen%(4) AS itemf$(4), _
          itemLen%(5) AS itemf$(5), itemLen%(6) AS itemf$(6), _
          itemLen%(7) AS itemf$(7)
      CASE 8
        FIELD #1, 1 AS statusf$, _
          itemLen%(1) AS itemf$(1), itemLen%(2) AS itemf$(2), _
          itemLen%(3) AS itemf$(3), itemLen%(4) AS itemf$(4), _
          itemLen%(5) AS itemf$(5), itemLen%(6) AS itemf$(6), _
          itemLen%(7) AS itemf$(7), itemLen%(8) AS itemf$(8)
      CASE 9
        FIELD #1, 1 AS statusf$, _
          itemLen%(1) AS itemf$(1), itemLen%(2) AS itemf$(2), _
          itemLen%(3) AS itemf$(3), itemLen%(4) AS itemf$(4), _
          itemLen%(5) AS itemf$(5), itemLen%(6) AS itemf$(6), _
          itemLen%(7) AS itemf$(7), itemLen%(8) AS itemf$(8), _
          itemLen%(9) AS itemf$(9)
      CASE 10
        FIELD #1, 1 AS statusf$, _
          itemLen%(1) AS itemf$(1), itemLen%(2) AS itemf$(2), _
          itemLen%(3) AS itemf$(3), itemLen%(4) AS itemf$(4), _
          itemLen%(5) AS itemf$(5), itemLen%(6) AS itemf$(6), _
          itemLen%(7) AS itemf$(7), itemLen%(8) AS itemf$(8), _
          itemLen%(9) AS itemf$(9), itemLen%(10) AS itemf$(10)
  END SELECT
END SUB

SUB SortArrays(recNum%(1),value$(1)) 'bubble sort implementation
  LOCAL size%, index1%, index2%, temp$, temp%, exchanged%
  size% = UBOUND(recNum%(1))
  FOR index1% = 1 TO size%
    exchanged% = %false
    FOR index2% = 1 TO size%-index1%
      IF value$(index2%) > value$(index2%+1) THEN
        'exchange index2% with index2%+1 in both arrays
        temp$ = value$(index2%)
        value$(index2%) = value$(index2%+1)
        value$(index2%+1) = temp$
        temp% = recNum%(index2%)
        recNum%(index2%) = recNum%(index2%+1)
        recNum%(index2%+1) = temp%
        exchanged% = %true
      END IF
    NEXT index2%
```

Program 12-22. *A master database management program* (continued)

```
      IF NOT exchanged% THEN EXIT SUB
   NEXT index1%
END SUB

SUB SortDatabase
   SHARED datafile$, itemf$(), itemName$()
   SHARED statusf$, recordLength%, lastRecord%
   LOCAL index%, recNum%(), value$()
   LOCAL file1f$, file2f$, fieldNumber%, holdName$
   IF FNDatabaseIsOpen THEN
      CALL GetFieldNumber(fieldNumber%)
      IF fieldNumber% = 0 THEN EXIT SUB
      PRINT
      PRINT "Sorting ";datafile$;".DB on ";itemName$(fieldNumber%)
      DIM recNum%(1:lastRecord%), value$(1:lastRecord%)
      FOR index% = 1 TO lastRecord%
         GET #1, index%
         recNum%(index%) = index%
         value$(index%) = itemf$(fieldNumber%)
      NEXT index%
      CALL SortArrays(recNum%(),value$())
      FIELD #1, 1 AS statusf$, recordLength%-1 AS file1f$
      CALL OpenAs2("zzzzzzzz.tmp")
      FIELD #2, recordLength% AS file2f$
      FOR index% = 1 TO lastRecord%
         GET #1, recNum%(index%)
         LSET file2f$ = statusf$ + file1f$
         PUT #2, index%
      NEXT index%
      holdName$ = datafile$
      CLOSE #2
      CALL CloseDatabase
      KILL holdName$ + ".DB"
      NAME "zzzzzzzz.tmp" AS holdName$ + ".DB"
      datafile$ = holdName$
      CALL OpenDatabase
   END IF
END SUB
```

Program 12-22. *A master database management program* (continued)

Appendixes

A ASCII Codes for the IBM PC

ASCII Value	Character	ASCII Value	Character
0	Null	12	Form-feed
1	☺	13	Carriage return
2	☻	14	♪
3	♥	15	☼
4	♦	16	►
5	♣	17	◄
6	♠	18	↕
7	Beep	19	‼
8	◘	20	¶
9	Tab	21	§
10	Linefeed	22	▬
11	Cursor home	23	↨

Table A-1. *ASCII Codes for the IBM PC*

ASCII Value	Character	ASCII Value	Character
24	↑	59	;
25	↓	60	<
26	→	61	=
27	←	62	>
28	Cursor right	63	?
29	Cursor left	64	@
30	Cursor up	65	A
31	Cursor down	66	B
32	Space	67	C
33	!	68	D
34	"	69	E
35	#	70	F
36	$	71	G
37	%	72	H
38	&	73	I
39	'	74	J
40	(	75	K
41	)	76	L
42	*	77	M
43	+	78	N
44	,	79	O
45	-	80	P
46	.	81	Q
47	/	82	R
48	0	83	S
49	1	84	T
50	2	85	U
51	3	86	V
52	4	87	W
53	5	88	X
54	6	89	Y
55	7	90	Z
56	8	91	[
57	9	92	\
58	:	93	]

Table A-1. ASCII Codes for the IBM PC (continued)

ASCII Codes for the IBM PC

ASCII Value	Character	ASCII Value	Character
94	^	129	ü
95	_	130	é
96	`	131	â
97	a	132	ä
98	b	133	à
99	c	134	å
100	d	135	ç
101	e	136	ê
102	f	137	ë
103	g	138	è
104	h	139	ï
105	i	140	î
106	j	141	ì
107	k	142	Ä
108	l	143	Å
109	m	144	É
110	n	145	ae
111	o	146	Æ
112	p	147	ô
113	q	148	ö
114	r	149	ò
115	s	150	û
116	t	151	ù
117	u	152	ÿ
118	v	153	Ö
119	w	154	Ü
120	x	155	¢
121	y	156	£
122	z	157	¥
123	{	158	Pt
124	¦	159	*f*
125	}	160	á
126	~	161	í
127	⌂	162	ó
128	Ç	163	ú

Table A-1. *ASCII Codes for the IBM PC* (continued)

ASCII Value	Character	ASCII Value	Character
164	ñ	199	╠
165	Ñ	200	╚
166	ª	201	╔
167	º	202	╩
168	¿	203	╦
169	⌐	204	╠
170	¬	205	═
171	½	206	╬
172	¼	207	╧
173	¡	208	╨
174	«	209	╤
175	»	210	╥
176	░	211	╙
177	▒	212	╘
178	▓	213	╒
179	│	214	╓
180	┤	215	╫
181	╡	216	╪
182	╢	217	┘
183	╖	218	┌
184	╕	219	█
185	╣	220	▄
186	║	221	▌
187	╗	222	▐
188	╝	223	▀
189	╜	224	α
190	╛	225	β
191	┐	226	Γ
192	└	227	π
193	┴	228	Σ
194	┬	229	σ
195	├	230	μ
196	─	231	τ
197	┼	232	Φ
198	╞	233	θ

Table A-1. *ASCII Codes for the IBM PC* (continued)

ASCII Value	Character	ASCII Value	Character
234	Ω	245	⌡
235	δ	246	÷
236	∞	247	≈
237	∅	248	°
238	∈	249	•
239	∩	250	·
240	≡	251	√
241	±	252	n
242	≥	253	2
243	≤	254	■
244	⌠	255	(blank 'FF')

Table A-1. *ASCII Codes for the IBM PC* (continued)

B An Abridged Reference Manual of Turbo Basic

Turbo Basic Metastatements, Statements, and Functions

Numbers in brackets follow some of the discussions. These numbers refer to supporting topics that are presented at the end of this appendix.

$COM The metastatement **$COM1** *bufSize,* where *bufSize* is a constant or a named constant, tells the compiler to allocate *bufSize* bytes for the receive buffer of communications adapter 1. The metastatement **$COM2** *bufSize* acts similarly for communications adapter 2. Allowable buffer sizes range from 0 to 32767 bytes. The default buffer size for each communications adapter is 256 bytes.

$DYNAMIC The metastatement **$DYNAMIC** specifies that any array that is dimensioned after this point in the program should have its memory allocated dynamically at run-time. Dynamic arrays have the advantage that you can **ERASE** them to free up memory.

By default, the computer allocates memory, where possible, to arrays *statically* (permanently) at compile-time. Array-memory allocation is automatically dynamic when you do one of the following: use the key word **DYNAMIC** in a **DIM** statement, declare the array to be **LOCAL** to a procedure or function, **DIM**ension the array by using a variable, or use the array in more than one **DIM** statement (not counting **LOCAL** declarations in procedures or functions). You can override the **$DYNAMIC** metastatement for a given **DIM** statement by inserting the word **STATIC**.

$EVENT The metastatement **$EVENT OFF** tells the compiler to compile subsequent lines of the program without the insertion of the additional code that is necessary to allow event trapping. The metastatement **$EVENT ON** tells the compiler to compile subsequent lines with the insertion of event-trapping code. [4]

$IF/$ELSE/$ENDIF When a block of statements is preceded by the metastatement **$IF** *namedConst* and followed by the metastatement **$ENDIF**, the compiler will compile the block only if *namedConst* has a nonzero value. If the metastatement **$ELSE** separates the block of statements into two parts, then the computer will compile the first part if *namedConst* has a nonzero value and the second part if the value is zero. These metastatements are useful for conditionally including or excluding statements that are meant for debugging only, and should not be compiled in the final version of the program. The metastatements are also used to compile conditionally one of several versions of a program that is maintained in a single source file.

$INCLUDE The metastatement **$INCLUDE** *filespec* directs the compiler to compile the program segment in the specified disk file as if that program segment appeared in the original program in place of the **$INCLUDE** statement. The **$INCLUDE** metastatement allows you to create a program in manageable chunks that the computer combines at compile-time. [3]

$INLINE The metastatement **$INLINE** *byte1, byte2, ...* indicates that *byte1, byte2,* and so on are actual bytes (with values 0 to 255) of machine-language code that the compiler does not need to com-

An Abridged Reference Manual of Turbo Basic

pile but should simply include in the compiled program as written. The metastatement **$INLINE** *filespec* indicates that the specified file contains actual bytes of machine-language code that should be placed as they are into the compiled program. [3]

$SEGMENT A single *segment* of machine code can be up to 64K bytes long. If a program becomes so large that the compiled program requires more than 64K bytes of machine code, you must place a **$SEGMENT** metastatement in the program to allow the computer to start a second code segment. You may use up to 15 **$SEGMENT** metastatements, in order to permit the compiled program to extend over 16 code segments.

$SOUND The music-background buffer holds notes that are specified by **PLAY** and **SOUND** statements, and that are played while the program continues to execute. The metastatement **$SOUND** *bufSize*, where *bufSize* is a named or numeric constant from 0 to 4096, reserves enough memory for the music-background buffer to store *bufSize* notes. (The computer counts pauses between notes as notes.) The default capacity is 32 notes.

$STACK The metastatement **$STACK** *stackSize*, where *stackSize* is a named or numeric constant from 1024 to 32768, directs the compiler to set aside stackSize bytes of memory for Turbo Basic's stack. The default stack size is 1024 bytes.

$STATIC The metastatement **$STATIC** tells the compiler to use a static—that is, permanent—allocation of memory, if possible, for arrays that appear in subsequent **DIM** statements. This action is the default unless the computer has encountered a **$DYNAMIC** metastatement. Static allocation will not occur if one of the following occurs: the **DIM** statement includes the key word **DYNAMIC**, you declare the array to be **LOCAL** to a procedure or function, you **DIM**ension the array by using a variable, or the array appears in more than one **DIM** statement (not counting **LOCAL** declarations in procedures or functions).

ABS The function **ABS** strips the minus signs from negative numbers while leaving other numbers unchanged. If x is any number, then the value of **ABS**(x) is the absolute value of x.

ASC The ASCII table in Appendix A associates a number from 0 to 255 with each of the characters available to the computer. The value of **ASC**(*a$*) is the ASCII value of the first character of the string *a$*.

ATN The trigonometric function **ATN**, or *arctangent*, is the inverse of the tangent function. For any number x, **ATN**(x) is the angle in radians between $-pi/2$ and $pi/2$, whose tangent is x.

BEEP The statement **BEEP** produces a sound of frequency 800 Hz that lasts a quarter of a second. The statement **BEEP** n produces n quarter-second beeps.

BIN$ If n is a whole number from 0 to 65535, then the value of the function **BIN$**($n$) is the string that consists of the binary representation of n.

BLOAD You can save the contents of successive memory locations in a file by using the **BSAVE** statement, and then later restore them by using the **BLOAD** statement. (This process is commonly used to save and later restore the contents of the screen.) The statement **BLOAD** *filespec*, m places the bytes that have been **BSAVE**d in the file *filespec* into successive memory locations, beginning with the location at offset m in the current segment of memory. [2], [3]

BSAVE The statement **BSAVE** *filespec*, n, m stores in the file *filespec* the contents of the m consecutive memory locations, beginning at the location of offset n in the current memory segment. [2], [3]

CALL You use a statement of the form **CALL** *ProcedureName(list of parameters)* to execute the named procedure, while passing to it the variables and values in the *list of parameters*. After the computer executes the statements in the procedure, program execution continues with the statement **CALL**.

CALL ABSOLUTE The **CALL ABSOLUTE** statement passes control to a machine-language subprogram in much the same way that **CALL** passes control to a procedure. The statement **CALL ABSOLUTE** *offvar (var1, var2,...)* passes control to the machine-language program that begins at the memory location whose offset in the current segment of memory is the value of the numeric variable *offvar*. The machine-language subprogram uses the values of the variables *var1, var2,* and so on. [2]

CALL INTERRUPT The statement **CALL INTERRUPT** *n* causes system interrupt *n* to occur. For example, **CALL INTERRUPT 5** invokes the Print Screen interrupt. Some interrupts require you to set certain processor registers before the interrupt occurs. You can set these registers by using the **REG** statement.

CDBL You use function **CDBL** to convert integer, long integer, and single-precision numbers to double-precision numbers. If x is any number, then the value of **CDBL**(x) is the double-precision number that x determines.

CEIL The value of the function **CEIL**(x) is the smallest whole number that is greater than or equal to x.

CHAIN The **CHAIN** statement passes control from the current program to another compiled program that is on disk. You may not run a program containing a **CHAIN** statement from within Turbo Basic, but rather must compile it to a stand-alone .EXE file and then execute it directly from DOS. Upon encountering the statement **CHAIN** *filespec*, the computer deletes the current program from memory, loads into memory the program denoted by *filespec*, and executes the new program. Execution begins with the first line of the new program. All variables assigned values prior to chaining will be lost unless you use an appropriate **COMMON** statement in both the "chained-from" and "chained-to" programs. [3]

CHDIR The statement **CHDIR** *p$* changes the current disk directory to the subdirectory that the path *p$* specifies. For example, **CHDIR** " \ " specifies the root directory as the current directory. [1]

CHR$ If n is a number from 0 to 255, then **CHR$**($n$) is the character in the ASCII table (as shown in Appendix A) that is associated with n.

CINT You use the function **CINT** to convert long integer, single-precision, and double-precision numbers to integer numbers. If x is any number from -32768 to 32767, then the value of **CINT**(x) is the possibly rounded integer constant that x determines. When x has the fractional part 0.5, rounding goes to the nearest even integer.

CIRCLE The statement **CIRCLE** (x,y),$r,c,r1,r2,a$ draws a portion, or all, of an ellipse. The center of the ellipse is the point (x,y) and the radius is r. The color of the circle is determined by c. If $r1$ and $r2$ are present, then the computer draws only the portion of the ellipse that extends in a counterclockwise direction from the radius line at an angle of **ABS**($r1$) radians with the horizontal radius to the radius line at an angle of **ABS**($r2$) radians with the horizontal radius line. If either $r1$ or $r2$ is negative, then the computer also draws its radius line. The ratio of the length of the vertical diameter to the length of the horizontal diameter will be a. (If a is missing, the figure drawn will be a circle.)

CLEAR The statement **CLEAR** is a holdover from Standard Basic that is of dubious value in Turbo Basic. The statement **CLEAR** resets all numeric variables and arrays to 0, resets all string variables and arrays to null, closes all files, and deletes all dynamic arrays from memory. Used in the wrong place, CLEAR can cause an infinite loop or a complete system lockup. Avoid using it.

CLNG You use the function **CLNG** to convert integer, single-precision, and double-precision numbers to long integer numbers. If x is any number from -2147483648 to 2147483647, then the value of **CINT**(x) is the possibly rounded long-integer constant that x determines. When x has the fractional part 0.5, rounding goes to the nearest even integer.

CLOSE The statement **CLOSE** #n closes the file that you opened with the reference number n. By itself, **CLOSE** closes all open files.

CLS In text mode (**SCREEN 0**), the statement **CLS** clears the screen—except for possibly the twenty-fifth line—and moves the cursor to the upper-left corner. In graphics mode, **CLS** clears just the viewport that **VIEW** sets (the default viewport is the whole screen), and makes the center of the screen the last point referenced.

COLOR In text mode (**SCREEN 0**), the **COLOR** statement produces either special effects or colors, depending on the type of monitor that you are using. The statement **COLOR** *f,b* sets the foreground color to *f* and the background color to *b*, where *f* ranges from 0 to 15 and *b* from 0 to 7. The statement **COLOR** *f+16, b* selects the same colors as the statement just given, but with a blinking foreground.

In medium-resolution graphics mode (**SCREEN 1**), two palettes, each of four colors, are available. The statement **COLOR** *b,p* specifies *b* as the background color and *p* as the palette. Text will appear in color 3 of the selected palette, and you can display graphics in any color of that palette.

In EGA mode (**SCREEN 7**, **SCREEN 8**, or **SCREEN 9**), a palette of 16 colors is available for text and graphics. The statement **COLOR** *f,b* sets the foreground color to *f* and the background color to *b*, where *f* and *b* range from 0 to 15.

COM(n) The statement **COM(***n***)** enables, disables, or defers trapping of the *n*th communications port, depending on whether the statement is followed by **ON**, **OFF**, or **STOP**, respectively. [4], [5]

***COMMAND$*** The value of the string function **COMMAND$** is a string that consists of all of the characters typed, if any, after the program name when you invoke a standalone program from DOS. For developmental purposes, you can use the **Parameter Line** selection from the Options pull-down menu to give **COMMAND$** a value before you run a program from within Turbo Basic.

COMMON If a statement of the form **COMMON** *fromVar1, fromVAR2,..., fromVarN* precedes a **CHAIN** statement, and a statement of the form **COMMON** *toVar1, toVar2,..., toVarN* appears in the chained-to program, then the computer assigns the value of the variable *fromVar1* to the variable *toVar1*, the value of *fromVar2* to *toVar2*, and so on. The same number of variables must appear in each **COMMON** statement. Although the names of corresponding **COMMON** variables need not be the same, corresponding variables must be of the same type: string, integer, long integer, single-precision, or double-precision.

COS The value of the trigonometric function **COS**(x) is the cosine of an angle of x radians.

CSNG You use the function **CSNG** to convert integer, long integer, and double-precision numbers to single-precision numbers. If x is any number, then the value of **CSNG**(x) is the single-precision constant that x determines.

CSRLIN At any time, the value of the function **CSRLIN** is a number from 1 to 25 that identifies the line of the screen that currently contains the cursor.

CVI, CVL, CVS, and CVD You must first transform numbers that will be recorded in random files into strings. To transform them back to their numeric form, you use these four functions. If you transformed an integer constant into the string *a$* of length 2, then the value of **CVI**(*a$*) will be the original constant. Similarly, **CVL**(*a$*), **CVS**(*a$*), or **CVD**(*a$*) will be the long integer, single-precision, or double-precision numeric constants that were transformed into *a$*, which is a string of length 4, 4, or 8, respectively.

CVMD and CVMS With the functions **CVMD** and **CVMS**, you can transfer back to numeric form single-precision and double-precision numbers that were converted to strings with Microsoft BASIC or IBM PC BASIC and then entered into random files.

DATA The statement **DATA** *const1, const2, . . .* holds the specified constants. **READ** statements can read these constants in order and assign them to variables.

DATE$** The statement **PRINT DATE$ displays the current date as a string of the form *mm-dd-yyyy*. If *d$* is a string of that form, then the statement **DATE$** = *d$* resets the date as specified by *d$*.

DECR The statement **DECR** *numvar* reduces the value of *numvar* by 1, and the statement **DECR** *numvar, amount* reduces the value of *numvar* by *amount*.

DEF FN/END DEF User-defined functions are created in one of two ways: by a single-line definition of the form **DEF FN**name(varlist) = expression using varlist; or by a multi-line block that begins with a statement of the form **DEF FN**name(varlist), which is followed by one or more statements that calculate the value of the function, and ending with the statement **END DEF**. Usually one of the statements in the block has the form **FN**name = expression. The variable list, *varlist*, can involve several variables of numeric type, string type, or both.

DEFINT, DEFLNG, DEFSNG, DEFDBL, and DEFSTR A statement of the form **DEFINT** *letter* specifies that all tagless variables whose names begin with the specified *letter* will have integer precision. A statement of the form **DEFINT** *letter1* − *letter2* specifies that all tagless variables whose names begin with a letter in the range *letter1* through *letter2* will have integer precision. The statements **DEFLNG, DEFSNG, DEFDBL**, and **DEFSTR** specify the corresponding levels of precision for long-integer, single-precision, double-precision, and string variables, respectively.

DEF SEG The statement **DEF SEG** = *n* specifies that the *current* memory segment should consist of memory locations 16∗*n* to 16∗*n* + 65535. Subsequently, all statements that access memory directly — such as **PEEK, POKE, BLOAD,** and **BSAVE** — will refer to memory locations in this range. [2]

DELAY The statement **DELAY** *n* causes program execution to pause for *n* seconds. For example, the statement **DELAY 1.25** suspends program execution for 1.25 seconds.

DIM The statement **DIM** *arrayName(m:n)* declares an array with subscripts that range from *m* to *n*, inclusive. A statement of the form **DIM** *arrayName(m:n,p:q)* declares a doubly subscripted, or two-dimensional, array. You may use similar statements to declare three- and higher-dimensional arrays. If *m* and *p* are zero, you can condense the **DIM** statements just given to **DIM** *arrayName(n)* and **DIM** *arrayName(n,q)*. Inserting **STATIC** or **DYNAMIC** after the word **DIM** tells the computer to allocate memory permanently at compile-time or temporarily at run-time, respectively.

DO/LOOP You use a statement of the form **DO, DO WHILE** *cond*, or **DO UNTIL** *cond*, to mark the beginning of a block of statements that will be repeated. You use a statement of the form **LOOP, LOOP WHILE** *cond*, or **LOOP UNTIL** *cond* to mark the end of the block of statements that will be repeated. Each time that the computer encounters a statement that contains **WHILE** *cond* or **UNTIL** *cond*, the truth value of the condition determines whether the computer should repeat the block or whether the program should jump to the statement that immediately follows the block.

DRAW You use the graphics statement **DRAW** *a$*, where *a$* is a string of directions and parameters, to draw figures on screen in much the same way that you draw figures with pencil and paper. The rich and varied command strings constitute a miniature graphics language. You can use the **DRAW** statement to produce straight lines that begin at the last point referenced and extend in several directions. After you draw each line, the end point of that line becomes the last point referenced for the next **DRAW** statement. The possible directions are shown here:

| U up | L left | E northeast | G southwest |
| D down | R right | F southeast | H northwest |

If *X* is one of these directions and *n* is a number, then the statement **DRAW** "*Xn*" draws a line of *n* units in the specified direction. You can combine several such statements into one statement of the form **DRAW** "*X1n X2n X3n* ...". If **N** precedes a direction, the last point referenced will not change after the computer draws the line. If **B** precedes a direction, the computer will draw an invisible line and the last point referenced will change to the end-point of that line. Some other variations of the **DRAW** statement are shown in Figure B-1.

END The statement **END** terminates the execution of the program and closes all files.

ENDMEM The value of the function **ENDMEM** is a long integer that gives the address of the last byte available in memory.

ENVIRON Turbo Basic has an environment table consisting of equations of the form "*name=value*" that is inherited from DOS when you invoke Turbo Basic. You use **ENVIRON** to alter this table. The statement **ENVIRON** "*name=;*" removes any equation whose left side is *name*. The statement **ENVIRON** "*name=value*" places the equation in quotes in the table.

ENVIRON$ If *name* is the left side of an equation in Turbo Basic's environment, then the value of the function **ENVIRON$** ("*name*") will be the string that consists of the right side of the equation. The value of **ENVIRON$**(*n*) is the *n*th equation in Turbo Basic's environment table.

DRAW "M x,y"	Draw a line from the last point referenced to (x,y)
DRAW "C n"	Draw subsequent lines in color n of the current palette
DRAW "S n"	Change the unit scale by a factor of n/4
DRAW "A n"	Draw subsequent lines rotated by n*90 degrees
DRAW "TA n"	Draw subsequent lines rotated by n degrees
DRAW "P c, b"	Fill in the closed region of boundary color b containing the last point referenced with color c of the current palette

Figure B-1. *Using DRAW*

EOF Suppose that a file has been opened for input with the reference number n. The value of the function **EOF**(n) will be -1 (true) if the computer has reached the end of the file and 0 (false) if not. (Note: The logical condition **NOT EOF** is true until the computer reaches the end of the file.)

ERADR When error trapping detects a run-time error, the function **ERADR** will give the value of the program-counter. The program can report the value to the user who can then use the **Run-time error** command in the Debug menu in order to obtain a display of the point within the program at which the error occurred. [4]

ERASE The statement **ERASE** *arrayName* resets numeric arrays to 0 and string arrays to the null string when the specified array is static. If the specified array is dynamic, the statement **ERASE** *arrayName* deletes the array from memory.

ERDEV and ERDEV$ After a device error occurs, the value of **ERDEV** provides information about the type of error and gives certain attributes of the device. The value of **ERDEV$** is the name of the device. [5]

ERR and ERL After an error occurs during program execution, the value of the function **ERR** will be a number that identifies the type of error, and the value of the function **ERL** will be the line number of the program statement in which the error occurred. (If the statement that contains the error has no line number, then **ERL** reports the line number of the most recently executed statement with a line number. If the computer has not executed a statement with a line number, **ERL** reports a value of 0.) You use these functions in error-trapping routines to correct errors. [4]

ERROR The statement **ERROR** n simulates the occurrence of the run-time error that the number n identifies, where n may range from 0 to 255. **ERROR** is a useful debugging tool.

EXIT You may use the **EXIT** statement in any of these seven forms: **EXIT DEF, EXIT FOR, EXIT IF, EXIT LOOP, EXIT SELECT, EXIT SUB,** or **EXIT WHILE**. The **EXIT** statement causes program execution to jump out of the specified structure prematurely: **EXIT FOR** jumps out of a **FOR/NEXT** loop to the statement that follows **NEXT, EXIT SELECT** jumps out of a **SELECT CASE/END SELECT** block to the statement that follows **END SELECT,** and so on.

EXP, EXP2, and EXP10 The value of the function **EXP**(x) is e^x, where e (about 2.71828) is the base of the natural logarithm function. Similarly, the value of the function **EXP2**(x) is 2^x, and the value of the function **EXP10**(x) is 10^x.

FIELD A statement of the form **FIELD** #n, $w1$ **AS** *strvar1*, $w2$ **AS** *strvar2*, ... partitions each record of the random file with reference number n into fields of widths $w1$, $w2$, and so on, and names *strvar1*, *strvar2*, and so on.

FILES The statement **FILES** *dirspec*, where *dirspec* specifies a directory of a disk, produces a listing of the files in the specified directory. Variations produce selected sublistings. [1]

FIX The value of the function **FIX**(x) is the whole number that is obtained if you discard the decimal part of the number x.

FOR/NEXT The statement **FOR** *index* $= a$ **TO** b **STEP** s sets the value of the variable *index* to a, and repeatedly executes the portion of the program contained between itself and the statement **NEXT** *index*. Each time that the computer reaches the **NEXT** statement, it adds s to the value of *index*. This process continues until the value of *index* passes b.

FRE At any time, the value of the function **FRE**(" ") is the number of memory locations available for storing new string data. The value of the function **FRE**(-1) is the number of memory locations available for new numeric arrays; this function is useful in determining whether or not sufficient memory remains to declare a new numeric array. The value of **FRE(−2)** is the amount of space left on the stack.

GET (Files) The statement **GET** #*n*,*r* retrieves record number *r* from the random file with the reference number *n*. You can then use assignment statements to access the record's individual fields.

GET (Graphics) A graphics statement of the form **GET** (*x1,y1*) − (*x2,y2*), *arrayName* stores a description of the rectangular portion of the screen having upper-left corner (*x1,y1*) and lower-right corner (*x2,y2*) in the array *arrayName*. You can then duplicate the rectangular region at another location of the screen by using a **PUT** statement. **GET** and **PUT** statements are the key tools for animation.

GET$** The statement **GET$ #*n,c,a$* reads *c* bytes from the binary file with the reference number *n*, and assigns them to the string variable *a$*. Reading starts with the current file position.

GOSUB A statement of the form **GOSUB** *label* causes a jump to the statements that begin at *label*. When the computer reaches the statement **RETURN**, the program jumps back to the statement after the **GOSUB** statement. [6]

GOTO The statement **GOTO** *label* causes an unconditional jump to the first statement after the specified *label*. [6]

HEX$ If *n* is a whole number from 0 to 65535, then the value of the function **HEX$**(*n*) is the string that consists of the hexadecimal representation of *n*.

IF (single line) A statement of the form **IF** *condition* **THEN** *action* causes the program to take the specified action if the condition is true. If the condition is false, execution continues at the next line. A statement of the form **IF** *condition* **THEN** *action1* **ELSE** *action2* causes the program to take *action1* if the *condition* is true and *action2* if the *condition* is false.

An Abridged Reference Manual of Turbo Basic 373

IF (block) A block of statements that begin with a statement of the form **IF** *condition* **THEN** and that end with the statement **END IF** indicates that the computer should execute the group of statements between **IF** and **END IF** only if the *condition* is true. If an **ELSE** statement separates the group of sta tements into two parts, then the computer will execute the first part when the *condition* is true and the second part when the *condition* is false. Statements of the form **ELSEIF** *condition* may also appear and they define groups of statements to be executed when alternate conditions are true.

INCR The statement **INCR** *numvar* increases the value of the numeric variable *numvar* by 1, and the statement **INCR** *numvar, amount* increases the value of *numvar* by *amount*.

INKEY$** The statement *a$* = **INKEY$** assigns to the variable *a$* the character that corresponds to the first keystroke waiting in the keyboard buffer. If no keystroke is waiting, the null string, " ", is assigned to *a$*. Non-ASCII keys—such as F1, HOME, and INS— produce two characters: **CHR$(0) followed by **CHR$(***n***)**, where *n* is the *extended code* for the non-ASCII key.

INP The value of the function **INP(***n***)** is the value of the byte read from port *n*. [5]

INPUT A statement of the form **INPUT** *var* causes the computer first to display a question mark and then to pause until the user enters a response. The statement then assigns this response to the variable *var*. Statements of the form **INPUT** *"prompt"*; *var* will insert a prompt before the question mark, and statements of the form **INPUT** *"prompt"*, *var* will display the prompt without the question mark.

INPUT# The statement **INPUT** #*n, var* reads the next item of data from a sequential file that has been opened for **INPUT** with the reference number *n*. The statement then assigns the item to the variable *var*.

INPUT$ A statement of the form $a\$ = $ **INPUT\$**(n) causes the program to pause until the user types n characters. The statement then assigns the string that consists of these n characters to $a\$$.

INSTAT The value of the function **INSTAT** is 0 (false) when the keyboard buffer is empty, and -1 (true) when a keystroke is waiting to be read. You can include a statement of the form **IF INSTAT THEN** *action* within a program to execute *action* only if a keystroke is waiting in the keyboard buffer.

INSTR The value of the function **INSTR**($a\$,b\$$) is the position of the string $b\$$ in the string $a\$$. The value of **INSTR**($n,a\$,b\$$) is the first position at or after the nth character of $a\$$ where the string $b\$$ occurs.

INT The value of the function **INT**(x) is the greatest whole number that is less than or equal to x.

IOCTL and IOCTL$ After you have opened a device with the reference number n, the value of the function **IOCTL\$**(n) is a control string read from the device driver, while a statement of the form **IOCTL** #$n,a\$$ sends the string $a\$$ to the driver. [5]

KEY The statement **KEY** n, $a\$$ assigns the string $a\$$ to the function key Fn. The string $a\$$ must have a length of 15 or less, and n can be any number from 1 to 10. After the computer executes the statement **KEY** n, $a\$$, pressing the key Fn has the same effect as typing in the characters in $a\$$. You may use the statement **KEY ON** to display the first six characters of the assigned strings on the twenty-fifth row of the Run window. The statement **KEY OFF** turns this display off. The statement **KEY LIST** displays all of the assigned strings in their entirety.

KEY(n) The statement **ON KEY**(n) **GOSUB** *label* sets up the trapping of function key Fn. After the computer executes **KEY**(n) **ON**, pressing Fn causes a **GOSUB** to the subroutine that begins at *label*. You disable trapping by using **KEY**(n) **OFF**, and defer trapping by using **KEY**(n) **STOP**. [4], [6]

KILL The statement **KILL** *filespec* erases the specified disk file. [3]

LBOUND The value of the function **LBOUND**(*arrayName*(*dimNum*)) is the smallest subscript value that can be used for the *dimNum*th subscript of the array *arrayName*. For example, after the computer executes **DIM example(1:31, 1:12, 1960:1989)**, the value of **LBOUND(example(3))** is the smallest value allowed for the subscript of **example( )**, which is 1960.

LCASE$** The value of the string function **LCASE$(*a$*) is a string identical to *a$*, except that all uppercase letters have been changed to lowercase.

LEFT$** The value of the function **LEFT$(*a$,n*) is the string that consists of the leftmost *n* characters of *a$*.

LEN The value of **LEN**(*a$*) is the number of characters (or the length) of the string *a$*.

LET The statement **LET** *variable = expression* assigns the value of the expression to the variable.

LINE The graphics statement **LINE** (*x1, y1*) − (*x2, y2*) draws a line that connects the two points. (If you omit the first point, then the computer draws the line from the last point referenced to the specified point.) In medium-resolution graphics mode, the line will be in color *c* of the current palette if the computer executes **LINE** (*x1, y1*) − (*x2, y2*), *c*. If you append **B** or **BF** (preceded by a comma) to the statement, the computer will draw a rectangle or solid rectangle. If *s* is a number from 0 to 32767, then **LINE** (*x1, y1*) − (*x2, y2*),,,*s* draws a styled line connecting the two points, using the pattern determined by *s*.

LINE INPUT The statements **LINE INPUT** *a$* and **LINE INPUT** *"prompt"; a$* are similar to the corresponding INPUT statements. However, the user can respond with *any* string—even a statement that contains commas, leading spaces, and quotation marks. The computer will assign the entire string to the string variable *a$*.

LINE INPUT# After you have opened a sequential file for input with the reference number n, the statement **LINE INPUT** #n, $a\$$ assigns to the string variable $a\$$ the string of characters from the file up to the next pair of carriage-return/linefeed characters.

LOC The function **LOC** gives the current location in a sequential, random, or binary file. For a sequential file with the reference number n, **LOC**(n) is the number of blocks of 128 characters read from or written to the file since it was opened. For a random file, **LOC**(n) is the last record read or written. For a binary file, **LOC**(n) is the number of bytes from the beginning of the file to the current file position.

LOCAL You may use a statement of the form **LOCAL** $var1$, $var2$,... at the beginning of the definition of a procedure or user-defined function block to specify that variables $var1$, $var2$, and so on are local to the procedure or function. Local variables have no connection to variables of the same name outside the procedure or function definition; so you may name them without regard to "outside" variables. The computer only allocates memory for local variables when the program invokes the procedure or function, and frees that memory when the program exits the procedure or function. As a consequence, local variables do not retain their values between successive invocations of the procedure or function. You may declare arrays to be local first by giving their names followed by empty parentheses in a **LOCAL** statement, and then by dimensioning the arrays in a subsequent **DIM** statement.

LOCATE The statement **LOCATE** r, c positions the cursor at row r, column c of the screen. The statement **LOCATE,,0** turns the display of the cursor off, while the statement **LOCATE,,1** turns the display back on. If m and n are whole numbers between 0 and 13, with $m < n$, then the statement **LOCATE,,,** m, n will change the size of the cursor.

LOF After you have opened a file with the reference number n, the statement **LOF**(n) gives the number of characters in the file—that is, the length of the file.

LOG, LOG2, and LOG10 If x is a positive number, then the value of **LOG**(x) is the natural logarithm (base e) of x. Similarly, the value of **LOG2**(x) is the base 2 logarithm of x, and the value of **LOG10**(x) is the base 10 logarithm of x.

LPOS The printer has a buffer that holds characters until they are ready to be printed. The value of **LPOS**(1) is the current position in the buffer.

LPRINT and LPRINT USING The statements **LPRINT** and **LPRINT USING** print data on the printer in the same way that **PRINT** and **PRINT USING** display data on the screen. In addition, you may use **LPRINT** to set various print modes, such as the width of the characters and the vertical spacing.

LSET If $af\$$ is a field variable of a random file, then the statement **LSET** $af\$ = b\$$ assigns to $af\$$ the string $b\$$, which is possibly truncated or padded on the right with spaces. If $a\$$ is an ordinary variable, then the statement **LSET** $a\$ = b\$$ replaces the value of $a\$$ with a string of the same length that consists of $b\$$ truncated or padded on the right with spaces.

MEMSET The statement **MEMSET** *address* specifies that the computer should treat the long-integer value *address* as the last address available in memory. Turbo Basic will attempt to reduce its use of memory so that it can accommodate this limiting address. You can then use memory beyond this limit for storing machine-language subroutines.

MID$** The value of the function **MID$($a\$, m, n$) is the substring of $a\$$ that begins with the mth character of $a\$$ and that contains up to n characters, if available. If you omit the parameter n, **MID$**($a\$, m$) consists of all of the characters of $a\$$ from the mth character onward. The statement **MID$**($a\$, m, n$) = $b\$$ replaces the characters of $a\$$, beginning with the mth character, with the first n characters of the string $b\$$.

MKDIR The statement **MKDIR** *p$* creates a new subdirectory. The string *p$* specifies the location and name of the subdirectory. [1]

MKI$, MKL$, MKS$, and MKD$ The functions **MKI$**, **MKL$**, **MKS$**, and **MKD$** convert integer, long integer, single-precision, and double-precision numbers into strings of lengths 2, 4, 4, and 8, respectively. You must do this conversion before you can place numbers into random files.

MKMD$ and MKMS$** The functions **MKMD$ and **MKMS$** convert single-precision and double-precision numbers into strings of lengths 4 and 8, respectively, in the Microsoft format. This conversion is necessary before you can place these numbers into random files that will be read with Microsoft BASIC or IBM PC BASIC.

MTIMER The statement **MTIMER** resets and starts the microtimer clock. The function **MTIMER** first gives the number of microseconds that have elapsed since the **MTIMER** statement started the clock, and then stops and resets the clock. Thus, you can only call the **MTIMER** function once after each **MTIMER** statement; if you call the **MTIMER** function more than once, it gives a value of zero.

NAME The statement **NAME** *filespec* **AS** *filename* changes the name of the specified file to the specified name. [3]

OCT$ If *n* is a whole number between 0 and 65535, then **OCT$**(*n*) is the octal—that is, base 8—representation of *n*.

ON COM(n) If *n* is the number 1 or 2, then the statement **ON COM**(*n*) **GOSUB** *label* sets up the trapping of the *n*th communications port. After the computer executes **COM**(*n*) **ON**, information coming into the port causes a **GOSUB** to *label*. [4], [5], [6]

ON ERROR The statement **ON ERROR GOTO** *label* sets up error trapping. An error then causes a jump to an error-handling routine that begins at *label*. (See the discussion of **RESUME** for further details.) [4], [6]

ON...GOSUB and ON...GOTO The statement **ON** *expression* **GOSUB** *label1, label2,...* causes a **GOSUB** to *label1, label2,* and so on, depending upon whether the value of the expression is 1, 2, and so on. Similarly, the **GOTO** variation causes an unconditional jump to the appropriate label. [6]

ON KEY(n) The statement **ON KEY**(*n*) **GOSUB** *label* sets up trapping of the function key F*n*. After the computer executes **KEY**(*n*) **ON**, pressing F*n* causes a **GOSUB** to *label*. [4], [6]

ON PEN The statement **ON PEN GOSUB** *label* sets up trapping of a light pen. After the computer executes **PEN ON**, pressing the metal clip on the light pen or pressing the light pen to the screen causes a **GOSUB** to *label*. [4], [6]

ON PLAY(n) The music-background buffer holds notes that **PLAY** statements have specified and that are waiting to be played. If *n* is a whole number, then the statement **ON PLAY**(*n*) **GOSUB** *label* sets up trapping of the music buffer. After the computer executes **PLAY ON**, as soon as the number of notes in the buffer decreases from *n* to *n*−1 the program **GOSUB**s to *label*. The capacity of the music-background buffer defaults to 32 notes, but you may set it to be as high as 4096 notes by using the **$SOUND** metastatement. [4], [6]

ON STRIG(n) If *n* is 0, 2, 4, or 6, the statement **ON STRIG**(*n*) **GOSUB** *label* sets up trapping of one of the joystick buttons. The numbers 0 and 4 are associated with the lower and upper buttons of the first joystick, and the numbers 2 and 6 are associated with the lower and upper buttons of the second joystick. After the computer executes **STRIG**(*n*) **ON**, pressing the button associated with *n* causes a **GOSUB** to *label*. [4], [6]

ON TIMER If *n* is an integer from 1 to 86400 (which represents 1 second to 24 hours), the statement **ON TIMER**(*n*) **GOSUB** *label* sets up trapping of the computer's internal clock. After the computer executes **TIMER ON**, every *n* seconds, the program **GOSUB**s to the subroutine that begins at *label*. You disable trapping with **TIMER OFF**, and defer trapping with **TIMER STOP**. [4], [6]

OPEN The statement **OPEN** *filespec* **FOR** *mode* **AS** *#n* allows access to the sequential file *filespec* in one of the following modes: **INPUT** (the computer can read information from the file), **OUTPUT** (the program creates a new file and the computer can write information to it), **APPEND** (the computer can add information to the end of a file), or **BINARY** (the computer can read or write information in an arbitrary fashion). Throughout the program, the file is referred to by the reference number n (usually 1, 2, or 3). The statement **OPEN** *filespec* **AS** *#n* **LEN** $=g$ allows access to the random file *filespec*, in which each record has length g. Some other variations of the OPEN statement are **OPEN "SCRN:" FOR OUTPUT AS** *#n*, **OPEN "LPT1:" FOR OUTPUT AS** *#n*, and **OPEN "KYBD:" FOR INPUT AS** *#n*. These variations allow access to the screen, printer, and keyboard as if they were sequential files. [3]

OPEN "COM... If n is 1 or 2, then **OPEN "COM** $n:b,p,d,s,L$**" AS** *#m* **LEN**$=g$ allows access to the nth communications port with the reference number m. The statement also specifies the record length (g), the speed of transmission (b), the parity (p), the number of data bits to be used when transmitting each character (d), the number of stop bits (s), and the line parameters (L).

OPTION BASE After the computer executes the statement **OPTION BASE** m, a statement of the form **DIM** *arrayName*(n) defines an array with subscripts that range from m to n, rather than the normal range of 0 to n. The value of m may range from 0 to 32767. Turbo Basic's extended **DIM** statement, which permits you to specify both lower and upper subscript bounds for each array, achieves the same results in a clearer fashion, making its use preferable to **OPTION BASE**.

OUT OUT n,m sends byte m to port n. For the definitive listing of the different uses of the **OUT** statement and its counterpart **INP**, see "PEEKing at Your PC's Memory, Parts 1 and 2," by David I. Schneider (*PC Magazine*, Nov. 12 and Nov. 26, 1985). [5]

PAINT If (x,y) is an unlit interior point of a region of the screen, then the statement **PAINT** (x,y) fills the region. In medium-resolution graphics mode, if the boundary has the color b of the current palette and if *c* is one of the colors of the current palette, then the statement **PAINT** (*x*,*y*),*c*,*b* fills the bounded region with the color *c*. If *t$* is a string of a maximum length of 64 characters, then the statement **PAINT** (*x*,*y*), *t$*,*b* fills the region with the repeating pattern, referred to as a tile, determined by *t$*.

PALETTE and PALETTE USING When a graphics monitor is attached to an Enhanced Graphics Adapter, you specify colors by using a palette that consists of the numbers from 0 through 15 to which colors have been assigned. The statement **PALETTE** *m*,*n* assigns the color *n* to the *m*th palette number. The statement **PALETTE USING** *integerArray*(0) specifies that the computer should assign to palette numbers 0 through 15 the values that are held in *integerArray*(0) through *integerArray*(15).

PEEK Each memory location contains a number from 0 to 255. If *n* is a number from 0 to 65535, the value of **PEEK**(*n*) is the number in the memory location of offset *n* in the current segment. [2]

PEN The statements **PEN ON**, **PEN OFF**, and **PEN STOP** enable, disable, and defer, respectively, the reading of the status of the light pen. For each *n* from 0 to 9, the value of the function **PEN**(*n*) gives a piece of information about the status of the light pen. See Table B-1.

n	Value of PEN(*n*)
0	−1 if pen down since last check; 0 if not
1	x-coordinate when pen was last activated
2	y-coordinate when pen was last activated
3	−1 if switch is down; 0 if not
4	Most-recent x-coordinate
5	Most-recent y-coordinate
6	Row when pen was last activated
7	Column when pen was last activated
8	Most-recent row
9	Most-recent column

Table B-1. *The **PEN** Statement*

PLAY The statement **PLAY** *a$*, where *a$* is a string of notes and parameters, produces musical notes with most of the embellishments that sheet music indicates. The rich and varied strings constitute a miniature music language. You can identify a note by using one of the letters A through G, possibly followed by a plus or minus sign to indicate a sharp or a flat. You specify a $1/n$ note pause by **P** *n*. The parameters **O, L, T, MF, MB, ML, MS,** and **MN** specify attributes of subsequent notes, and are sometimes combined with a number that gives a magnitude for the attribute. The parameter **O** *n*, where *n* ranges from 0 through 6, specifies the octave of subsequent notes. The parameter **L** *n*, where *n* ranges from 1 to 64, causes subsequent notes to be $1/n$th notes. (For instance, if *n* equals 4, **L4** produces quarter notes.) The parameter **T** *n*, where *n* ranges from 32 to 255, sets the tempo of subsequent notes to *n* quarter notes per minute. The default values for the parameters **O, L,** and **T** are 4, 4, and 120, respectively. The parameter **MF** (*music foreground*) causes the computer to play all notes before it executes additional statements; **MB** (music background) places up to 32 notes in a buffer that plays the notes while the program continues to execute. The parameters **ML** (*music legato*) and **MS** (*music staccato*) decrease and increase, respectively, the durations of notes, with **MN** returning the durations to normal articulation.

PLAY(n) The value of the function **PLAY(0)** is the number of notes that are currently in the music-background buffer waiting to be played.

PMAP The graphics function **PMAP** converts the world coordinates of a point to the physical coordinates, and vice versa, as shown in Table B-2.

POINT In graphics mode, the value of the function **POINT**(x,y) is the number of the color of the point with coordinates (x,y). When the monitor is attached to an Enhanced Graphics Adapter, **POINT**(x,y) gives the palette number that is assigned to the point.

An Abridged Reference Manual of Turbo Basic   **383**

The values of the functions **POINT(0)** and **POINT(1)** are the first and second physical coordinates of the last point referenced, and the values of **POINT(2)** and **POINT(3)** are the first and second world coordinates of the last point referenced.

POKE Each memory location contains a number from 0 to 255. If n is a number from 0 to 65535, then the statement **POKE** n,m places the number m in the memory location of offset n in the current segment. [2]

POS The value of the function **POS(0)** is the column number of the current text position of the cursor.

PRESET See **PSET**.

PRINT You use the **PRINT** statement to display data on screen. The statement **PRINT** *expression* displays the value of the *expression* at the current cursor position, and moves the cursor to the beginning of the next row of the screen. (The statement displays numbers with a trailing space and positive numbers with a leading space.) If a semicolon or comma follows the statement, then the cursor will not move to the next row after the display, but rather will move to the next position or print zone, respectively. You may place several expressions in the same **PRINT** statement if you separate the expressions with semicolons (to display them adjacent to one another) or with commas (to display them in successive zones).

n	c	Value of PMAP(c, n)
0	First world coordinate	First physical coordinate
1	Second world coordinate	Second physical coordinate
2	First physical coordinate	First world coordinate
3	Second physical coordinate	Second world coordinate

Table B-2. *The* **PMAP** *Function*

PRINT USING The statement **PRINT USING** *a$; list of expressions* displays the values of the expressions (possibly interspersed with text from *a$*) in the formats that *a$* specifies. You can use the statement to align and display financial quantities with dollar signs, commas, asterisks, two decimal places, and preceding or trailing signs. You format numbers by using the symbols #, +, $, $$, *, **, ^^^^, comma, and period. You format strings by using the symbols &, !, and \ \.

PRINT# and PRINT# USING After you have opened a sequential file for input or append with reference number *n*, the statements **PRINT** #*n,expression* and **PRINT** #*n*,**USING** *a$;expression* record the value of the expression into the file in the same way that **PRINT** and **PRINT USING** display it on screen.

PSET and PRESET In high-resolution graphics mode, the statement **PSET** (*x,y*) turns on the point with coordinates (*x,y*), and the statement **PRESET** (*x,y*) turns that point off. In medium-resolution graphics mode, the statement **PSET** (*x,y*),*c* or the statement **PRESET**(*x,y*),*c* causes the point (*x,y*) to be displayed in color *c* of the current palette.

PUT (Files) After you have opened a random file with reference number *n* and assigned values to the field variables, the statement **PUT** #*n,r* places these values in record *r*.

PUT (Graphics) After you have stored a rectangular region of the screen in the array *arrayName* by using a **GET** statement, the statement **PUT** (*x,y*),*arrayName*,**PSET** places an exact image of the rectangular region on screen positioned with its upper-left corner at the point (*x,y*). The following list shows the possible alternatives to **PSET** in the statement and, for each alternative, the conditions for which a point on the high-resolution graphics screen will be white:

XOR	The point is white in the stored image or was originally white, but not both.
AND	The point was originally white and is also white in the stored image.

OR   The point was originally white or is white in the stored image.

PRESET   The point is black in the stored image.

PUT$**   The statement **PUT$ *#n,a$* writes the characters in the string variable *a$* into the binary file with reference number *n*. Writing starts at the current file position.

RANDOMIZE   The statement **RANDOMIZE TIMER** automatically uses the computer's clock to seed the random-number generator **RND**. The statement **RANDOMIZE** requests a seed, and the statement **RANDOMIZE** *n* seeds the generator with a number that *n* determines.

READ   The statement **READ** *var1, var2,...* assigns to *var1* the first unused constant stored in DATA statements, to *var2* the next unused constant, and so on.

REG   The statement **REG** *register,value* sets the processor register that *register* specifies to *value*. The function **REG**(*register*) returns the current value of the processor register that corresponds to *register*. The *register* is a whole number from 0 to 9, which corresponds to processor registers Flags, AX, BX, CX, DX, SI, DI, BP, DS, and ES, respectively.

REM   **REM** allows you to document the program by inserting remarks, which are nonexecutable lines, into the program.

RESET   The statement **RESET** closes all open files. Using **RESET** is equivalent to using **CLOSE** without file-reference numbers.

RESTORE   **RESTORE** *label* causes the next request to **READ** an item of data to take the first item in the **DATA** statement that follows the indicated *label*. If you omit parameter *label*, the computer will access the first **DATA** statement in the program. [6]

RESUME   The combination of **ON ERROR** and **RESUME** is similar to the combination of **GOSUB** and **RETURN**. When the computer encounters the statement **RESUME** at the end of an error-handling routine, the program branches back to the statement in which the error was encountered. The variations **RESUME** *label* and **RESUME NEXT** cause the program to branch to the statement that follows the indicated *label* or to the statement that follows the statement in which the error occurred, respectively. [6]

RETURN When the computer encounters the statement **RETURN** at the end of a subroutine, the program branches back to the statement that follows the one containing the most recently executed **GOSUB**. The variation **RETURN** *label* causes the program to branch back to the statement that follows the indicated *label*. [6]

RIGHT$** The value of the function **RIGHT$(*a$,n*) is the string that consists of the rightmost *n* characters of *a$*.

RMDIR If *p$* is a string that specifies the location and name of a subdirectory containing no files, then the statement **RMDIR** *p$* removes the subdirectory. [1]

RND The value of the function **RND** is a pseudo-randomly selected number from 0 to 1, which does not include 1.

RSET If *af$* is a field variable of a random file, then the statement **RSET** *af$* = *b$* assigns the string *b$* — possibly truncated or padded on the left with spaces — to *af$*. If *a$* is an ordinary variable, then the statement **RSET** *a$* = *b$* replaces the value of *a$* with a string of the same length that consists of *b$* truncated or padded on the left with spaces.

RUN The statement **RUN** restarts the program currently in memory. The computer deletes values that you have previously assigned to variables. The variation **RUN** *filespec* loads the specified program from a disk and executes it. [3]

SCREEN (Function) The value of the function **SCREEN**(*r,c*) is the ASCII value of the character in the *r*th row, *c*th column of the screen. You can use value of **SCREEN**(*r,c*,1) to determine the color of the character.

SCREEN (Statement) You can place a color monitor in the desired screen mode — text or graphics — by using one of the statements in Table B-3. The first four statements also have the effect of enabling or disabling color on non-RGB monitors, such as TV sets.

When you use a graphics monitor in text mode, the computer can store the contents of several different screens called *pages*. At any time, the page currently displayed is called the *visual page*, and the page currently being written to is called the *active page*. If a and v are numbers from 0 to 3 (or are numbers from 0 to 7 on a WIDTH-40 screen), then the statement **SCREEN** ,,a,v specifies page a as the active page and page v as the visual page.

SEEK The statement **SEEK** #n,p sets the current file position in the binary file that n references to the pth byte of the file. After the computer executes the statement, the next **GET$** or **PUT$** statement will read or write bytes, respectively, beginning with the pth byte.

SELECT CASE The **SELECT CASE** statement provides a compact method of selecting for execution one of several blocks of statements, based on the value of an expression. The **SELECT**

Statement	Resulting screen mode
SCREEN 0,1	Text mode, color enabled
SCREEN 0,0	Text mode, color disabled
SCREEN 1,0	Medium-resolution graphics mode, color enabled
SCREEN 1,1	Medium-resolution graphics mode, color disabled
SCREEN 2	High-resolution graphics mode
SCREEN 7	320 horizontal by 200 vertical 16-color EGA mode
SCREEN 8	640 horizontal by 200 vertical 16-color EGA mode
SCREEN 9	640 horizontal by 350 vertical 4 to 16-color EGA mode
SCREEN 10	640 horizontal by 350 vertical monochrome EGA mode
SCREEN 11	640 horizontal by 480 black-and-white IBM PC/2 mode
SCREEN 12	640 horizontal by 480 16-color IBM PC/2 mode

Table B-3. *The **SCREEN** Statement*

CASE block begins with a line of the form **SELECT CASE** *expression*, and ends with the line **END SELECT**. Between the two lines are statements of the form **CASE** *value list* and perhaps the statement **CASE ELSE**. A block of one or more statements follows each of these **CASE** statements. The block of statements following the first **CASE** *value list* statement for which *value list* includes the value of *expression*, is the only block of statements executed. If none of the *value lists* include the value of *expression* and if a **CASE ELSE** statement is present, then the computer executes the block of statements that follow the **CASE ELSE** statement.

SGN   The value of the function **SGN**(*x*) is 1, 0, or −1, depending upon whether *x* is positive, zero, or negative, respectively.

SHARED   You can use a statement of the form **SHARED** *var1*, *var2*, ... at the beginning of the definition of a procedure or user-defined function to specify that variables *var1*, *var2*, and so on, are shared with the main program. Shared variables are often called *global variables*. Any change that the procedure or function makes to a shared variable will change the variable of the same name in the main program, and vice versa. Declaring a variable as **SHARED** allows both the main program and a procedure to use the variable without a variable having to be added to the parameter list. You may declare arrays to be **SHARED** by listing their names followed by empty parentheses in a **SHARED** statement. You should not redimension shared arrays within the procedure or function definition.

SHELL   If *c$* is a DOS command, then the statement **SHELL** *c$* suspends execution of the Turbo Basic program, executes the DOS command that *c$* specifies, and then resumes executing the Turbo Basic program. **SHELL** suspends program execution and invokes a copy of DOS. When you have finished all of your work with DOS, typing **EXIT** resumes execution of the Turbo Basic program.

SIN   For any number *x*, the value of the trigonometric function **SIN**(*x*) is the sine of the angle of *x* radians.

SOUND The statement **SOUND** *f,d* generates a sound of pitch *f* Hz for a duration of *d*∗0.055 seconds. (Note: The keys of the piano have frequencies that range from 55 Hz to 8372 Hz.)

SPACE$ If *n* is an integer from 0 to 32767, then the value of the function **SPACE$**(*n*) is the string that consists of *n* spaces.

SPC You use the function **SPC** in **PRINT**, **LPRINT**, and **PRINT#** statements to generate spaces. For instance, the statement **PRINT** *a$* **SPC**(*n*) *b$* skips *n* spaces between the displays of the two strings *a$* and *b$*.

SQR For any nonnegative number *x*, the value of the square root function **SQR**(*x*) is the nonnegative number whose square is *x*.

STATIC You can use a statement of the form **STATIC** *var1, var2,...* at the beginning of the definition of a procedure of user-defined function to specify that the variables *var1, var2,* and so on, are permanent local variables in the procedure or function. Static variables have no connection to variables of the same name outside the procedure or function definition; thus, you may name them without regard to "outside" variables. The computer sets aside memory for static variables permanently when the program is compiled, allowing static variables to retain their values between successive invocations of the procedure or function. You may declare arrays to be STATIC by listing their names followed by empty parentheses in a **STATIC** statement, and then dimensioning them in a subsequent **DIM** statement.

STICK If *n* equals 0 or 1, the value of the function **STICK**(*n*) is the x-coordinate or y-coordinate, respectively, of the first joystick lever. If *n* equals 2 or 3, the function gives the corresponding information for the second joystick.

STOP The statement **STOP** terminates the execution of a program and closes all files. The **STOP** and **END** statements are equivalent.

STR$** The **STR$ function converts numbers to strings. The value of the function **STR$**(*n*) is the string that consists of the number *n* in the form that the computer normally displays it in.

STRIG The statements **STRIG ON**, **STRIG OFF**, and **STRIG STOP** enable, disable, and defer, respectively, the reading of the status of the joystick buttons. For each *n* from 0 to 7, the value of the function **STRIG**(*n*) gives a piece of information about the status of the joystick buttons, as indicated in Table B-4.

STRIG(n) The statement **ON STRIG**(*n*) **GOSUB** *label* sets up the trapping of one of the joystick buttons. Pressing F*n* anytime after the computer executes **STRIG**(*n*) **ON** causes a **GOSUB** to the subroutine at *label*. You disable trapping with **STRIG**(*n*) **OFF**, and

n	Value of STRIG(*n*)
0	−1 if button 1 on joystick A has been pressed since the last check of STRIG (1); 0 if not.
1	−1 if button 1 on joystick A is currently being held down; 0 if not.
2	−1 if button 1 on joystick B has been pressed since the last check of STRIG(2); 0 if not.
3	−1 if button 1 on joystick B is currently being held down; 0 if not.
4	−1 if button 2 on joystick A has been pressed since the last check of STRIG(1); 0 if not.
5	−1 if button 2 on joystick A is currently being held down; 0 if not.
6	−1 if button 2 on joystick B has been pressed since the last check of STRIG(2); 0 if not.
7	−1 if button 2 on joystick B is currently being held down; 0 if not.

Table B-4. *The STRIG Function*

defer trapping with **STRIG**(*n*) **STOP**. The numbers $n = 0$ and $n = 4$ are associated with the lower and upper buttons of the first joystick, respectively, and the numbers $n = 2$ and $n = 6$ are associated with the lower and upper buttons of the second joystick. [4], [6]

STRING$ If *n* is a whole number from 0 to 32767, then the value of **STRING$**(*n*,*a$*) is the string that consists of the first character of *a$* repeated *n* times. If *m* is a whole number from 0 to 255, then the value of the function **STRING$**(*n*,*m*) is the string that consists of the character of ASCII value *m* repeated *n* times.

SUB/END SUB   You create a procedure, or subprogram, by writing a multi-statement block that begins with a statement of the form **SUB** *name(varlist)*, has on subsequent lines one or more statements for carrying out the task of the procedure, and ends with the statement **END SUB**. The variable list, *varlist*, gives a list of formal parameters that will be passed to the procedure whenever you invoke the procedure with a **CALL** statement. Formal parameters may be simple numeric or string variables, or arrays. You may pass actual parameters used in the **CALL** of a procedure by value or reference. You may declare **LOCAL**, **STATIC**, and **SHARED** variables within procedure definitions. Procedures may invoke themselves or other procedures and functions.

SUB INLINE/END SUB   A statement of the form **SUB** *ProcName* **INLINE** begins the definition of an assembly language subprogram within a Turbo Basic program. The statement **END SUB** ends the subprogram definition. The body of the definition consists of one or more **$INLINE** metastatements.

SWAP   If *var1* and *var2* are two variables of the same type—that is, if they are both numeric variables of the same precision or both string variables—then the statement **SWAP** *var1*, *var2* exchanges the values of the two variables.

SYSTEM   The statement **SYSTEM** terminates program execution and closes all files. **SYSTEM** and **END** statements are equivalent.

TAB The function **TAB**(*n*) is used in **PRINT**, **LPRINT**, and **PRINT**# statements to move the cursor to position *n* and place spaces in all positions that were skipped over.

TAN For any number *x* (except when *x* equals pi/2, −pi/2, 3∗pi/2, −3∗pi/2, and so on), the value of the trigonometric function **TAN**(*x*) is the tangent of the angle of *x* radians.

TIME$** The value of the function **TIME$ is the current time expressed as a string of the form *hh:mm:ss*. (The hours range from 0 to 23.) If *t$* is such a string, then the statement **TIME$** = *t$* sets the computer's internal clock to the time that corresponds to *t$*.

TIMER The value of the function **TIMER** is the number of seconds from midnight to the time currently stored in the computer's internal clock. The clock is set to midnight when you first turn the computer on, but can be set to the correct time in DOS or Turbo Basic.

TRON and TROFF You use the statements **TRON** and **TROFF**, which are abbreviations of *trace on* and *trace off*, to debug programs. **TRON** causes the trace windows to display any labels or line numbers that the computer encounters while executing a program. **TROFF** terminates this tracing. [6]

UBOUND The value of the function **UBOUND**(*arrayName* (*dimNum*)) is the largest subscript value that can be used for the *dimNum*th subscript of the array *arrayName*. For example, after the computer executes the statement **DIM example(1:31,1:12,1960:1989)**, the value of **UBOUND(example(3))** is the largest value allowed for the third subscript of **example( )**, which is 1989.

UCASE$** The value of the string function **UCASE$(*a$*) is a string that is identical to *a$*, except that all lowercase letters are changed to uppercase.

VAL You use the **VAL** function to convert strings to numbers. If the leading characters of the string *a$* correspond to a number, then **VAL**(*a$*) will be the number that these characters represent. For any number *n*, **VAL(STR$(***n***))** is *n*.

VARPTR and VARSEG The values of the functions **VARSEG**(*variable*) and **VARPTR**(*variable*) are the segment of memory and the offset in that segment where the value of *variable* (if it is numeric) or the descriptor of *variable* (if it is a string or an array variable) is located.

VARPTR$** The value of the function **VARPTR$(*variable*) is a five-character string whose first character identifies the type of the variable (string or numeric and its precision), and whose last four characters can be used to determine the location of the variable in memory.

VIEW The graphics statement **VIEW** establishes a rectangular portion of the screen as a *viewport*, which will contain all subsequent figures that graphics statements will draw. There are three variations of the **VIEW** statement. For the first variation, in medium-resolution graphics mode, the pair of statements **WINDOW SCREEN (0,0) — (319,199): VIEW** (*x1,y1*) — (*x2,y2*),*c*,*b* establish a viewport with the upper-left corner being (*x1,y1*) and the lower-right corner being (*x2,y2*). The rectangle will have a background of color *c* and a boundary of color *b*, where *b* and *c* are two colors of the current palette. Subsequent graphics statements will scale their displays and place them into the viewport as if it were the entire screen. For high-resolution graphics mode, you should change the number 319 in the statements to 639, the number *c* to 0, and the number *b* to 1 or 0, depending upon whether the rectangle is to have a border or not.

In the second variation, if no **WINDOW** statement is active, then the statement **VIEW** (*x1,y1*) — (*x2,y2*),*c*,*b* causes no future scaling, but the computer will draw figures by translating *x1* points to the right and *y1* points down, with only the portion of the figure that lies inside the viewport displayed.

In the third variation, if you replace the **VIEW** statement in the second variation with **VIEW SCREEN** (*x1,y1*) — (*x2,y2*),*c*,*b*, then no scaling or relocation takes place. However, when the computer executes graphics statements, it will draw only the portions of the figures that lie inside the viewport.

WAIT If p is a port number, q is the value of a byte received at port p, and n and m are integers from 0 to 255, then the statement **WAIT** p,n,m suspends the execution of the program until the condition $((q$ **XOR** $m)$ **AND** $n) <> 0$ is true for the byte received at port p. [5]

WHILE/WEND A **WHILE...WEND** loop is a sequence of statements that begin with a statement of the form **WHILE** *condition* and that end with the statement **WEND**. The computer repeatedly executes the entire sequence of statements inside the loop as long as the specified condition is true.

WIDTH When used with a graphics monitor, the statement **WIDTH 40** causes text to be displayed in wide characters with 40 characters per line. (The first print zone contains 14 positions and the second 26 positions.) You can restore the standard 80-character-per-line format with the statement **WIDTH 80**. If s is an integer, the statement **WIDTH "LPT1:"**,s causes standard printers to print s characters per line.

WINDOW The graphics statement **WINDOW** $(x1,y1) - (x2,y2)$ imposes a standard (right-hand) coordinate system on screen, with the x-coordinates of points ranging from $x1$ to $x2$ and the y-coordinates ranging from $y1$ to $y2$. Subsequent graphics statements place figures on screen according to this coordinate system. If you replace the statement **WINDOW** with **WINDOW SCREEN**, then the computer imposes a left-hand coordinate system; that is, the y-coordinate of a point decreases as the point moves higher on screen.

WRITE The statement **WRITE** $exp1,exp2,...$ displays the values of the expressions one after the other on screen. Strings appear surrounded by quotation marks, and numbers do not have leading or trailing spaces. All commas are displayed and do not induce jumps to successive print zones. After the computer displays all of the values, the cursor moves to the beginning of the next line.

An Abridged Reference Manual of Turbo Basic **395**

WRITE# After you open a sequential file for output or append with reference number *n*, **WRITE** #*n*, *exp1,exp2,...* records the values of the expressions one after the other into the file. Strings appear surrounded by quotation marks, numbers do not have leading or trailing spaces, all commas are recorded, and the characters for a carriage return and a linefeed are placed after the data.

Supporting Topics

[1] Subdirectories Think of a directory as a folder and each file in the directory as a sheet of paper in the folder. If you insert a second folder inside the original folder, then you can place sheets of paper in either of the two folders. The second folder corresponds to a *subdirectory* of the original directory. You can then place a third folder either inside the second folder or the original folder. You can expand this example to include as many folders as necessary. You can identify each sheet of paper by giving first the sequence of folders that must be opened to get to the folder actually containing the sheet, and then the title of the sheet of paper. In Turbo Basic and DOS, you write the names of the successive subdirectories of the sequence (and the filename) one after the other, separated by backslashes, in a string called a *path*. The directory that corresponds to the first, or outermost, folder is called the *root directory*. The *current directory*, which is initially the root directory, is the default directory for specifying files.

[2] Memory Each memory location holds an integer from 0 to 255. Certain overlapping blocks of 64K (65536) consecutive memory locations are called *segments*. Segment 0 extends from location 0 to location 65535, segment 1 extends from location 16 to location 65551, segment 2 extends from location 32 to location 65567, and so on. Within each segment, the memory locations are said to have offsets 0, 1,..., 65535. For instance, you can identify the thirty-fourth memory location as segment 0:offset 34, segment 1:offset 18, or segment 2:offset 2. Turbo Basic reserves a special segment, the *default data segment*, where it stores special values such as the current cursor row and column, and the value of the random seed.

[3] Filespec   The filespec of a file on disk is a string that consists of the letter of the drive, a colon, and the name of the file. If you are using subdirectories, then the identifying path precedes the filename.

[4] Event trapping   You can set up special events, such as the pressing of a function key or the occurrence of an error, to trigger a jump to a subroutine. You specify these events using statements of the general form *EVENT* **ON** and **ON** *EVENT* **GOSUB** *label*. These statements cause the computer to check for the event after executing each statement. If the event has occurred, the computer then performs a **GOSUB** to the subroutine at *label*.

[5] Device   Some examples of devices are the video screen, keyboard, printer, modem, and diskette drives. The PC's microprocessor receives data from and sends data to the various devices of the computer through *ports*. A number from 0 to 65535 identifies each port. A *byte* of data consists of a number from 0 to 255.

[6] Label   Turbo Basic supports two mechanisms for identifying program lines that are the destinations of statements such as **GOTO** and **GOSUB**. These mechanisms are line numbers and descriptive labels. Descriptive labels appear on lines by themselves, are named by using the same rules as variables, and are followed by a colon. When a label appears in a **GOTO** or **GOSUB** statement, execution jumps to the statement that follows the line containing the label. This text uses the word *label* to refer to either a descriptive label or a line number.

C Converting BASICA Programs to Turbo Basic

Statements That Must Be Removed

Turbo Basic and BASICA are not totally compatible. Some of the BASICA commands that you have used in your programs must be removed in order to run your program in Turbo Basic.

Unsupported Statements

Turbo Basic does not support the following BASICA statements:

```
AUTO    RENUM
DELETE  EDIT    LIST   LLIST   LOAD   MERGE   NEW   SAVE
CONT
DEF USR USR     MOTOR
```

BASICA principally executes the first three lines of commands in *direct mode* (also known as *immediate* or *nonprogram mode*). However, Turbo Basic does not have a direct mode. The statements in the first line affect line numbers, which are optional and not recommended for use in Turbo Basic. However, you can execute the commands in the second line easily from the main menu or with the editor in Turbo Basic; Chapters 2 and 3 describe the details of the way to do this.

When debugging a BASICA program, you can stop the program at some point, and then continue it by using **CONT** from that point after you examine the values of variables in direct mode. Since Turbo Basic does not have a direct mode, there is no need for the **CONT** command. After you terminate a Turbo Basic program by using **STOP** or **END**, or by pressing CTRL-BREAK, there is no way to continue execution at the stopping point.

You use **DEF USR** and **USR** in BASICA as a means to access a machine-language program. There are better ways to access this type of program in both BASICA and Turbo Basic. In Turbo Basic, the **CALL ABSOLUTE** statement does the job.

Certain models of the IBM PC (not including the PC XT, PC AT, or the PS/2) contain a cassette connector to which you can attach a cassette player. If you do so, you can use the **MOTOR** statement in BASICA to turn the cassette motor on and off. This feature is rarely used in BASICA programs.

Turbo Basic does not support these statements from BASICA 3.2 and later releases of BASICA: **EXTERR**(*n*), **LOCK**, **PCOPY**, and **UNLOCK**. Turbo Basic does not support these statements from BASICA 2.1 that are valid only for the IBM PCjr: **PCOPY, NOISE, SOUND ON, SOUND OFF**, and **TERM**. Also, unlike with the PCjr, screen modes 3 through 6 are not available, the **SOUND** statement has no "voice" parameter, and the **CLEAR** statement has no video-memory parameter.

Converting BASICA Programs to Turbo Basic   **399**

Unsupported Variations of Supported Statements and Their Alternatives

CHAIN *filespec*, **ALL**   Instead of using this statement, list all of the variables in a **COMMON** statement.

CHAIN MERGE *filespec*   Sometimes, you can accomplish the task by using **$INCLUDE** *filespec*.

CLEAR ,*n*   This statement is equivalent to **DEF SEG: MEMSET** *n*. A better way to free *b* bytes is to use **MEMSET ENDMEM** $-$ *b*.

CLEAR ,,*m*   Replace this statement with the metastatement **$STACK** *m*.

RUN *linenum*   This statement is equivalent to **CLEAR: GOTO** *linenum*.

VARPTR(#filenum)

Statements That Must Be Converted

In BASICA, you use the **CALL** statement only to call a machine-language subroutine. You must convert a statement of the form

CALL *numvar* (*var1*, *var2*, ...)

to the Turbo Basic statement

CALL ABSOLUTE *numvar* (*var1*, *var2*, ...)

BASICA statement	Converted Turbo Basic statement
PLAY "O = A;"	PLAY "O=" + VARPTR$(A)
PLAY "T = B;"	PLAY "T=" + VARPTR$(B)
PLAY "XA$;"	PLAY "X=" + VARPTR$(A$)
DRAW "U = A;"	DRAW "U =" + VARPTR$(A)
DRAW "S = B;"	DRAW "S =" + VARPTR$(B)
DRAW "XA$;"	DRAW "X =" + VARPTR$(A$)
DRAW "M = A;,=B;"	DRAW "M =" + VARPTR$(A) + ",=" + VARPTR$(B)
DRAW "M +=a;, −=B"	DRAW "M +=" + VARPTR$(A) + ",−=" + VARPTR$(B)

Table C-1. *Some Conversions for PLAY and DRAW*

In BASICA, the statement

CHAIN *filespec*

can pass control to any program. In Turbo Basic, you must compile the program being chained to disk as either a Chain file or an .EXE file, as described in Chapter 10. The same considerations apply to the statement **RUN** *filespec*.

In BASICA, when the statement

COMMON *var1, var2,...*

appears in a program that chains to another program, the program that contains the statement will pass the specified variables to the chained-to program. In Turbo Basic, this **COMMON** statement must also be present in the program being chained to. A BASICA **COMMON** statement lists array variables followed by an empty pair of parentheses, whereas a Turbo Basic **COMMON** statement lists array variables followed by a pair of parentheses that enclose a constant giving the number of dimensions in the array.

In BASICA, you can give the numeric argument of a **DRAW** command or a **PLAY** command as the value of a numeric variable. If you do so, you can give the numeric argument in the form *var =*; or in the form **VARPTR$**(*var*). A string of commands, **A$**, can be included as either **XA$;** or **VARPTR$(A$)**. In Turbo Basic, you may only use the **VARPTR$** forms. Table C-1 shows the format of several conversions.

In BASICA, the **FRE** function always returns the number of bytes in memory that are not being used by BASIC. In Turbo Basic, **FRE** can return three different pieces of information, depending on the type and value in the parentheses that follow **FRE**.

BASICA Program Segments That Produce Different Results in Turbo Basic

In each of the following programs, the output in BASICA is shown after the statement **RUN**, and the output in Turbo Basic is shown after the word **Run**. Comments follow most of the programs.

```
10 STOP
RUN
Break in 10
Run
(No message)
```

In Turbo Basic, the **STOP** statement is identical to the **END** statement.

```
10 SYSTEM
RUN
C> (Returns to DOS)
Run
(For non-stand alone program, returns to Turbo Basic, for .EXE or Chain
program, returns to DOS.)

10 PRINT EXP(1419)
RUN
Overflow
 1.701412E+38
Run
 1.835987925529816E+616
```

When BASICA overflows, the value displayed is the largest number that the computer can store. This number is referred to as *machine infinity*. In Turbo Basic, mathematical functions can return values beyond the range of double-precision variables. For the second program just given, **EXP(1420)** would produce an overflow even in Turbo Basic.

```
10 x# = EXP(100)
20 PRINT x#
RUN
Overflow
 1.7014117331926440+38
Run
 2.688117141816136E+043
```

You can assign numbers between 1.7×10^{38} and about 10^{307} to variables in Turbo Basic, but not in BASICA.

```
10 x# = EXP(710)
20 PRINT x#
RUN
Overflow
 1.7014117331926440+38
Run
Error 6: Overflow
```

The value of **EXP(710)** is about 10^{309}. You cannot assign values greater than about 10^{307} to double-precision variables.

```
10 a = 1234.567
20 PRINT a
RUN
 1234.567
Run
 1234.567016601562
```

Turbo Basic often displays single-precision numbers with more than seven digits. You can use the statement **PRINT USING** to format the display.

```
10 a = 1.2
20 PRINT a
RUN
 1.2
Run
 1.200000047683716
```

In both BASICA and Turbo Basic, single-precision numbers that are not integers are only approximate. Since BASICA is more conservative in what it displays, it appears to be more accurate; however, it is not.

```
10 ON ERROR GOTO 50
20 x = 0
30 PRINT 1/x
40 END
50 REM Correct error
60 x = 1
70 RESUME
RUN
Division by zero

 1.701412E+38
Run
 1
```

You cannot trap the error **Division by zero** in BASICA, whereas you can trap it in Turbo Basic.

```
10 REM BASICA 2.1
20 PLAY "CDEFG>AB"
30 PRINT "C Major"
RUN
C Major
(Displays "C Major" as soon as scale starts playing)
Run
C Major
(Displays "C Major" only after scale finishes playing)
```

In BASICA 2.1, the default mode for music is **Music Background**. In Turbo Basic and all other versions of BASICA, the default mode is **Music Foreground**.

```
10 SCREEN 1
20 PSET (1,1),1
30 PSET (2,2),2
40 PSET (3,3),3
RUN
(Turns on green, red and brown points.)
Run
(Turns on cyan, red, and white points.)
```

When you omit the second parameter of the **SCREEN** statement, Turbo Basic presents high-intensity versions of the two medium-resolution palettes of BASICA.

```
10 PRINT CINT(2.5)
RUN
 3
Run
 2
```

Turbo Basic rounds numbers with decimal part .5 to the nearest even integer. Actually, in Turbo Basic, all functions and statements that expect an integer value will round numbers with decimal part .5 to the nearest even integer. For instance, **LOCATE 3.5,4.5** is the same as **LOCATE 4,4**.

```
10 DEF FNF(X,X)=2*X
20 PRINT FNF(3,4)
RUN
 8
Run
Error 463: Duplicate variable declaration
```

BASICA allows you to use a variable more than once as a formal parameter in a function definition. However, Turbo Basic does not allow this.

```
10 REM Previously executed program used graphics mode
20 PSET (1,1)
RUN
(Turns on point)
Run
Error 5: Illegal function call
```

In BASICA, the **RUN** statement does not restore the screen mode to its default state **SCREEN 0,0**. However, in Turbo Basic, the **RUN** statement does.

```
10 REM Assume that the previously executed program contained
20 REM single statement PRINT "Hello";
30 PRINT "Goodbye"
RUN
Hello
Goodbye
Run
HelloGoodbye
```

When BASICA terminates the execution of a program, if the last **PRINT** statement suppressed a carriage return and a line feed by using a comma or a semicolon, then BASICA performs a carriage return and a line feed. Since Turbo Basic does not do this, one program can begin to display its output where another program left off. You can easily avoid this by beginning each program with a **CLS** statement.

```
10 PRINT FRE(-1)
20 DIM A(2000)
30 PRINT FRE(-1)
```

Converting BASICA Programs to Turbo Basic **405**

```
40 ERASE A
50 PRINT FRE(-1)
RUN
 36200
 35454
 36200
Run
 216336
 216336
 216336
```

BASICA allocates memory for all arrays dynamically. Therefore, when you erase these arrays, additional space in memory becomes available. Turbo Basic allocates memory statically to arrays whenever possible. Doing so speeds up access to arrays. However, you cannot recover this memory space. If you are concerned about the size of available memory, you can use the metastatement **$DYNAMIC** to create arrays that can be completely erased from memory.

```
10 GOTO 30
20 DEFINT bar
30 bar = 3.2
40 PRINT bar
RUN
 3.2
Run
 3
```

In Turbo Basic, the compiler took the statements in order and processed **DEFINT**. Although Turbo Basic will skip over the statement during run-time, it still determined the variable type of **bar**. Similar considerations apply to **TRON**, **TROFF**, **OPTION BASE**, and the other **DEF***type* statements.

Other Concerns

There are many reserved words in Turbo Basic that are not reserved words in BASICA. Some of those most likely to occur as variable names in BASICA programs are **ABSOLUTE, AT, BIN$, BINARY, CASE, DECR, DELAY, DO, EXIT, EXP10, EXP2, INCR, INTERRUPT, LBOUND, LOCAL, LOG10, LOG2, LOOP, PALETTE, SEEK, SELECT, SERVICE, SHARED, UBOUND,** and **UNTIL.**

PEEK and **POKE** statements that access low memory (**DEF SEG = 0**) or ROM will serve the same purpose in Turbo Basic. However, **PEEK**s and **POKE**s in BASIC's data segment will usually fail to perform as you will expect. A notable exception is the statement **POKE 78**,*c*, which sets the text color to *c* in medium-resolution graphics mode.

In BASICA, you can save programs in three formats—compressed binary, ASCII, and protected. However, only programs saved in ASCII format (which you can accomplish with the command **SAVE** *filespec*,**A**) can be executed in Turbo Basic. If you see unexpected characters—such as the characters with ASCII values either less than 32 or greater than 127—when you load a BASICA program into Turbo Basic's editor, then it has probably been saved in compressed binary or protected format. You can convert programs in compressed binary format to ASCII format by **LOAD**ing them in BASICA and then **SAVE**ing them in ASCII format. Programs in protected format are more difficult to convert. The following steps will convert such a program in IBM PC BASICA. (These steps will not work with other versions of BASICA.) Suppose that the protected program is named PROGRAM.BAS.

1. Enter **DEF SEG: NEW**.

2. Enter **BSAVE "UNPROT.ECT",1124,1**.

3. Enter **LOAD "PROGRAM.BAS"**.

4. Enter **BLOAD "UNPROT.ECT"**.

5. Enter **SAVE "PROGRAM.BAS",A**.

It is recommended that you remove all line numbers that are not referenced. They are not needed in Turbo Basic and take up space in the compiler's symbol table. In addition, they slow down the compiler and might result in the message **Compiler out of memory**.

D Turbo Basic Reserved Words

This appendix presents a list of the reserved words of Turbo Basic.

$COM1	AT	COM	DIM	EXP2	INSTR
$COM2	ATN	COMMAND	DO	FIELD	INT
$DEBUG	BASE	COMMON	DRAW	FILES	INTERRUPT
$DYNAMIC	BEEP	COS	DYNAMIC	FIX	IOCTL
$ELSE	BIN$	CSNG	ELSE	FN	IOCTL$
$ENDIF	BINARY	CSRLIN	ELSEIF	FOR	KEY
$EVENT	BLOAD	CVD	END	FRE	KILL
$IF	BSAVE	CVI	ENDMEM	GET	LBOUND
$INCLUDE	CALL	CVL	ENVIRON	GET$	LCASE$
$INLINE	CASE	CVMD	ENVIRON$	GOSUB	LEFT$
$LIST	CDBL	CVMS	EOF	GOTO	LEN
$OPTION	CEIL	CVS	EQV	HEX$	LET
$SEGMENT	CHAIN	DATA	ERADR	IF	LINE
$SOUND	CHDIR	DATE$	ERASE	IMP	LIST
$STACK	CHR$	DECR	ERDEV	INCR	LOC
$STATIC	CINT	DEF	ERDEV$	INKEY$	LOCAL
ABS	CIRCLE	DEFDBL	ERL	INLINE	LOCATE
ABSOLUTE	CLEAR	DEFINT	ERR	INP	LOF
AND	CLNG	DEFLNG	ERROR	INPUT	LOG
APPEND	CLOSE	DEFSNG	EXIT	INPUT#	LOG10
AS	CLS	DEFSTR	EXP	INPUT$	LOG2
ASC	COLOR	DELAY	EXP10	INSTAT	LOOP

LPOS	OPTION	REG	SPACE$	UCASE$	WIDTH
LPRINT	OR	REM	SPC	UNTIL	WINDOW
LPRINT#	OUT	RESET	SQR	USING	WRITE
LSET	OUTPUT	RESTORE	STATIC	USR	WRITE#
MEMSET	PAINT	RESUME	STEP	USR0	XOR
MID$	PALETTE	RETURN	STICK	USR1	
MKD$	PEEK	RIGHT$	STOP	USR2	
MKDIR	PEN	RMDIR	STR$	USR3	
MKI$	PLAY	RND	STRIG	USR4	
MKL$	PMAP	RSET	STRING#	USR5	
MKMD$	POINT	RUN	SUB	USR6	
MKMS$	POKE	SAVE	SWAP	USR7	
MKS$	POS	SCREEN	SYSTEM	USR8	
MOD	PRESET	SEEK	TAB	USR9	
MTIMER	PRINT	SEG	TAN	VAL	
NAME	PRINT#	SELECT	THEN	VARPTR	
NEXT	PSET	SERVICE	TIME$	VARPTR$	
NOT	PUT	SGN	TIMER	VARSEG	
OCT$	PUT$	SHARED	TO	VIEW	
OFF	RANDOM	SHELL	TROFF	WAIT	
ON	RANDOMIZE	SIN	TRON	WEND	
OPEN	READ	SOUND	UBOUND	WHILE	

E Installing Turbo Basic

Hard-Disk Installation

Place the Turbo Basic Program Disk into drive A. From the **C>** prompt, use the following set of DOS commands to create a new directory and to copy the Turbo Basic Program Disk to the hard disk. (Assume the standard drive specifier, **C:**, for the hard disk.)

```
MD \TB
CD \TB
COPY A:*.*
```

If you wish to copy the Turbo Basic sample programs onto your hard disk, place the Sample Programs diskette into drive A and give the command

```
COPY A:*.*
```

After copying the master Turbo Basic disks to your hard disk, store them in a safe place.

Hard-Disk Startup

In general, to start Turbo Basic, type the following commands from the **C>** prompt:

```
CD \TB
TB
```

Floppy-Disk Installation

First, prepare a formatted system disk by placing the DOS disk that contains the program FORMAT.COM in drive A, and a new disk in drive B. From the **A>** prompt, type the DOS command

```
FORMAT B:
```

When the prompt **Format another?** appears, type **N**. Remove the DOS disk from drive A and replace it with the original copy of the Turbo Basic disk. Now type the DOS commands

```
COPY TB.EXE B:
COPY TBHELP.TBH B:
```

Your disk in drive B now contains Turbo Basic.

Floppy-Disk Startup

In general, to start Turbo Basic, place your working copy of the Turbo Basic diskette into drive A, and type the following command from the **A>** prompt:

```
TB
```

You might also want to have a formatted disk in drive B on which you can save the programs that you create.

F A Summary of Turbo Basic's Predefined Functions Grouped by Use

Notation

This appendix uses the following notation: *x* denotes values that may naturally have a fractional part; *n* and *m* denote values that are naturally whole numbers, though Turbo Basic may be given values with fractional parts and will round them to whole numbers before use.

Array Functions

LBOUND(*arrayName*(*n*))   This function produces the smallest value allowed for the *n*th subscript.

412 *Using Turbo Basic*

      UBOUND(*arrayName*(*n*))   This function produces the largest value allowed for the *n*th subscript.

Conversion Functions

BIN$(*n*)	This function produces the string that consists of the binary representation of *n*.
CDBL(*x*)	This function produces the double-precision constant that *x* determines.
CINT(*x*)	This function produces the integer constant that *x* determines.
CLNG(*x*)	This function produces the long integer constant that *x* determines.
CSNG(*x*)	This function produces the single-precision constant that *x* determines.
CVD(*a$*)	This function produces the double-precision constant encoded as *a$*.
CVI(*a$*)	This function produces the integer constant encoded as *a$*.
CVL(*a$*)	This function produces the long integer constant encoded as *a$*.
CVS(*a$*)	This function produces the single-precision constant encoded as *a$*.
CVMD(*a$*)	This function produces the double-precision constant that Microsoft BASIC encodes as *a$*.
CVMS(*a$*)	This function produces the single-precision constant that Microsoft BASIC encodes as *a$*.
HEX$(*n*)	This function produces the string that consists of the hexadecimal representation of *n*.
MKD$(*x*)	This function produces the string that encodes the double-precision constant *x*.

A Summary of Turbo Basic's Predefined Functions **413**

MKI$(*n*)	This function produces the string that encodes the integer constant *n*.
MKL$(*n*)	This function produces the string that encodes the long integer constant *n*.
MKS$(*x*)	This function produces the string that encodes the single-precision constant *x*.
MKMD$(*x*)	This function produces the Microsoft BASIC string that encodes the double-precision constant *x*.
MKMS$(*x*)	This function produces the Microsoft BASIC string that encodes the single-precision constant *x*.
OCT$(*n*)	This function produces the string that consists of the octal representation of *n*.
STR$(*x*)	This function produces the string that consists of the standard decimal representation of *x*.
VAL(*a$*)	This function produces the value of the number given in decimal string format in *a$*.

Error-Control Functions

ERADR	This function produces the value of the program-counter at the time of a run-time error.
ERDEV	This function produces information about errors.
ERDEV$	This function produces the name of the device responsible for an error.
ERR	This function produces the error number of a run-time error.
ERL	This function produces the current or most-recent line number when a run-time error occurs.

File Functions

EOF(*n*)	This function produces −1 if the end of file *n* has been reached, or 0 if not.
LOC(*n*)	For sequential file *n*, this function produces the number of 128-character blocks read or written. For random file *n*, this function produces the number of the last record read or written. For binary file *n*, this function produces the number of bytes from the beginning of the file.
LOF(*n*)	This function produces the number of characters in file *n*.

Graphics Functions

PMAP(*x,n*)	This function produces the physical or world coordinate for *x* as indicated by *n*.
POINT(*n*)	This function produces the last-point-referenced coordinate that *n* indicates.
POINT(*x,y*)	This function produces the number of the color of the point with coordinates (*x,y*).

Input Functions

INKEY$	This function produces the character or characters for the next keystroke in the keyboard buffer, if any.
INSTAT	This function produces −1 if a keystroke is waiting in the keyboard buffer, or 0 if not.

A Summary of Turbo Basic's Predefined Functions

Mathematical Functions

ABS(x)	This function produces the absolute value of x.
ATN(x)	This function produces the arctangent of the angle of x radians.
CEIL(x)	This function produces the smallest whole number greater than or equal to x.
COS(x)	This function produces the cosine of the angle of x radians.
EXP(x)	This function produces the natural log base e (2.71828...) to the x power, which is e^x.
EXP2(x)	This function produces 2 to the x power; which is 2^x.
EXP10(x)	This function produces ten to the x power; which is 10^x.
FIX(x)	This function produces the whole number obtained by discarding the decimal part of x.
INT(x)	This function produces the greatest whole number less than or equal to x.
LOG(x)	This function produces the natural logarithm of x.
LOG2(x)	This function produces the logarithm base 2 of x.
LOG10(x)	This function produces the logarithm base 10 of x.
RND	This function produces a pseudo-randomly selected number from 0 to 1, but not including 1.
SIN(x)	This function produces the sine of the angle of x radians.
SGN(x)	This function produces the sign of x: thus, 1 if x is greater than 0, 0 if x is equal to 0, or −1 if x is less than 0.
SQR(x)	This function produces the square root of x.
TAN(x)	This function produces the tangent of the angle of x radians.

Print Functions

LPOS(1)	This function produces the current "cursor position" in the print buffer.
SPC(n)	This function prints n spaces.
TAB(n)	This function moves to print position n, and places spaces in all skipped-over positions.

Screen Functions

CSRLIN	This function produces the line of the screen that currently contains the cursor.
POS	This function produces the column number of the current text position of the cursor.
SCREEN(r,c)	This function produces the ASCII value of the character in row r, column c of the screen.
SCREEN($r,c,1$)	This function is used to obtain the foreground and background colors of the character at row r, column c of the screen.

String-Analysis Functions and String-Manipulation Functions

ASC($a$$)	This function produces the ASCII value of the first character of the string $a$$.
**CHR$**($n$)	This function produces the character whose ASCII value is n.

A Summary of Turbo Basic's Predefined Functions **417**

INSTR(*n,a$,b$*)	This function produces the first position at or after the *n*th character of *a$* at which the string *b$* occurs.
**LCASE$**(*a$*)	This function produces the string *a$* with all uppercase letters converted to lowercase.
**LEFT$**(*a$,n*)	This function produces the string that consists of the leftmost *n* characters of *a$*.
LEN(*a$*)	This function produces the number of characters (or length) in the string *a$*.
**MID$**(*a$,m,n*)	This function produces the string that consists of *n* characters of *a$*, starting with character *m*.
**RIGHT$**(*a$,n*)	This function produces the string that consists of the rightmost *n* characters of *a$*.
SPACE$(*n*)	This function produces the string that consists of *n* spaces.
**STRING$**(*n,a$*)	This function produces the string that consists of the first character of *a$* repeated *n* times.
STRING$(*n,m*)	This function produces the string that consists of the character of ASCII value *m* repeated *n* times.
**UCASE$**(*a$*)	This function produces the string *a$* with all lowercase letters converted to uppercase.

System-Related Functions

COMMAND$	This function produces the string that consists of the DOS command-line parameters.
ENDMEM	This function produces the absolute address of the last byte available in memory.

418   Using Turbo Basic

**ENVIRON$**(*a$*)	This function produces the right side of the environment-table entry that *a$* names.
ENVIRON$(*n*)	This function produces the *n*th equation in the environment table.
FRE(" ")	This function produces the number of memory locations available for storing new string data.
FRE(−1)	This function produces the number of memory locations available for new numeric arrays.
FRE(−2)	This function produces the amount of space left on the stack.
INP(*n*)	This function produces the value of the byte read from port *n*.
IOCTL$(*n*)	This function produces the control string that is returned upon opening a device driver as *n*.
PEEK(*n*)	This function produces the value of the byte at offset *n* in the current memory segment.
REG(*regnum*)	This function produces the current value of the system register that corresponds to *regnum*.
VARPTR(*var*)	This function produces the offset in **VARSEG**(*var*) of the value or descriptor for *var*.
VARPTR$(*var*)	This function produces the five-character string that identifies *var*'s type and location.
VARSEG(*var*)	This function produces the memory segment that contains the value or descriptor for *var*.

Time Functions

DATE$	This function produces the current date in the form *mm-dd-yyyy*.

A Summary of Turbo Basic's Predefined Functions

MTIMER	This function produces the number of microseconds elapsed since you reset the microtimer.
TIME$	This function produces the current time expressed as a string of the form "*hh:mm:ss*".
TIMER	This function produces the number of seconds elapsed on the computer's internal clock.

Miscellaneous Functions

PEN(*n*)	This function produces the light pen status that *n* indicates.
PLAY(0)	This function produces the number of notes that remain in the music-background buffer.
STICK(*n*)	This function produces the joystick coordinate that *n* indicates.
STRIG(*n*)	This function produces the joystick status that *n* indicates.

G Editor Commands

Notation

Table G-1 summarizes all of the commands that the Turbo Basic editor understands. This appendix then describes the details of each command.

Table G-1 uses the following notation: A word or words in small caps, such as LEFT ARROW, indicates that you should use a *single key* of the given name. When a caret (^) precedes a letter, such as ^S, you must hold down CTRL as you press the key for the letter. When two letters follow a caret, such as ^QS, you must hold down CTRL as you press the key for the first letter, and you may optionally hold down CTRL for the key for the second letter. Although all commands are shown in uppercase letters, you may use lowercase letters also.

DESCRIPTION	COMMAND
Commands to move cursor	
Left one character	^S or LEFT ARROW
Right one character	^D or RIGHT ARROW
Left to beginning of word	^A or ^LEFT ARROW
Right to beginning of word	^F or ^RIGHT ARROW
Left to beginning of line	^QS or HOME
Right to end of line	^QD or END
Up one line	^E or UP ARROW
Down one line	^X or DOWN ARROW
Up to first line in window	^QE or ^HOME
Down to last line in window	^QX or ^END
Up to a new page	^R or PGUP
Down to a new page	^C or PGDN
Up to first line of program	^QR or ^PGUP
Down to last line of program	^QC or ^PGDN
Scroll up one line in program	^W
Scroll down one line in program	^Z
Move to beginning of block	^QB
Move to end of block	^QK
Move to last cursor position	^QP
Set place marker n ($n=0-3$)	^K n (not ^n)
Find place marker n ($n=0-3$)	^Q n (not ^n)
Commands to delete text	
Delete character left of cursor	^H or BACKSPACE
Delete character at cursor	^G or DEL
Delete from cursor to end of word	^T
Delete from cursor to end of line	^QY
Delete entire line	^Y

Table G-1. *The Turbo Basic Editor Commands*

Editor Commands

DESCRIPTION	COMMAND
Commands to act on blocks of text	
Mark beginning of a block	^KB or F7
Mark end of a block	^KK or F8
Mark a word that contains cursor as block	^KT
Print marked block	^KP
Delete marked block	^KY
Copy marked block to cursor position	^KC
Move marked block to cursor position	^KV
Write marked block to disk file	^KW
Read file from disk as a block	^KR
Hide or display marked block	^KH
Mode toggles	
Auto-indent mode on or off	^OI
Insert mode on or off	^V or INS
Tab mode on or off	^OT
Commands to search and replace	
Search for text	^QF
Search for and replace text	^QA
Repeat last search or replace	^L
Commands to save, load, and exit	
Save current program to disk file	^KS or F2
Load new program from disk file	F3
Exit editor to main menu	^KD, ^KQ, ^KX, or ESC

Table G-1. *The Turbo Basic Editor Commands (continued)*

DESCRIPTION	COMMAND
Miscellaneous commands	
Abort operation	^U
Enter control character	^P
Move end of line to new line	^N
Tab	^I or TAB
Restore error message	^QW
Restore line	^QL

Table G-1. *The Turbo Basic Editor Commands* (continued)

Commands to Move Cursor

This section describes the commands of the Turbo Basic editor that move the cursor.

Left One Character (^S or LEFT ARROW) This command moves the cursor one character to the left. Turbo Basic ignores this command when the cursor is at the beginning of the line.

Right One Character (^D or RIGHT ARROW) This command moves the cursor one character to the right. This command does not consider the last nonblank character on a line as the end of the line, but will continue to move the cursor to the right until it reaches the maximum line length (248 characters).

Left to Start of Word (^A or ^LEFT ARROW) This command moves the cursor to the beginning of the first word to the left. A *word* is defined as a sequence of characters that occurs between any two of the following 17 separators: *space* $ ' ( ) * + , - . / ; < > [ ] ^

If the cursor is in a word but not at the beginning of that word, the cursor moves to the beginning of this word. If the cursor is not in a word, it moves to the beginning of the first word that is to its left. If no word lies to the left of the cursor and if a line lies above the current line, the cursor moves to the position that follows the last nonblank character of the previous line.

Right to Start of Word (^F or ^RIGHT ARROW) This command moves the cursor to the beginning of the first word to the right. If the cursor is in the last word of a line, the cursor moves to the position that follows the end of this word. If the cursor is at the end of the line and another line follows the current line, the cursor moves to the beginning of the first word in the next line.

Left to Start of Line (^QS or HOME) This command moves the cursor to column 1 of the current line.

Right to End of Line (^QD or END) This command moves the cursor to the position that follows the last nonblank character in the line. In some cases, this command may move the cursor to the left.

Up One Line (^E or UP ARROW) If a line exists above the current line, this command moves the cursor up to that line. The command preserves the column of the cursor—it encounters a tab character, in which case the cursor will move farther right.

Down One Line (^X or DOWN ARROW) If a line exists below the current line, this command moves the cursor down to that line. The command preserves the column of the cursor—unless it encounters a tab character, in which case the cursor will move farther right.

Up to First Line in Window (^QE or ^HOME) This command moves the cursor to the first line visible in the Edit window. The command preserves the column of the cursor—unless it encounters a tab character, in which case the cursor will move farther right.

Down to Last Line in Window (^QX or ^END) This command moves the cursor to the last line visible in the Edit window. The command preserves the column of the cursor—unless it encounters a tab character, in which case the cursor will move further right.

Up to a New Page (^R or ^PGUP) This command displays an earlier section of the program in the Edit window. In general, what was the first line visible in the window becomes the last line visible in the window.

Down to a New Page (^C or ^PGDN) This command displays later section of the program in the Edit window. In general, what was the last line visible in the window becomes the first line visible in the window.

Up to First Line of Program (^QR or ^PGUP) This command moves the cursor to the beginning of the first line of the program, and displays this line at the top of the Edit window.

Down to Last Line of Program (^QC or ^PGDN) This command moves the cursor to the end of the last line of the program, and displays this line at the bottom of the Edit window.

Scroll View Up One Line (^W) If more program lines exist above the first line displayed in the Edit window, then this command scrolls each line in the Edit window down one line to bring in a new line of the program at the top of the Edit window. The command preserves the position of the cursor, unless the cursor lies on the last visible line in the Edit window.

Scroll View Down One Line (^Z) If more program lines exist below the last line displayed in the Edit window, then the command scrolls each line in the Edit window up one line to bring in a new line of the program at the bottom of the Edit window. The command preserves the position of the cursor, unless the cursor lies on the first line visible in the Edit window.

Editor Commands **427**

Move to Beginning of Block (^QB) If you marked the beginning of a block of text earlier, this command moves the cursor to the location of this "start block" mark.

Move to End of Block (^QK) If you marked the end of a block of text earlier, this command moves the cursor to the location of this "end block" mark.

Move to Last Cursor Position (^QP) This command moves the cursor to the location where it was before you issued the last command or typed the last character. This command is useful after you issue a cursor-moving command, including ^QF, for returning to the location at which you were working.

Set Place Marker n (^K n) This command places a temporary marker at the current cursor position; n can be any one of the four single digits 0 to 3. (Note: Do not hold CTRL down when pressing the digit key.) After setting a marker, you may return immediately from any other location in the program to the location where the marker is by using the Find Place Marker n command with the appropriate value of n. You may move place markers by simply setting them in a new location. Turbo Basic does not save place markers with the program.

Find Place Marker n (^Q n) This command moves the cursor to the location where you last set place marker n; n can be any one of the four single digits 0 to 3.

Commands to Delete Text

This section describes the commands of the Turbo Basic editor that delete text.

Delete Character Left of Cursor (^H or BACKSPACE) This command deletes the character immediately to the left of the cursor. If the cursor is at the beginning of the line and there is a line above the current line, the command joins the current line to the end of the previous line.

Delete Character at Cursor (^G or DEL) This command deletes the character located at the current cursor position. If the cursor is located after the last nonblank character on the line and there is a line below the current line, the command joins the next line to the end of the current line.

Delete from Cursor to End of Word (^T) This command deletes all characters from the character located at the current cursor position to the end of the word in which the cursor lies. If the cursor is located at a space character, the command deletes all spaces from the cursor position to the next nonblank character. If the cursor is located after the last nonblank character in the current line and there is a line below the current line, the command joins the next line to the end of the current line.

Delete from Cursor to End of Line (^QY) This command deletes any and all characters from the character located at the current cursor position to the last character on the line.

Delete Entire Line (^Y) This command deletes all characters in the line that contains the cursor, and moves subsequent lines up to fill in the gap.

Commands to Act on Blocks of Text

This section describes the commands of the Turbo Basic editor that act on blocks of text.

Mark Beginning of a Block (^KB or F7) This command marks the character located at the current cursor position as the first character in a block of text. When you also mark the end of the block, the command highlights the text within the block. You may print, move, copy, or delete marked blocks of text in a single operation, as described later in this section.

Mark End of a Block (^KK or F8) This command marks the character located just left of the current cursor position as the last character in a block of text. When you also mark the beginning of the block, the command highlights the text within the block. You may print, move, copy, or delete marked blocks of text in a single operation, as described later in this section.

Mark a Word Containing Cursor as Block (^KT) This command marks the word that contains the cursor as a block. If the cursor is not inside a word, the command marks the first word to the right of the cursor.

Print Marked Block (^KP) This command prints on the printer the text within the currently marked block. If you do not mark a block or if the marked block is hidden, then the command prints the entire program in memory.

Delete Marked Block (^KY) This command deletes from memory the entire block of text that you marked in the current program.

Copy Marked Block to Cursor Position (^KC) This command copies the block of text that you marked in the current program to the point where the cursor currently resides. Any text lying at or after the cursor is pushed down to make room for the copied block. The cursor is left at the beginning of the copied block. This command does not affect the block of text originally marked.

Move Marked Block to Cursor Position (^KV) This command moves the block of text that you marked in the current program to the point where the cursor currently resides, and deletes the block of text from its original location. The command pushes down any text lying at or after the cursor to make room for the moved block. The cursor is left at the beginning of the moved block.

Write Marked Block to Disk File (^KW) This command copies the block of text that you marked in the current program to a disk file, and asks for the name of the file to create (or overwrite). If the disk file already exists, the command warns you and gives an option to cancel or to give a new name. This command does not affect the block of text originally marked.

Read in File from Disk as a Block (^KR) This command requests the name of an existing disk file, and then inserts the contents of this file into the current program at the current cursor position. The command pushes down any text lying at or after the cursor to make room for the text inserted from the disk file. The command automatically marks the inserted text as a block, and the cursor is left at the beginning of this block. This command does not affect the disk file from which the inserted text was read.

Hide or Display Marked Block (^KH) If a marked block of text is being displayed in the current program, this command hides the fact that a marked block exists by not highlighting the block. When a block is hidden, you cannot perform block commands, such as block copy, block move, and block write, on a hidden block. If a marked block exists but is hidden, then the command redisplays the block highlighting and permits you to execute block commands.

Mode Toggles

This section describes the commands of the Turbo Basic editor that toggle the various modes.

Auto-indent Mode On/Off (^OI) This command changes the status of the Auto-indent mode from OFF to ON, or from ON to OFF.

Editor Commands

When Auto-indent mode is ON, Turbo Basic automatically positions the cursor in the same column as the first nonblank character of the previous line whenever you press ENTER to create a new line. (Note: Pressing ENTER can create a new line only if Insert mode is on.)

Insert Mode On/Off (^V or INS) This command changes the status of the Insert mode from OFF to ON, or from ON to OFF. When Insert mode is ON, Turbo Basic moves existing text to the right to make room for new text that you are entering. When Insert mode is OFF, newly entered text replaces, or overwrites, existing text. Note: You can add new lines to the bottom of a program only when Insert mode is ON.

Tab Mode On/Off (^OT) This command changes the status of Tab mode from OFF to ON, or from ON to OFF. When Tab mode is ON, you can use TAB to place tabs in your program for the sake of readability. Turbo Basic preset tab stops at columns 9, 17, 25, 33, 41, and so on. When Tab mode is OFF, Turbo Basic ignores the use of TAB.

Commands to Search and Replace

This section describes the commands of the Turbo Basic editor that search and replace.

Search for Text (^QF) This command requests a string of characters to search for, requests search options, and finds the string in the program. Search options can be any number, or none, of the following:

- B   Search backwards through the program.
- G   Search globally (through the entire program), rather than just the section after (or before) the current cursor location.

n   Ignore the first $n-1$ matches to the search string, and move the cursor to the nth match found. For example, giving 4 as a search option causes Turbo Basic to ignore the first three matches with the search string, and moves the cursor to the fourth match.

U   Ignore whether letters are uppercase or lowercase when checking for a match with the search string. For example, if you give the **U** option, a search for **time** will match **Time**, **TIME**, and so on.

W   Match the search string with whole words only. Turbo Basic will not make a match when the search string is part of a larger word. For example, if you give the **W** option, a search for **end** will not match **ends**, **send**, or **friend**.

Two examples of search options are **GB** to search from the end to the beginning of the program for a match of the search string, and **3W** to search forwards from the current cursor location for the third whole word match of the search string.

Search for and Replace Text (^QA)   This command requests a string of characters to search for, requests a string of replacement characters, requests search and replacement options, finds the search string in the program according to the search options, and replaces the match with the replacement string. Search options are as described for the Search for Text command. The following replacement option is also available:

N   Make the replacement without first asking for a verification that the string found should be replaced.

Repeat Last Search or Replace (^L)   This command executes again the last search or search-and-replace command by using the same search string, replacement string (if appropriate), and options.

Editor Commands

Commands to Save, Load, and Exit

This section describes the commands of the Turbo Basic editor for saving, loading, and exiting.

Save Current Program to Disk File (^KS or F2) This command saves the program currently in memory in a disk file with the program name. If the program name is NONAME.BAS, the command asks you to give another name. If a disk file of the same name already exists, the command asks if it should overwrite the old disk file with the new program.

Load New Program from Disk File (F3) This command asks for the name of a disk file to be loaded into memory. If you have not saved the current program in memory, the command gives you the option to do so. Any text currently in memory is lost as the command loads the new file into memory.

Exit Editor to Main Menu (^KD, ^KQ, ^KX, or ESC) This command stops editing and returns control to the main menu. The program that you edited remains in memory, ready to be compiled, run, or saved. Note: Exiting the editor does not automatically cause Turbo Basic to save the program on disk. You must save the program explicitly by, for example, pressing F2 while in the Editor.

Miscellaneous Commands

This section describes the remaining commands of the Turbo Basic editor.

Abort Operation (^U) This command stops the command currently being entered or executed. You must press ESC next. This command is particularly useful for stopping a global search-and-replace command before it finishes.

Enter Control Character (^P)   This command interprets the next character entered as a control character, rather than as a standard character. For example, the editor interprets pressing CTRL-P and then typing **M** as the character ^M (ASCII character 13). You use this command primarily when specifying search-and-replacement strings. The command allows the strings to contain control characters, such as the tab character, ^I, and the end-of-line characters ^M^J.

Move End of Line to New Line (^N)   This command creates a new line below the current lines, and moves any text lying at or right of the cursor to the beginning of this new line. The cursor remains at the new end of the current line.

Tab (^I or TAB)   If Tab mode is ON, this command places a tab character in the program and moves the cursor to the next tab stop. Turbo Basic presets tab stops at columns 9, 17, 25, 33, 41, and so on.

Restore Error Message (^QW)   This command redisplays the last compiler-error message at the top of the Edit window, and moves the cursor back to the place in the program text where this error occurred.

Restore Line (^QL)   This command restores the current line to its "original" form, which is the form that the current line had when you moved the cursor to the line from another line. Use this command to undo the changes that you just made to the current line.

H The Differences Between WordStar and the Turbo Basic Editor

If you are familiar with the WordStar word-processing package, this appendix provides Table H-1 and Table H-2 to compare the different meanings of certain commands in WordStar and Turbo Basic, and to show which commands in Turbo Basic you can use in place of certain WordStar commands. In both tables, (3) indicates that the description applies to WordStar version 3.x only, and (4) indicates that the description applies to WordStar version 4.0 only. In addition, both tables use the following notation: A word or words in small caps, such as LEFT ARROW, indicates that you should use a *single key* of the given name. When a caret (^) precedes a letter, such as ^S, you must hold down CTRL while pressing the key for the letter. When two letters follow a caret, such as ^QS, you must hold down CTRL while pressing the key for the first letter, and may optionally hold down CTRL while pressing the key for the second letter. Although both tables show all commands in uppercase letters, you may use lowercase letters as well.

Turbo Basic does not support the following WordStar commands:

^B   ^KL
^Q DEL   ^KF
^KN   ^J...
^KO   ^O...
^KJ   ^QQ...
^KE

Command	In WordStar	In Turbo Basic
BACKSPACE or ^H	(3) Move one space to the left (no deletion). If at the beginning of line, move to end of previous line. (4) Same as Turbo Basic.	Delete character the left of cursor. If at beginning of line, join current line to previous line.
DEL	(3) Delete character to left of cursor. If at beginning of line, join current line to previous line. (4) Same as Turbo Basic.	Delete character at cursor position. If at end of line, join next line to current line.
^S	Move left one column. If at beginning of line, move to end of previous line.	Move left one column. No effect if at beginning of line.
^D	Move right one column. If at end of current line, move to beginning of next line.	Move right one column. (Ignores end of line.)
^QD	Move cursor to end of current line.	Move cursor to just after last nonblank character on current line.
HOME	Move cursor to first line on screen.	Move cursor to beginning of current line.
END	Move cursor to last line on screen.	Move cursor to just after last nonblank character on current line.

Table H-1. *The Meanings of Commands in WordStar and Turbo Basic*

Differences Between WordStar and Turbo Basic Editor

Command	In WordStar	In Turbo Basic
^HOME	(3) No effect. (4) Move cursor to the beginning of the document.	Move to first line of Edit window.
^END	(3) No effect. (4) Move cursor to the end of the document.	Move to last line of Edit window.
^PGUP	(3) Same as Turbo Basic. (4) Scroll screen up one line in document.	Move cursor to start of program.
^PGDN	(3) Same as Turbo Basic. (4) Scroll screen down one line in document.	Move cursor to end of program.
^KD	Save document and go to main menu.	Leave editor and go to main menu. Program is not saved to disk, but is still in memory.
^KX	Save document and exit WordStar.	Leave editor and go to main menu. Program is not saved to disk, but is still in memory.
^KQ	Forget any changes made to document and return to main menu.	Leave editor and go to main menu. Changes to program are not lost. Program is still in memory.
^KP	Print a disk file while editing continues.	Print the block that you marked with ^KB and ^KK. No editing allowed while block is printed.
^OI	Set tab stops.	Toggle Auto-indent mode ON or OFF.
^OT	Toggle display of ruler line.	Toggle whether tabbing will insert spaces or will skip over existing text.
^QL	Find misspelling.	Undo changes just made to current line.
^J...	Call up a help screen.	Not supported. Press F1 instead.
F1	(3) Set help level. (4) After pressing, press another key to call up a help screen.	Call up a help screen.

Table H-1. *The Meanings of Commands in WordStar and Turbo Basic* (continued)

Command	In WordStar	In Turbo Basic
F2	(3) Do a temporary margin indent. (4) Undo last command.	Save current form of program in memory to a disk file. After save, continue editing.
F3	(3) Set left margin. (4) Toggle underlining.	Load a new file.
F4	(3) Set right margin. (4) Toggle boldface.	No effect.
F5	(3) Toggle underlining. (4) Delete a line.	Zoom Edit window either in or out.
F6	(3) Toggle boldface. (4) Delete to end of word.	Make next (Trace) window active.
F7	(3) Same as Turbo Basic. (4) Reform paragraph and return cursor to previous location.	Mark beginning of block.
F8	(3) Same as Turbo Basic. (4) Imbed a ruler line.	Mark end of block.
F9	(3) Move cursor to the beginning of the document. (4) Save document and then continue editing.	No effect.
F10	(3) Move cursor to the end of the document. (4) Save document and go to main menu.	No effect.

Table H-1. *The Meanings of Commands in WordStar and Turbo Basic* (continued)

Differences Between WordStar and Turbo Basic Editor 439

WordStar command	Effect of WordStar command	Equivalent Turbo Basic command
BACKSPACE or ^H	(3) Move one space to the left (no deletion). If at beginning of line, move to end of previous line.	Cursor left
DEL	(3) Delete character to left of cursor. If at beginning of line, join current line to previous line.	^G
F9	(3) Go to top of document. May also use ^QR.	^PGUP or ^QR
HOME	(4) Go to top of document. May also use ^QR.	^PGUP or ^QR
F10	(3) Go to end of document. May also use ^QC.	^PGDN or ^QC
^END	(4) Go to end of document. May also use ^QC.	^PGDN or ^QC
HOME	Move cursor to first line on screen.	^HOME
END	Move cursor to last line on screen.	^END
^QD	Move cursor to end of current line.	END or ^QD
^KS	Save document and remain in Edit mode.	F2 or ^KS
^KD	Save document and go to main menu.	F2 followed by ESC
^KX	Save document and exit WordStar.	F2 followed by ALT-X
^KQ	Forget any changes made to document and return to main menu.	ALT-X and type **N**
^J...	Call up a help screen.	F1

Table H-2. WordStar Commands and Their Turbo Basic Equivalents

Trademarks

AT™	International Business Machines Corporation
Color/Graphics Adapter™	International Business Machines Corporation
Epson®	Seiko Epson Corporation
Etch A Sketch®	Ohio Art
IBM®	International Business Machines Corporation
Microsoft BASIC®	Microsoft Corporation
PCjr™	International Business Machines Corporation
Turbo Basic®	Borland International, Inc.
Turbo Pascal®	Borland International, Inc.
WordStar®	Micropro International Corporation
XT™	International Business Machines Corporation

INDEX

Symbols

_ (formatting character), 59
_ (program line extender), 22
! (formatting character), 58
! (suffix for single-precision variable), 32, 35
(formatting character), 57
(suffix for double-precision variable), 32, 35
$ (formatting character), 57-58
$ (suffix for string variable), 39
^ (formatting character), 60
^ (exponentiation arithmetic operator), 33
* (formatting character), 60
* (multiplication arithmetic operator), 33
/ (formatting character), 58-59
/ (division arithmetic operator), 33
+ (addition arithmetic operator), 33
+ (concatenation string operator), 40
+ (formatting character), 60
& (formatting character), 59
& (prefix for binary and hexadecimal notation), 188, 294
& (suffix for long integer variables), 32, 34
− (subtraction arithmetic operator), 33
\ (integer division arithmetic operator), 32-33
% (suffix for integer variables), 32, 34
: (statement separator), 42
, (formatting character), 57
' (REM), 36
> (greater-than relational operator), 71
< (less-than relational operator), 70
= (equal relational operator), 71

$

$COM, 359
$COM1, 266, 407
$COM2, 266, 407
$DEBUG, 407
$DYNAMIC, 267, 359, 407
$ELSE, 260, 360, 407
$ENDIF, 259, 360, 407
$EVENT, 264, 360, 407
$IF, 360, 407, 259-262
$INCLUDE, 245, 267-271, 360, 407
$INLINE, 264, 360, 407
$LIST, 407
$OPTION, 407
$SEGMENT, 271-272, 361, 407
$SOUND, 220, 266, 361, 407
$STACK, 238, 265, 361, 407
$STATIC, 267, 361, 407

A

ABS, 37, 362, 407, 415
ABSOLUTE, 363, 407
Absolute coordinates, 170
Absolute value function, 362
Action of a PUT statement, 198
Active page, 387
Active window, 16, 247
Actual parameters, 100, 105, 112
ALT-C, 18
ALT-F1, 13
ALT-F5, 17
ALT-R, 15
Amortization of a loan, 306-310
Ampersand character in text formatting, 59
AND, 71-72
AND (PUT), 199, 201
Animation, 194-202
    detecting collisions in, 202
Apostrophe, 36
APPEND, 136, 380, 407
Arctangent function, 362
Arithmetic operators, 32-33

Arrays, 44
    allocation of memory for, 267
    checking bounds for, 236
    declaring, inside procedures, 118
    deleting, 370
    dimensioning, 45-46, 368
    dynamic, 48-50, 120
    elements of, 44
    functions acting on, 411
    higher-dimensional, 47
    indices of, 44
    local, 120
    lower bound of subscripts in, 375
    maximum sizes of, 48
    memory allocation for, 47, 266-267, 360-361
    merging, 118
    one-dimensional, 44-45
    passing, to procedures, 118
    range of subscripts in, 380
    shared, 120
    static, 48-50, 120
    subscripts of, 44
    two-dimensional, 45-46
    upper bound of subscripts in, 392
ASC, 362, 407, 416
ASCII table, 353, 362, 364
Assigning values to variables, 50
ATN, 362, 407, 415
Attribute, 65, 183
AUTO, 397
Auto-indent mode (editor), 24
Auto save edit option, 92, 245

B

Background color, 61, 63, 182-183
Backslash character in text formatting, 58, 395
Backup source files option, 245
Bar chart program, generic, 323
Bar charts, 316-328
BASE, 407

BASIC, 1
BASICA, 2-4
    converting, to Turbo Basic, 397-406
BEEP, 362, 407
BIN$, 362, 407, 412
BINARY, 380, 407
Binary files, 154-161
    moving file pointer in, 154
    opening, 154
    reading data from, 155
    writing data to, 154
Binary representation, 362
Binary search, 84
Blinking characters, 61
BLOAD, 299, 362, 407
Block editor commands, 423, 428-430
Border, 240
Bounds option, 236
BSAVE, 298, 362, 407
Buffer
    communications, 359
    music-background, 361
Business programming, 305
Byte, 294

C

CALL, 112, 115-116, 362, 399, 407
CALL ABSOLUTE, 363
CALL INTERRUPT, 363
Caret (^), 421
Carriage-return/linefeed pair, 134
CASE, 79, 388, 407
CASE ELSE, 81, 388
Cassette motor, 398
CDBL, 363, 407, 412
CEIL, 36, 363, 407, 415
CGA board, 164
CHAIN, 255, 363, 407
Chain file compilation option, 255
CHAIN MERGE, 287, 398
Chain programs (TBC), 254

Chaining, 363, 365
Change Dir option, 233
Character table, 295
Characters, specifying, 295
CHDIR, 363, 407
CHR$, 293, 298, 364, 407, 416
CINT, 364, 407, 412
CIRCLE, 168, 183, 314-315, 364, 407
CLEAR, 364, 398-399, 407
Clearing the screen, 365
Clearing a viewport, 217
CLNG, 364, 407, 412
Clock, 378, 392
    trapping the, 379
CLOSE, 364, 407
Close (window) option, 247
Closing a file, 136
CLS, 365, 407
Colons in multiple-statement lines, 42
COLOR, 61, 63, 66, 182, 365, 407
Color, 181-187
    background, 61, 63
    foreground, 61, 63
Color monitor, 62
Color of character on screen, 386
Colors
    16 basic, 62
    63 with EGA, 63-64
Colors option, 239-244
Column number (editor), 23
COM, 407
COM(n), 365
COMMAND$, 253, 365, 407, 417
Command-line parameter, 253
COMMON, 255-257, 365, 400, 407
Communications
    port, opening, 380
    trapping, 378
Communications buffer, 239, 266, 359
Communications port, 365
Compilation
    conditional, 260, 360

Compilation, *continued*
    of a program, 18
    segments, 361
Compile command, main menu, 9
Compile-time error, 18
Compile to chain file option, 255
Compile to option, 234
Compiler, 2
Compiler directive, 258
Composite monitors, 164
Concatenation operator, 40
Condition, 71
Conditional compilation, 260, 360
Conditions, in loops, 85
Configuration file, 246
CONT, 397
Control characters, 134
Control structures
    DO loops, 83-87
    FOR...NEXT loops, 88-90
    If blocks, 75-79
    IF...THEN...ELSE statements, 74-75
    SELECT CASE blocks, 79-82
    WHILE...WEND loops, 86-87
Conversion functions, 412-413
Converting
    Microsoft BASIC strings to numbers, 366
    numbers to Microsoft BASIC strings, 378
    numbers to strings, 378
    strings to lowercase, 375
    strings to numbers, 366
    strings to uppercase, 392
Coordinates, 164, 170, 207
    physical, 207
    user-defined, 207
    world, 208
COS, 366, 407, 415
Cosine function, 274, 366
Counter variable, 89

Creating a program, 14-18
CSNG, 366, 407, 412
CSRLIN, 366, 407, 416
CTRL-ALT-DEL, 91
CTRL-BREAK, 11, 90-92, 235
Current directory, 395
Current (binary) file position, 154, 387
Current (memory) segment, 294
Cursor
    changing size of, 376
    column, 383
    locating, 376
Cursor line, 366
Cursor-moving editor commands, 422, 424-427
Custom-designed characters, 293
CVD, 151, 366, 407, 412
CVI, 151, 366, 407, 412
CVL, 151, 366, 407, 412
CVMD, 366, 407, 412
CVMS, 366, 407, 412
CVS, 151, 366, 407, 412

D

DATA, 51, 366, 407
Data files, 133-161
Database, 328
Database management, 328-350
Database management program, generic, 342-350
DATE$, 40, 367, 407, 418
Debug command, main menu, 9
Debug menu commands, 249
Debug pull-down menu, 258
Debugging, 254, 260, 392
DECR, 123, 367, 407
DEF, 407
DEF FN, 99, 105, 367
DEF SEG, 294, 298, 367
DEF USR, 397-398
Default data segment, 395

DEFDBL, 43, 367, 407
DEFINT, 43, 367, 407
DEFLNG, 43, 367, 407
DEFSNG, 43, 367, 407
DEFSTR, 43, 367, 407
DEFtype statements, 43, 100
DELAY, 367, 407
DELETE, 397
Deleting a program from memory, 20, 230
Deletion commands, text editor, 427-428
Detecting errors, 6
Device, 396
    driver, 374
    error, 370
DIM, 45-47, 120, 266, 368, 407
Direct mode, 398
Directives, compiler, 251
Directories option, 232, 244
Directory, 395
    changing, 363
    creating, 378
    removing, 386
Directory box, 241, 244
Division by zero, 404
DO loops, 83
DOS, invoking, 388, 391
Double-precision number, 363
Double-precision numeric variables, 35
DRAW, 173-181, 183, 368, 407
    angle subcommands in, 178
    direction subcommands in, 175-178
    relative coordinates in, 174
    scale subcommands in, 180
    selecting color in, 185
    using substrings in, 180
    using variables in, 180
DYNAMIC, 118, 120, 407
Dynamic allocation of arrays, 267
Dynamic arrays, 48-50
DYNAMIC dimensioning, 368

E

Edit, 5, 397
Edit command, main menu, 9
Edit window, 5, 8-9
Editor, 4, 7
    auto-indent mode, 24
    capabilities of, 21-22
    column number, 23
    insert mode, 23
    line number, 23
    overwrite mode, 23
    Status line, 23
    tabbing, 24
    and WordStar, differences between, 435-439
Editor commands, 24, 421
    abort operation, 433
    block, 423, 428-430
    delete text, 422, 427-428
    file, 423, 430, 433
    miscellaneous, 424, 433
    mode toggles, 423, 430
    move cursor, 422, 424-427
    place marker, 427
    restore current line, 26, 434
    restore message, 434
    scroll view, 426
    search and replace, 423, 431-432
EGA board, 164, 203-207
8087 coprocessor, 6
8087 required option, 235
Ellipse, 364
ELSEIF, 77, 373, 407
END, 110, 369, 407
END DEF, 105, 367
End-of-file, 370
End-of-file character, 134
END SELECT, 81
END SUB, 112, 391

ENDMEM, 296, 369, 407, 417
Enhanced Graphics Adapter, 163
   special capabilities of, 381
Enhanced graphics display, 63
ENVIRON, 369, 407
ENVIRON$, 369, 407, 418
Environment table, 369
EOF, 139, 370, 407, 414
EQV, 73-74, 407
ERADR, 370, 407, 413
ERASE, 49, 266, 370, 407
ERDEV, 370, 407, 413
ERDEV$, 370, 407, 413
ERL, 370, 407, 413
ERR, 104, 370, 407, 413
ERROR, 370, 407
Error
   device, 370
   line, 370
   number, 370
Error box, 241, 244
Error-control functions, 413
Error message, 240-241
   restore, 434
Error number, 258
Error trapping, 370, 378, 385
ESC key, 10
Event trapping, 262-264, 360, 396
   terminating, 263
Exclamation mark in text formatting, 58
.EXE file, 245, 252, 255
EXIT, 93, 371, 388, 407
EXIT SUB, 112
Exiting decision structures, 93
Exiting Turbo Basic, 20
EXP, 277, 371, 407, 415
EXP10, 277, 371, 407, 415
EXP2, 277, 371, 407, 415
Exponential functions, 276, 371, 415
EXTERR(n), 398

F

F1 key, 12
Field, 57, 134, 149-150, 371, 407
File command, main menu, 5, 9
File commands (editor), 423, 430, 433
File menu commands, 229-234
FILES, 371, 407
Files
   binary, 154-161
   closing, 364, 385
   current location in, 376
   editing arbitrary, 156-161
   end of, 370
   erasing, 375
   examining, 156-157
   functions acting on, 414
   length of, 376
   maximum number open, 148
   naming, 135
   opening, 380
   outputting data to, 384
   placing data in, 384
   placing values into random, 377, 386
   random, 149-154
   reading data from arbitrary, 374
   reading data from binary, 372
   reading data from sequential, 373, 376
   renaming, 378
   retrieving records from, 372
   sequential, 134-149
   setting current file position in (binary), 387
   specifying, 23
   specifying fields, 371
   writing data to binary, 385
Filespec, 23, 148, 232, 396
First letter, 244
FIX, 371, 407, 415
Floating-point variables, 35
FN, 98, 407
FOR...NEXT loops, 89-90
Foreground color, 61, 63
Formal parameters, 100, 115-116, 103-105, 112
Format string, 57
Formatting characters on screen, 55, 57

Index

FRE, 371, 401, 407, 418
Freeing memory, 49
Function key, trapping, 374, 379
Function keys, 374
Functions
    actual parameters in, 100, 105
    array, 411-412
    conversion, 412-413
    effect of chaining, 256
    error-control, 413
    file, 414
    formal parameters of, 100, 105
    graphics, 414
    input, 414
    invoking other functions, 125
    mathematical, 415
    miscellaneous, 419
    multiline, 105
    numeric, 36
    parameterless, 104
    predefined, 36-37, 40
    print, 416
    recursion of, 129-132
    screen, 416
    string, 40, 416-417
    system related, 417-418
    time, 418-419
    user-defined, 98-110
    using logical expressions in, 101-103
    versus procedures, 123

G

Generating random numbers, 385-386
GET, 407
GET (files), 151, 153, 372
GET (graphics), 195-197, 372
GET$, 155, 372, 407
Global file name character, 230
Global variables, 3
GOSUB, 110, 113-114, 372, 407
GOTO, 372, 407
Goto (window) option, 248
GRAFTABL.COM, 298
Graphics, 163-217

Graphics commands
    CIRCLE, 168
    DRAW, 173-181
    general description of, 164-167
    LINE, 167
    PAINT, 183
    POINT, 167
Graphics functions, 414
Graphics modes using IBM PS/2, 207
Graphics monitors, 163
Graphics screen modes using EGA, 204-207
Graphics coordinate system, specifying, 394
GRAPHICS.COM, 322
Graphing functions, 282-287
GW BASIC, 2, 4

H

Help line, 8, 10
Help screens, 10, 12-13, 241
HEX$, 372, 407, 412
Hexadecimal representation, 372
Hierarchy
    of arithmetic operations, 38
    of logical operators, 74
High-resolution graphics mode, 164
Higher-dimensional arrays, 47
Horizontal radius line, 314
Horizontal screen scrolling, 22

I

IBM PCjr BASIC, 398
IBM PS/2, special graphics modes on, 66
IF block, 75-78, 373
IF...THEN...ELSE, 74-75
IMP, 73-74, 407
Include directories, 245, 270
INCR, 106, 373, 407
Indentation, 94
Index, 371
Infinite loops, 90-92
INKEY$, 373, 407, 414

INLINE, 391, 407
INP, 373, 407, 418
INPUT, 50-51, 138, 373, 380, 407
Input box, 241, 244
Input functions, 414
INPUT#, 139, 373, 407
INPUT$, 52, 142, 374, 407
Insert mode (editor), 23
Installing Turbo Basic, 409-410
INSTAT, 374, 407, 414
INSTR, 40, 374, 407, 417
INT, 37, 374, 407, 415
Integer, converting number to, 364
Integer division, 32
Integer variables, 33-34
Intense white, 61
Interpreter, 2
INTERRUPT, 363, 407
Interrupt, executing, 363
Invoking DOS, 388, 391
IOCTL, 374, 407
IOCTL$, 374, 407, 418

J

Jars (color), 64, 182
Joystick, 389
Joystick buttons
    status of, 390
    trapping of, 379, 390-391
Jump, unconditional, 372, 379

K

KEY, 374, 407
KEY(n), 374
KEY LIST, 374
KEY OFF, 374
KEY ON, 374
Key words. *See* reserved words
Keyboard, opening, as a file, 380
Keyboard break, 235
Keyboard break option, 11, 90
Keyboard buffer, 373-374
Keywords, 244
KILL, 375, 407

L

Label, 4, 110, 262, 396
Last point referenced, 169, 172, 368, 383
LBOUND, 375, 407, 411
LCASE$, 40, 375, 407, 417
LEFT$, 40, 375, 407, 417
LEN, 40, 375, 407, 417
Less than, 70
LET, 50, 53, 375, 407
Light pen
    status, 381
    trapping, 379
LINE, 167, 183, 189, 375, 407
LINE INPUT, 375
LINE INPUT#, 142, 376
Line label, 110
Line number (editor), 23
Line number (program), 3-4, 110
Line styling, 188-190
LIST, 397, 407
Listing a program, 19
LLIST, 397
LOAD, 397
Load option, 229
Load Options/Window/Setup
    option, 246
Loading a program, 20
LOC, 153, 155, 376, 407, 414
LOCAL, 108, 112, 376, 407
Local variables, 3, 108, 112
LOCATE, 56, 376, 407
LOCK, 398
Lock keys, 244
LOF, 152, 155, 376, 407, 414
LOG, 281, 377, 407, 415
LOG2, 281, 377, 407, 415
LOG10, 281, 377, 407, 415
Logarithmic functions, 281, 377, 415
Logical expressions, 101
    numerical evaluation of, 101
Logical operators, 71-74
Long integer variables, 33-34
Long integers, 305

Index

LOOP, 368, 407
Loops
   condition-controlled, 88
   counter-controlled, 88-90
   DO, 83
   exiting, 93
   FOR...NEXT, 89-90, 371
   infinite, 90-92
   nested, 94-95
   terminal conditions for, 90
   WHILE...WEND, 86-88, 394
Lowercase, converting strings to, 375
LPOS, 377, 407, 416
LPRINT, 67, 377, 407
LPRINT USING, 67, 377
LPRINT#, 407
LSET, 150, 153, 377, 407

M

Machine infinity, 402
Machine language, 2, 360, 363, 391
   programs, 264-265
Main file, 271
Main File option, 232
Main menu, 5, 8
   selecting item from, 10
Main/pull downs, 241
Manageable chunk, 98
Marked block, 240-241
Mathematical
   characters, 298
   functions, 415
   programming, 273-304
Matrices
   addition, 300
   inversion, 302-304
   multiplication, 300-302
Medium-resolution graphics mode, 164
Memory, 293, 395
   allocation of, for arrays, 47, 266

Memory, *continued*
   amount of, available, 371-372
   freeing, 49
   last byte available in, 369
   placing a value in, 381
   reading a value from, 383
   specifying current segment of, 367
   specifying last address of, 377
MEMSET, 296, 377, 407
MERGE, 397
Merging two programs, 20
Message window, 5, 8-9
Metastatements, 258-272, 359-361
Metastatements option, 238-239
Microtimer clock, 378
MID$, 40, 377, 407, 417
Miscellaneous functions, 419
Miscellaneous option, 245
MKD$, 151, 378, 407, 412
MKDIR, 378, 407
MKI$, 150, 378, 407, 412
MKL$, 150, 378, 407, 412
MKMD$, 378, 407, 412
MKMS$, 378, 407, 412
MKS$, 151, 378, 407, 412
MOD, 32, 407
Modulo operator, 32
Monochrome display, 61, 163, 206
MOTOR, 397
Moving file pointer in binary file, 154
MTIMER, 378, 407, 419
Multi-statement function definition block, 367
Multiline functions, 105-111
Multiple-statement lines, 42
Music, 382
Music background buffer, 220, 239, 266, 361
   status, 382
   trapping, 379
Music background mode, 220
Music foreground mode, 220

N

NAME, 378, 407
Named constant, 258-259
Naming a sequential file, 135
Naming variables, 6, 31
Nested IF...THEN...ELSE
  statements, 79
Nested loops, 94-95
NEW, 397
New option, 230
NEXT, 89, 371, 407
Next option (window), 247
NOISE, 398
NONAME.BAS, 23
Normal text, 241
NOT, 71-72
Nucleus of an .EXE file, 252
Null string, 39
Numbers, 31-32
  accuracy, 35
  converting, to strings, 390
  rounding, 38, 53, 404
  rounding, to integers, 34
Numeric
  expressions, 38
  functions, 36
  variables, 32

O

Object code, 251
  Chain program, 254
  standalone program, 252
  standard memory-resident, 251
OCT$, 378, 407, 412
Octal representation, 378
Offset, 294, 395
ON COM(n), 378
ON ERROR, 263, 286, 378
ON KEY(n), 379
ON PEN, 379
ON PLAY(n), 379
ON STRIG(n), 379
ON TIMER, 379

ON...GOSUB, 262, 379
ON...GOTO, 379
One-dimensional arrays, 44-45
OPEN, 150, 154, 380, 407
OPEN "COM..., 380
Open option (window), 247
Opening
  binary files, 154
  random files, 150
  sequential files for append, 136
  sequential files for input, 138
  sequential files for output, 135
Operators
  arithmetic, 32-33
  hierarchy of, 74
  logical, 71-74
  relational, 70-71
OPTION, 407
OPTION BASE, 380
Options command, main menu, 9, 234
OR, 71-74
OR (PUT), 199, 201
OS Shell option, 233
OUTPUT, 135, 380, 407
Overflow, 402
Overflow option, 237
Overwrite mode (editor), 23

P

Packing a database, 335
Page, specifying, 387
PAINT, 183, 193, 380, 407
PALETTE, 65-66, 182, 204-207, 365, 381, 407
PALETTE USING, 381
Palettes, undocumented, 185-186
Parameter Line, 365
Parameter line option, 238
Parameterless functions, 104
Parameters
  actual, 100, 105, 112
  formal, 100, 103-105, 112, 115-116

Index

Pass-by-reference, 115-116, 123
Pass-by-value, 116, 123
Path, 232, 395
PCOPY, 398
PEEK, 294, 381, 405, 407, 418
PEN, 381, 407, 419
Pgm-ctr, 257
Physical coordinates, 207, 382
Pi, 274
Pie chart program, generic, 311
Pie charts, 308-316
Pixel, 164. *See also* point
   color of, 382
Place marker commands (editor), 427
PLAY, 217-226, 382, 407, 419
   identifying notes by number in, 225
   legato in, 223
   length of notes in, 220
   music background in, 220
   music foreground in, 220
   octave subcommand in, 218
   pause in, 222
   staccato in, 223
   tempo in, 224
PLAY(n), 382
PMAP, 208, 382, 407, 414
POINT, 201-202
Point, 164, 167, 382, 407, 414
POKE, 294, 383, 405, 407
Ports, 396
   reading values from, 373, 394
   sending values to, 380
POS, 383, 407, 416
Predefined functions, 36-41, 98, 411-419
PRESET, 167, 198, 201, 383-385, 407
PRINT, 54-56, 383, 407
Print functions, 416
PRINT USING, 57-60, 384
PRINT zones, 54-55
PRINT#, 141, 384, 407

PRINT# USING, 141, 384
Printer
   controlling, 67
   formatting output on, 377
   line width, 68
   specifying line width for, 394
Printer buffer, current position in, 377
Printing a program, 19
Problem solving, 97
Procedures, 3, 112-132, 391
   actual parameters in, 112
   effect of chaining, 256
   formal parameters in, 112
   invoking, 362
   invoking other procedures, 125
   passing arrays to, 118
   recursion in, 129-132
   versus functions, 123
   versus subroutines, 113-114
Program
   chain (TBC), 254
   deleting, from memory, 230
   designating, as main file, 232
   extending lines in, 22
   loading, from disk, 229
   machine language, 264-265
   managing a large, 269, 271-272
   running a, 15-18, 19
   saving, to disk, 231, 245
   saving, under a new name, 231
   standalone (.EXE), 252
   standard memory-resident, 251
Program counter, 249-250, 258, 370
Prompt, 51, 373
PS/2, special graphics modes on, 66
PSET, 167, 183, 197, 200, 384, 407
Pseudo-random, 289
Pseudocolors, 206-207
Pull-down menu, 10, 240
PUT, 407
PUT (files), 150, 153, 384
PUT (Graphics), 197-202, 384

PUT$, 154, 385, 407

Q

Question mark, 51
Quit option, 234

R

Radians, 274
RANDOM, 407
Random files, 149-154
  converting numbers to strings for, 151
  fields in records of, 149
  opening, 150
  packing, 335
  reading data from, 151
  records in, 149
  record length in, 149
  writing data to, 150
Random number generator, 385-386
Random numbers, 288-293
RANDOMIZE, 385, 407
RANDOMIZE TIMER, 288, 385
READ, 51, 385, 407
Reading data from binary file, 155
Reading data from random file, 151
Reading data from sequential file, 137-139
Record, 134, 149
Rectangle, 167
  solid, 168
Recursion, 129-132
Reference number of file, 135
REG, 385, 407, 418
Register, processor, 385
Relational expression, 71
Relational operators, 70-71
Relative coordinates, 170, 172
REM, 36, 385, 407
RENUM, 397
Reserved words, 407
RESET, 385, 407
RESTORE, 385, 407
Restore-line command (editor), 26

RESUME, 263, 385, 407
RETURN, 110, 386, 407
Returning to DOS, 20
Reverse video, 61
RIGHT$, 40, 386, 407, 417
RMDIR, 386, 407
RND, 288, 386, 407, 415
Root directory, 232, 395
Rounding numbers, 404
RSET, 154, 386, 407
Rule of 72, 99
RUN, 386, 399, 407
Run command, main menu, 5, 9
Run-time error option, 249
Run-time errors, 19, 257
Run window, 5, 8, 10
  zooming, 17
Running a program, 15-18, 19

S

Sampling, 292
SAVE, 397, 407
Save option, 231
Save Options/Window/Setup option, 246
Saving a program, 17, 19
Saving graphs, 298-299
Scientific notation, 36
Scientific programming, 273-304
SCREEN, 166, 394, 404, 407, 416
SCREEN (function), 386
SCREEN (statement), 387
Screen
  clearing, 365
  controlling placement of graphics on, 393
  displaying formatted text on, 384, 392
  displaying text on, 383, 394
  dump, 265, 322
  formatting characters on, 55, 57
  functions, 416
  modes, specifying, 167, 387

Index

Screen, *continued*
    number of characters per line, 55, 394
    opening, as a file, 380
    placing characters on, 56
Scroll lock, 250
Scrolling commands (editor), 426
Search and replace commands (editor), 423, 431-432
Seeding the random number generator, 385
SEEK, 154, 387, 407
SEG, 407
Segment, 272, 293, 395
SELECT, 407
SELECT CASE, 79-82, 387
Selected keyword, 244
Selecting cases, 388
Selection bar, 240, 244
Sentinel value, 136
Sequential files, 134
    closing, 136
    fields in, 134
    naming, 135
    opening, for append, 136
    opening, for input, 138
    opening, for output, 135
    reading, data from, 137-139
    records, 134
    reference number for, 135
    sorting, 143-146
    writing to, 135
SERVICE, 407
Setup command, main menu, 9, 239
SGN, 37, 388, 407, 415
SHARED, 108, 112, 120, 388, 407
Shared variables, 108, 112
SHELL, 146, 388, 407
Shell sort, 95
Simulation, 292
SIN, 388, 407, 415
Sine function, 274, 388
Single-precision numbers, 366
Single-precision numeric variables, 35

SORT (DOS command), 145-146
Sorting
    sequential files, 143-146
    arrays, 95
    with pointers, 339
SOUND, 226, 389, 407
Sound, 217-227
Sound effects, 227
SOUND OFF, 398
SOUND ON, 398
Source code, 251
SPACE$, 389, 407, 417
Spaces, generating, 389
SPC, 389, 407, 416
Specifying current segment of memory, 367
Specifying variable types, 367
SQR, 273, 389, 407, 415
Square root function, 273, 389
Stack, 238, 265, 361
    LIFO, 121
Stack (window) option, 248
Stack test option, 237
Standard BASIC, 1-4
Starting Turbo Basic, 7
STATIC, 108, 112, 120, 389, 407
Static allocation of arrays, 267
Static arrays, 48-50
STATIC dimensioning, 368
Static variables, 108, 112
Status line, 241, 244
    editor, 23
STEP (graphics), 171
STEP (loop increment), 89, 407
Stepwise refinement, 98, 125-129
    chart, 127
STICK, 389, 407, 419
STOP, 389, 407
STR$, 390, 407, 412
Straight line, 375
STRIG, 390, 407, 419
STRIG(n), 390
STRING$, 391, 407, 417
Strings, 39
    converting, to numbers, 392

Strings, *continued*
    functions of, 40, 416-417
    number of characters in, 375
Structured programming, 6, 97-98
Style, 189
Styled line, 187
SUB, 112, 391, 407
SUB INLINE, 391
Subdirectories, 232, 395
Subroutines, 110, 372, 386
SWAP, 391, 407
SYSTEM, 391, 407
System-related functions, 417-418
System reset, 91

T

TAB, 55, 67, 392, 408, 416
Tab mode (editor), 24
Tagless variables, 42
TAN, 392, 407, 415
Tangent function, 274, 392
TB file, 245
TBC file, 254
TBCONFIG.TB, 246
TERM, 398
Text-deleting editor commands, 422
Text mode, 166
Tile option (window), 248
Tile patterns, 190-194
Tile specifier, 193
Tiled region, 187
Time functions, 418-419
TIME$, 104, 392, 407, 419
TIMER, 392, 407, 419
Title, 240
Toggle mode editor commands, 423, 430-431
Top-down design, 98
Trace option, 249
Trace window, 5, 8, 10
Tracing, 392
Trapping, 262-264, 360
    clock, 379

Trapping, *continued*
    communications, 365, 378
    error, 370, 378, 385
    function key, 374, 379
    joystick buttons, 379, 390-391
    light pen, 379
    music background buffer, 379
Trigonometric functions, 274-276
TROFF, 392, 407
TRON, 392, 407
Turbo Basic, 1, 2
    features of, 3
    installing, 409-410
    screen, 5
Two-dimensional arrays, 45-46
Type declaration tags, 32, 41
    in naming functions, 100

U

UBOUND, 392, 407, 411
UCASE$, 40, 392, 407, 417
Unconditional jump, 372, 379
Undeclared variables, 124
Underline character, 22
Underlined characters, 61
Undocumented palettes, 185-186
Unit circle, 274
UNLOCK, 398
Uppercase, converting strings to, 392
User-defined coordinate systems, 207
User-defined functions, 98-110, 367
USING, 407
USR, 397-398, 407

V

VAL, 40, 392, 407, 412
Variables, 31
    assigning values to, 50
    checking, for overflow, 237
    double-precision numeric, 35
    exchanging values of, 391
    floating-point, 35

Variables, *continued*
    integer, 33-34
    local, 108, 112
    location of values of, 393
    long integer, 33-34
    naming, 31
    numeric, 32
    passing-by-reference, 115-116
    passing-by-value, 116-117
    shared, 108, 112
    single-precision numeric, 35, 42
    specifying, as local, 376
    specifying, as shared, 388
    specifying, as static, 389
    specifying types of, 367
    static, 108, 112
    type declaration tags of, 32
    type mismatches with, 53
VARPTR, 393, 399, 407, 418
VARPTR$, 180, 222, 393, 407, 418
VARSEG, 393, 407, 418
Verify box, 241, 244
VIEW, 212-217, 393, 407
VIEW SCREEN, 215
Viewport, 209, 365, 393
    clearing, 217
Visual page, 387

W

WAIT, 394, 407
WEND, 394, 407
WHILE, 407
WHILE...WEND loops, 86-88, 394
WIDTH, 55, 68, 394, 407
Width of a field, 150
Wild card character, 229
WINDOW, 207, 394, 407
Window
    active, 16
    command, main menu, 9, 246-249
WINDOW SCREEN, 207-209
Windows, 8
    adjusting, 250
    custom-coloring of, 239
Word-wrapping, 22
WordStar and Turbo Basic editor, difference between, 435-439
Work file, 271
World coordinates, 208, 382
WRITE, 394, 407
Write to option, 231
WRITE#, 135, 395, 407
Writing to
    binary files, 154
    random files, 150
    sequential files, 135

X

XOR, 72-74, 384, 394, 407
XOR (PUT), 199, 201

Z

Zones, PRINT, 54-55
Zoom option (window), 249
Zooming, 17

The manuscript for this book was prepared and submitted to Osborne/McGraw-Hill in electronic form. The acquisitions editor for this project was Jeffrey Pepper and the technical reviewer was Richard Guion.

Text design by Pamela Webster, using Baskerville for text body and Megaron for display.

Cover art by Bay Graphics Design Associates. Color separation by Colour Image. Cover supplier, Phoenix Color Corp. Book printed and bound by R.R. Donnelly & Sons Company, Crawfordsville, Indiana.

Osborne/McGraw-Hill's Indispensable Complete Reference Series

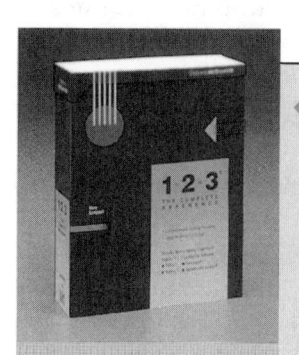

◀ 1-2-3®: The Complete Reference
by Mary Campbell

Every Lotus® 1-2-3® command, function, and procedure is thoroughly explained and demonstrated in "real-world" business applications. Includes money-saving coupons for add-on products. 892 pages.

$22.95, A Quality Paperback,
ISBN 0-07-881005-1

◀ DOS: The Complete Reference
by Kris Jamsa

Has all the answers to all your questions on DOS through version 3.X. This essential resource is for every PC-DOS and MS-DOS® user. 1045 pages.

$24.95, A Quality Paperback,
ISBN 0-07-881259-3

◀ dBASE III PLUS™: The Complete Reference
by Joseph-David Carrabis

Conveniently organized so you can quickly pinpoint all dBASE III® and dBASE III PLUS™ commands, functions, and features. 768 pages.

$22.95, A Quality Paperback,
ISBN 0-07-881012-4

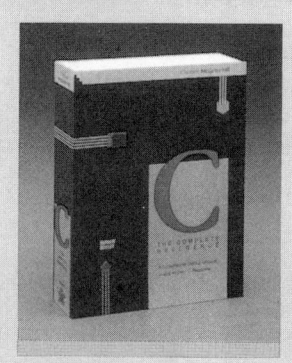

◀ C: The Complete Reference
by Herbert Schildt

For all C programmers, beginners and seasoned pros, here's an encyclopedia of C terms, functions, codes, and applications. Covers C++ and the proposed ANSI standard. 740 pages.

$24.95, A Quality Paperback,
ISBN 0-07-881263-1

AVAILABLE NOW   **ORDER TOLL-FREE**

Dealers & Wholesalers   **1-800-772-4726**
Colleges & College Bookstores   **1-800-338-3987**
Available in Canada through McGraw-Hill Ryerson. Ltd. Phone 416-293-1911

Osborne McGraw-Hill
2600 Tenth Street
Berkeley, California 94710

Trademarks: Lotus and 1-2-3 are registered trademarks of Lotus Development Corp. dBASE is a registered trademark and dBASE III PLUS is a trademark of Ashton-Tate. MS-DOS is a registered trademark of Microsoft Corp.

MAXIT™ increases your DOS addressable conventional memory beyond 640K for only $195.

- Add up to 256K above 640K for programs like **FOXBASE+** and **PC/FOCUS**.

- Short card works in the IBM PC, XT, AT, and compatibles.

- Top off a 512 IBM AT's memory to 640K and add another 128K beyond that.

- Run resident programs like Sidekick above 640K.

- Add up to 96K above 640K to all programs, including **PARADOX** and 1-2-3.

- Compatible with EGA, Network, and other memory cards.

Break through the 640 barrier.
MAXIT increases your PC's available memory by making use of the vacant unused address space between 640K and 1 megabyte. (See illustrations)

Big gain—no pain.
Extend the productive life of your, IBM PC, XT, AT or compatible. Build more complex spreadsheets and databases without upgrading your present software.

Installation is a snap.
The MAXIT 256K memory card and software works automatically. You don't have to learn a single new command.

If you have questions, our customer support people will answer them, fast. MAXIT is backed by a one-year warranty and a 30-day money-back guarantee.

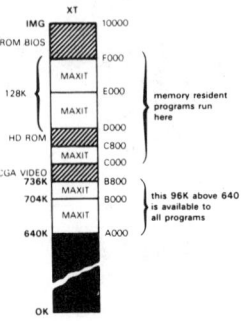

XT class machine (8088, 8086) w/640K and a CGA Color Monitor or a Compaq Type Dual Mode Display

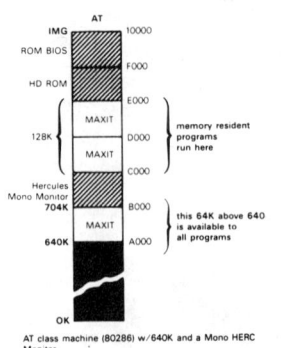

AT class machine (80286) w/640K and a Mono HERC Monitor

Order toll free 1-800-227-0900. MAXIT is just $195 plus $4 shipping, and applicable state sales tax. Buy MAXIT today and solve your PC's memory crisis. Call Toll free 1-800-227-0900 (In California 800-772-2531). Outside the U.S.A. call 1-415-548-2805. We accept VISA, MC.

MAXIT is a trademark of Osborne **McGraw-Hill**. IBM is a registered trademark of International Business Machines Corporation; 1-2-3 and Symphony are registered trademarks of Lotus Development Corporation; Sidekick is a registered trademark of Borland International, Inc; PARADOX is a trademark of ANSA Software; FOXBASE+ is a trademark of Fox Software; Hercules is a trademark of Hercules Computer Technology, Inc; XT and AT are registered trademarks of International Business Machines Corporation; Compaq is a registered trademark of Compaq Computer Corporation.